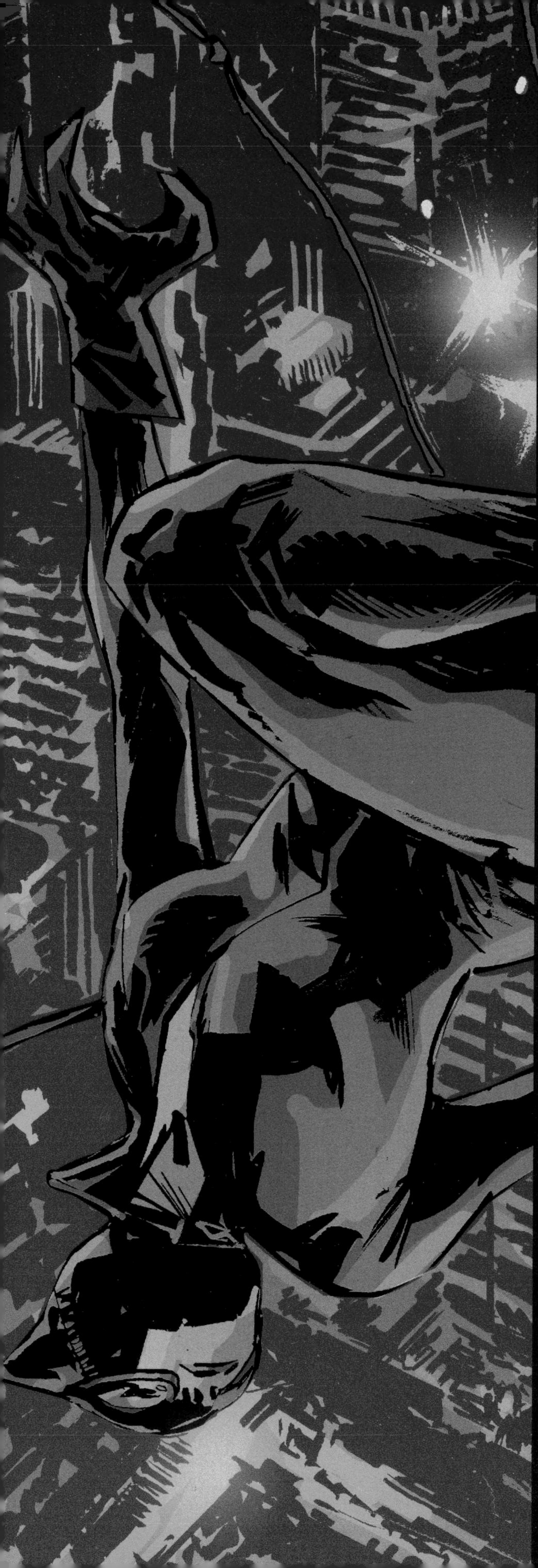

KEEPER OF
THE CASTLE

ATWOMAN

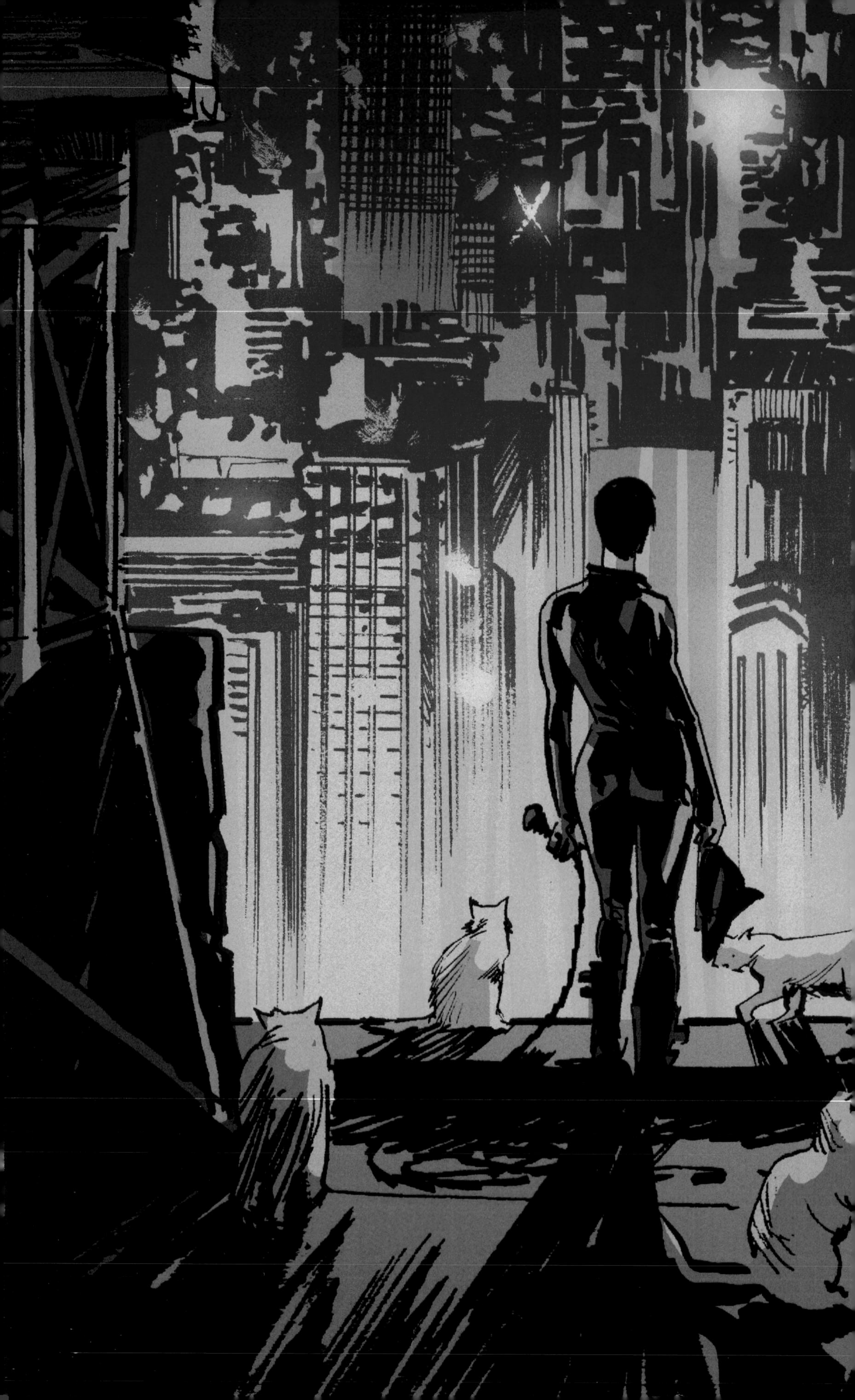

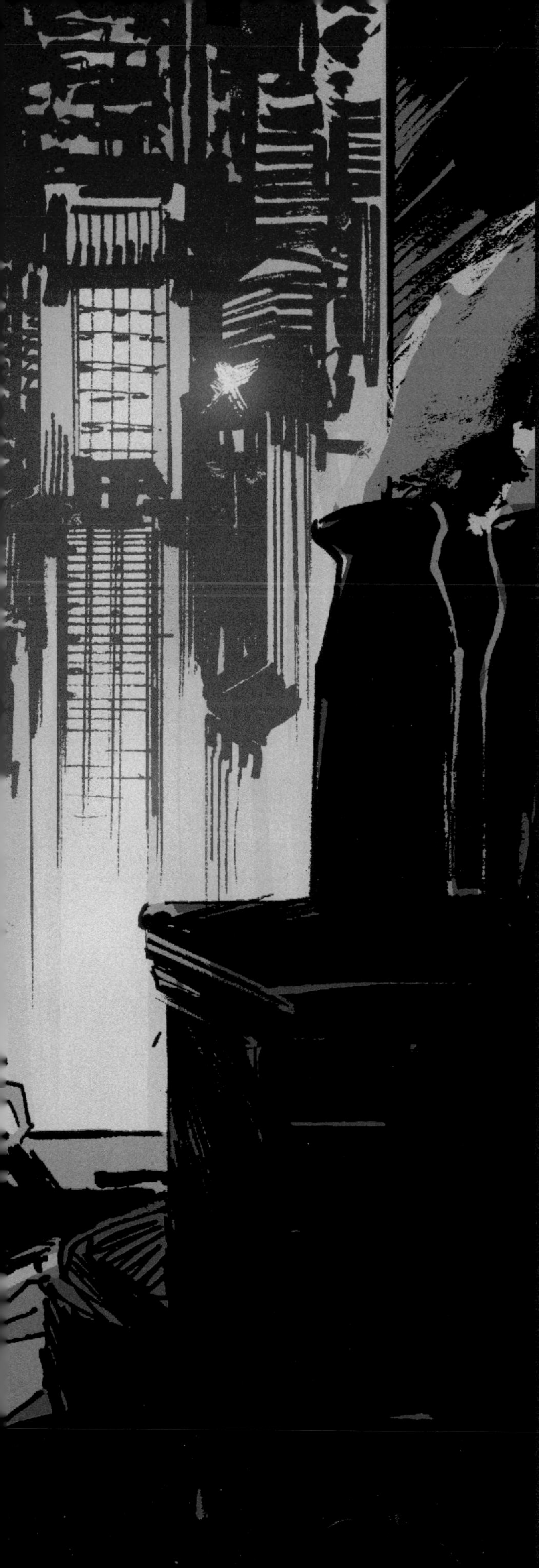

CATWOMAN

VOLUME 6
KEEPER OF THE CASTLE

WRITER
GENEVIEVE VALENTINE

ARTISTS
GARRY BROWN
PAT OLLIFFE
TOM NGUYEN
JOHN MCCREA

COLORIST
LEE LOUGHRIDGE

LETTERERS
SAL CIPRIANO
TAYLOR ESPOSITO
TRAVIS LANHAM
CARLOS M. MANGUAL

COLLECTION COVER ARTISTS
JAE LEE AND
JUNE CHUNG

CATWOMAN VOLUME 6: KEEPER OF THE CASTLE

Published by DC Comics. Compilation Copyright © 2015 DC Comics. All Rights Reserved.

Originally published in single magazine form in CATWOMAN 35-40, CATWOMAN ANNUAL 2 © 2014, 2015 DC Comics. All Rights Reserved.
All characters, their distinctive likenesses and related elements featured in this publication are trademarks of DC Comics.
The stories, characters and incidents featured in this publication are entirely fictional.
DC Comics does not read or accept unsolicited ideas, stories or artwork.

DC Comics, 4000 Warner Blvd., Burbank, CA 91522
A Warner Bros. Entertainment Company.
Printed by RR Donnelley, Owensville, MO, USA. 6/22/15. First Printing.
ISBN: 978-1-4012-5469-8

Library of Congress Cataloging-in-Publication Data

Valentine, Genevieve, author.
Catwoman. Volume 6, Keeper of the castle / Genevieve Valentine,
writer ; Garry Brown, artist.
pages cm. — (The New 52!)
ISBN 978-1-4012-5469-8 (paperback)
1. Graphic novels. I. Brown, Garry, 1981- illustrator. II. Title. III.
Title: Keeper of the castle.
PN6728.C39V35 2015
741.5'973—dc23
2015008027

SUSTAINABLE   Certified Chain of Custody
FORESTRY   20% Certified Forest Content,
INITIATIVE   80% Certified Sourcing
               www.sfiprogram.org
               SFI-01042
               APPLIES TO TEXT STOCK ONLY

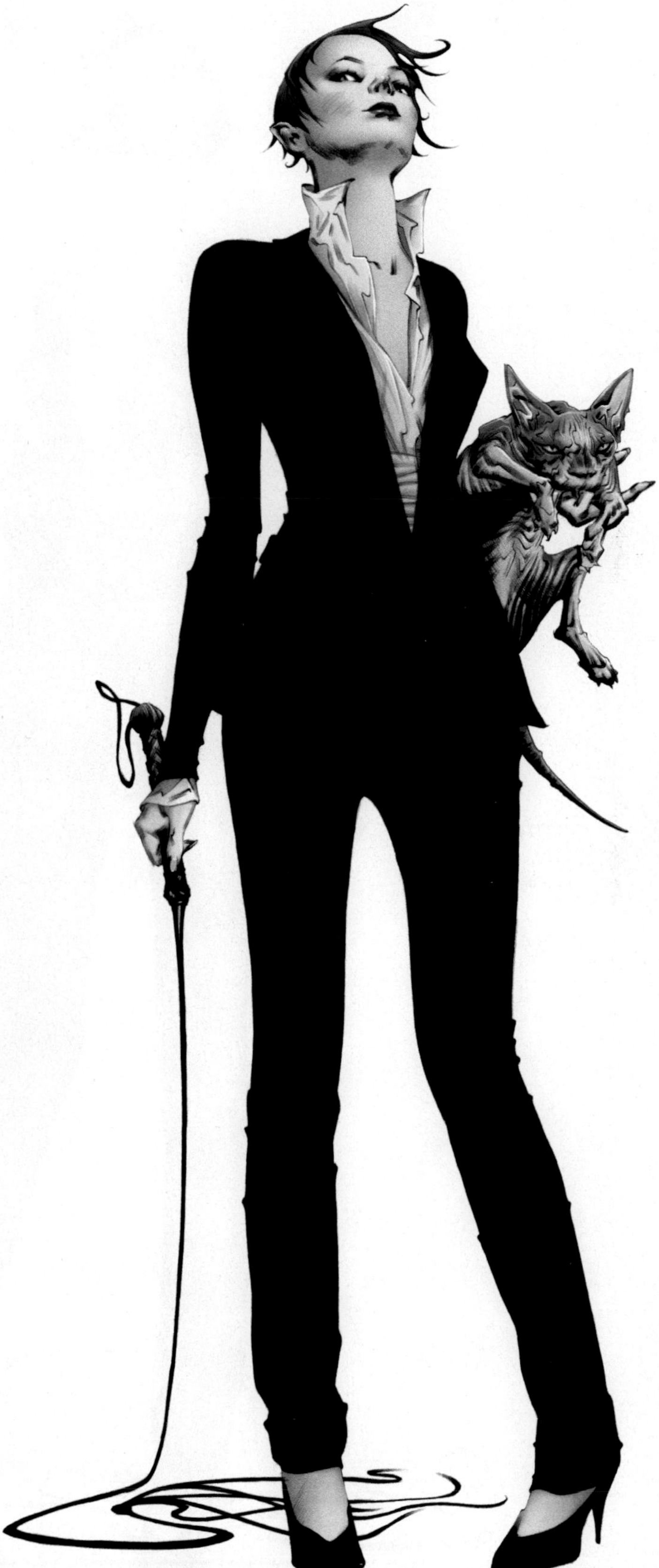

COMFORT TO THE HURT OF THE KING

GENEVIEVE VALENTINE writer **GARRY BROWN** artist cover art by **JAE LEE & JUNE CHUNG**

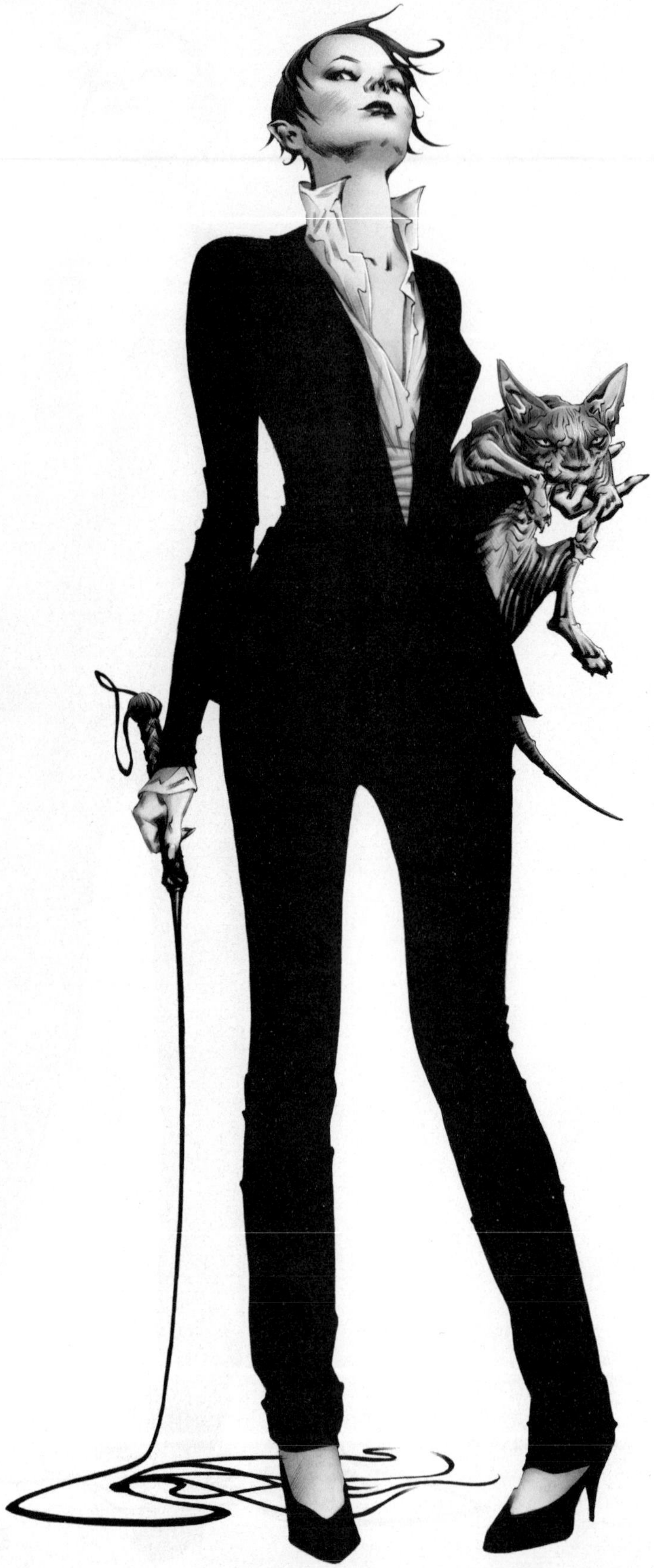

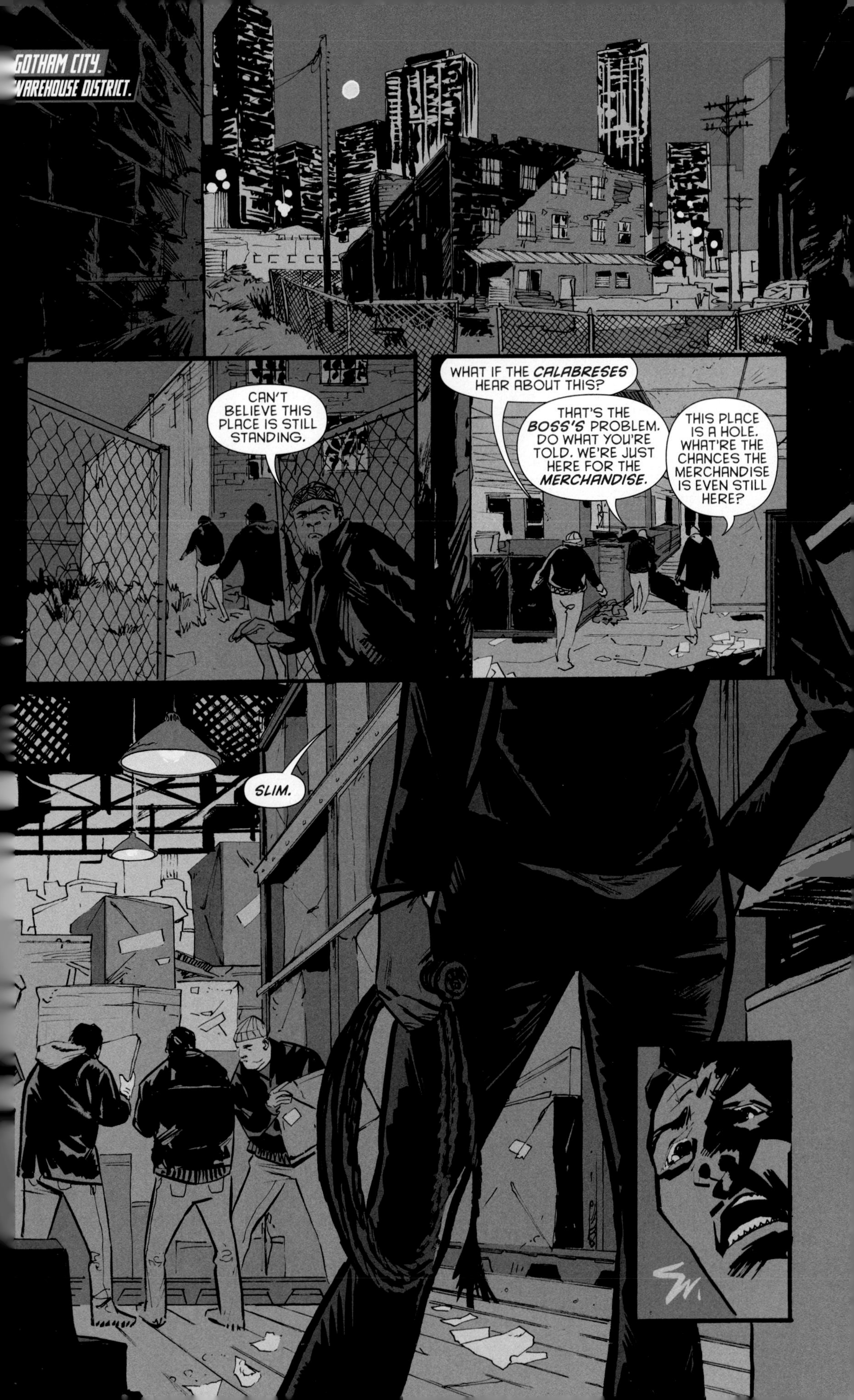
GOTHAM CITY.
WAREHOUSE DISTRICT.
CAN'T BELIEVE THIS PLACE IS STILL STANDING.
WHAT IF THE CALABRESES HEAR ABOUT THIS?
THAT'S THE BOSS'S PROBLEM. DO WHAT YOU'RE TOLD. WE'RE JUST HERE FOR THE MERCHANDISE.
THIS PLACE IS A HOLE. WHAT'RE THE CHANCES THE MERCHANDISE IS EVEN STILL HERE?
SLIM.

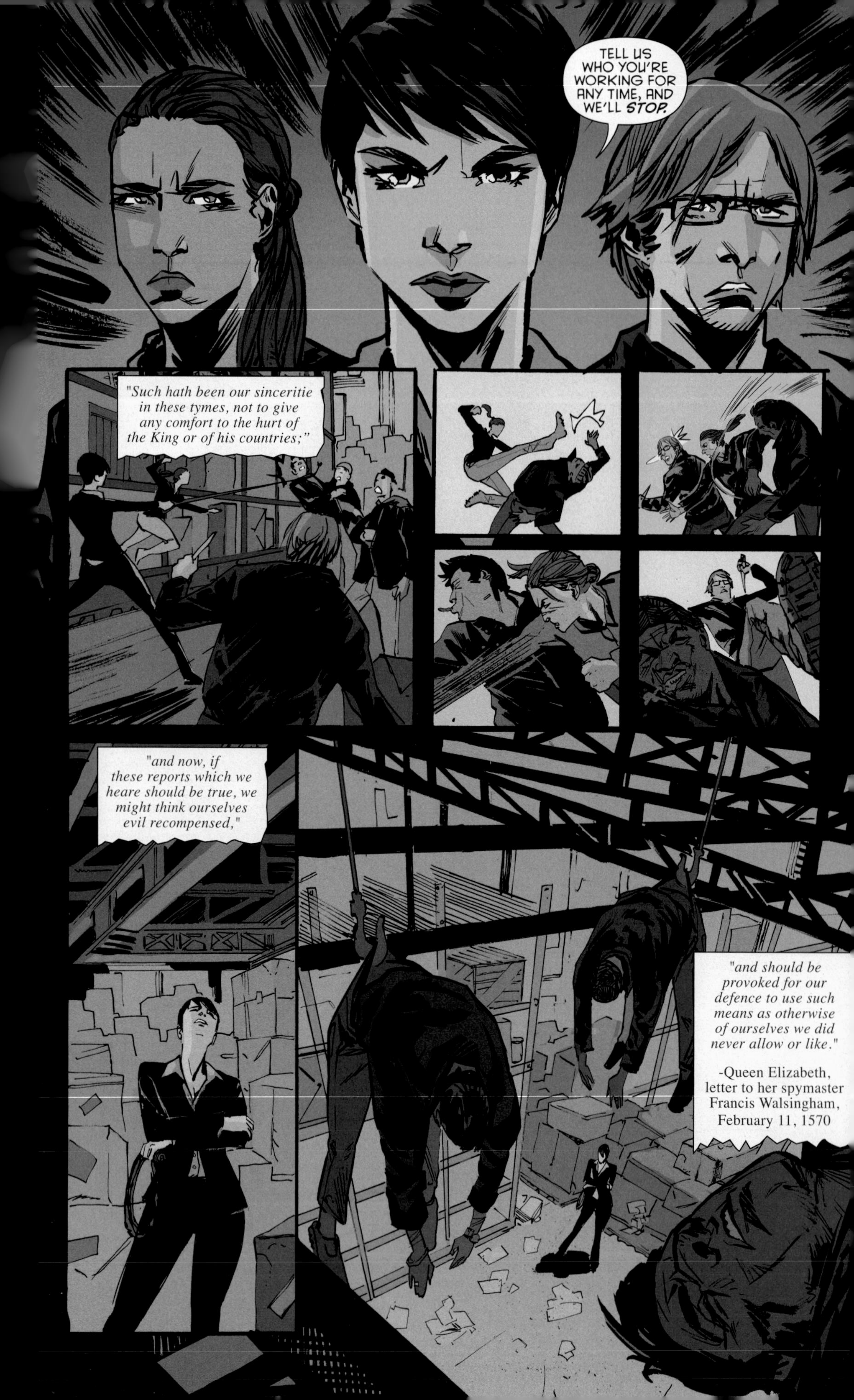
TELL US WHO YOU'RE WORKING FOR ANY TIME, AND WE'LL STOP.
"Such hath been our sinceritie in these tymes, not to give any comfort to the hurt of the King or of his countries;"
"and now, if these reports which we heare should be true, we might think ourselves evil recompensed,"
"and should be provoked for our defence to use such means as otherwise of ourselves we did never allow or like."
-Queen Elizabeth, letter to her spymaster Francis Walsingham, February 11, 1570

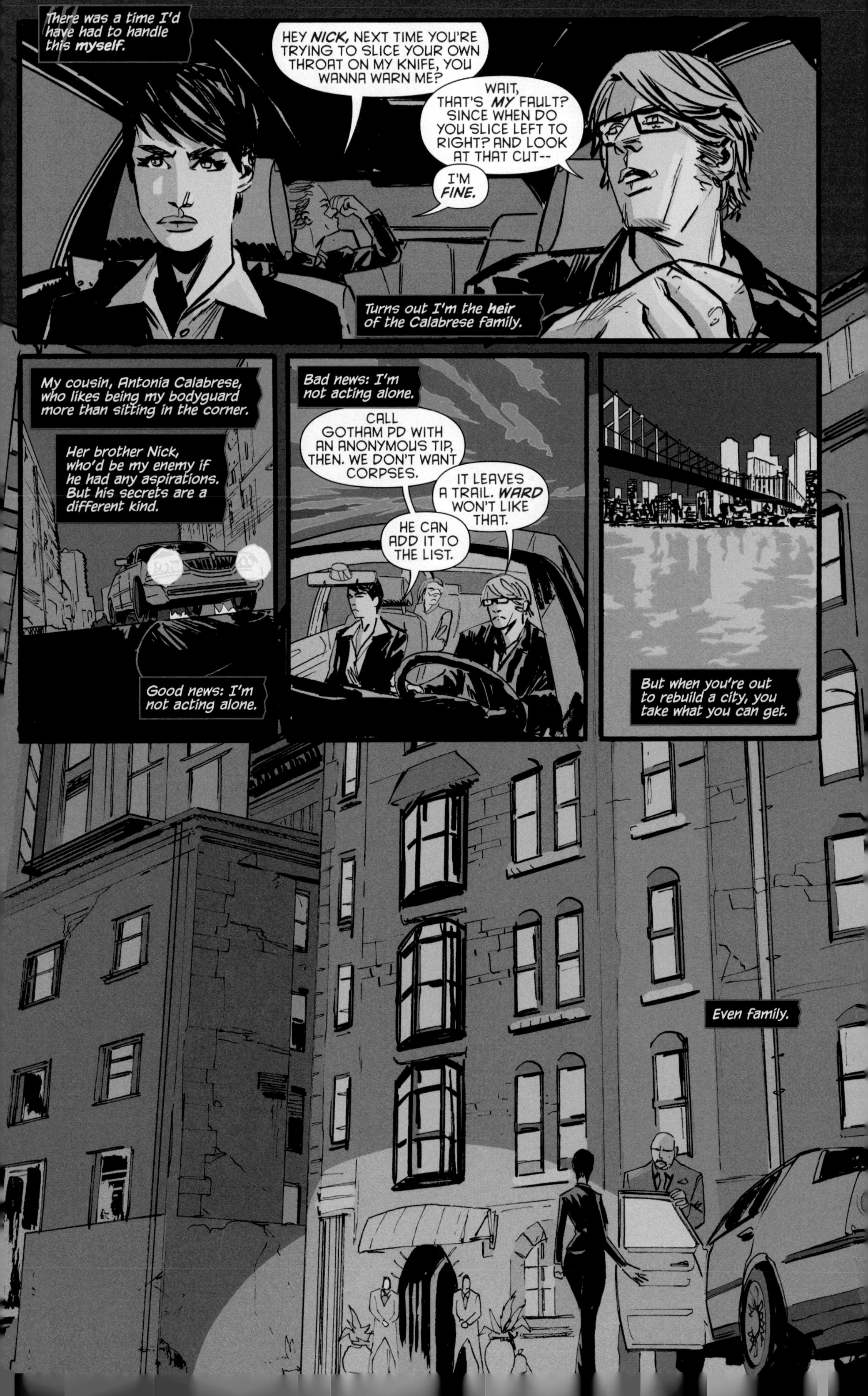

There was a time I'd have had to handle this myself.
HEY NICK, NEXT TIME YOU'RE TRYING TO SLICE YOUR OWN THROAT ON MY KNIFE, YOU WANNA WARN ME?
WAIT, THAT'S MY FAULT? SINCE WHEN DO YOU SLICE LEFT TO RIGHT? AND LOOK AT THAT CUT--
I'M FINE.
Turns out I'm the heir of the Calabrese family.
My cousin, Antonia Calabrese, who likes being my bodyguard more than sitting in the corner.
Her brother Nick, who'd be my enemy if he had any aspirations. But his secrets are a different kind.
Good news: I'm not acting alone.
Bad news: I'm not acting alone.
CALL GOTHAM PD WITH AN ANONYMOUS TIP, THEN. WE DON'T WANT CORPSES.
IT LEAVES A TRAIL. WARD WON'T LIKE THAT.
HE CAN ADD IT TO THE LIST.
But when you're out to rebuild a city, you take what you can get.
Even family.

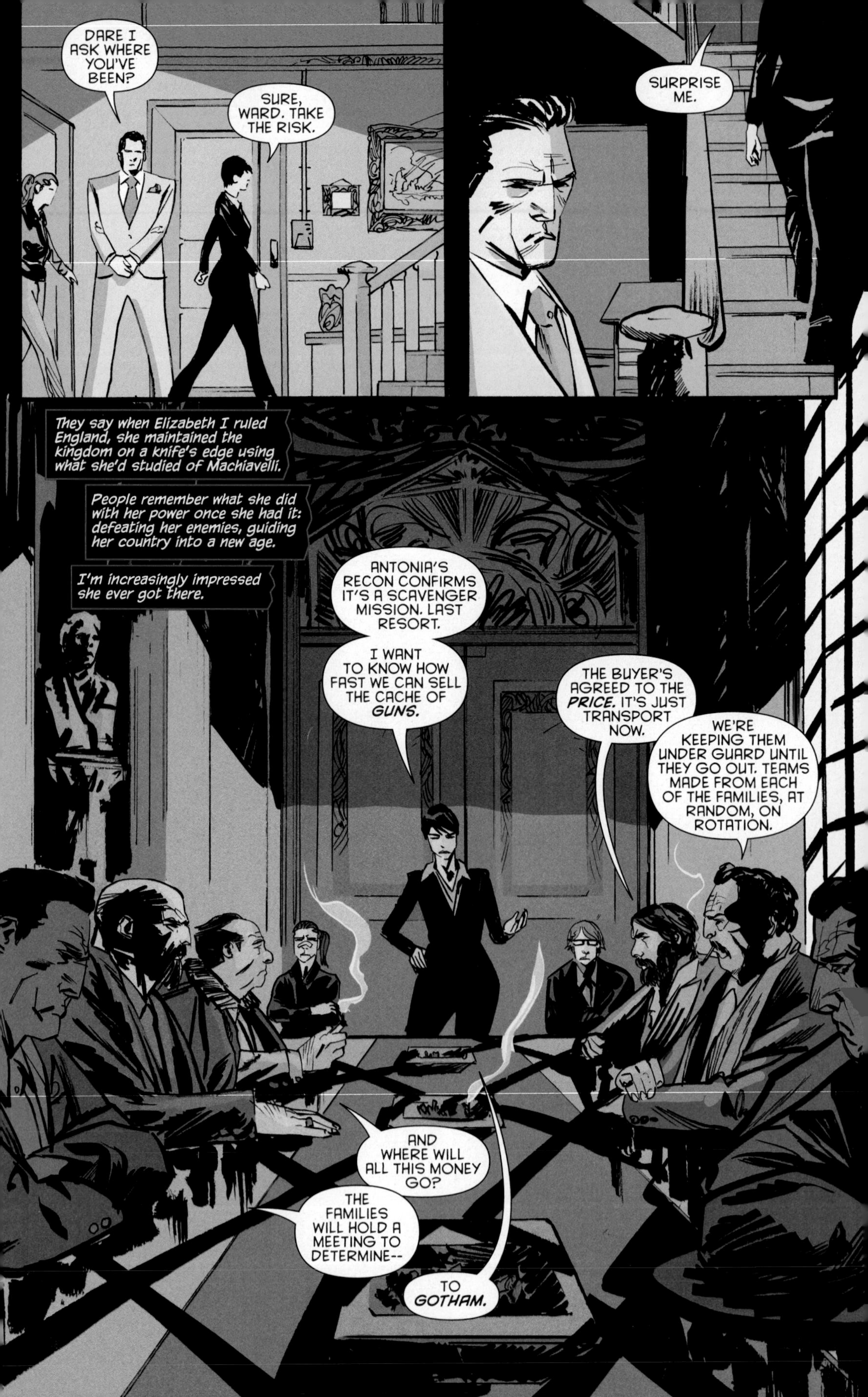
DARE I ASK WHERE YOU'VE BEEN?
SURE, WARD. TAKE THE RISK.
SURPRISE ME.
They say when Elizabeth I ruled England, she maintained the kingdom on a knife's edge using what she'd studied of Machiavelli.
People remember what she did with her power once she had it: defeating her enemies, guiding her country into a new age.
I'm increasingly impressed she ever got there.
ANTONIA'S RECON CONFIRMS IT'S A SCAVENGER MISSION. LAST RESORT.
I WANT TO KNOW HOW FAST WE CAN SELL THE CACHE OF GUNS.
THE BUYER'S AGREED TO THE PRICE. IT'S JUST TRANSPORT NOW.
WE'RE KEEPING THEM UNDER GUARD UNTIL THEY GO OUT. TEAMS MADE FROM EACH OF THE FAMILIES, AT RANDOM, ON ROTATION.
AND WHERE WILL ALL THIS MONEY GO?
THE FAMILIES WILL HOLD A MEETING TO DETERMINE--
TO GOTHAM.

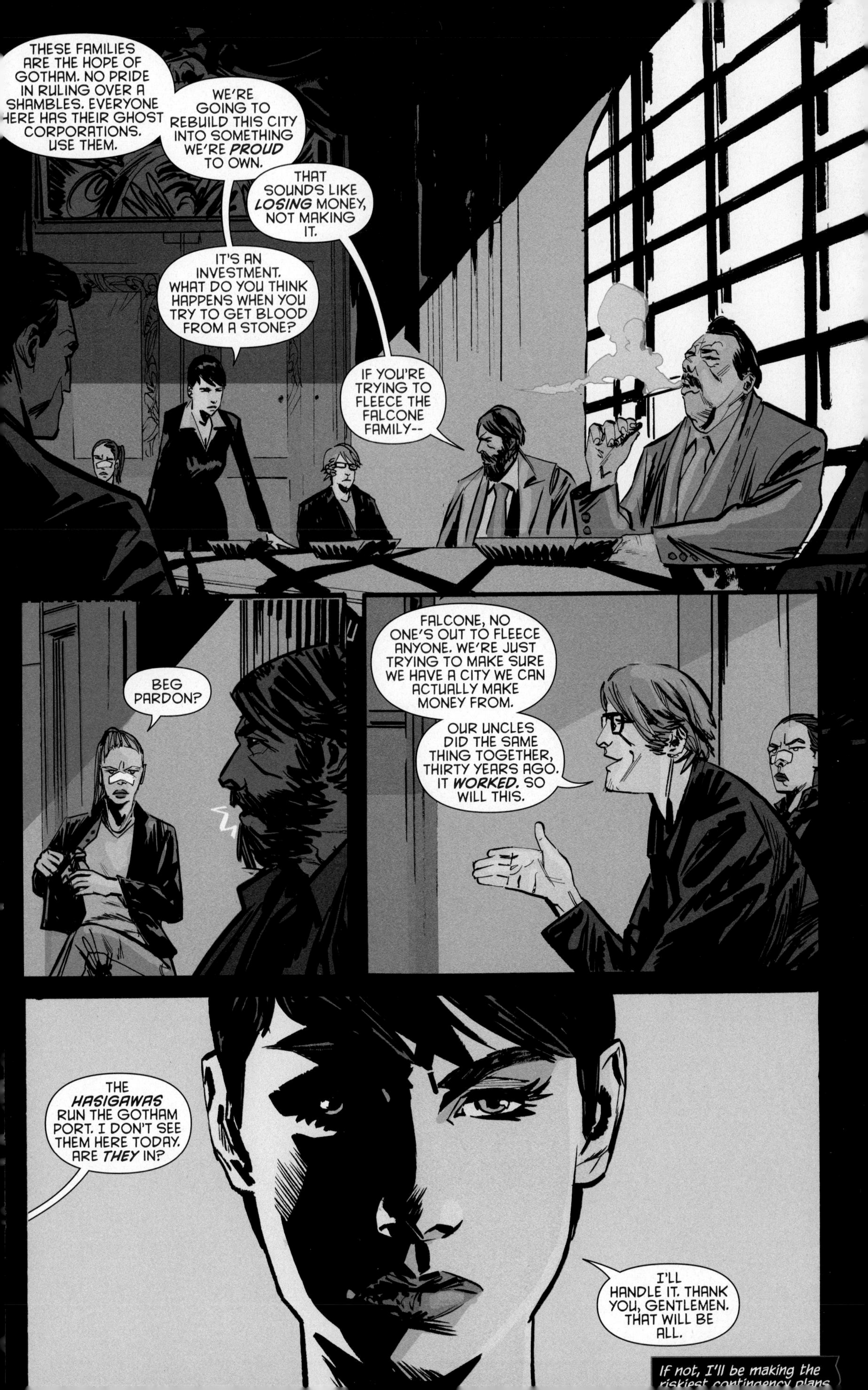
THESE FAMILIES ARE THE HOPE OF GOTHAM. NO PRIDE IN RULING OVER A SHAMBLES. EVERYONE HERE HAS THEIR GHOST CORPORATIONS. USE THEM.
WE'RE GOING TO REBUILD THIS CITY INTO SOMETHING WE'RE PROUD TO OWN.
THAT SOUNDS LIKE LOSING MONEY, NOT MAKING IT.
IT'S AN INVESTMENT. WHAT DO YOU THINK HAPPENS WHEN YOU TRY TO GET BLOOD FROM A STONE?
IF YOU'RE TRYING TO FLEECE THE FALCONE FAMILY--
BEG PARDON?
FALCONE, NO ONE'S OUT TO FLEECE ANYONE. WE'RE JUST TRYING TO MAKE SURE WE HAVE A CITY WE CAN ACTUALLY MAKE MONEY FROM.
OUR UNCLES DID THE SAME THING TOGETHER, THIRTY YEARS AGO. IT WORKED. SO WILL THIS.
THE HASIGAWAS RUN THE GOTHAM PORT. I DON'T SEE THEM HERE TODAY. ARE THEY IN?
I'LL HANDLE IT. THANK YOU, GENTLEMEN. THAT WILL BE ALL.
If not, I'll be making the

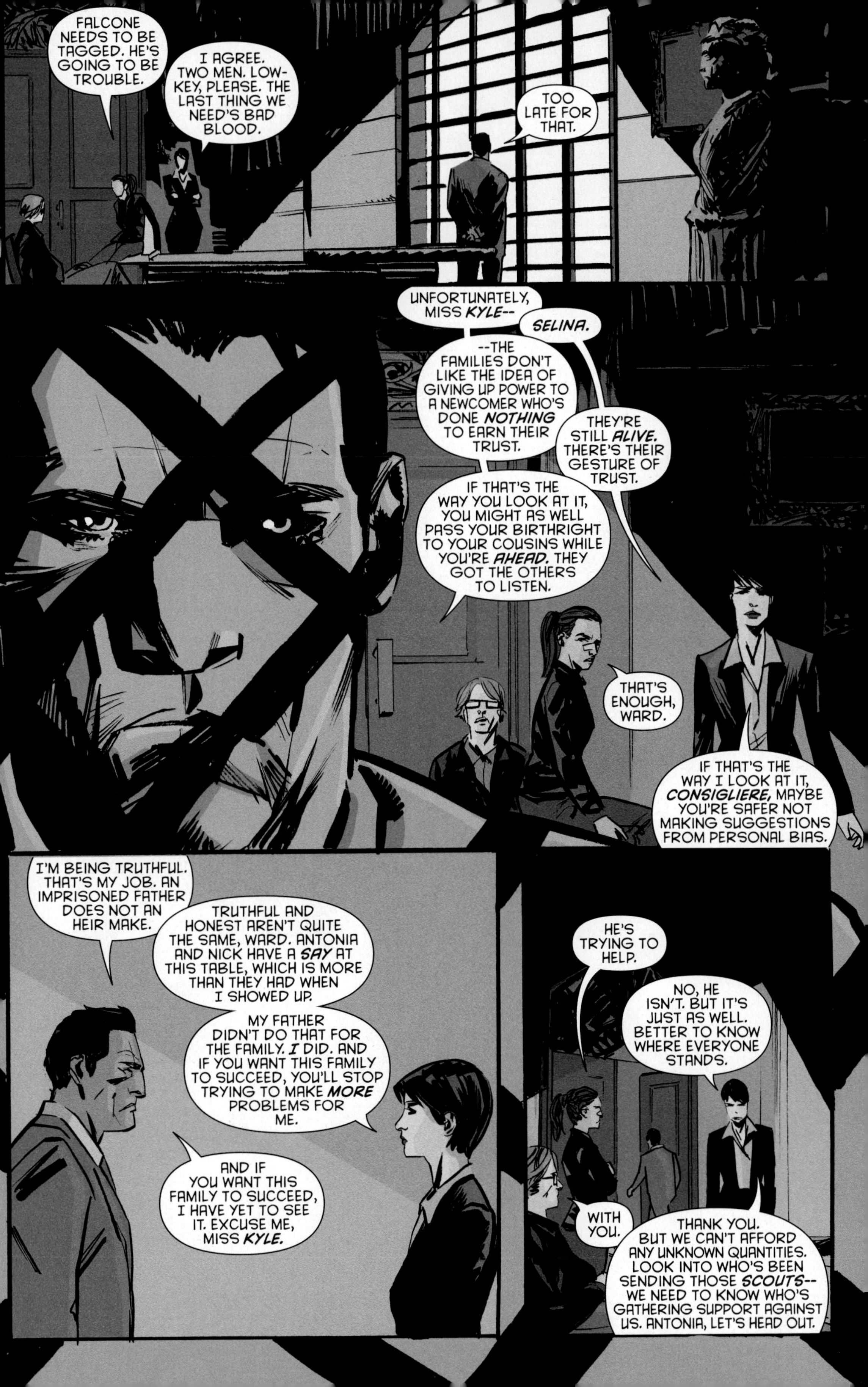

FALCONE NEEDS TO BE TAGGED. HE'S GOING TO BE TROUBLE.
I AGREE. TWO MEN. LOW-KEY, PLEASE. THE LAST THING WE NEED'S BAD BLOOD.
TOO LATE FOR THAT.
UNFORTUNATELY, MISS KYLE--
SELINA.
--THE FAMILIES DON'T LIKE THE IDEA OF GIVING UP POWER TO A NEWCOMER WHO'S DONE NOTHING TO EARN THEIR TRUST.
THEY'RE STILL ALIVE. THERE'S THEIR GESTURE OF TRUST.
IF THAT'S THE WAY YOU LOOK AT IT, YOU MIGHT AS WELL PASS YOUR BIRTHRIGHT TO YOUR COUSINS WHILE YOU'RE AHEAD. THEY GOT THE OTHERS TO LISTEN.
THAT'S ENOUGH, WARD.
IF THAT'S THE WAY I LOOK AT IT, CONSIGLIERE, MAYBE YOU'RE SAFER NOT MAKING SUGGESTIONS FROM PERSONAL BIAS.
I'M BEING TRUTHFUL. THAT'S MY JOB. AN IMPRISONED FATHER DOES NOT AN HEIR MAKE.
TRUTHFUL AND HONEST AREN'T QUITE THE SAME, WARD. ANTONIA AND NICK HAVE A SAY AT THIS TABLE, WHICH IS MORE THAN THEY HAD WHEN I SHOWED UP.
MY FATHER DIDN'T DO THAT FOR THE FAMILY. I DID. AND IF YOU WANT THIS FAMILY TO SUCCEED, YOU'LL STOP TRYING TO MAKE MORE PROBLEMS FOR ME.
AND IF YOU WANT THIS FAMILY TO SUCCEED, I HAVE YET TO SEE IT. EXCUSE ME, MISS KYLE.
HE'S TRYING TO HELP.
NO, HE ISN'T. BUT IT'S JUST AS WELL. BETTER TO KNOW WHERE EVERYONE STANDS.
WITH YOU.
THANK YOU. BUT WE CAN'T AFFORD ANY UNKNOWN QUANTITIES. LOOK INTO WHO'S BEEN SENDING THOSE SCOUTS-- WE NEED TO KNOW WHO'S GATHERING SUPPORT AGAINST US. ANTONIA, LET'S HEAD OUT.

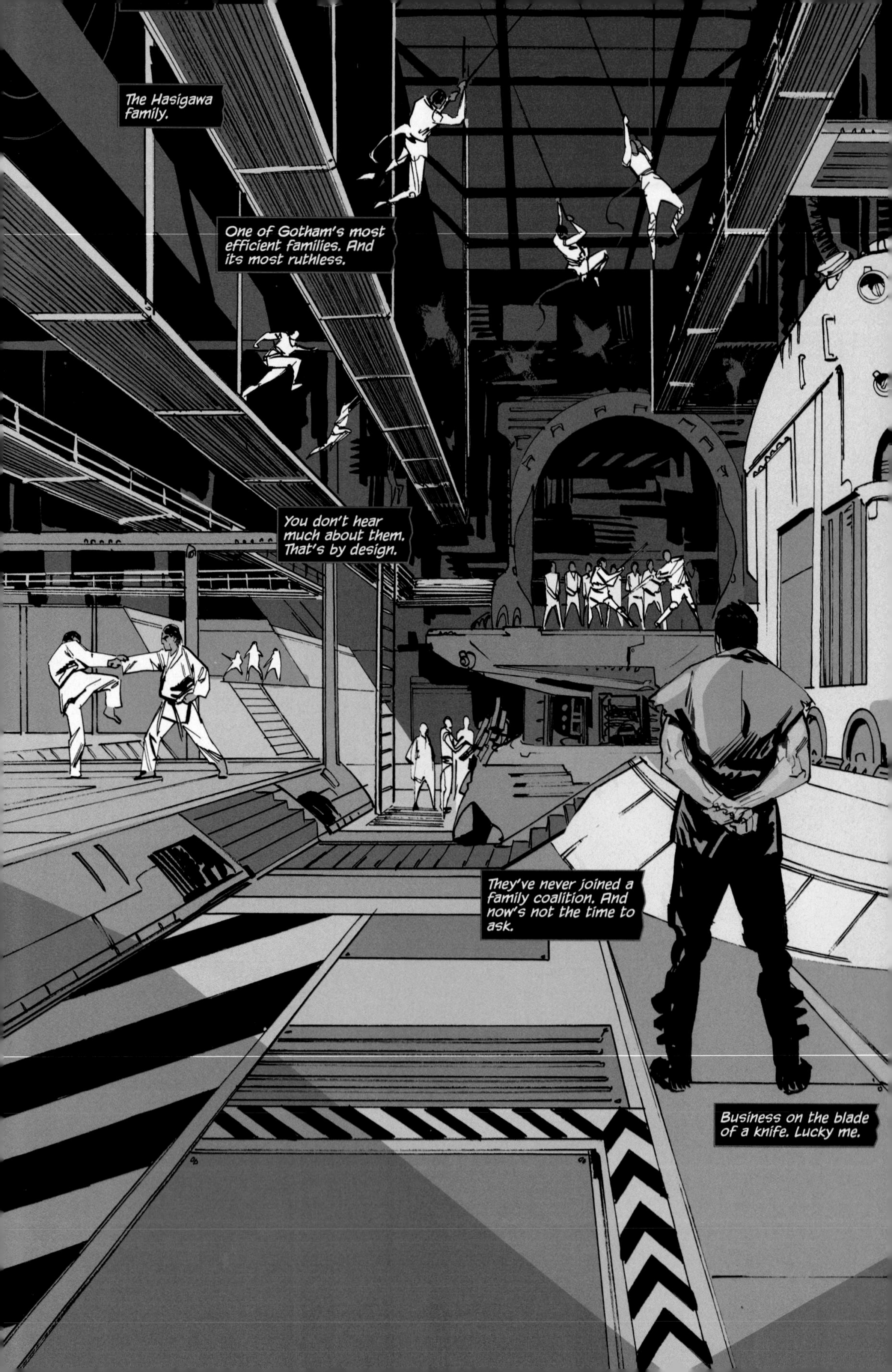
The Hasigawa family.
One of Gotham's most efficient families. And its most ruthless.
You don't hear much about them. That's by design.
They've never joined a family coalition. And now's not the time to ask.
Business on the blade of a knife. Lucky me.

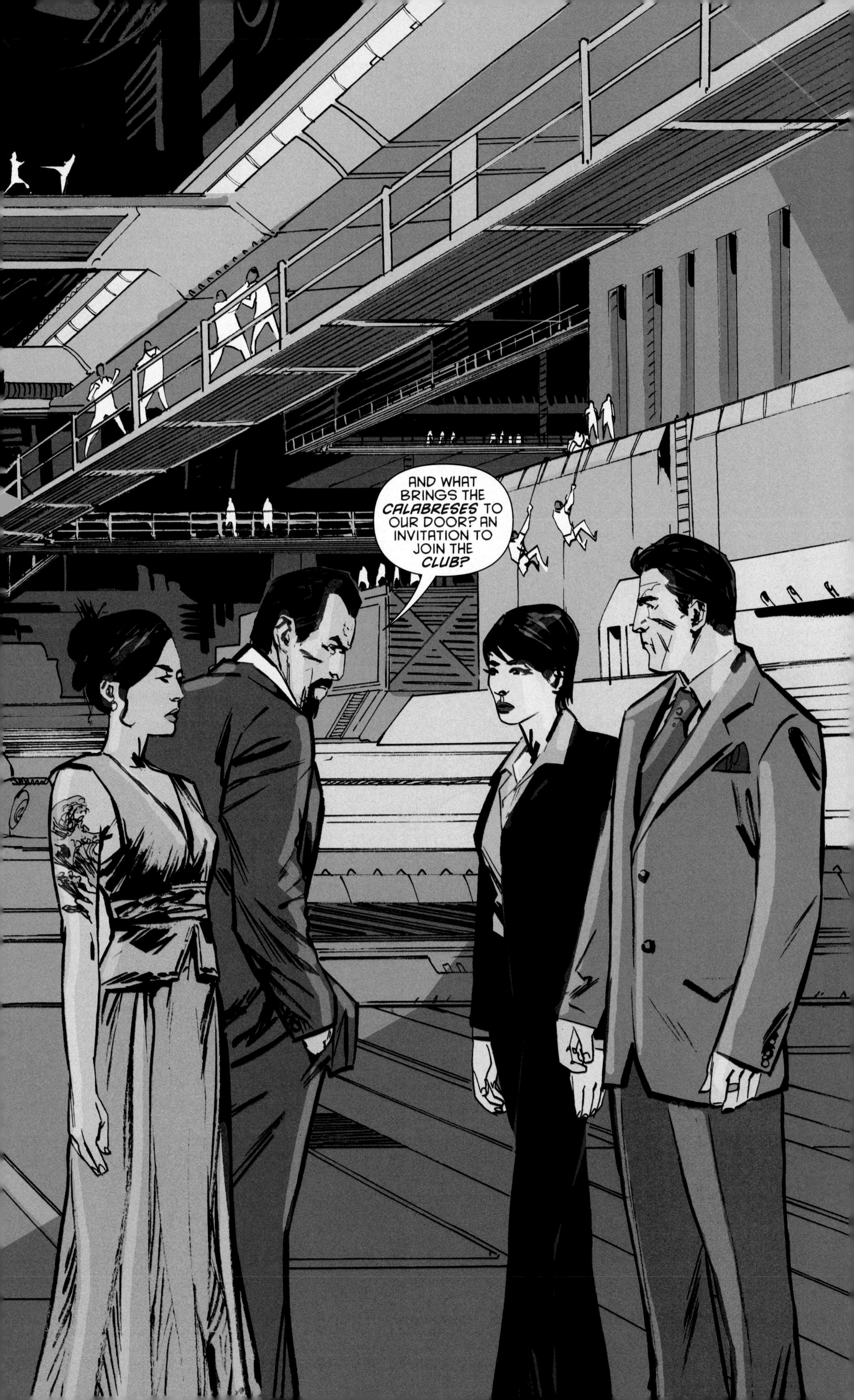
AND WHAT BRINGS THE *CALABRESES* TO OUR DOOR? AN INVITATION TO JOIN THE *CLUB?*

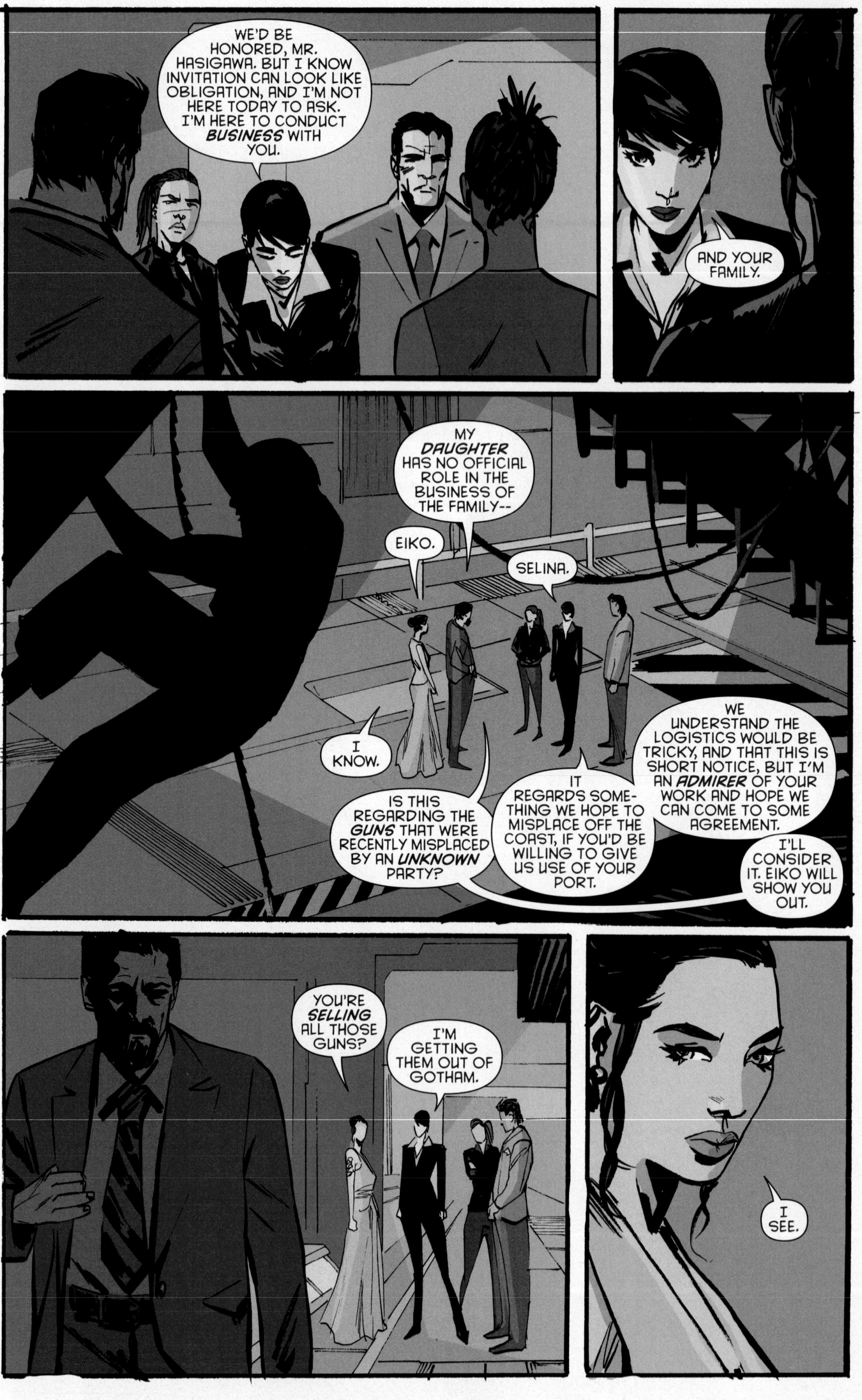
WE'D BE HONORED, MR. HASIGAWA. BUT I KNOW INVITATION CAN LOOK LIKE OBLIGATION, AND I'M NOT HERE TODAY TO ASK. I'M HERE TO CONDUCT BUSINESS WITH YOU.
AND YOUR FAMILY.
MY DAUGHTER HAS NO OFFICIAL ROLE IN THE BUSINESS OF THE FAMILY--
EIKO.
SELINA.
I KNOW.
WE UNDERSTAND THE LOGISTICS WOULD BE TRICKY, AND THAT THIS IS SHORT NOTICE, BUT I'M AN ADMIRER OF YOUR WORK AND HOPE WE CAN COME TO SOME AGREEMENT.
IT REGARDS SOME-THING WE HOPE TO MISPLACE OFF THE COAST, IF YOU'D BE WILLING TO GIVE US USE OF YOUR PORT.
IS THIS REGARDING THE GUNS THAT WERE RECENTLY MISPLACED BY AN UNKNOWN PARTY?
I'LL CONSIDER IT. EIKO WILL SHOW YOU OUT.
YOU'RE SELLING ALL THOSE GUNS?
I'M GETTING THEM OUT OF GOTHAM.
I SEE.

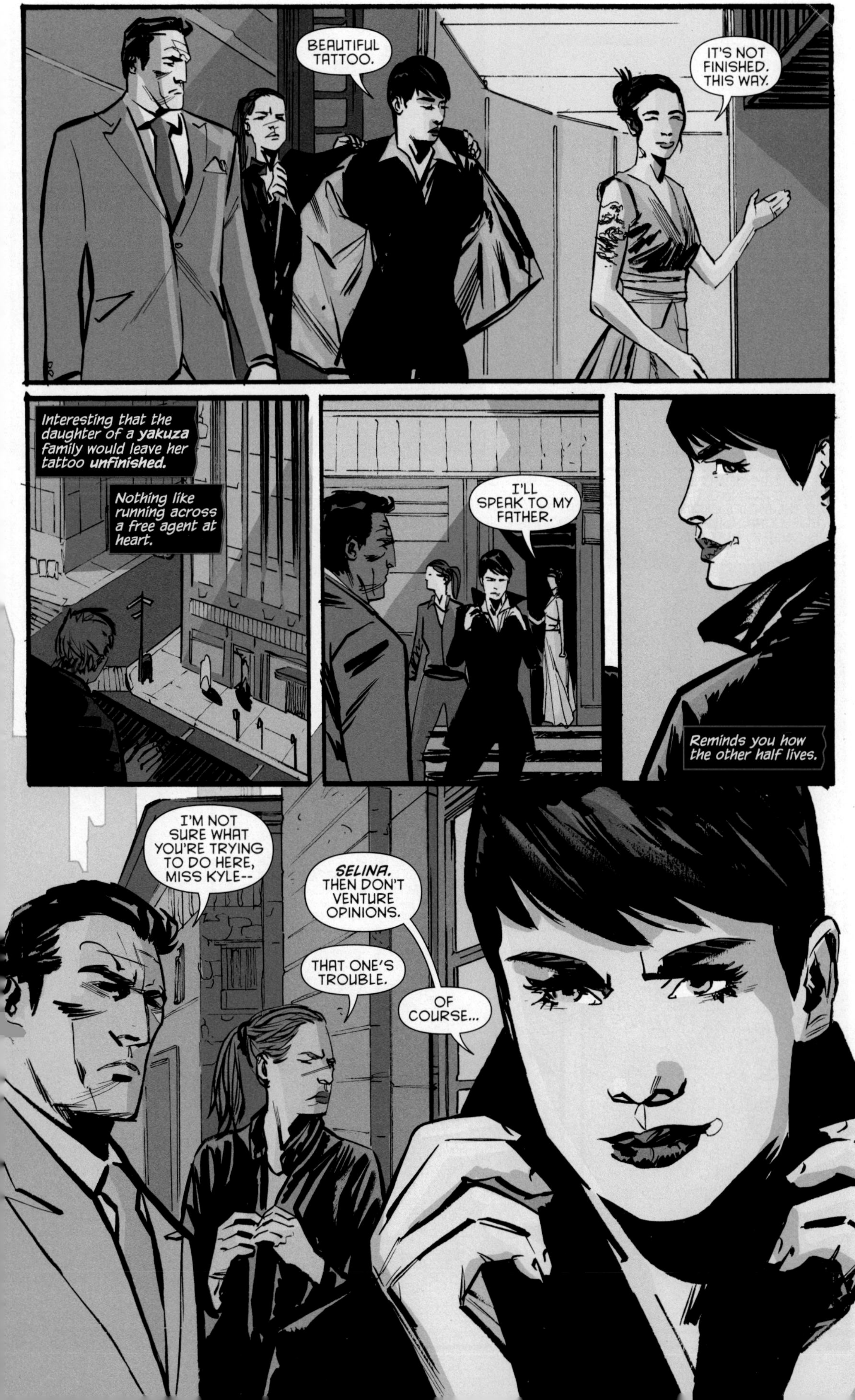

BEAUTIFUL TATTOO.
IT'S NOT FINISHED. THIS WAY.
Interesting that the daughter of a yakuza family would leave her tattoo unfinished.
Nothing like running across a free agent at heart.
I'LL SPEAK TO MY FATHER.
Reminds you how the other half lives.
I'M NOT SURE WHAT YOU'RE TRYING TO DO HERE, MISS KYLE--
SELINA. THEN DON'T VENTURE OPINIONS.
THAT ONE'S TROUBLE.
OF COURSE...

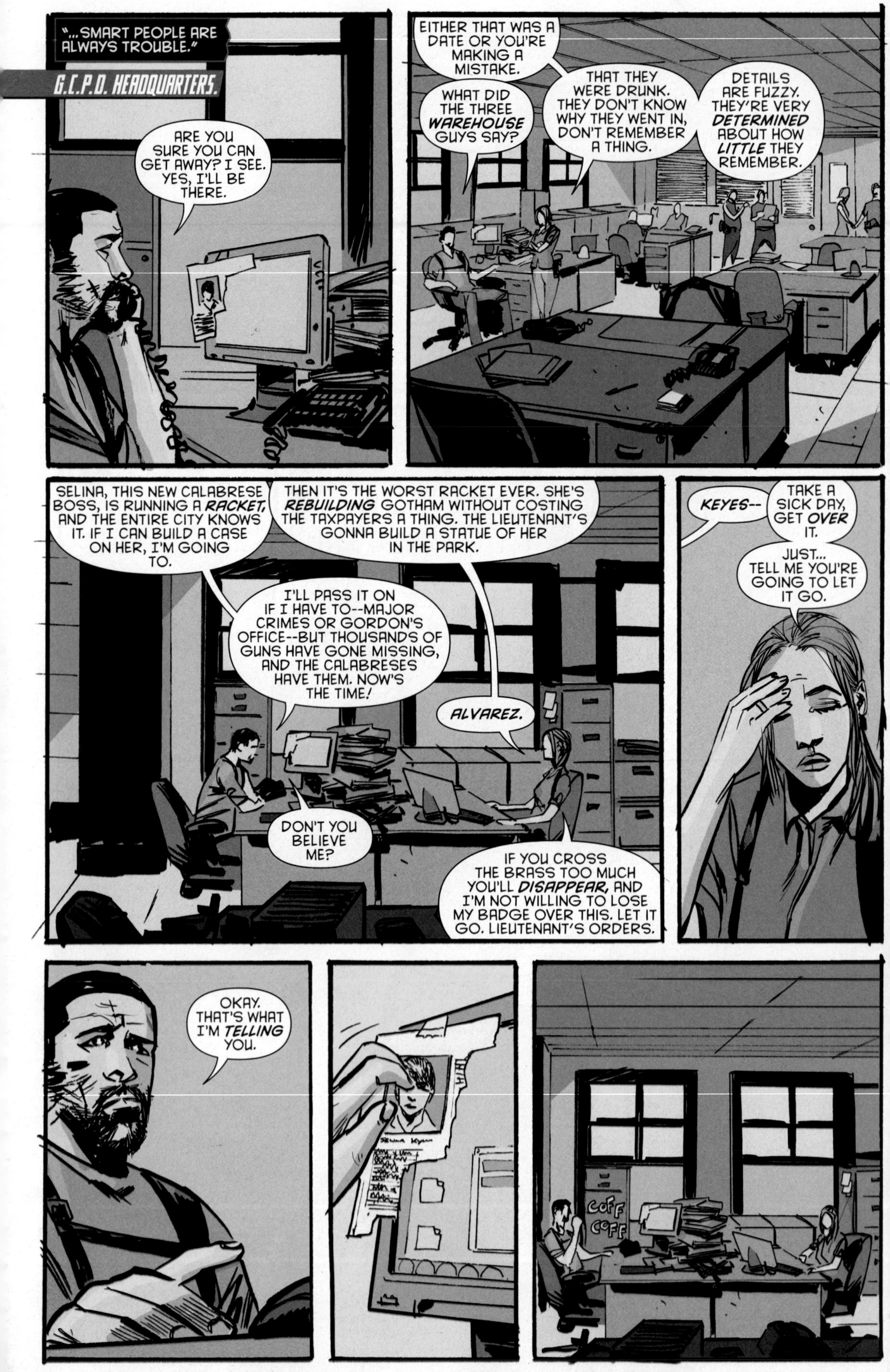

"...SMART PEOPLE ARE ALWAYS TROUBLE."
G.C.P.D. HEADQUARTERS.
ARE YOU SURE YOU CAN GET AWAY? I SEE. YES, I'LL BE THERE.
EITHER THAT WAS A DATE OR YOU'RE MAKING A MISTAKE.
WHAT DID THE THREE WAREHOUSE GUYS SAY?
THAT THEY WERE DRUNK. THEY DON'T KNOW WHY THEY WENT IN, DON'T REMEMBER A THING.
DETAILS ARE FUZZY. THEY'RE VERY DETERMINED ABOUT HOW LITTLE THEY REMEMBER.
SELINA, THIS NEW CALABRESE BOSS, IS RUNNING A RACKET, AND THE ENTIRE CITY KNOWS IT. IF I CAN BUILD A CASE ON HER, I'M GOING TO.
THEN IT'S THE WORST RACKET EVER. SHE'S REBUILDING GOTHAM WITHOUT COSTING THE TAXPAYERS A THING. THE LIEUTENANT'S GONNA BUILD A STATUE OF HER IN THE PARK.
I'LL PASS IT ON IF I HAVE TO--MAJOR CRIMES OR GORDON'S OFFICE--BUT THOUSANDS OF GUNS HAVE GONE MISSING, AND THE CALABRESES HAVE THEM. NOW'S THE TIME!
ALVAREZ.
DON'T YOU BELIEVE ME?
IF YOU CROSS THE BRASS TOO MUCH YOU'LL DISAPPEAR, AND I'M NOT WILLING TO LOSE MY BADGE OVER THIS. LET IT GO. LIEUTENANT'S ORDERS.
KEYES--
TAKE A SICK DAY, GET OVER IT.
JUST... TELL ME YOU'RE GOING TO LET IT GO.
OKAY. THAT'S WHAT I'M TELLING YOU.
COFF COFF

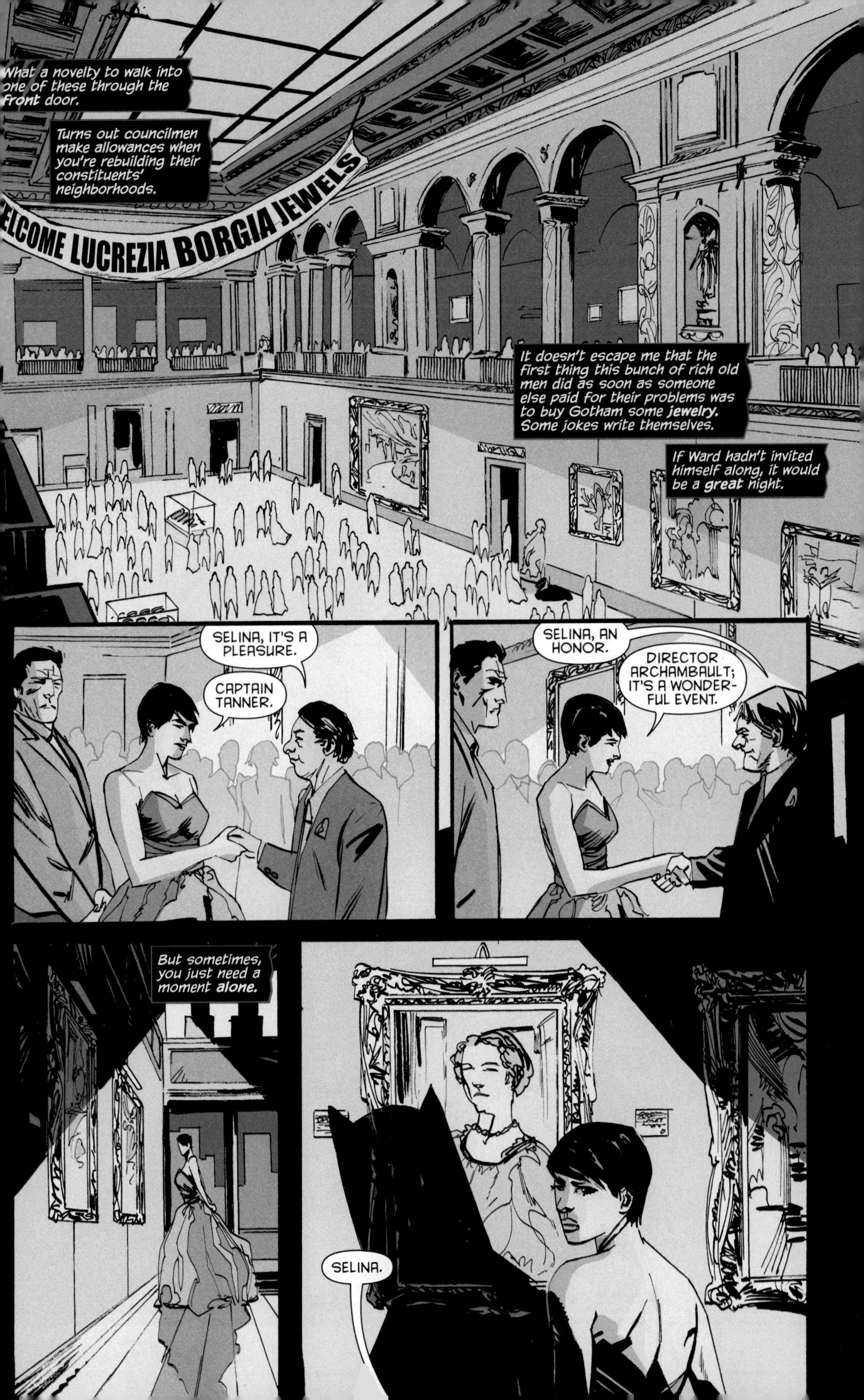
What a novelty to walk into one of these through the front door.
Turns out councilmen make allowances when you're rebuilding their constituents' neighborhoods.
WELCOME LUCREZIA BORGIA JEWELS
It doesn't escape me that the first thing this bunch of rich old men did as soon as someone else paid for their problems was to buy Gotham some jewelry. Some jokes write themselves.
If Ward hadn't invited himself along, it would be a great night.
SELINA, IT'S A PLEASURE.
CAPTAIN TANNER.
SELINA, AN HONOR.
DIRECTOR ARCHAMBAULT; IT'S A WONDERFUL EVENT.
But sometimes, you just need a moment alone.
SELINA.

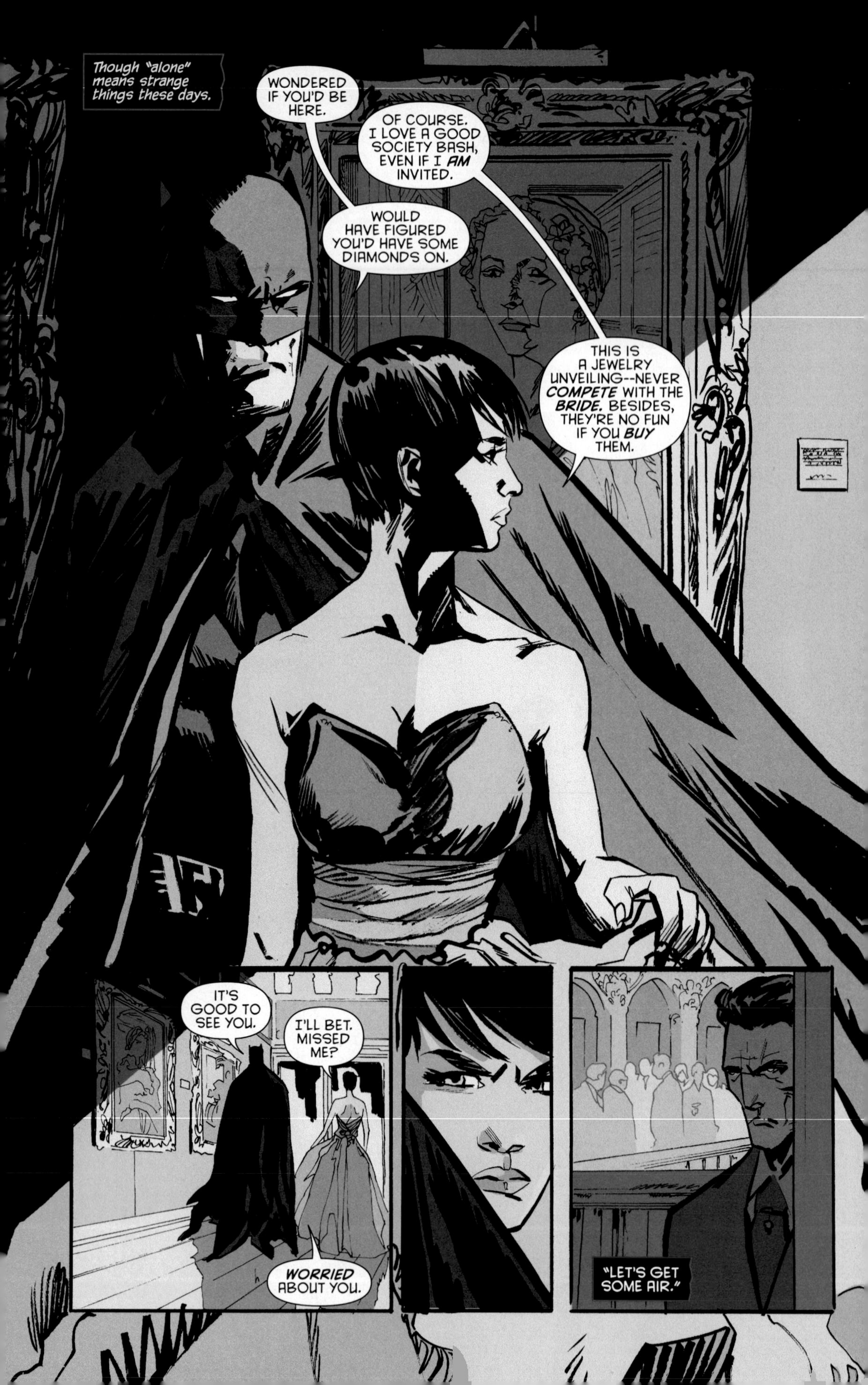

Though "alone" means strange things these days.
WONDERED IF YOU'D BE HERE.
OF COURSE. I LOVE A GOOD SOCIETY BASH, EVEN IF I *AM* INVITED.
WOULD HAVE FIGURED YOU'D HAVE SOME DIAMONDS ON.
THIS IS A JEWELRY UNVEILING--NEVER *COMPETE* WITH THE *BRIDE.* BESIDES, THEY'RE NO FUN IF YOU *BUY* THEM.
IT'S GOOD TO SEE YOU.
I'LL BET. MISSED ME?
WORRIED ABOUT YOU.
"LET'S GET SOME AIR."

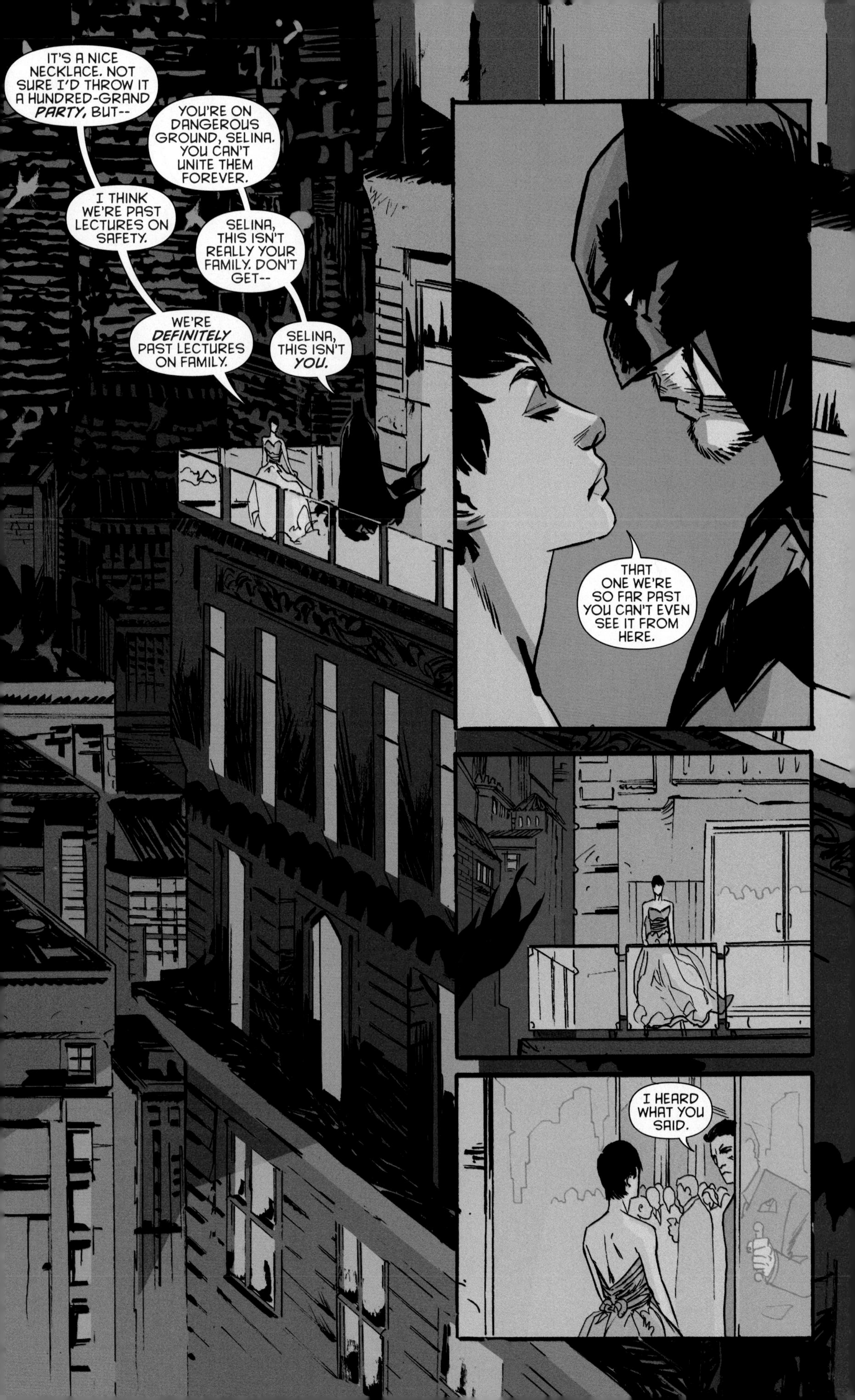
IT'S A NICE NECKLACE. NOT SURE I'D THROW IT A HUNDRED-GRAND PARTY, BUT--
YOU'RE ON DANGEROUS GROUND, SELINA. YOU CAN'T UNITE THEM FOREVER.
I THINK WE'RE PAST LECTURES ON SAFETY.
SELINA, THIS ISN'T REALLY YOUR FAMILY. DON'T GET--
WE'RE DEFINITELY PAST LECTURES ON FAMILY.
SELINA, THIS ISN'T YOU.
THAT ONE WE'RE SO FAR PAST YOU CAN'T EVEN SEE IT FROM HERE.
I HEARD WHAT YOU SAID.

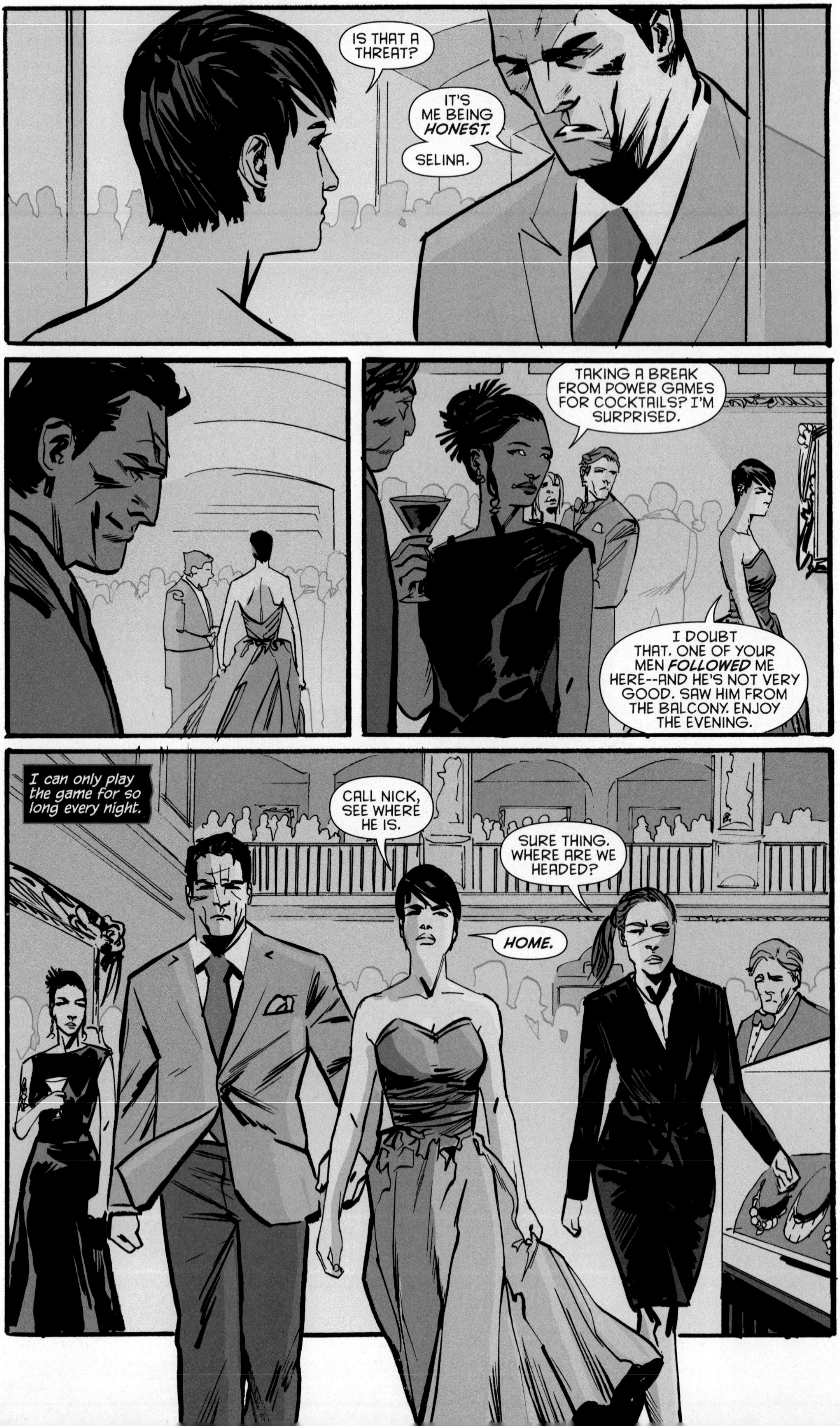

IS THAT A THREAT?
IT'S ME BEING HONEST.
SELINA.
TAKING A BREAK FROM POWER GAMES FOR COCKTAILS? I'M SURPRISED.
I DOUBT THAT. ONE OF YOUR MEN FOLLOWED ME HERE--AND HE'S NOT VERY GOOD. SAW HIM FROM THE BALCONY. ENJOY THE EVENING.
I can only play the game for so long every night.
CALL NICK, SEE WHERE HE IS.
SURE THING. WHERE ARE WE HEADED?
HOME.

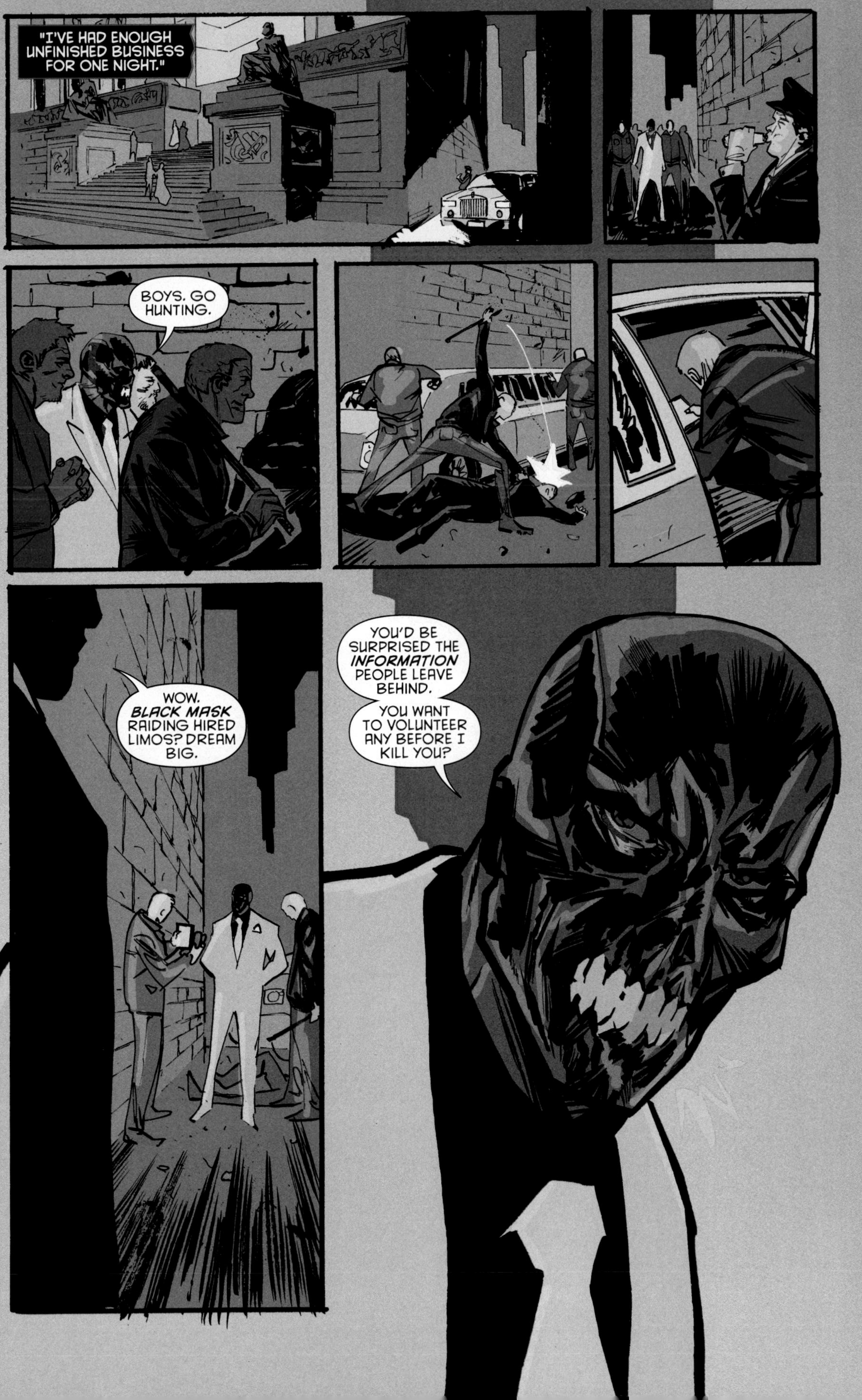
"I'VE HAD ENOUGH UNFINISHED BUSINESS FOR ONE NIGHT."
BOYS. GO HUNTING.
WOW. BLACK MASK RAIDING HIRED LIMOS? DREAM BIG.
YOU'D BE SURPRISED THE INFORMATION PEOPLE LEAVE BEHIND.
YOU WANT TO VOLUNTEER ANY BEFORE I KILL YOU?

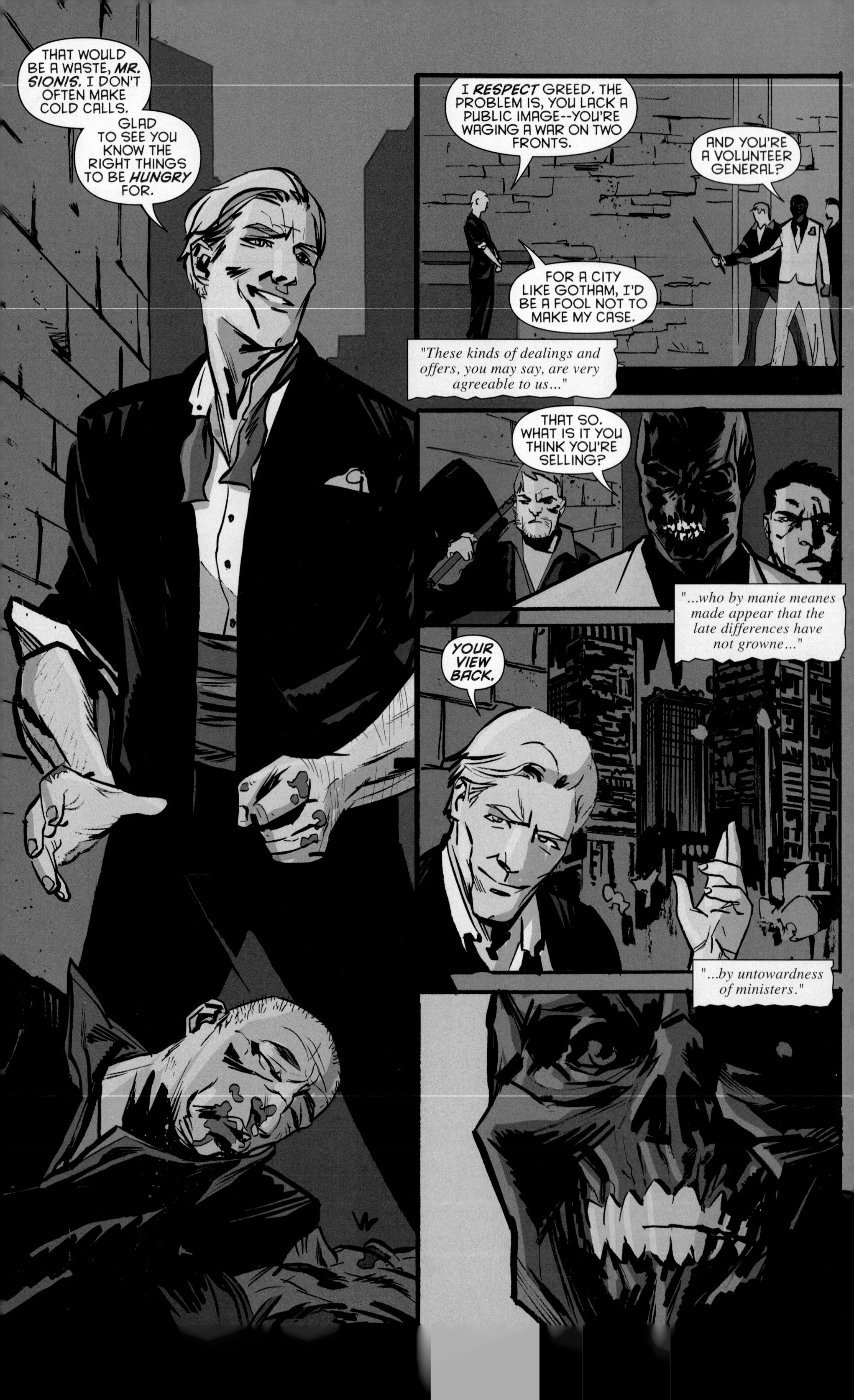
THAT WOULD BE A WASTE, MR. SIONIS. I DON'T OFTEN MAKE COLD CALLS.
GLAD TO SEE YOU KNOW THE RIGHT THINGS TO BE HUNGRY FOR.
I RESPECT GREED. THE PROBLEM IS, YOU LACK A PUBLIC IMAGE--YOU'RE WAGING A WAR ON TWO FRONTS.
AND YOU'RE A VOLUNTEER GENERAL?
FOR A CITY LIKE GOTHAM, I'D BE A FOOL NOT TO MAKE MY CASE.
"These kinds of dealings and offers, you may say, are very agreeable to us..."
THAT SO. WHAT IS IT YOU THINK YOU'RE SELLING?
"...who by manie meanes made appear that the late differences have not growne..."
YOUR VIEW BACK.
"...by untowardness of ministers."

can raise a city.

But this will break if anyone gets *careless*. All machines do.

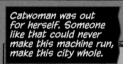

Catwoman was out for herself. Someone like that could never make this machine run, make this city whole.

I will.

Not bad, as ninth lives go.

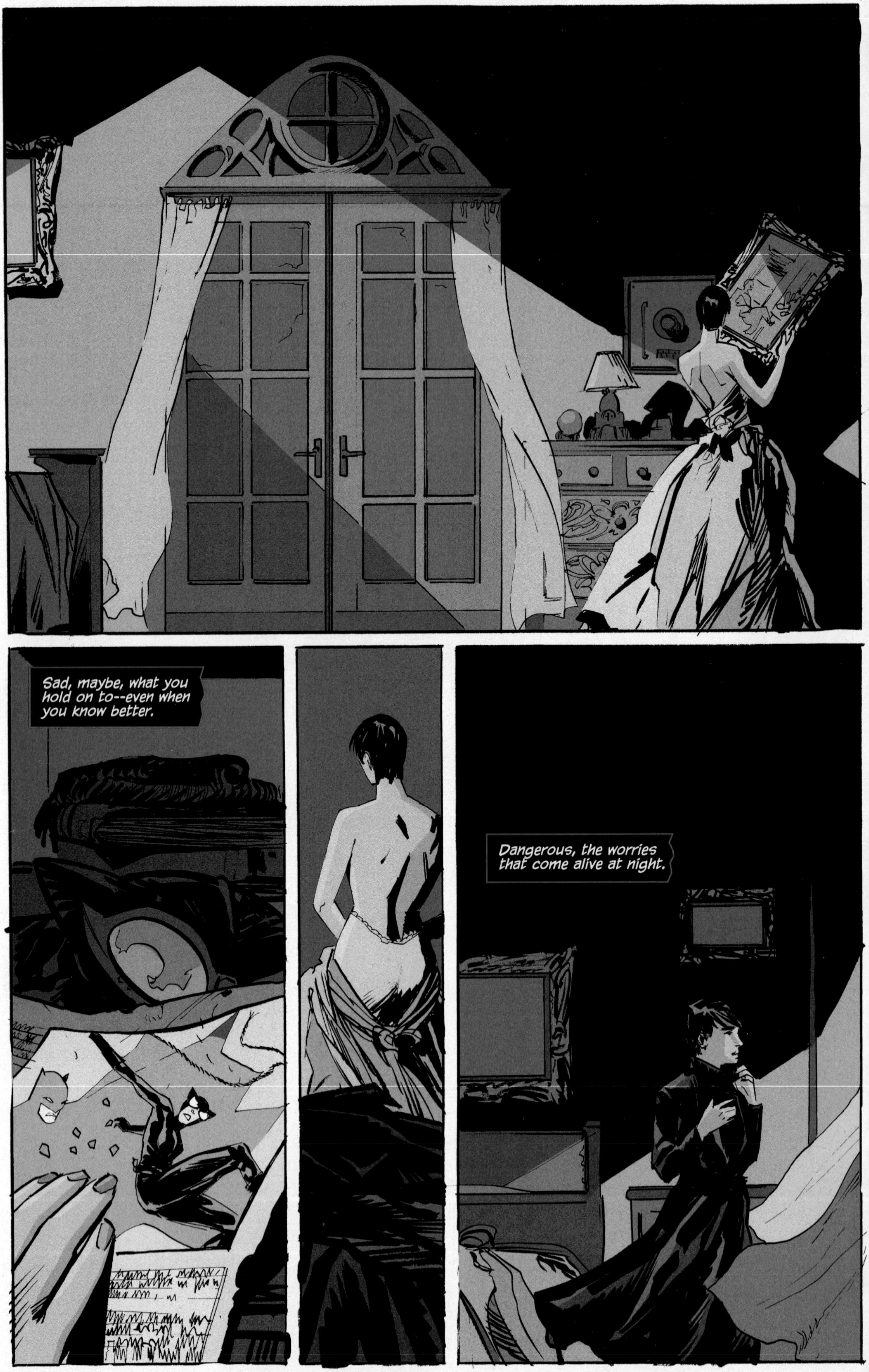
Sad, maybe, what you hold on to--even when you know better.
Dangerous, the worries that come alive at night.

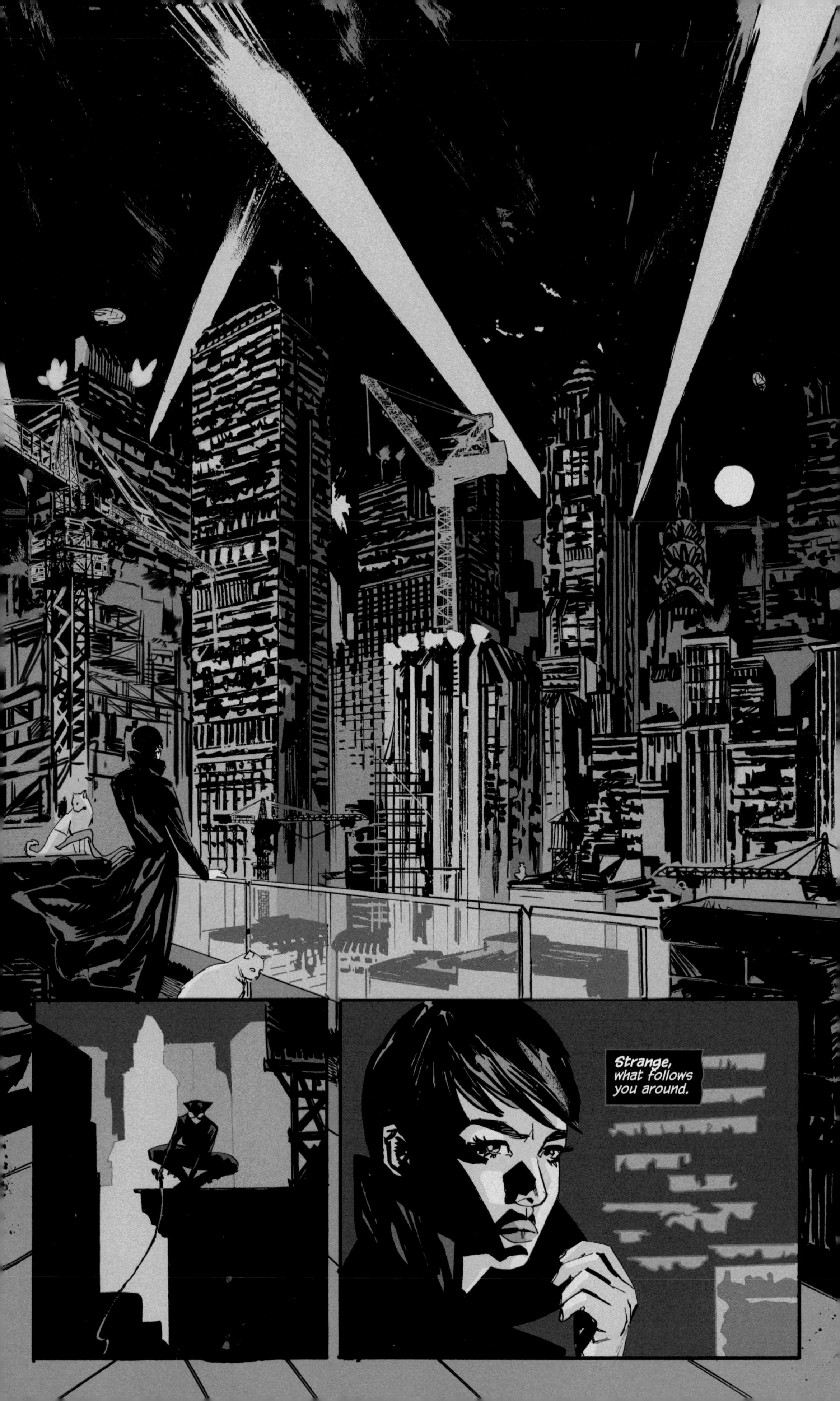
Strange, what follows you around.

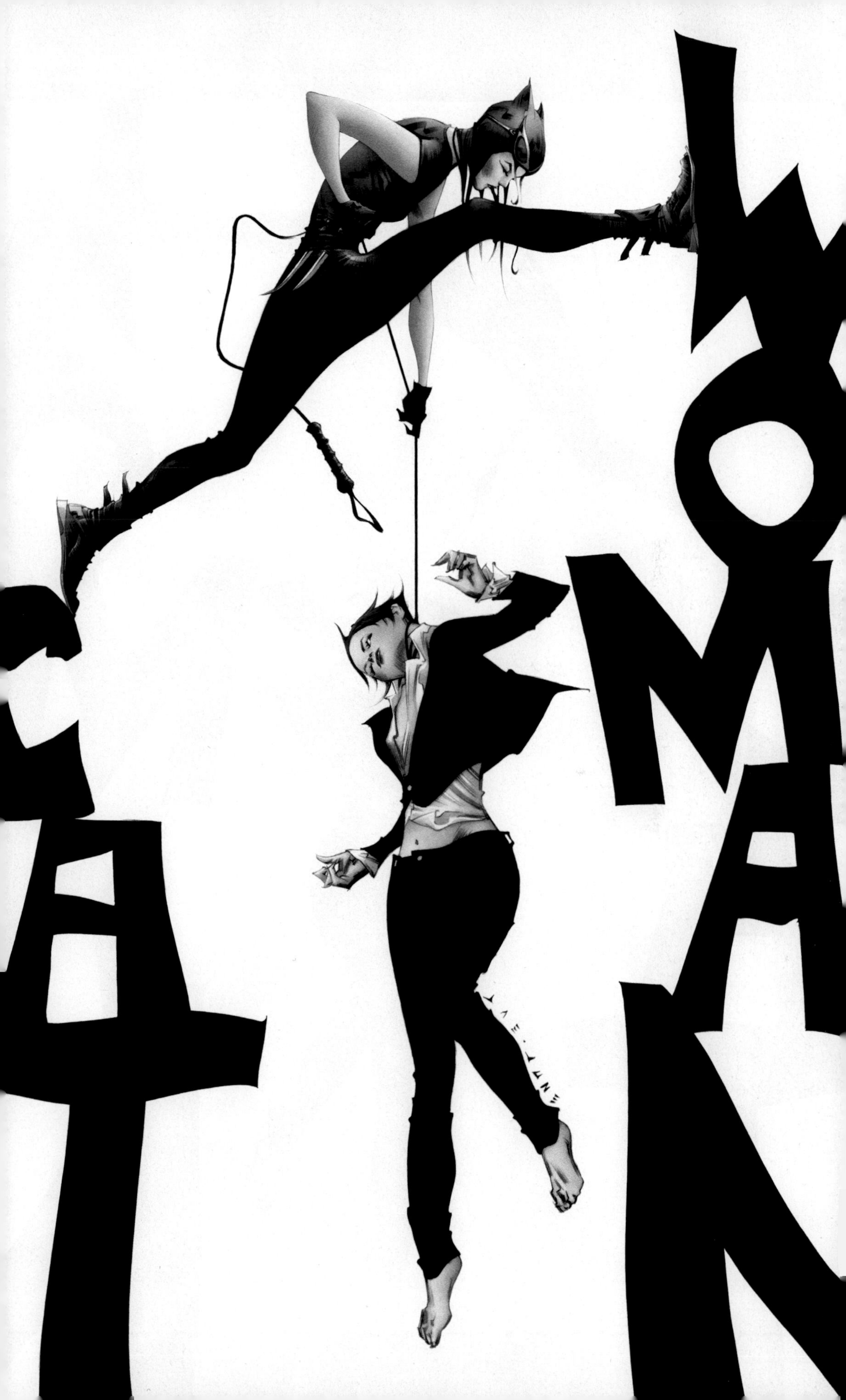
CAT
WOMAN

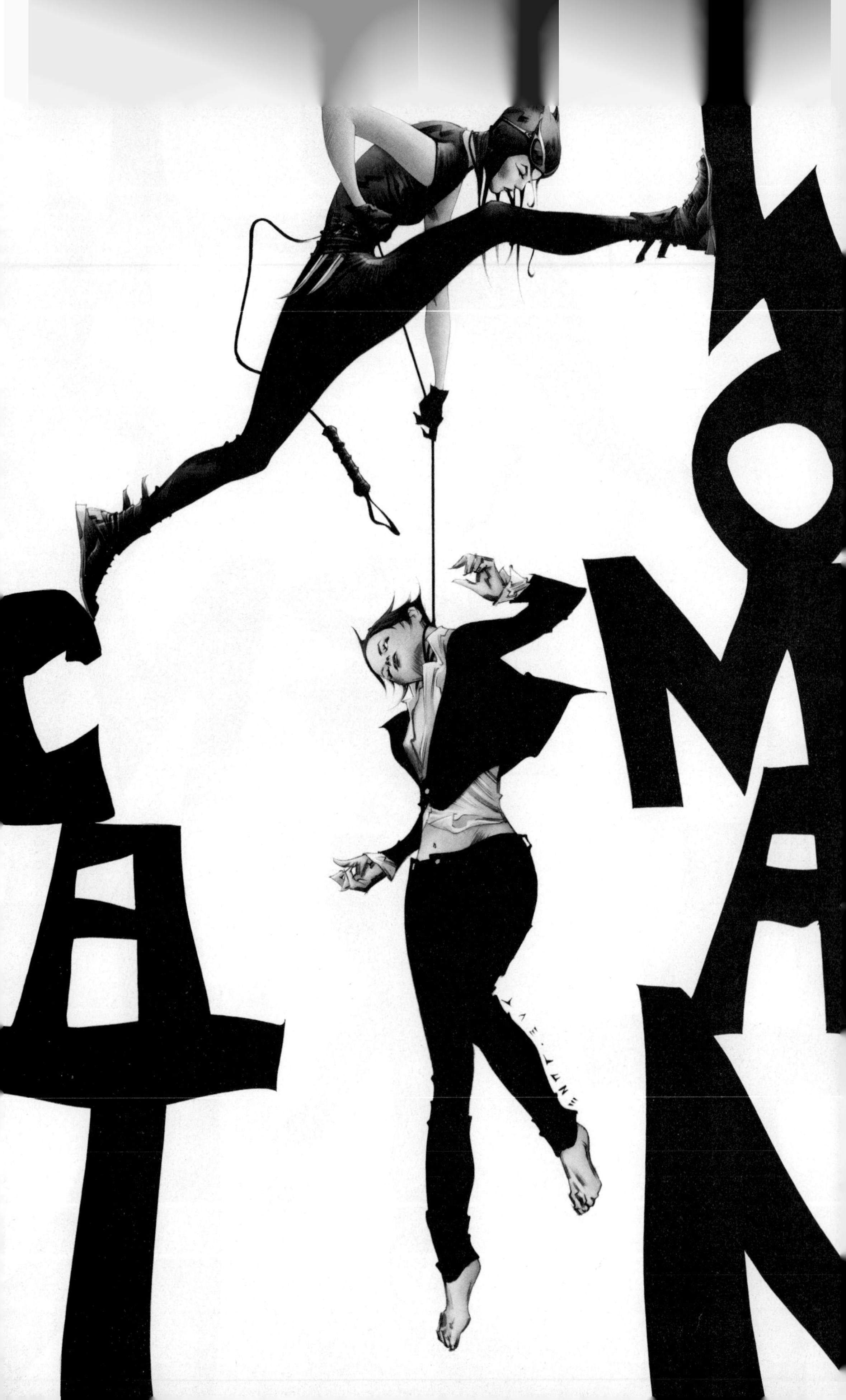
CAT
WOMAN

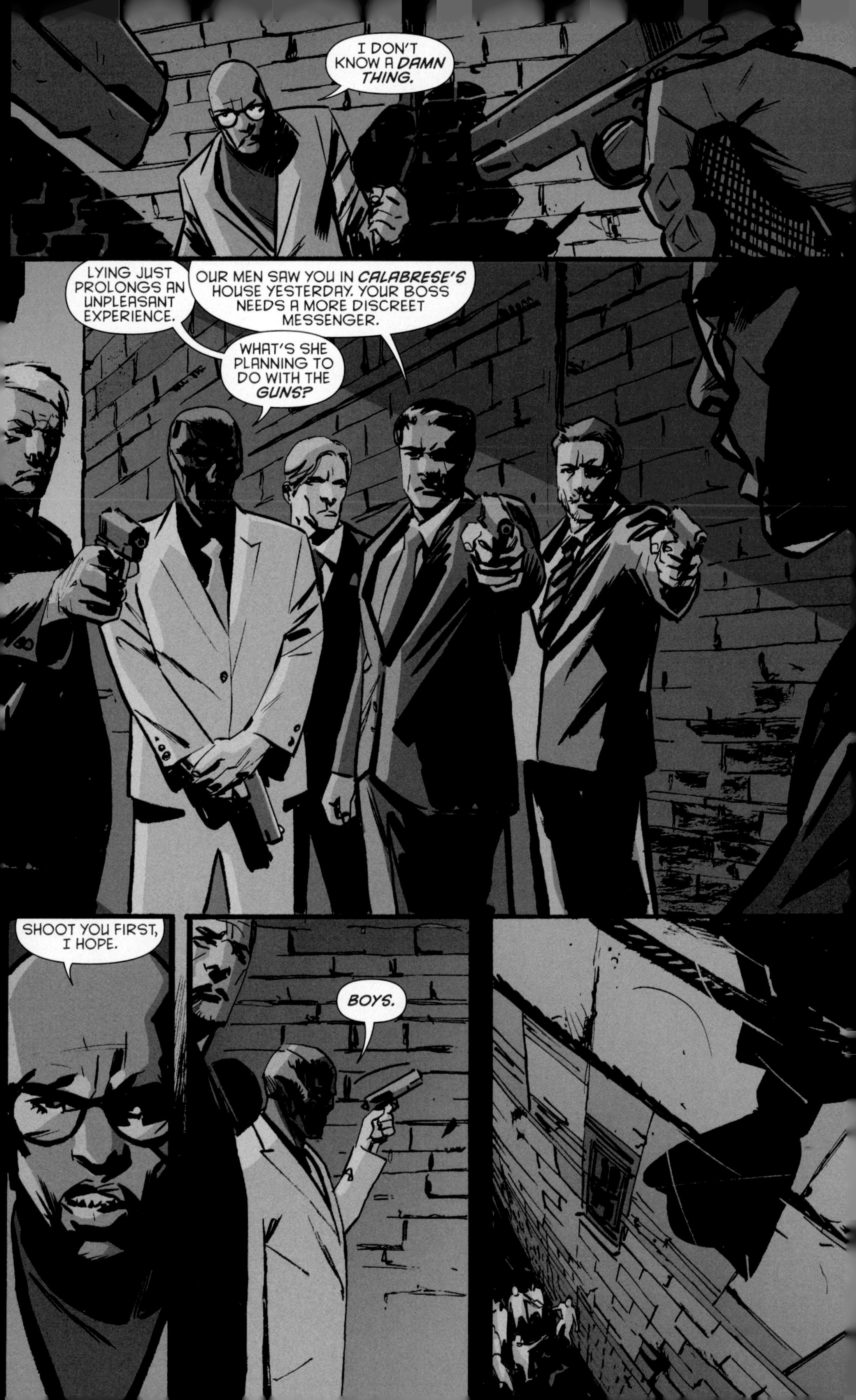
I DON'T KNOW A *DAMN THING.*
LYING JUST PROLONGS AN UNPLEASANT EXPERIENCE.
OUR MEN SAW YOU IN *CALABRESE'S* HOUSE YESTERDAY. YOUR BOSS NEEDS A MORE DISCREET MESSENGER.
WHAT'S SHE PLANNING TO DO WITH THE *GUNS?*
SHOOT YOU FIRST, I HOPE.
BOYS.

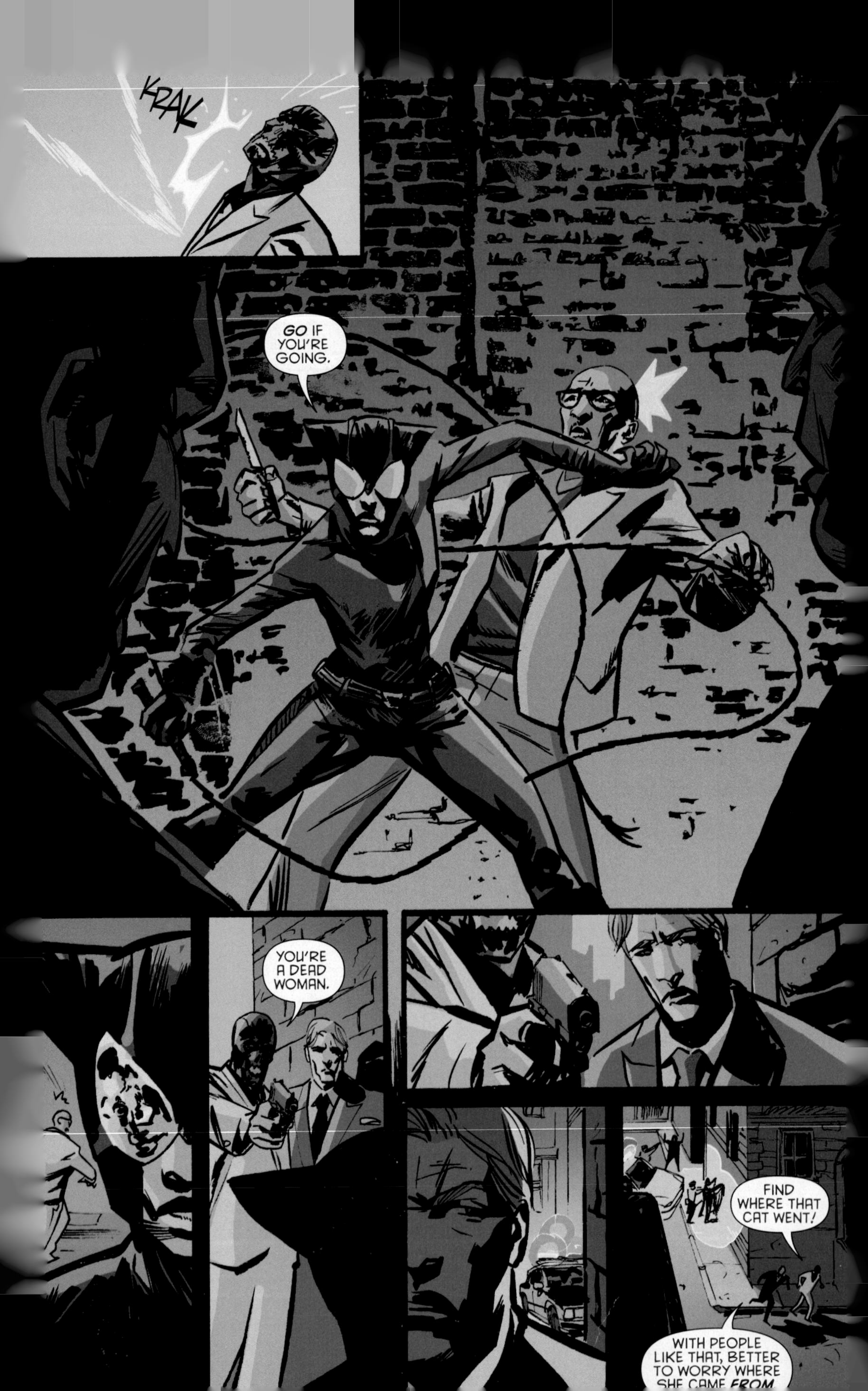
KRAK
GO IF YOU'RE GOING.
YOU'RE A DEAD WOMAN.
FIND WHERE THAT CAT WENT!
WITH PEOPLE LIKE THAT, BETTER TO WORRY WHERE SHE CAME FROM.

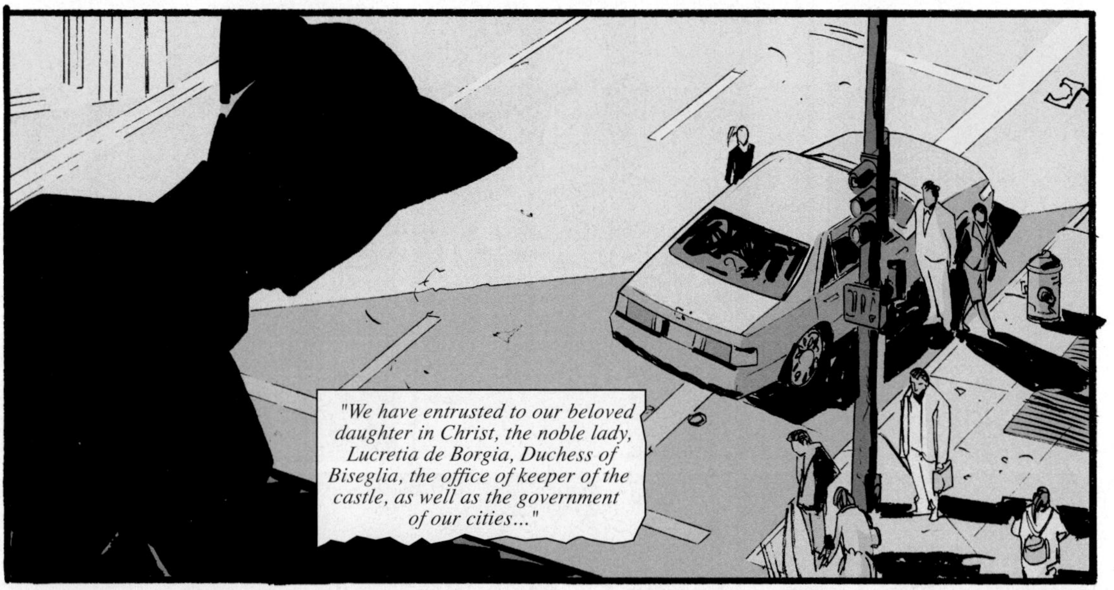
"We have entrusted to our beloved daughter in Christ, the noble lady, Lucretia de Borgia, Duchess of Biseglia, the office of keeper of the castle, as well as the government of our cities..."

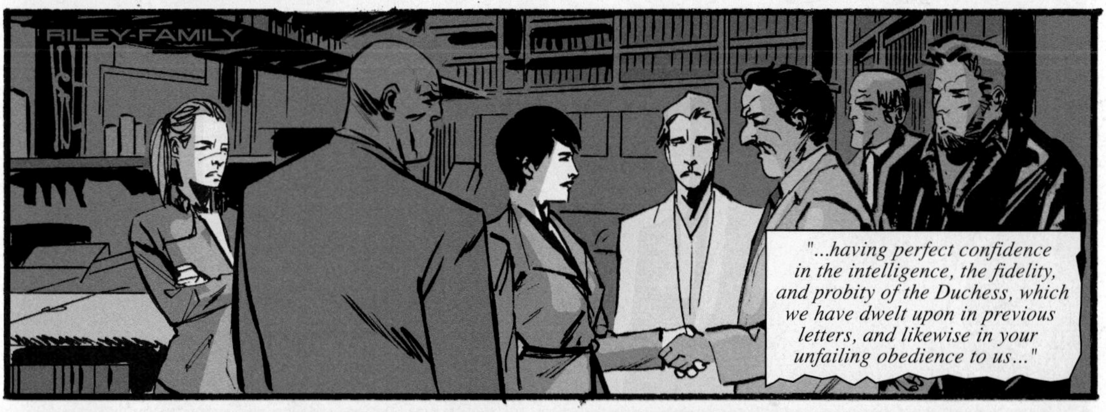
RILEY-FAMILY
"...having perfect confidence in the intelligence, the fidelity, and probity of the Duchess, which we have dwelt upon in previous letters, and likewise in your unfailing obedience to us..."

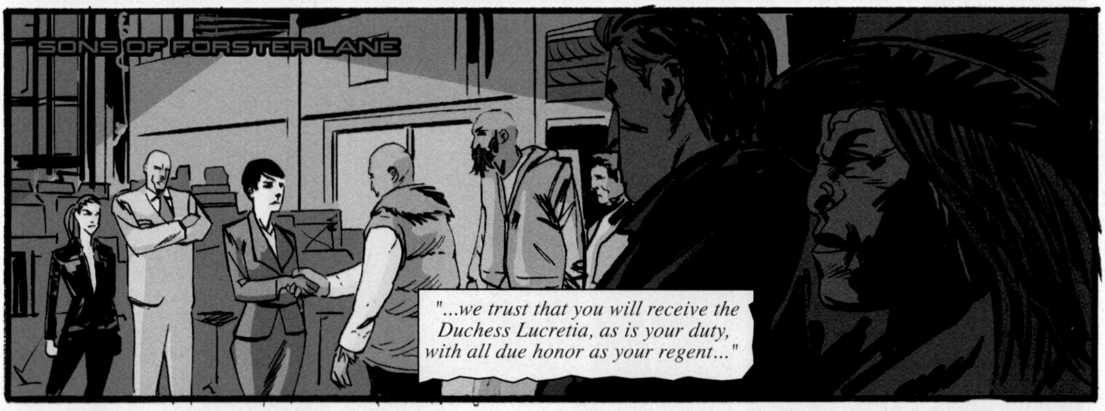
SONS OF FORSTER LANE
"...we trust that you will receive the Duchess Lucretia, as is your duty, with all due honor as your regent..."

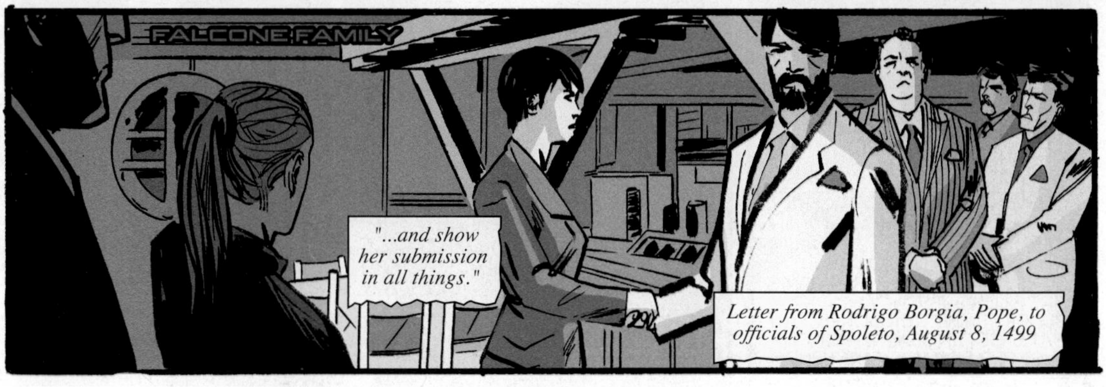
FALCONE FAMILY
"...and show her submission in all things."
Letter from Rodrigo Borgia, Pope, to officials of Spoleto, August 8, 1499

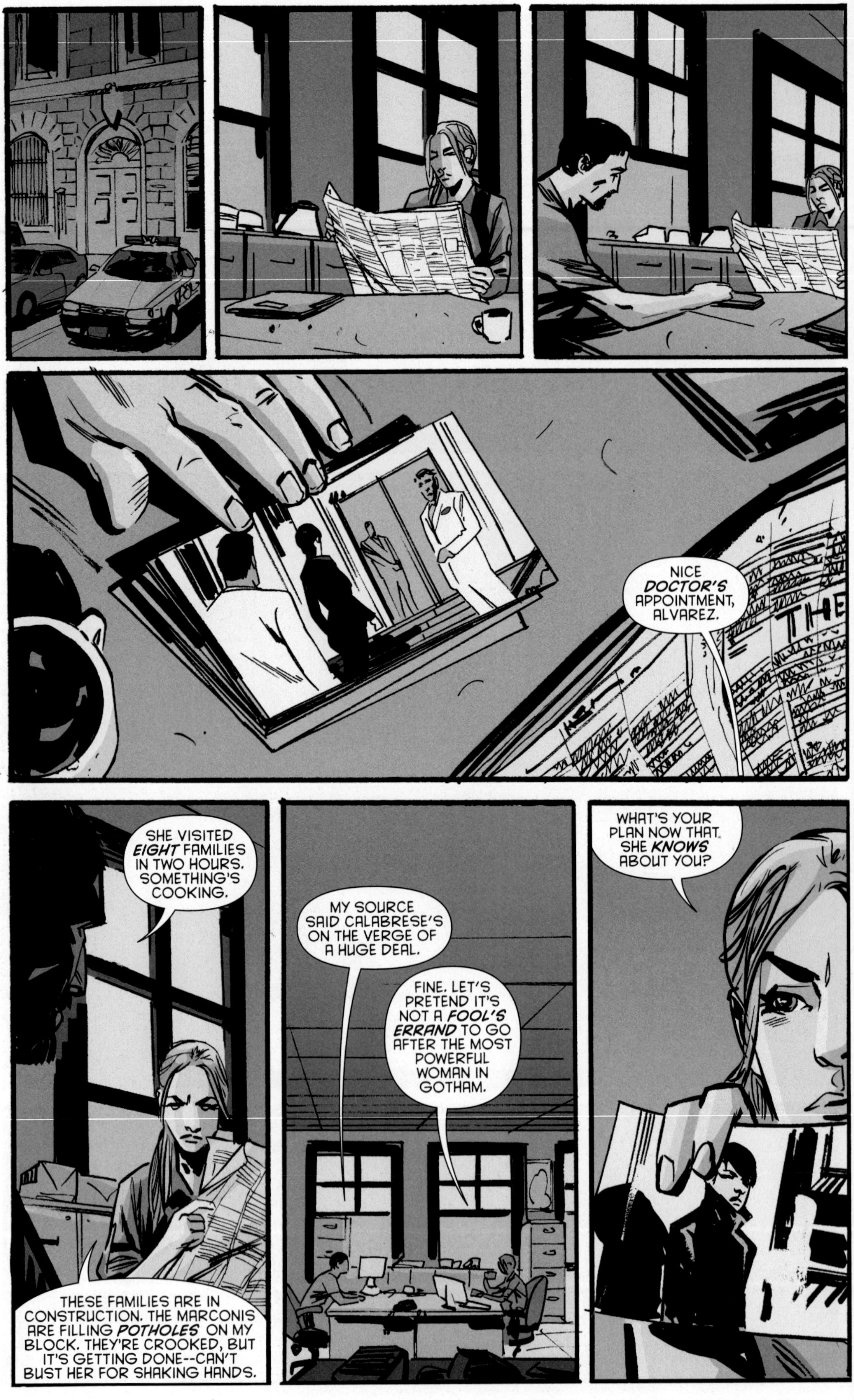
NICE DOCTOR'S APPOINTMENT, ALVAREZ.
SHE VISITED EIGHT FAMILIES IN TWO HOURS. SOMETHING'S COOKING.
THESE FAMILIES ARE IN CONSTRUCTION. THE MARCONIS ARE FILLING POTHOLES ON MY BLOCK. THEY'RE CROOKED, BUT IT'S GETTING DONE--CAN'T BUST HER FOR SHAKING HANDS.
MY SOURCE SAID CALABRESE'S ON THE VERGE OF A HUGE DEAL.
FINE. LET'S PRETEND IT'S NOT A FOOL'S ERRAND TO GO AFTER THE MOST POWERFUL WOMAN IN GOTHAM.
WHAT'S YOUR PLAN NOW THAT SHE KNOWS ABOUT YOU?

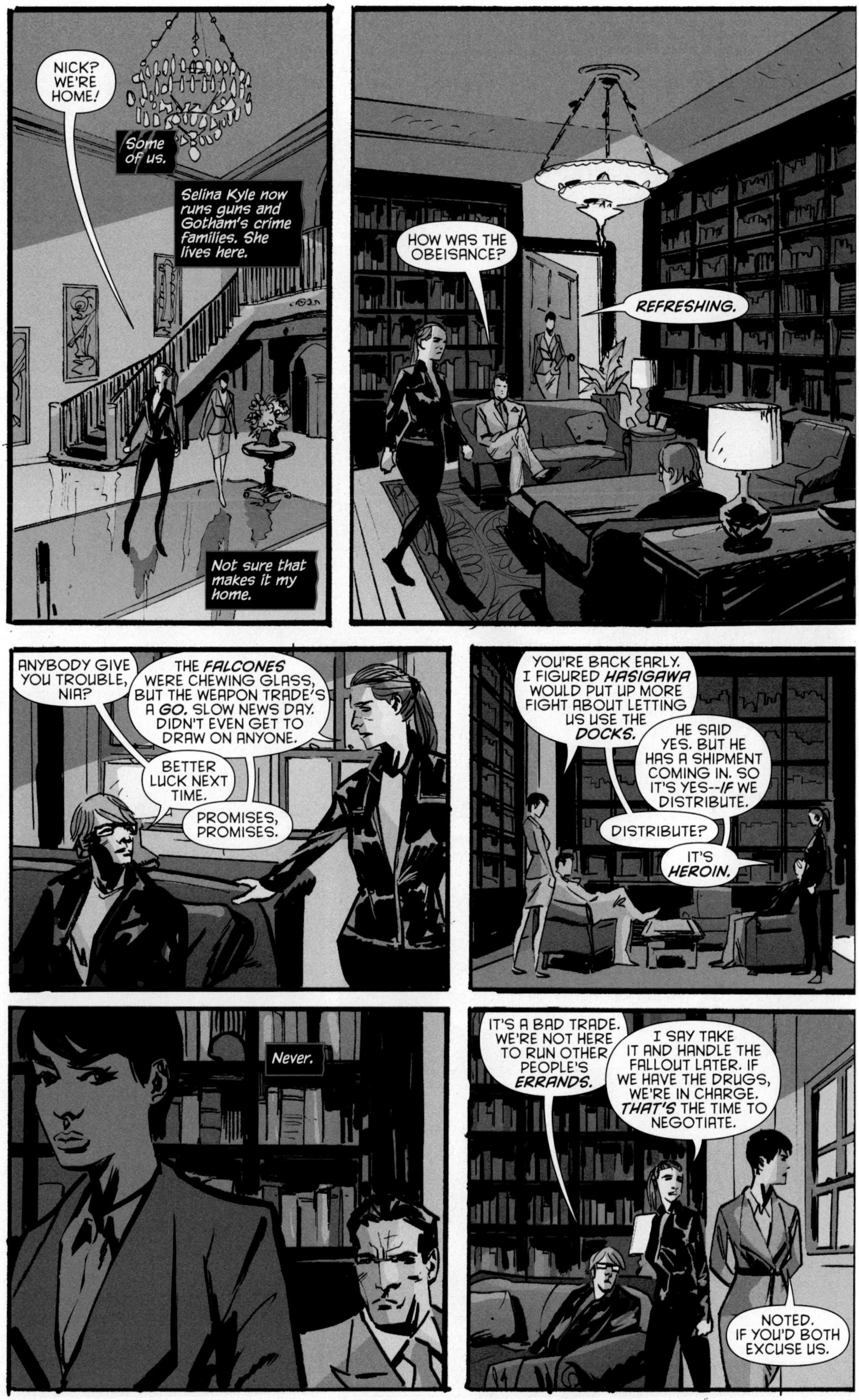

NICK? WE'RE HOME!
Some of us.
Selina Kyle now runs guns and Gotham's crime families. She lives here.
Not sure that makes it my home.
HOW WAS THE OBEISANCE?
REFRESHING.
ANYBODY GIVE YOU TROUBLE, NIA?
THE FALCONES WERE CHEWING GLASS, BUT THE WEAPON TRADE'S A GO. SLOW NEWS DAY. DIDN'T EVEN GET TO DRAW ON ANYONE.
BETTER LUCK NEXT TIME.
PROMISES, PROMISES.
YOU'RE BACK EARLY. I FIGURED HASIGAWA WOULD PUT UP MORE FIGHT ABOUT LETTING US USE THE DOCKS.
HE SAID YES. BUT HE HAS A SHIPMENT COMING IN. SO IT'S YES--IF WE DISTRIBUTE.
DISTRIBUTE?
IT'S HEROIN.
Never.
IT'S A BAD TRADE. WE'RE NOT HERE TO RUN OTHER PEOPLE'S ERRANDS.
I SAY TAKE IT AND HANDLE THE FALLOUT LATER. IF WE HAVE THE DRUGS, WE'RE IN CHARGE. THAT'S THE TIME TO NEGOTIATE.
NOTED. IF YOU'D BOTH EXCUSE US.

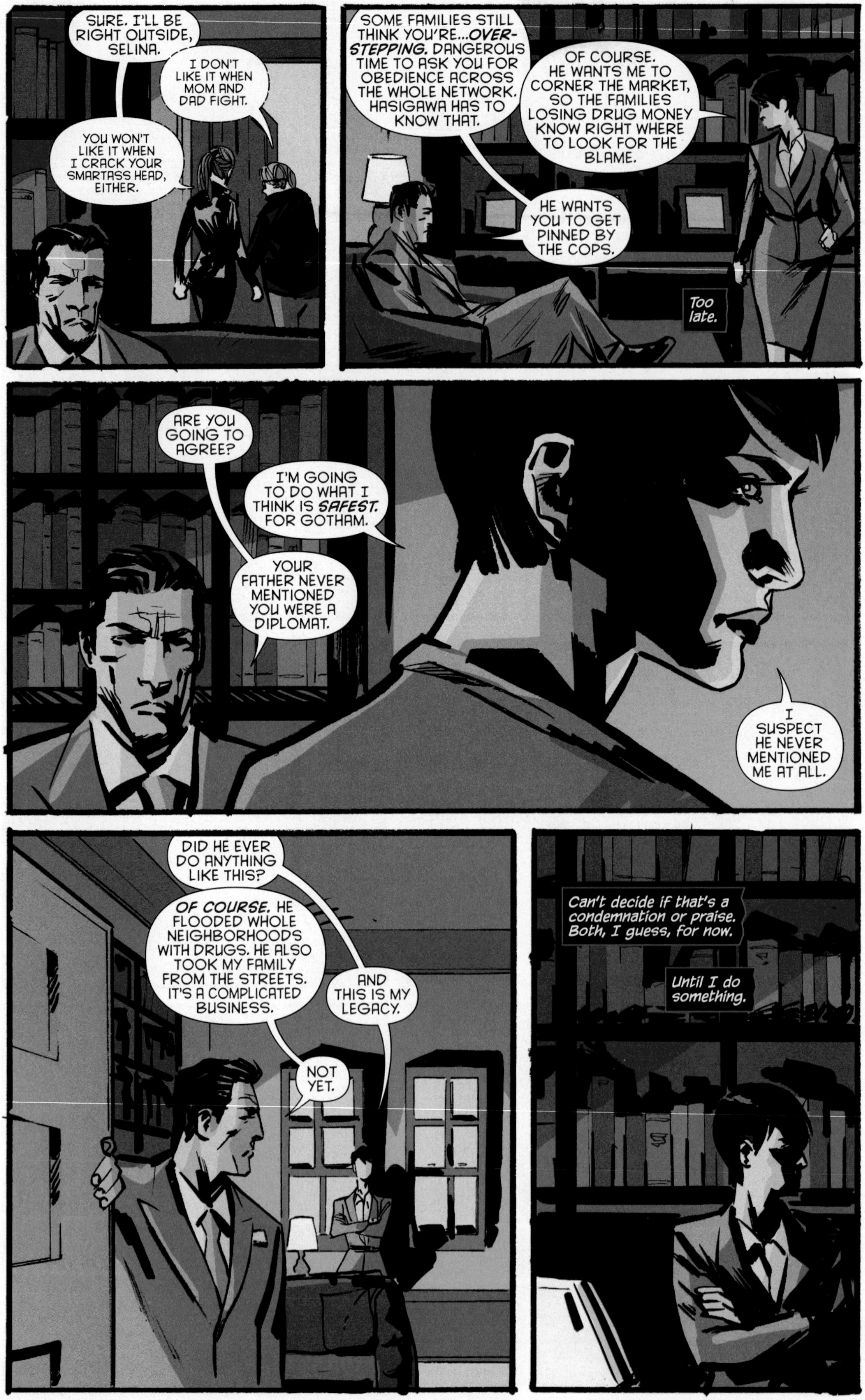
SURE. I'LL BE RIGHT OUTSIDE, SELINA.
I DON'T LIKE IT WHEN MOM AND DAD FIGHT.
YOU WON'T LIKE IT WHEN I CRACK YOUR SMARTASS HEAD, EITHER.
SOME FAMILIES STILL THINK YOU'RE...OVER-STEPPING. DANGEROUS TIME TO ASK YOU FOR OBEDIENCE ACROSS THE WHOLE NETWORK. HASIGAWA HAS TO KNOW THAT.
OF COURSE. HE WANTS ME TO CORNER THE MARKET, SO THE FAMILIES LOSING DRUG MONEY KNOW RIGHT WHERE TO LOOK FOR THE BLAME.
HE WANTS YOU TO GET PINNED BY THE COPS.
Too late.
ARE YOU GOING TO AGREE?
I'M GOING TO DO WHAT I THINK IS SAFEST. FOR GOTHAM.
YOUR FATHER NEVER MENTIONED YOU WERE A DIPLOMAT.
I SUSPECT HE NEVER MENTIONED ME AT ALL.
DID HE EVER DO ANYTHING LIKE THIS?
OF COURSE. HE FLOODED WHOLE NEIGHBORHOODS WITH DRUGS. HE ALSO TOOK MY FAMILY FROM THE STREETS. IT'S A COMPLICATED BUSINESS.
AND THIS IS MY LEGACY.
NOT YET.
Can't decide if that's a condemnation or praise. Both, I guess, for now.
Until I do something.

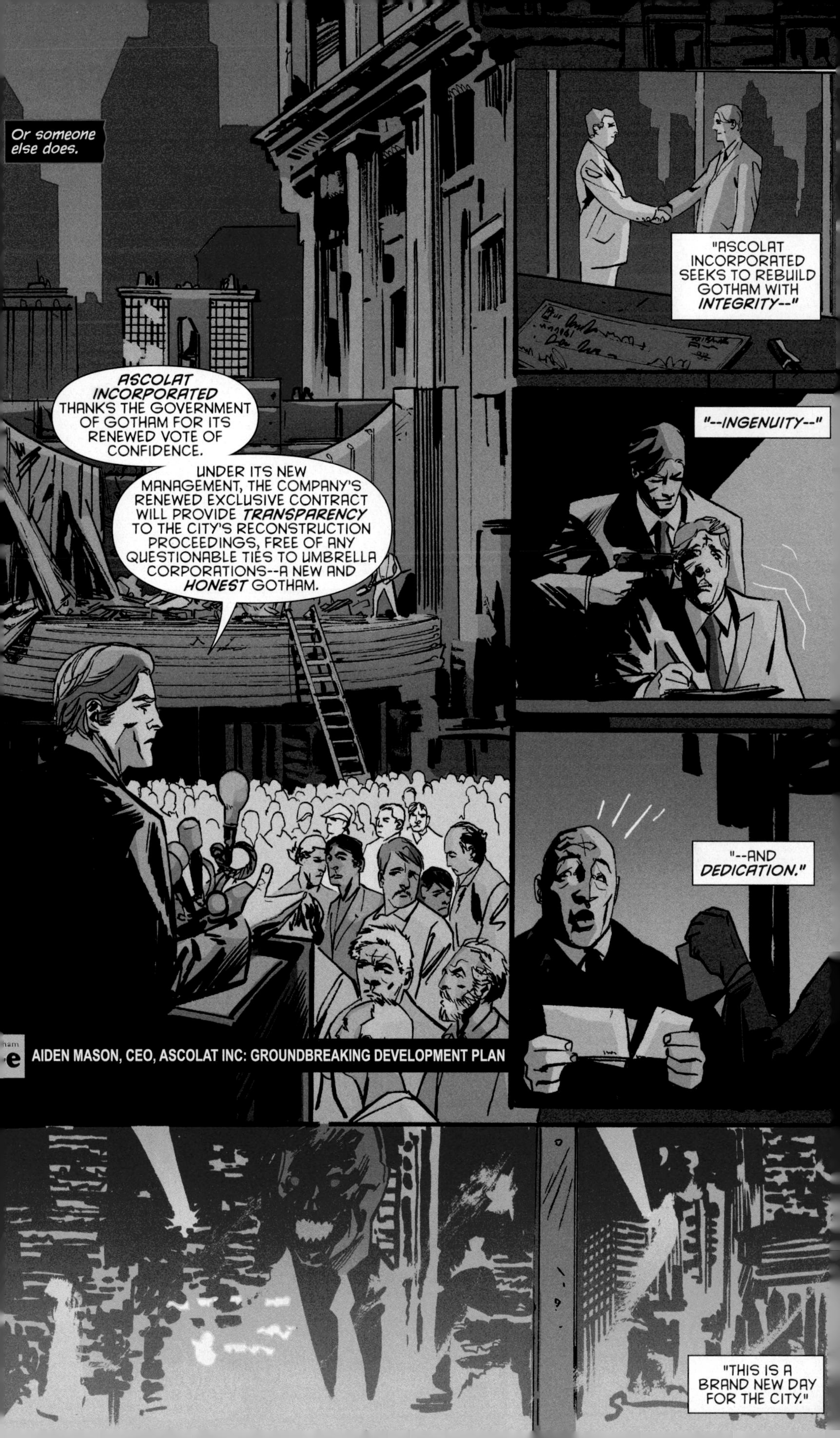
Or someone else does.
"ASCOLAT INCORPORATED SEEKS TO REBUILD GOTHAM WITH INTEGRITY--"
ASCOLAT INCORPORATED THANKS THE GOVERNMENT OF GOTHAM FOR ITS RENEWED VOTE OF CONFIDENCE.
UNDER ITS NEW MANAGEMENT, THE COMPANY'S RENEWED EXCLUSIVE CONTRACT WILL PROVIDE TRANSPARENCY TO THE CITY'S RECONSTRUCTION PROCEEDINGS, FREE OF ANY QUESTIONABLE TIES TO UMBRELLA CORPORATIONS--A NEW AND HONEST GOTHAM.
AIDEN MASON, CEO, ASCOLAT INC: GROUNDBREAKING DEVELOPMENT PLAN
"--INGENUITY--"
"--AND DEDICATION."
"THIS IS A BRAND NEW DAY FOR THE CITY."

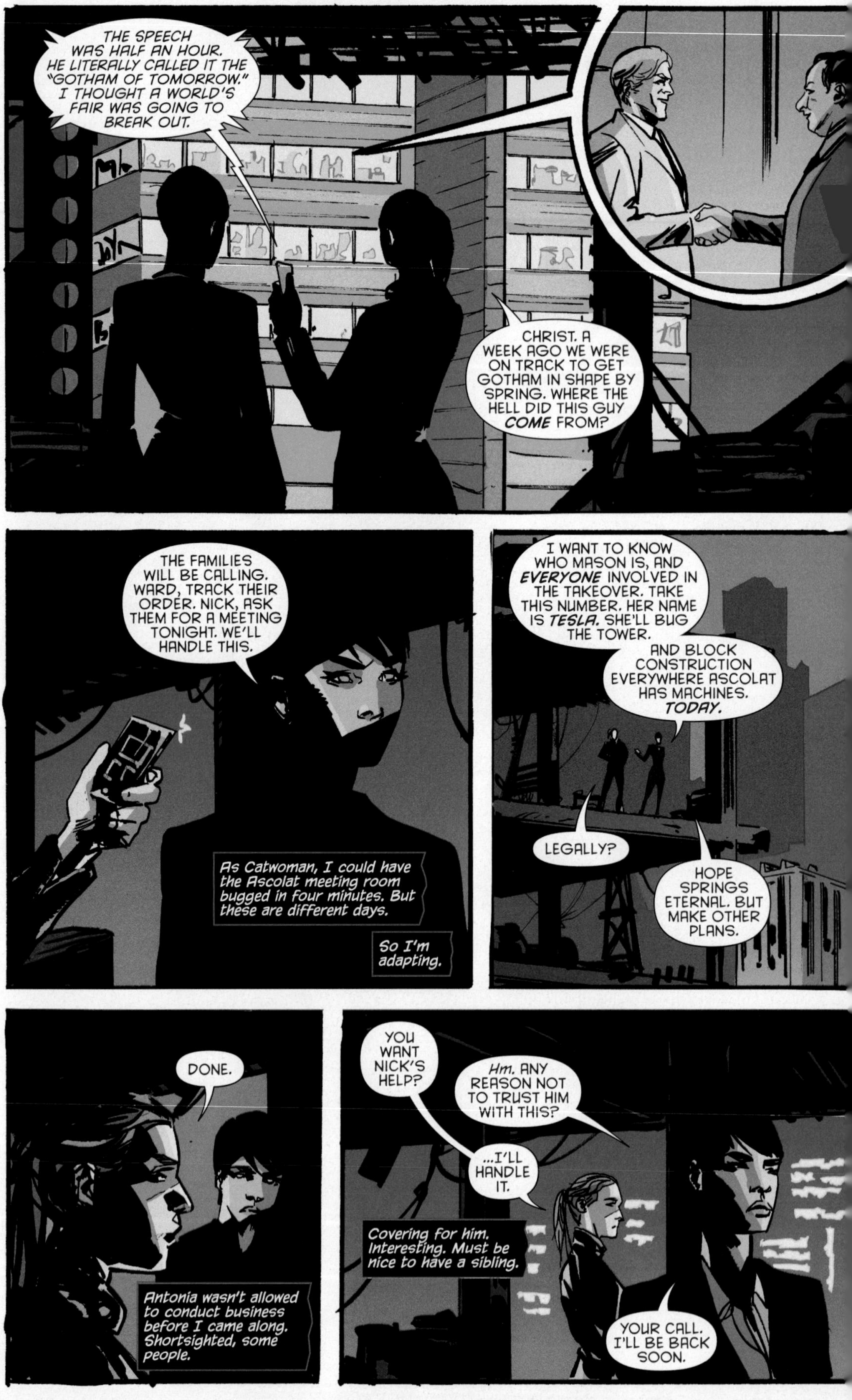
THE SPEECH WAS HALF AN HOUR. HE LITERALLY CALLED IT THE "GOTHAM OF TOMORROW." I THOUGHT A WORLD'S FAIR WAS GOING TO BREAK OUT.
CHRIST. A WEEK AGO WE WERE ON TRACK TO GET GOTHAM IN SHAPE BY SPRING. WHERE THE HELL DID THIS GUY COME FROM?
THE FAMILIES WILL BE CALLING. WARD, TRACK THEIR ORDER. NICK, ASK THEM FOR A MEETING TONIGHT. WE'LL HANDLE THIS.
As Catwoman, I could have the Ascolat meeting room bugged in four minutes. But these are different days.
So I'm adapting.
I WANT TO KNOW WHO MASON IS, AND EVERYONE INVOLVED IN THE TAKEOVER. TAKE THIS NUMBER. HER NAME IS TESLA. SHE'LL BUG THE TOWER.
AND BLOCK CONSTRUCTION EVERYWHERE ASCOLAT HAS MACHINES. TODAY.
LEGALLY?
HOPE SPRINGS ETERNAL. BUT MAKE OTHER PLANS.
DONE.
Antonia wasn't allowed to conduct business before I came along. Shortsighted, some people.
YOU WANT NICK'S HELP?
Hm. ANY REASON NOT TO TRUST HIM WITH THIS?
...I'LL HANDLE IT.
Covering for him. Interesting. Must be nice to have a sibling.
YOUR CALL. I'LL BE BACK SOON.

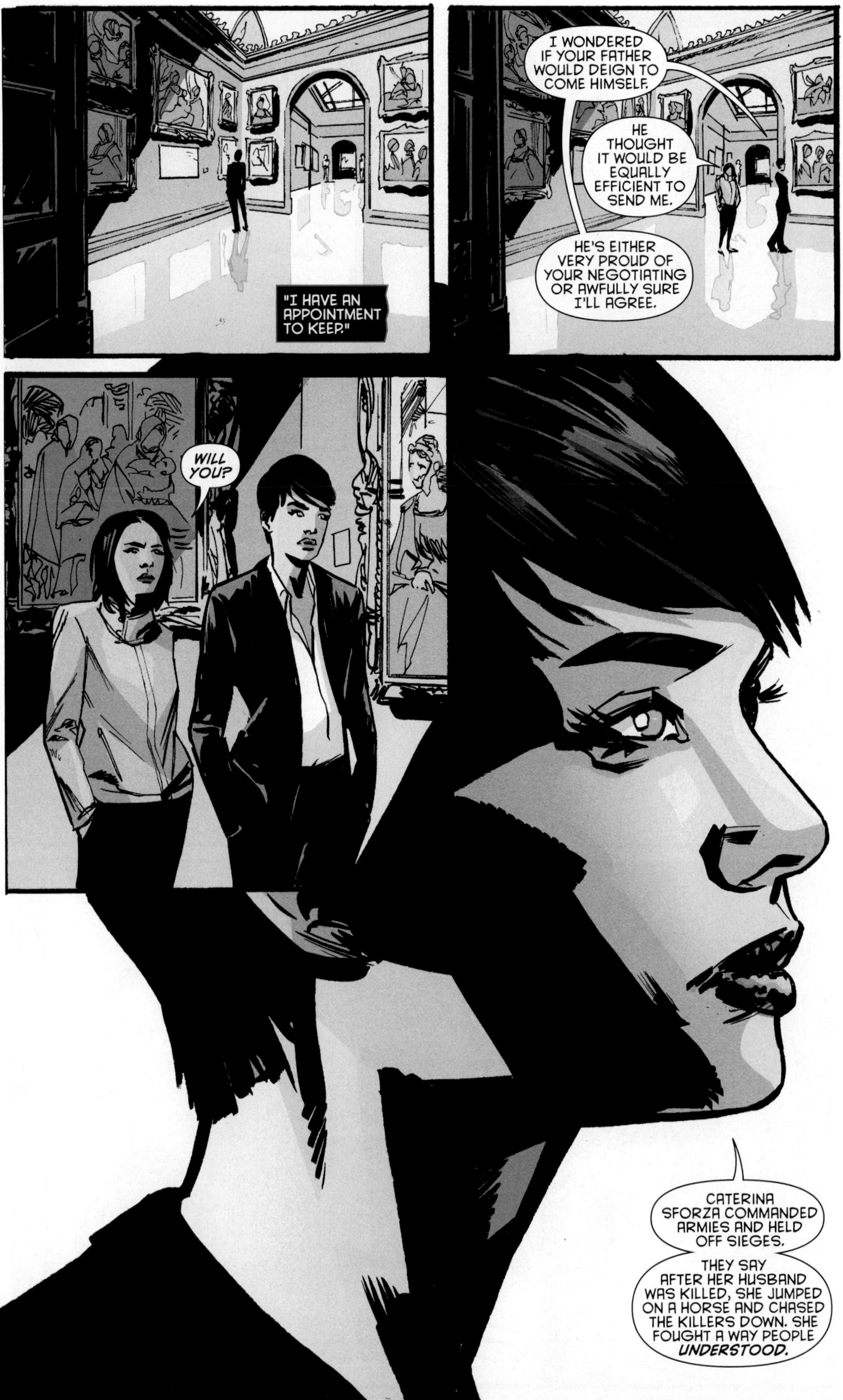
"I HAVE AN APPOINTMENT TO KEEP."
I WONDERED IF YOUR FATHER WOULD DEIGN TO COME HIMSELF.
HE THOUGHT IT WOULD BE EQUALLY EFFICIENT TO SEND ME.
HE'S EITHER VERY PROUD OF YOUR NEGOTIATING OR AWFULLY SURE I'LL AGREE.
WILL YOU?
CATERINA SFORZA COMMANDED ARMIES AND HELD OFF SIEGES.
THEY SAY AFTER HER HUSBAND WAS KILLED, SHE JUMPED ON A HORSE AND CHASED THE KILLERS DOWN. SHE FOUGHT A WAY PEOPLE *UNDERSTOOD.*

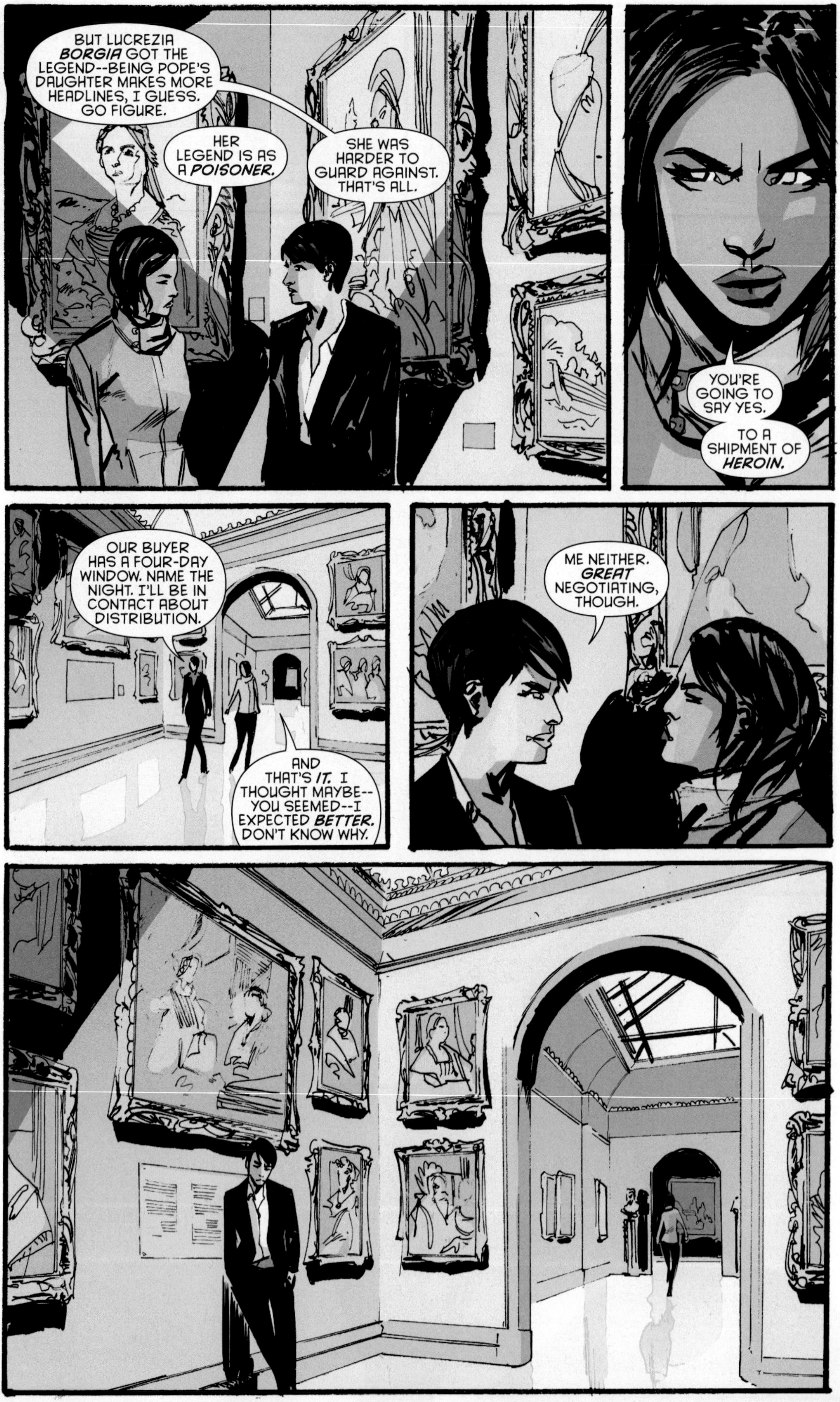
BUT LUCREZIA BORGIA GOT THE LEGEND--BEING POPE'S DAUGHTER MAKES MORE HEADLINES, I GUESS. GO FIGURE.
HER LEGEND IS AS A POISONER.
SHE WAS HARDER TO GUARD AGAINST. THAT'S ALL.
YOU'RE GOING TO SAY YES.
TO A SHIPMENT OF HEROIN.
OUR BUYER HAS A FOUR-DAY WINDOW. NAME THE NIGHT. I'LL BE IN CONTACT ABOUT DISTRIBUTION.
AND THAT'S IT. I THOUGHT MAYBE--YOU SEEMED--I EXPECTED BETTER. DON'T KNOW WHY.
ME NEITHER. GREAT NEGOTIATING, THOUGH.

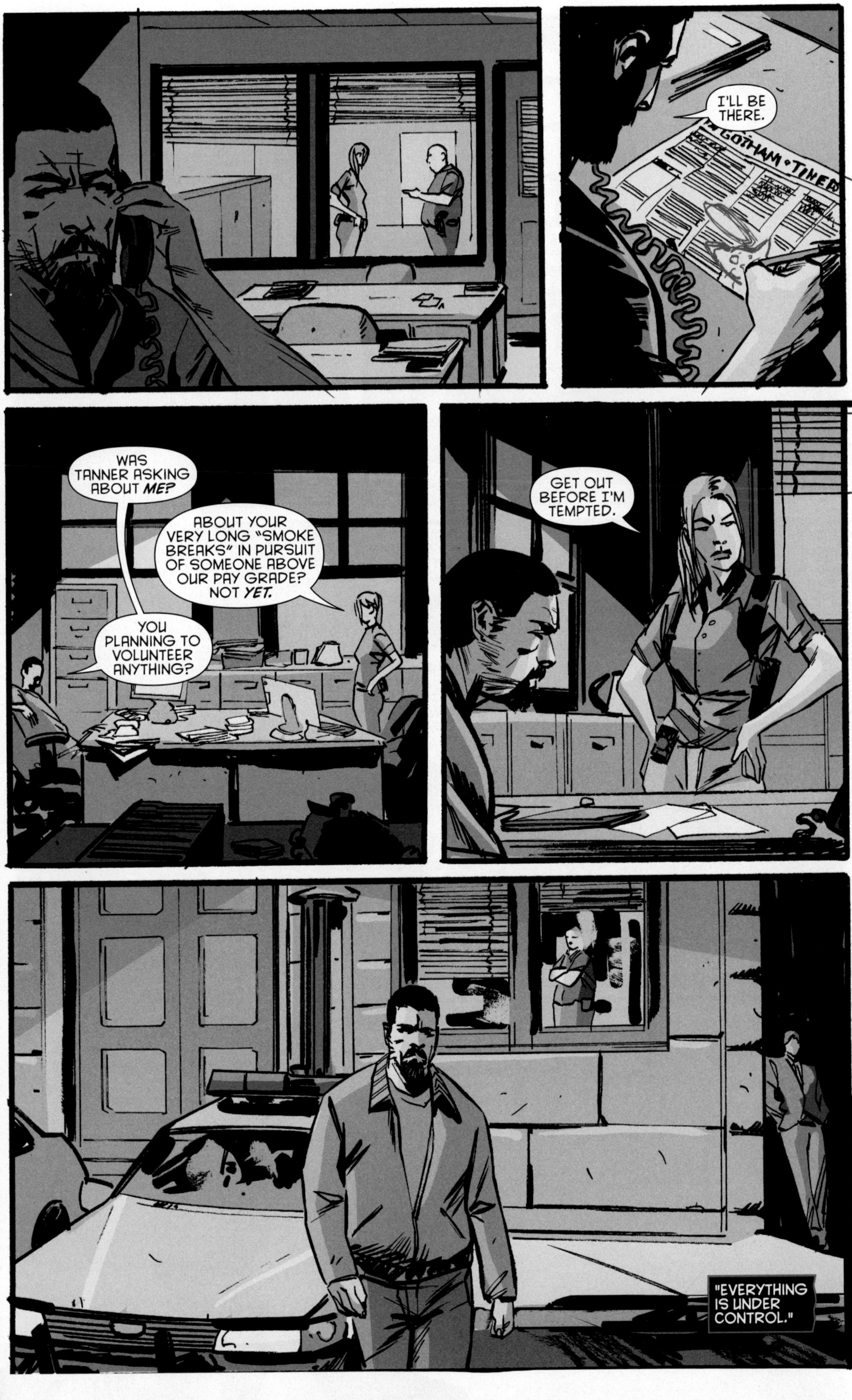
I'LL BE THERE.
GOTHAM TIMES
WAS TANNER ASKING ABOUT *ME?*
ABOUT YOUR VERY LONG "SMOKE BREAKS" IN PURSUIT OF SOMEONE ABOVE OUR PAY GRADE? NOT *YET.*
YOU PLANNING TO VOLUNTEER ANYTHING?
GET OUT BEFORE I'M TEMPTED.
"EVERYTHING IS UNDER CONTROL."

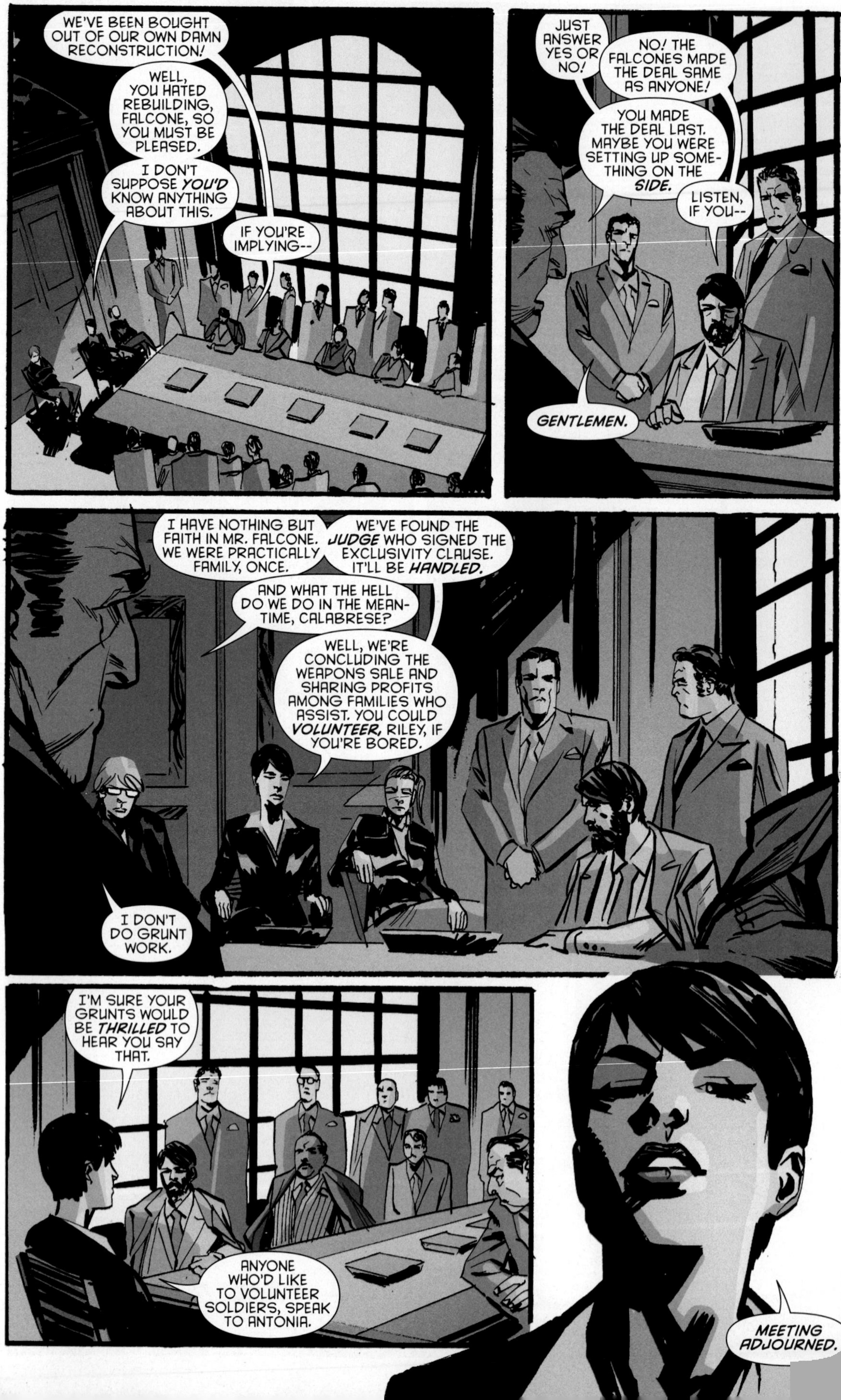
WE'VE BEEN BOUGHT OUT OF OUR OWN DAMN RECONSTRUCTION!
WELL, YOU HATED REBUILDING, FALCONE, SO YOU MUST BE PLEASED.
I DON'T SUPPOSE YOU'D KNOW ANYTHING ABOUT THIS.
IF YOU'RE IMPLYING--
JUST ANSWER YES OR NO!
NO! THE FALCONES MADE THE DEAL SAME AS ANYONE!
YOU MADE THE DEAL LAST. MAYBE YOU WERE SETTING UP SOME-THING ON THE SIDE.
LISTEN, IF YOU--
GENTLEMEN.
I HAVE NOTHING BUT FAITH IN MR. FALCONE. WE WERE PRACTICALLY FAMILY, ONCE.
WE'VE FOUND THE JUDGE WHO SIGNED THE EXCLUSIVITY CLAUSE. IT'LL BE HANDLED.
AND WHAT THE HELL DO WE DO IN THE MEAN-TIME, CALABRESE?
WELL, WE'RE CONCLUDING THE WEAPONS SALE AND SHARING PROFITS AMONG FAMILIES WHO ASSIST. YOU COULD VOLUNTEER, RILEY, IF YOU'RE BORED.
I DON'T DO GRUNT WORK.
I'M SURE YOUR GRUNTS WOULD BE THRILLED TO HEAR YOU SAY THAT.
ANYONE WHO'D LIKE TO VOLUNTEER SOLDIERS, SPEAK TO ANTONIA.
MEETING ADJOURNED.

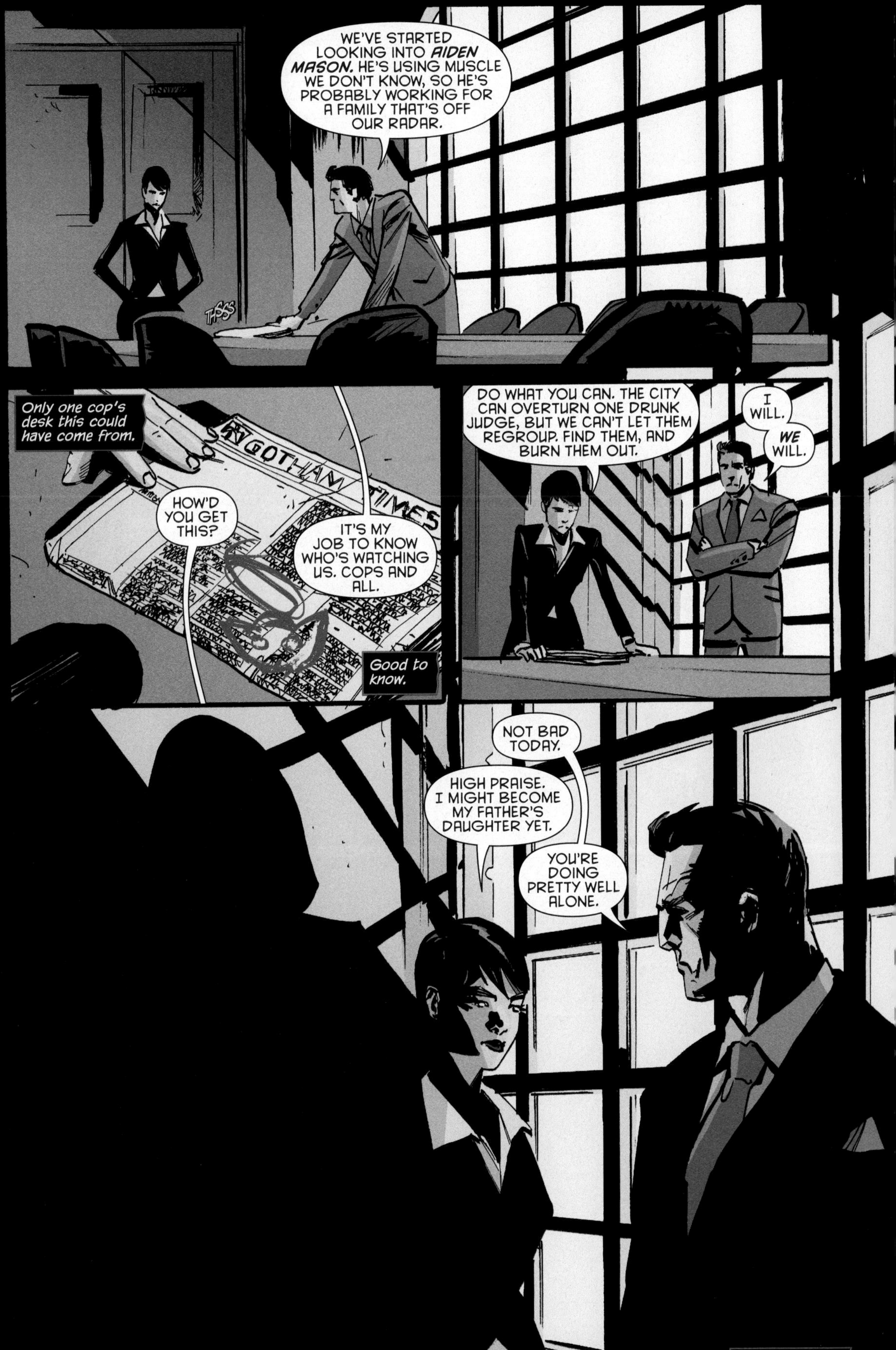
WE'VE STARTED LOOKING INTO AIDEN MASON. HE'S USING MUSCLE WE DON'T KNOW, SO HE'S PROBABLY WORKING FOR A FAMILY THAT'S OFF OUR RADAR.
Only one cop's desk this could have come from.
GOTHAM TIMES
HOW'D YOU GET THIS?
IT'S MY JOB TO KNOW WHO'S WATCHING US. COPS AND ALL.
Good to know.
DO WHAT YOU CAN. THE CITY CAN OVERTURN ONE DRUNK JUDGE, BUT WE CAN'T LET THEM REGROUP. FIND THEM, AND BURN THEM OUT.
I WILL.
WE WILL.
NOT BAD TODAY.
HIGH PRAISE. I MIGHT BECOME MY FATHER'S DAUGHTER YET.
YOU'RE DOING PRETTY WELL ALONE.
That's what I'm afraid of.

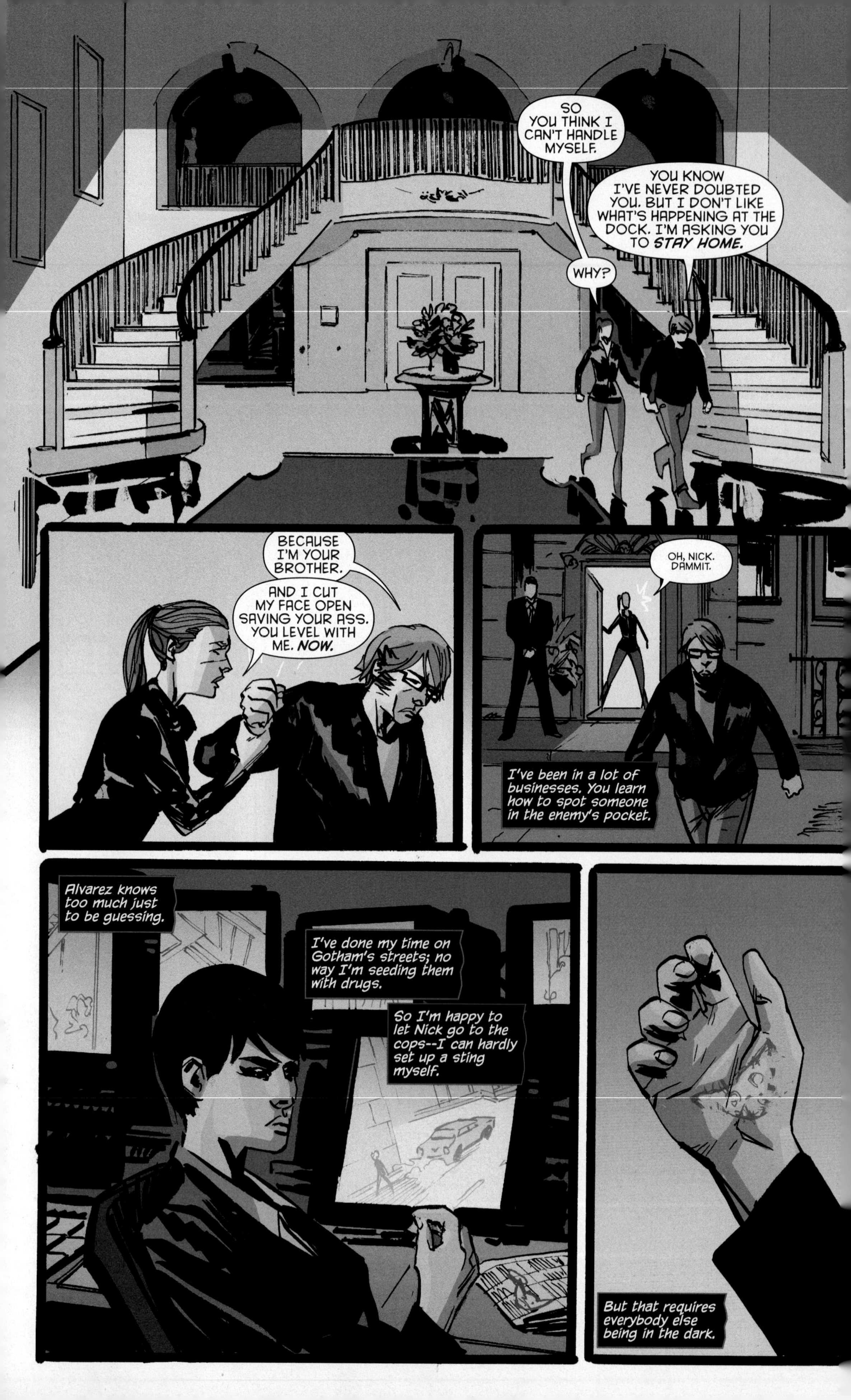
SO YOU THINK I CAN'T HANDLE MYSELF.
YOU KNOW I'VE NEVER DOUBTED YOU. BUT I DON'T LIKE WHAT'S HAPPENING AT THE DOCK. I'M ASKING YOU TO STAY HOME.
WHY?
BECAUSE I'M YOUR BROTHER.
AND I CUT MY FACE OPEN SAVING YOUR ASS. YOU LEVEL WITH ME. NOW.
OH, NICK. DAMMIT.
I've been in a lot of businesses. You learn how to spot someone in the enemy's pocket.
Alvarez knows too much just to be guessing.
I've done my time on Gotham's streets; no way I'm seeding them with drugs.
So I'm happy to let Nick go to the cops--I can hardly set up a sting myself.
But that requires everybody else being in the dark.

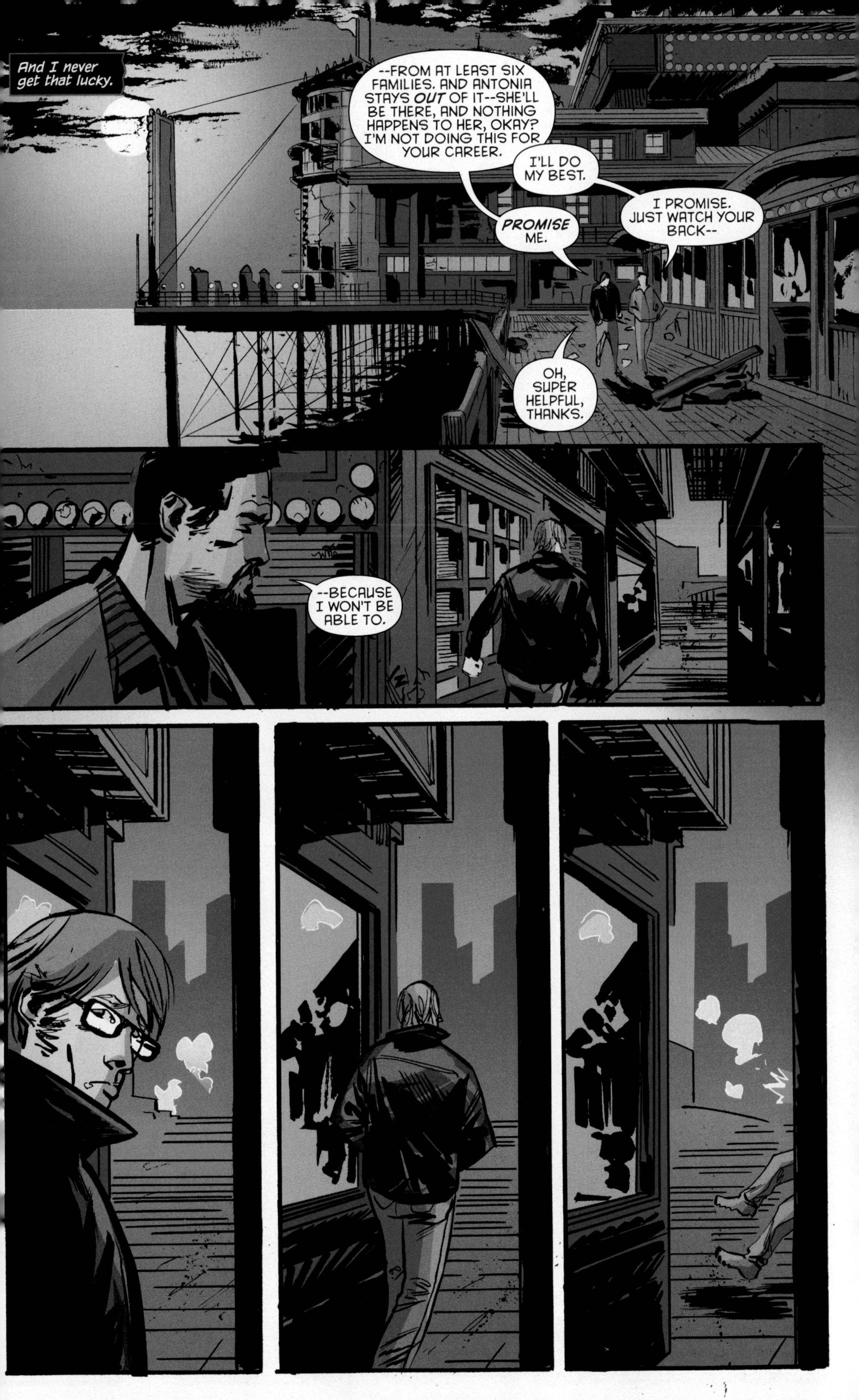
And I never get that lucky.
--FROM AT LEAST SIX FAMILIES. AND ANTONIA STAYS OUT OF IT--SHE'LL BE THERE, AND NOTHING HAPPENS TO HER, OKAY? I'M NOT DOING THIS FOR YOUR CAREER.
I'LL DO MY BEST.
PROMISE ME.
I PROMISE. JUST WATCH YOUR BACK--
OH, SUPER HELPFUL, THANKS.
--BECAUSE I WON'T BE ABLE TO.

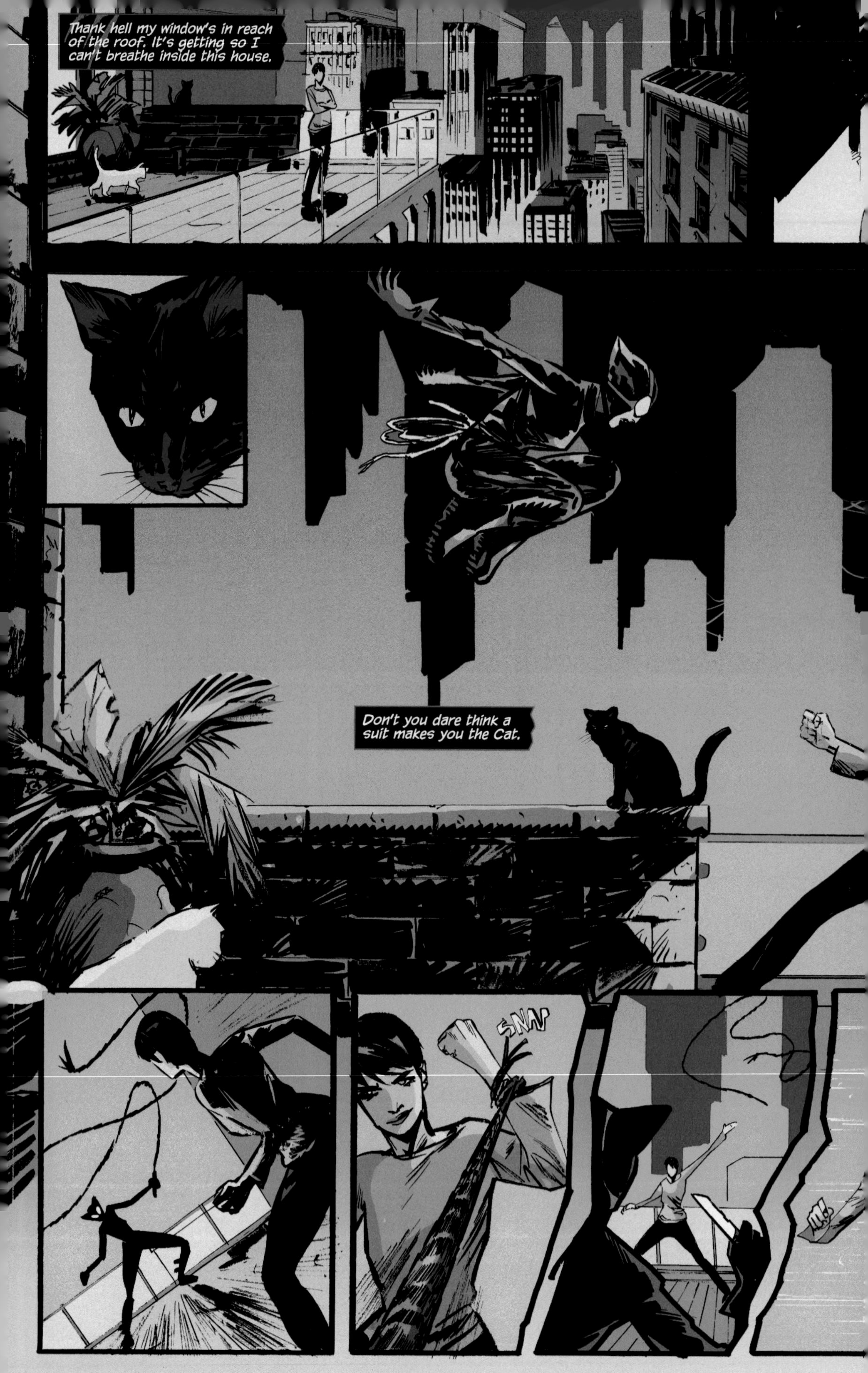
Thank hell my window's in reach of the roof. It's getting so I can't breathe inside this house.
Don't you dare think a suit makes you the Cat.
SNAP

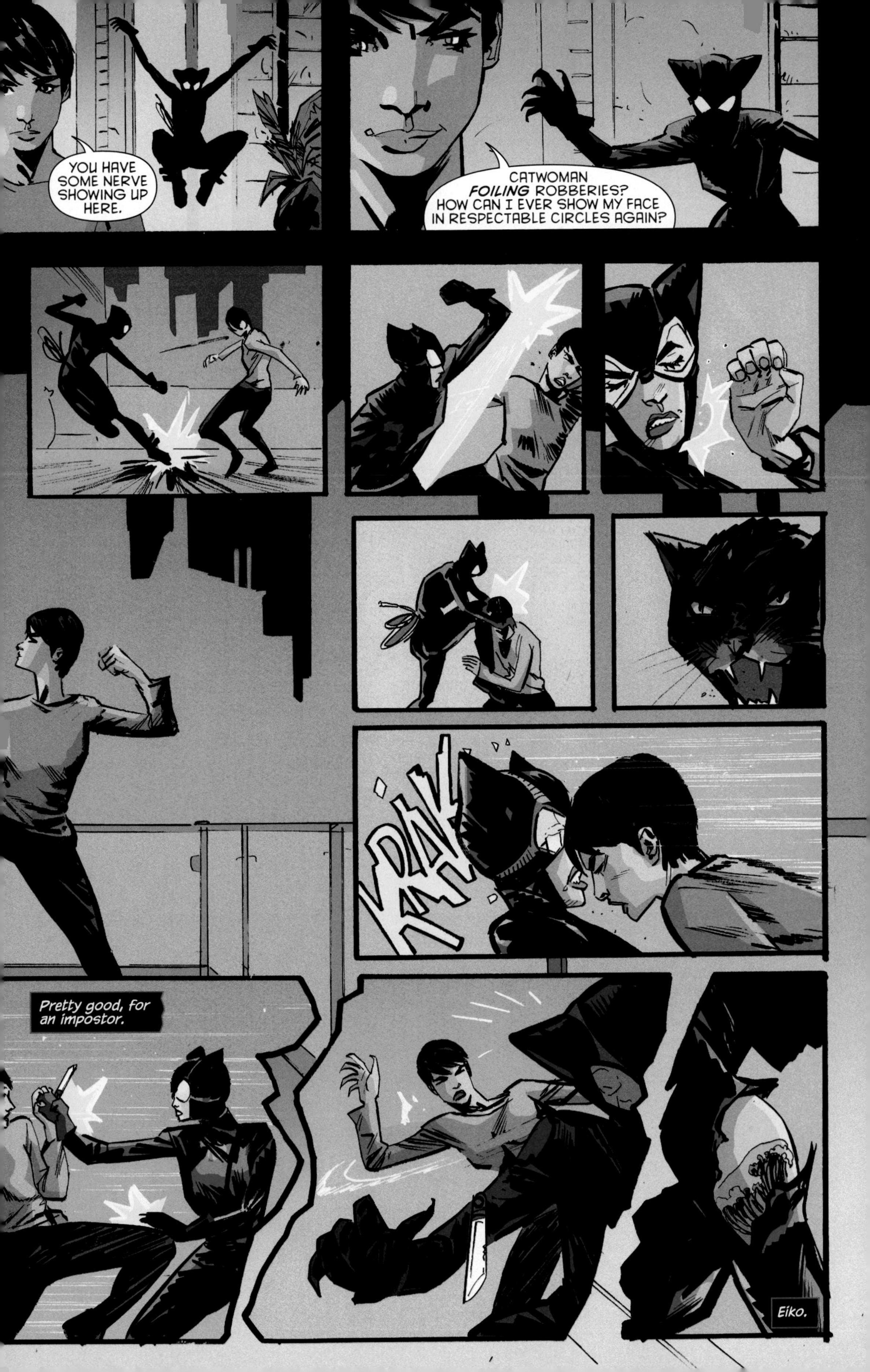
YOU HAVE SOME NERVE SHOWING UP HERE.
CATWOMAN FOILING ROBBERIES? HOW CAN I EVER SHOW MY FACE IN RESPECTABLE CIRCLES AGAIN?
Pretty good, for an impostor.
Eiko.

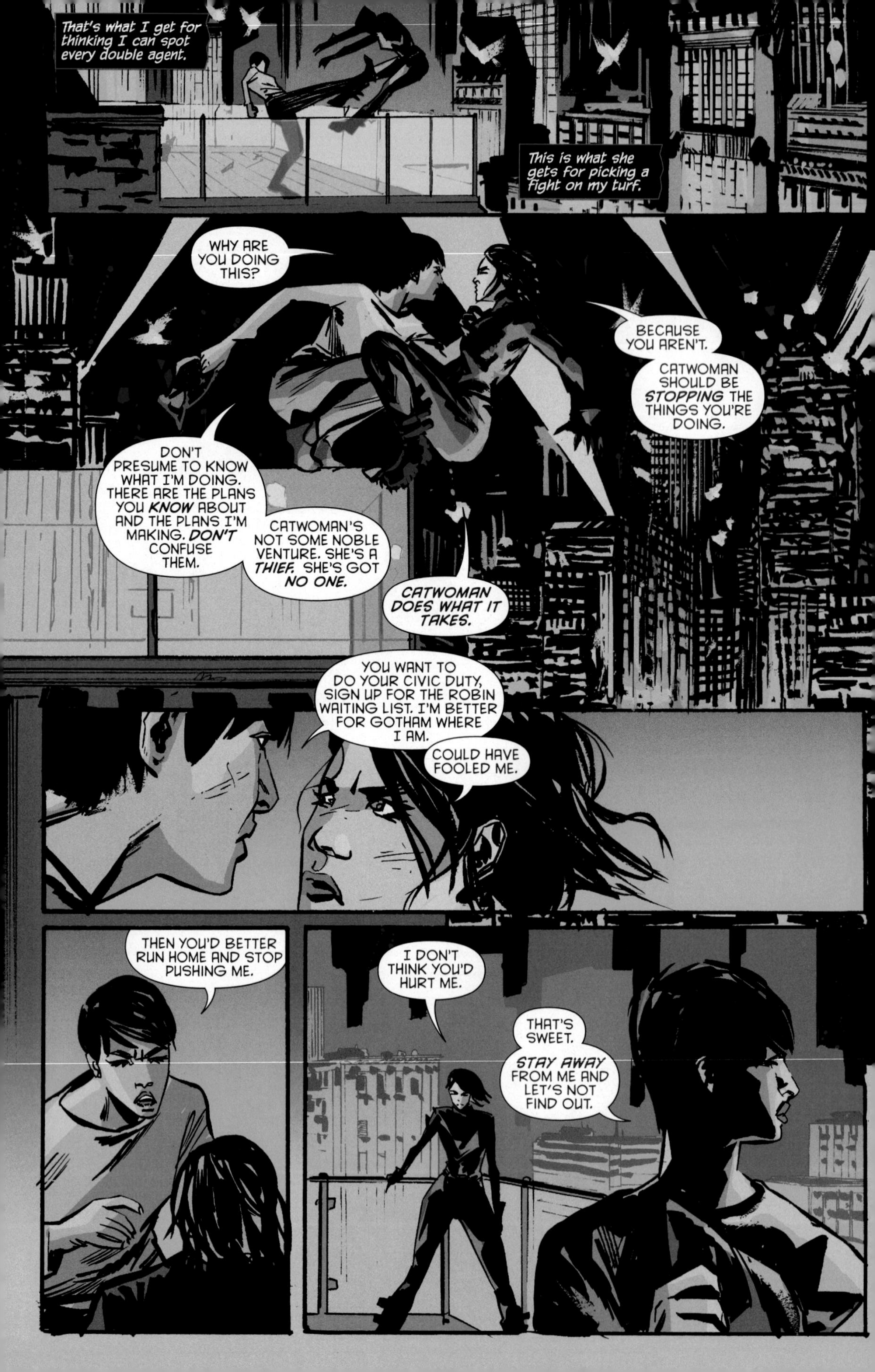

That's what I get for thinking I can spot every double agent.
This is what she gets for picking a fight on my turf.
WHY ARE YOU DOING THIS?
BECAUSE YOU AREN'T.
CATWOMAN SHOULD BE *STOPPING* THE THINGS YOU'RE DOING.
DON'T PRESUME TO KNOW WHAT I'M DOING. THERE ARE THE PLANS YOU *KNOW* ABOUT AND THE PLANS I'M MAKING. *DON'T* CONFUSE THEM.
CATWOMAN'S NOT SOME NOBLE VENTURE. SHE'S A *THIEF.* SHE'S GOT *NO ONE.*
CATWOMAN DOES WHAT IT TAKES.
YOU WANT TO DO YOUR CIVIC DUTY, SIGN UP FOR THE ROBIN WAITING LIST. I'M BETTER FOR GOTHAM WHERE I AM.
COULD HAVE FOOLED ME.
THEN YOU'D BETTER RUN HOME AND STOP PUSHING ME.
I DON'T THINK YOU'D HURT ME.
THAT'S SWEET.
STAY AWAY FROM ME AND LET'S NOT FIND OUT.

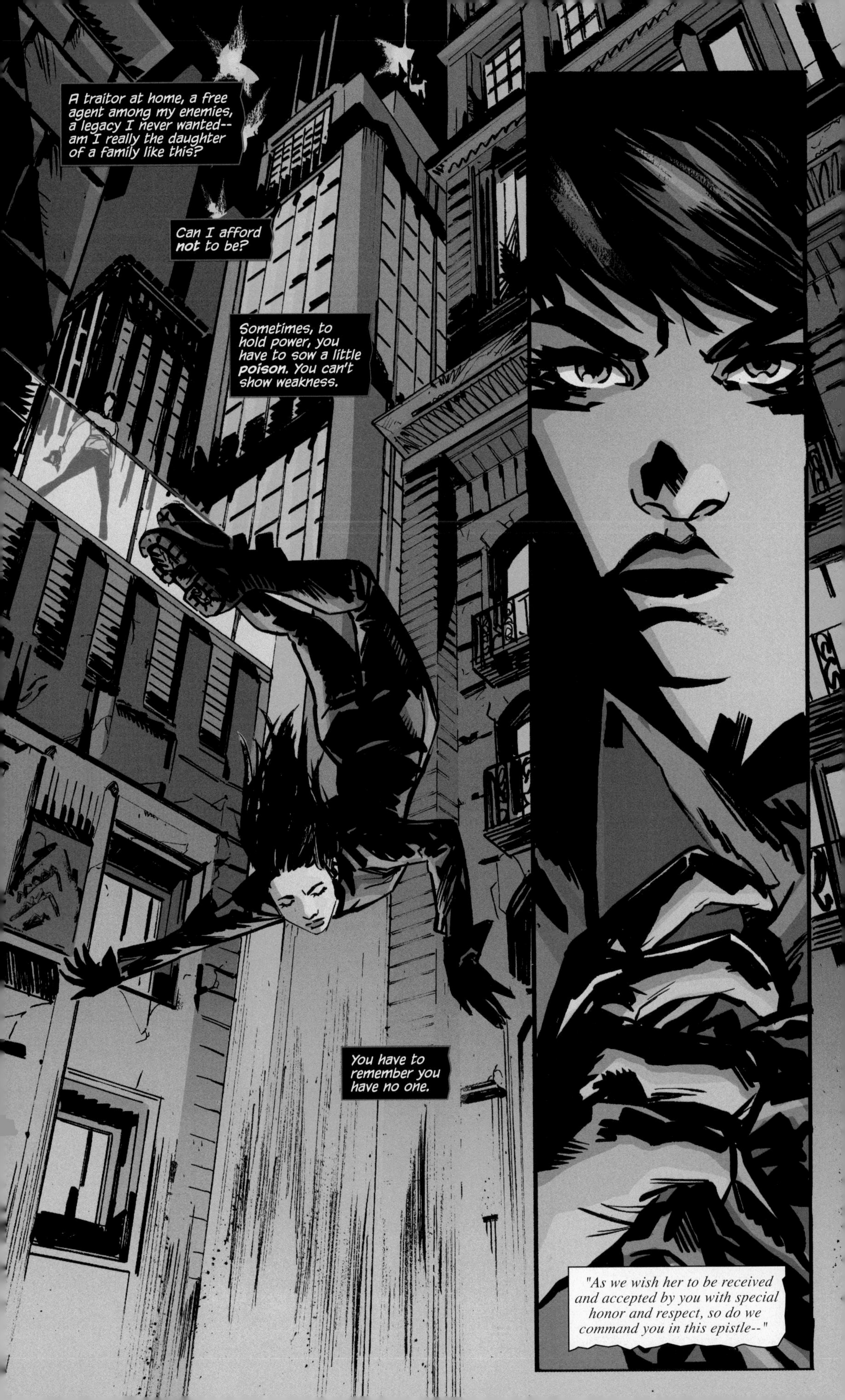
A traitor at home, a free agent among my enemies, a legacy I never wanted--am I really the daughter of a family like this?
Can I afford **not** to be?
Sometimes, to hold power, you have to sow a little **poison.** You can't show weakness.
You have to remember you have no one.
"As we wish her to be received and accepted by you with special honor and respect, so do we command you in this epistle--"

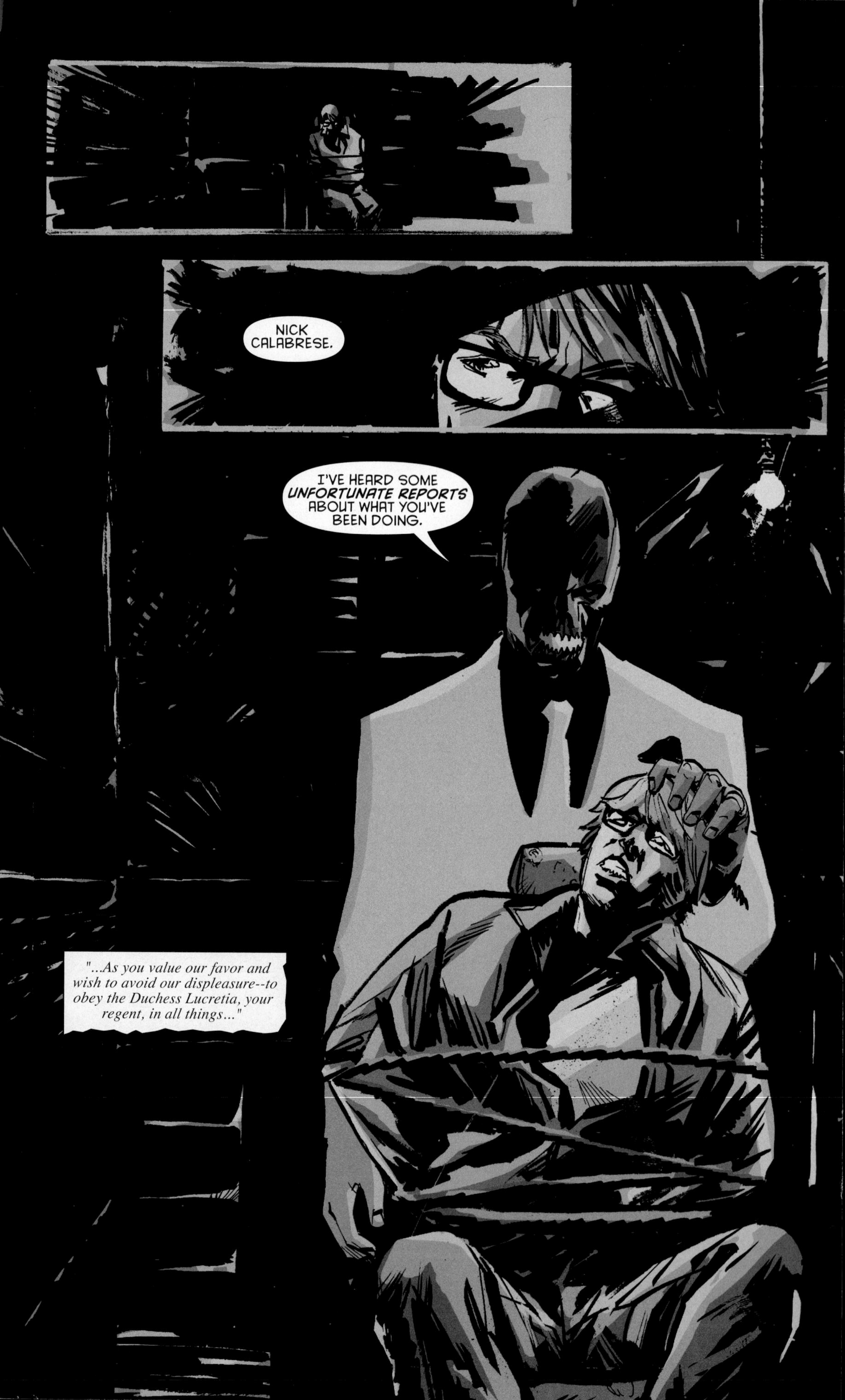
NICK CALABRESE.
I'VE HEARD SOME UNFORTUNATE REPORTS ABOUT WHAT YOU'VE BEEN DOING.
"...As you value our favor and wish to avoid our displeasure--to obey the Duchess Lucretia, your regent, in all things..."

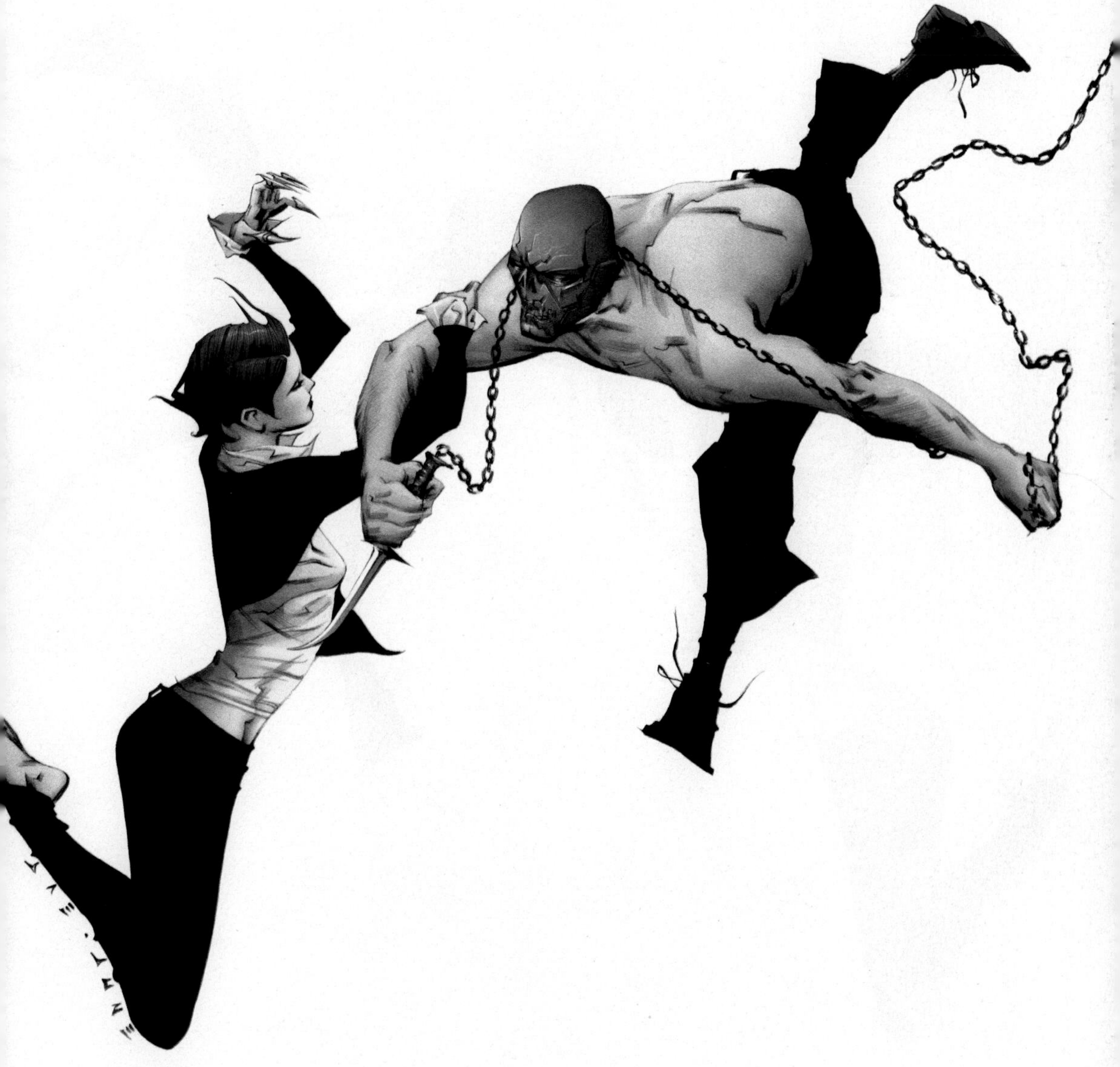

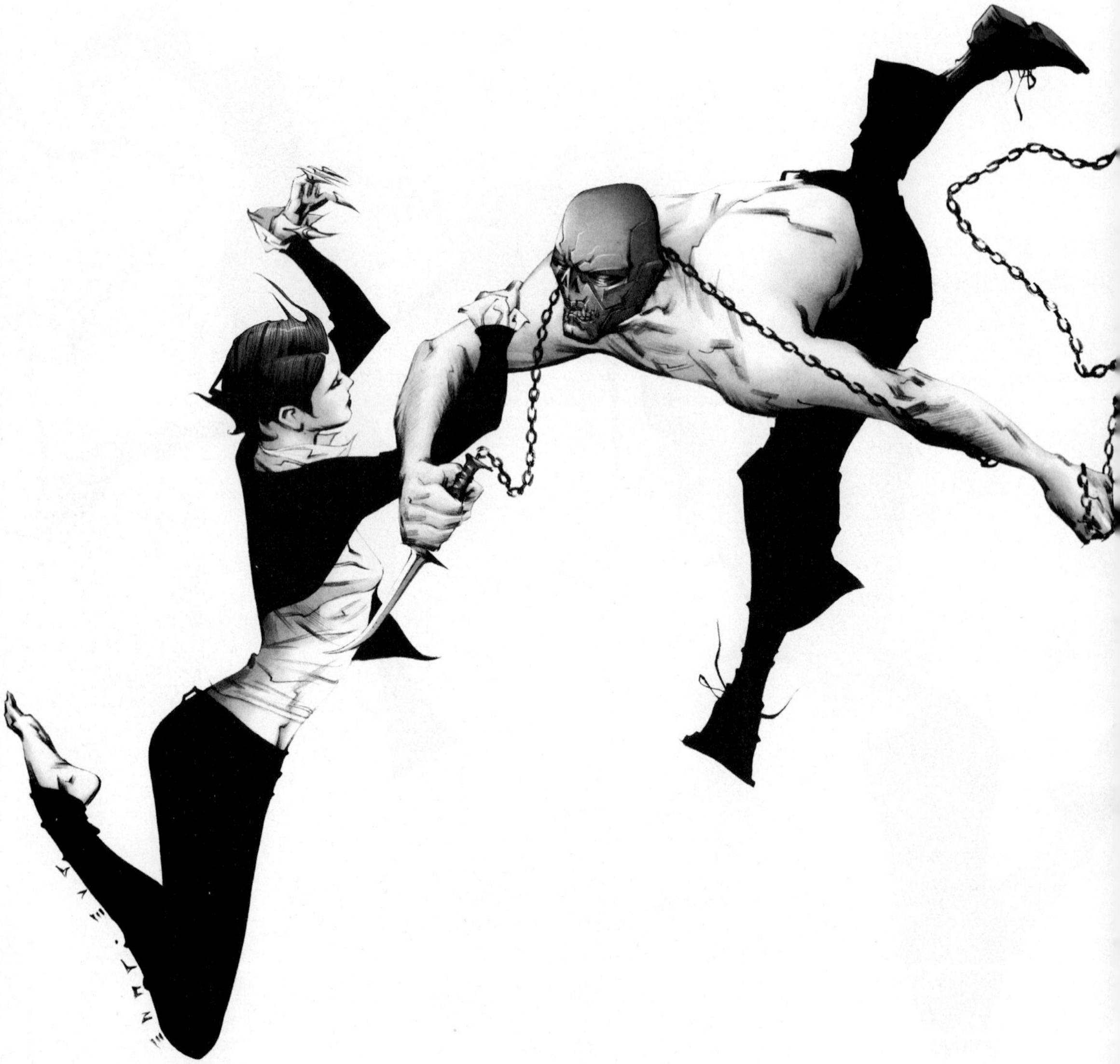

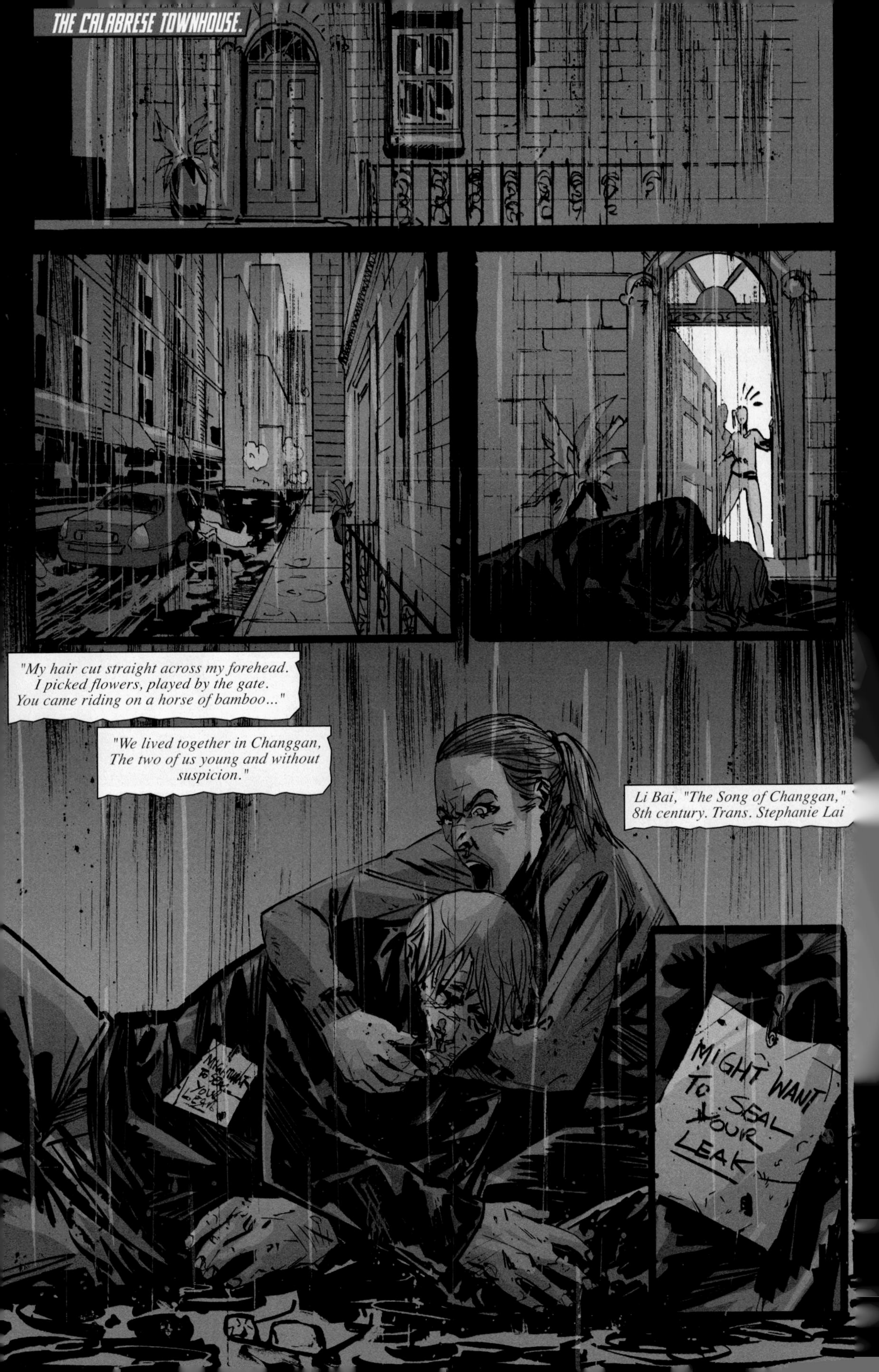
THE CALABRESE TOWNHOUSE.
"My hair cut straight across my forehead. I picked flowers, played by the gate. You came riding on a horse of bamboo..."
"We lived together in Changgan, The two of us young and without suspicion."
Li Bai, "The Song of Changgan," 8th century. Trans. Stephanie Lai
MIGHT WANT TO SEAL YOUR LEAK

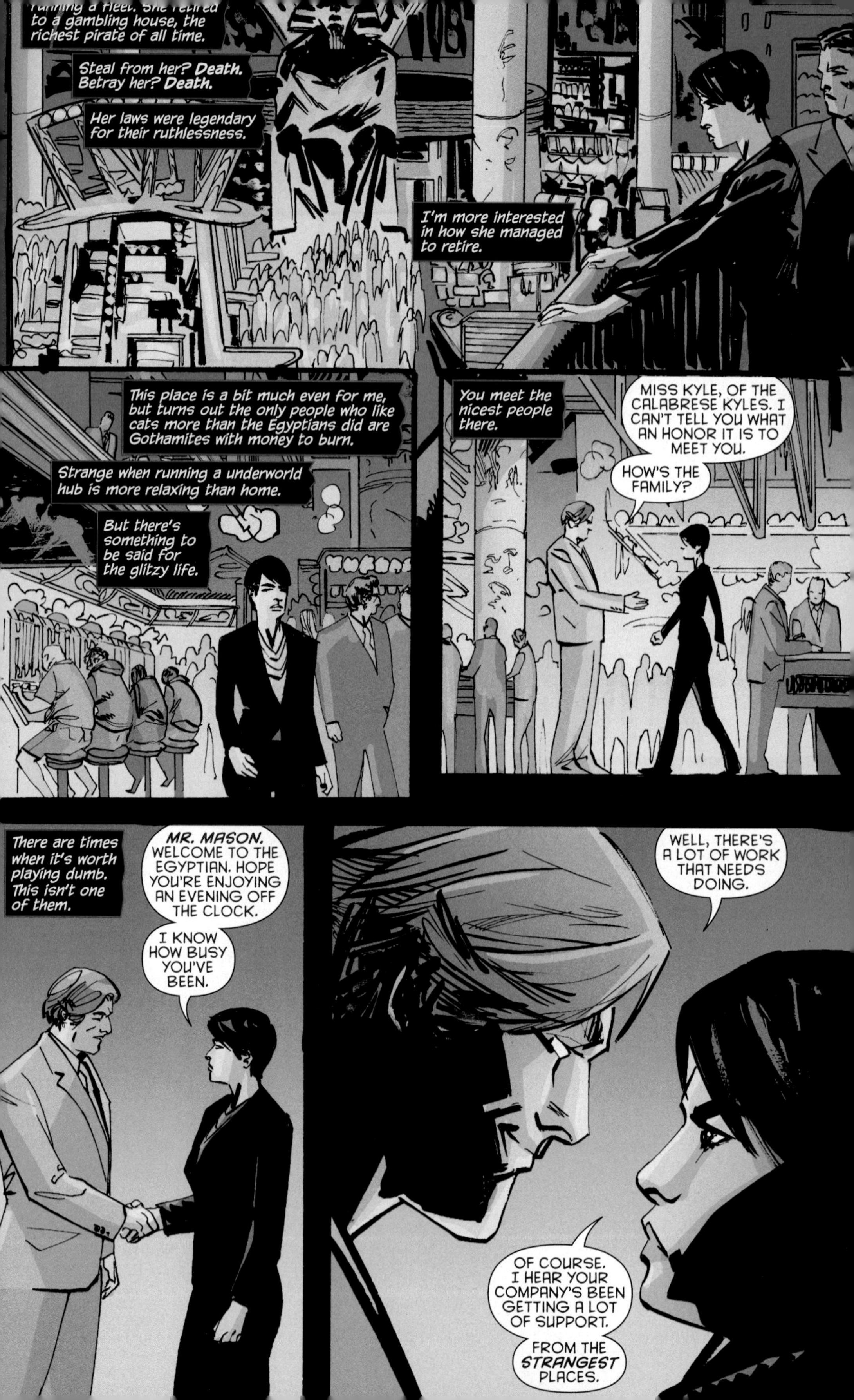
running a fleet. She retired to a gambling house, the richest pirate of all time.
Steal from her? Death. Betray her? Death.
Her laws were legendary for their ruthlessness.
I'm more interested in how she managed to retire.
This place is a bit much even for me, but turns out the only people who like cats more than the Egyptians did are Gothamites with money to burn.
Strange when running a underworld hub is more relaxing than home.
But there's something to be said for the glitzy life.
You meet the nicest people there.
MISS KYLE, OF THE CALABRESE KYLES. I CAN'T TELL YOU WHAT AN HONOR IT IS TO MEET YOU.
HOW'S THE FAMILY?
There are times when it's worth playing dumb. This isn't one of them.
MR. MASON. WELCOME TO THE EGYPTIAN. HOPE YOU'RE ENJOYING AN EVENING OFF THE CLOCK.
I KNOW HOW BUSY YOU'VE BEEN.
WELL, THERE'S A LOT OF WORK THAT NEEDS DOING.
OF COURSE. I HEAR YOUR COMPANY'S BEEN GETTING A LOT OF SUPPORT.
FROM THE STRANGEST PLACES.

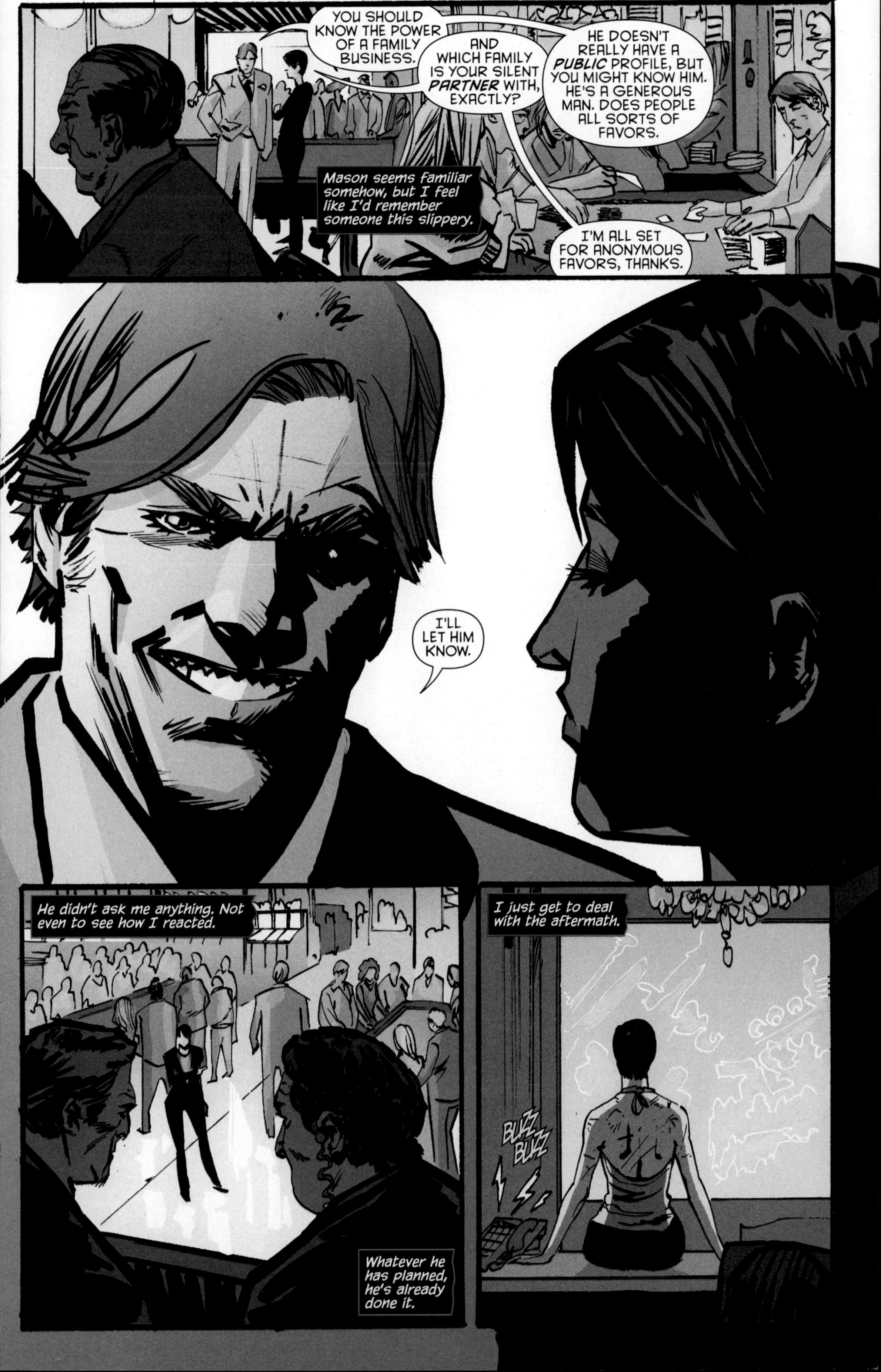
YOU SHOULD KNOW THE POWER OF A FAMILY BUSINESS.
AND WHICH FAMILY IS YOUR SILENT PARTNER WITH, EXACTLY?
HE DOESN'T REALLY HAVE A PUBLIC PROFILE, BUT YOU MIGHT KNOW HIM. HE'S A GENEROUS MAN. DOES PEOPLE ALL SORTS OF FAVORS.
Mason seems familiar somehow, but I feel like I'd remember someone this slippery.
I'M ALL SET FOR ANONYMOUS FAVORS, THANKS.
I'LL LET HIM KNOW.
He didn't ask me anything. Not even to see how I reacted.
Whatever he has planned, he's already done it.
I just get to deal with the aftermath.
BLIZZ BLIZZ

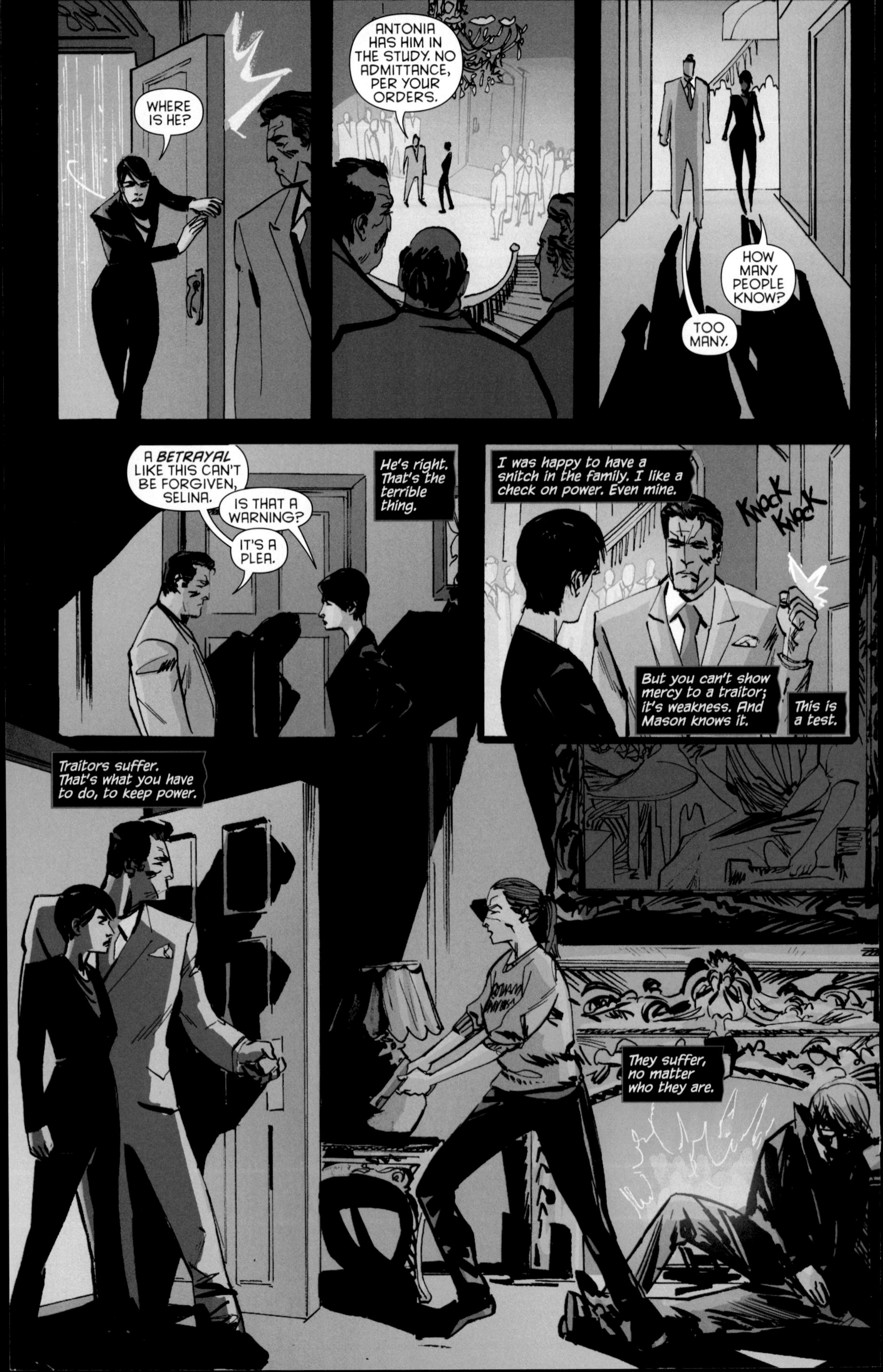
WHERE IS HE?
ANTONIA HAS HIM IN THE STUDY. NO ADMITTANCE, PER YOUR ORDERS.
HOW MANY PEOPLE KNOW?
TOO MANY.
A BETRAYAL LIKE THIS CAN'T BE FORGIVEN, SELINA.
IS THAT A WARNING?
IT'S A PLEA.
He's right. That's the terrible thing.
I was happy to have a snitch in the family. I like a check on power. Even mine.
KNOCK KNOCK
But you can't show mercy to a traitor; it's weakness. And Mason knows it.
This is a test.
Traitors suffer. That's what you have to do, to keep power.
They suffer, no matter who they are.

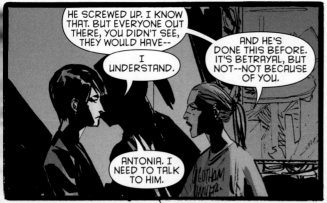

HE SCREWED UP. I KNOW THAT. BUT EVERYONE OUT THERE, YOU DIDN'T SEE, THEY WOULD HAVE--

I UNDERSTAND.

AND HE'S DONE THIS BEFORE. IT'S BETRAYAL, BUT NOT--NOT BECAUSE OF YOU.

ANTONIA. I NEED TO TALK TO HIM.

JUST TALK.

I KNOW YOU WOULDN'T.

Cold comfort.

I DIDN'T TALK.

I MEAN, YES, THE *COPS*, OBVIOUSLY. THAT'S WHY YOU'RE GOING TO KILL ME.

Traitor, maybe, but he's no coward, I'll give him that.

BUT *BLACK MASK* DID THIS TO ME, AND I DIDN'T SAY A DAMN WORD. *PROMISE.*

And he didn't care that Nick knew him. That's terrifying.

BETTER START FROM THE BEGINNING.

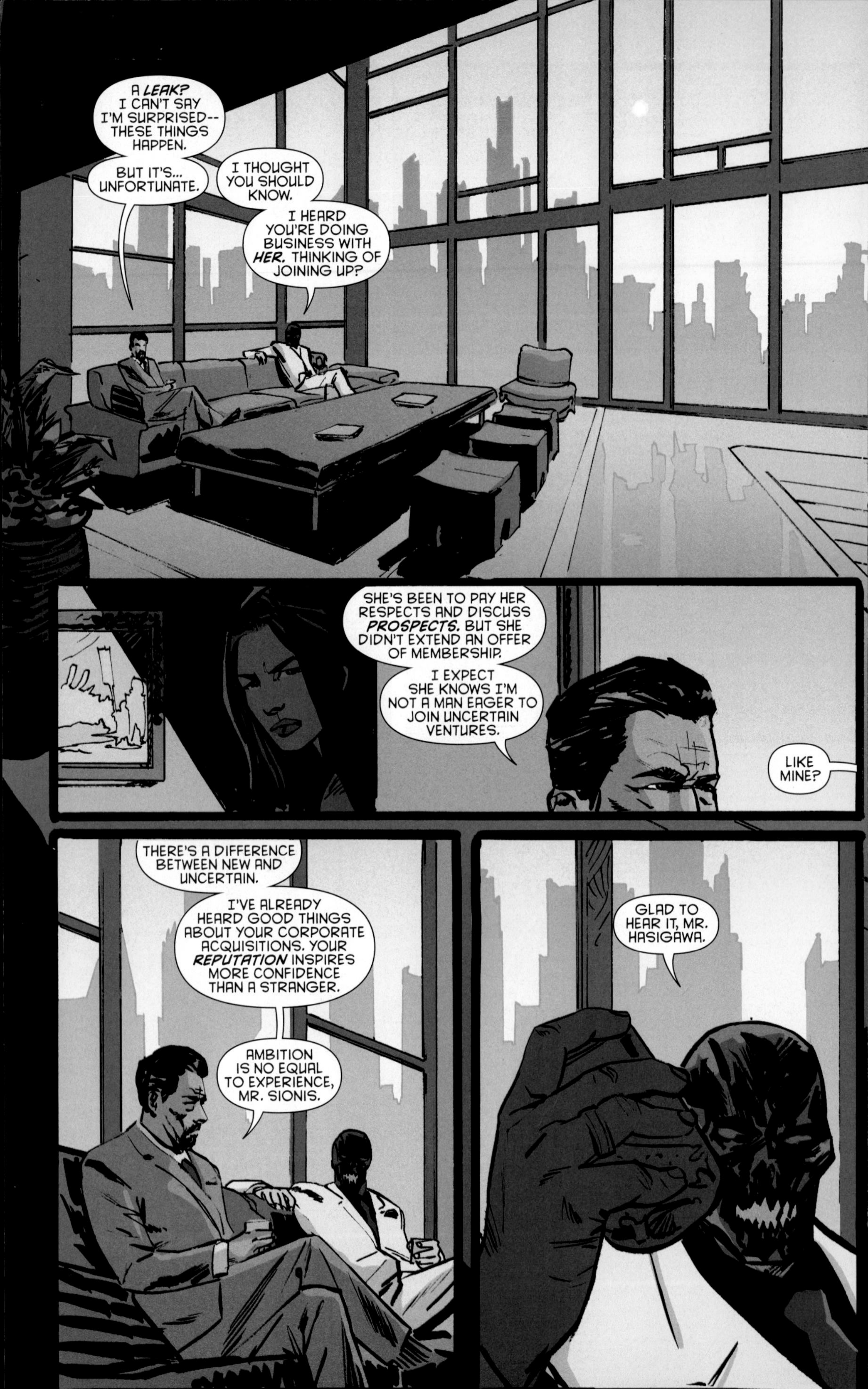
A LEAK? I CAN'T SAY I'M SURPRISED-- THESE THINGS HAPPEN.
BUT IT'S... UNFORTUNATE.
I THOUGHT YOU SHOULD KNOW.
I HEARD YOU'RE DOING BUSINESS WITH HER. THINKING OF JOINING UP?
SHE'S BEEN TO PAY HER RESPECTS AND DISCUSS PROSPECTS. BUT SHE DIDN'T EXTEND AN OFFER OF MEMBERSHIP.
I EXPECT SHE KNOWS I'M NOT A MAN EAGER TO JOIN UNCERTAIN VENTURES.
LIKE MINE?
THERE'S A DIFFERENCE BETWEEN NEW AND UNCERTAIN.
I'VE ALREADY HEARD GOOD THINGS ABOUT YOUR CORPORATE ACQUISITIONS. YOUR REPUTATION INSPIRES MORE CONFIDENCE THAN A STRANGER.
AMBITION IS NO EQUAL TO EXPERIENCE, MR. SIONIS.
GLAD TO HEAR IT, MR. HASIGAWA.

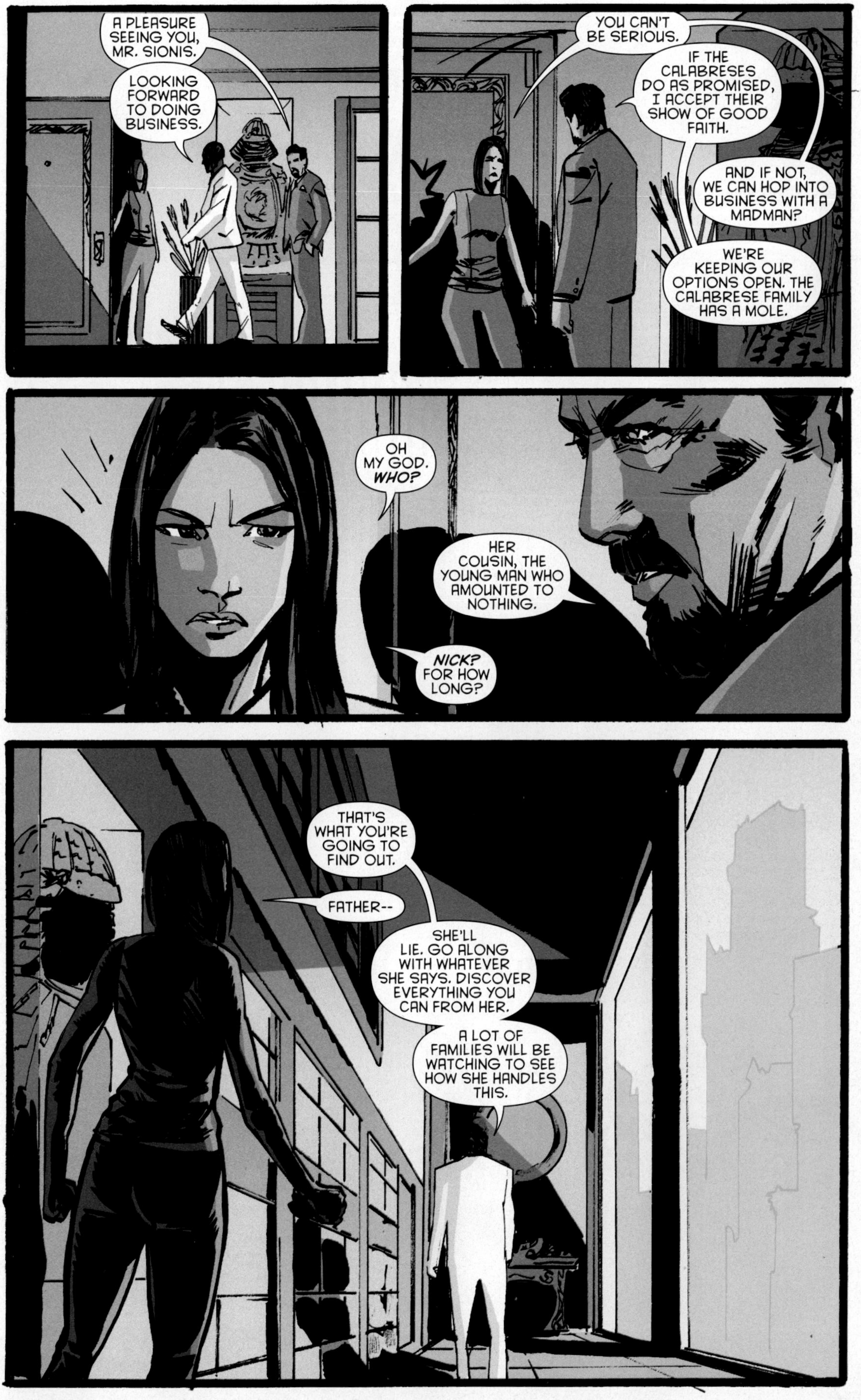
A PLEASURE SEEING YOU, MR. SIONIS.
LOOKING FORWARD TO DOING BUSINESS.
YOU CAN'T BE SERIOUS.
IF THE CALABRESES DO AS PROMISED, I ACCEPT THEIR SHOW OF GOOD FAITH.
AND IF NOT, WE CAN HOP INTO BUSINESS WITH A MADMAN?
WE'RE KEEPING OUR OPTIONS OPEN. THE CALABRESE FAMILY HAS A MOLE.
OH MY GOD. *WHO?*
HER COUSIN, THE YOUNG MAN WHO AMOUNTED TO NOTHING.
NICK? FOR HOW LONG?
THAT'S WHAT YOU'RE GOING TO FIND OUT.
FATHER--
SHE'LL LIE. GO ALONG WITH WHATEVER SHE SAYS. DISCOVER EVERYTHING YOU CAN FROM HER.
A LOT OF FAMILIES WILL BE WATCHING TO SEE HOW SHE HANDLES THIS.

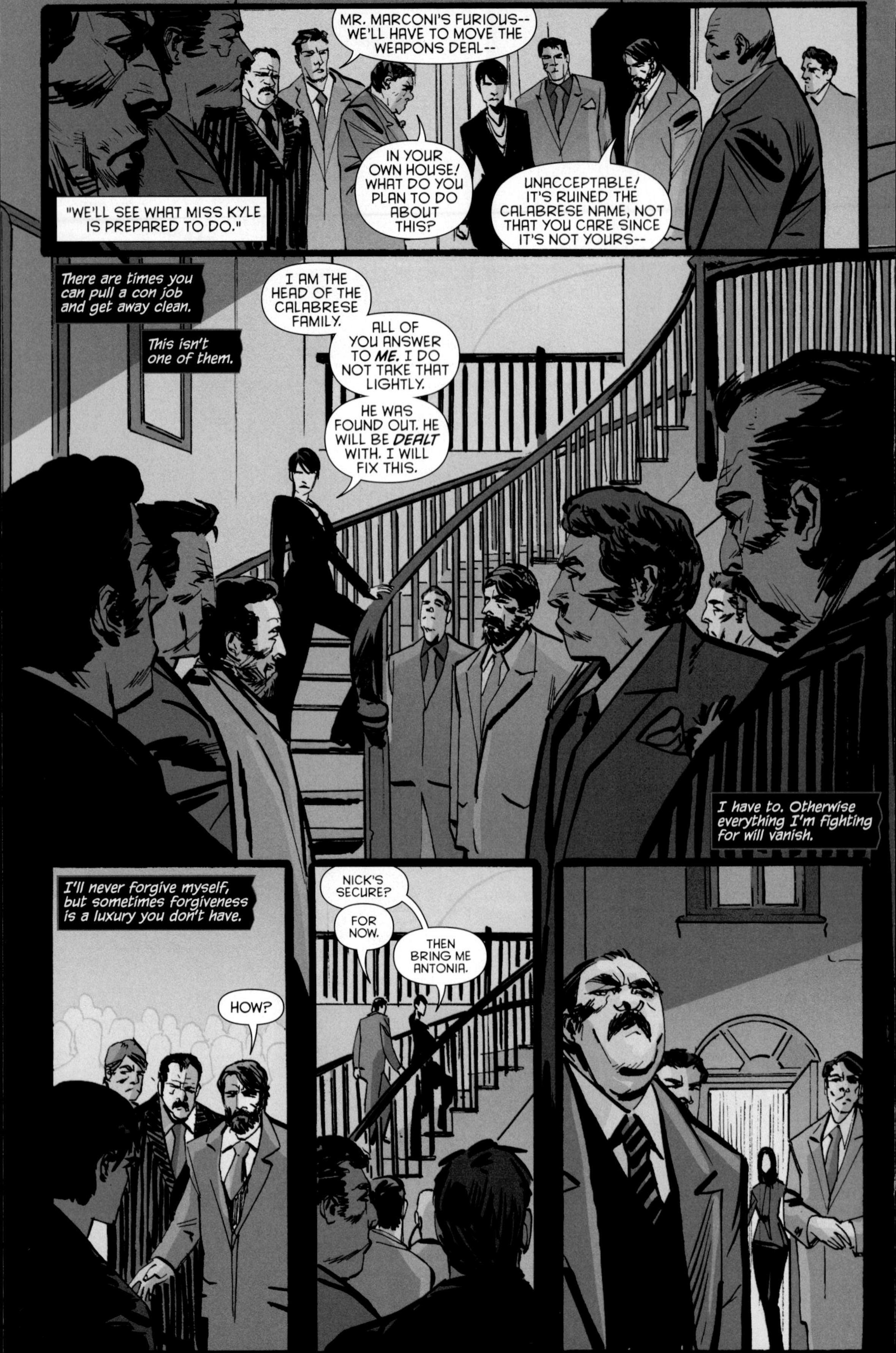
MR. MARCONI'S FURIOUS-- WE'LL HAVE TO MOVE THE WEAPONS DEAL--
IN YOUR OWN HOUSE! WHAT DO YOU PLAN TO DO ABOUT THIS?
UNACCEPTABLE! IT'S RUINED THE CALABRESE NAME, NOT THAT YOU CARE SINCE IT'S NOT YOURS--
"WE'LL SEE WHAT MISS KYLE IS PREPARED TO DO."
There are times you can pull a con job and get away clean.
This isn't one of them.
I AM THE HEAD OF THE CALABRESE FAMILY.
ALL OF YOU ANSWER TO ME. I DO NOT TAKE THAT LIGHTLY.
HE WAS FOUND OUT. HE WILL BE DEALT WITH. I WILL FIX THIS.
I have to. Otherwise everything I'm fighting for will vanish.
I'll never forgive myself, but sometimes forgiveness is a luxury you don't have.
HOW?
NICK'S SECURE?
FOR NOW.
THEN BRING ME ANTONIA.

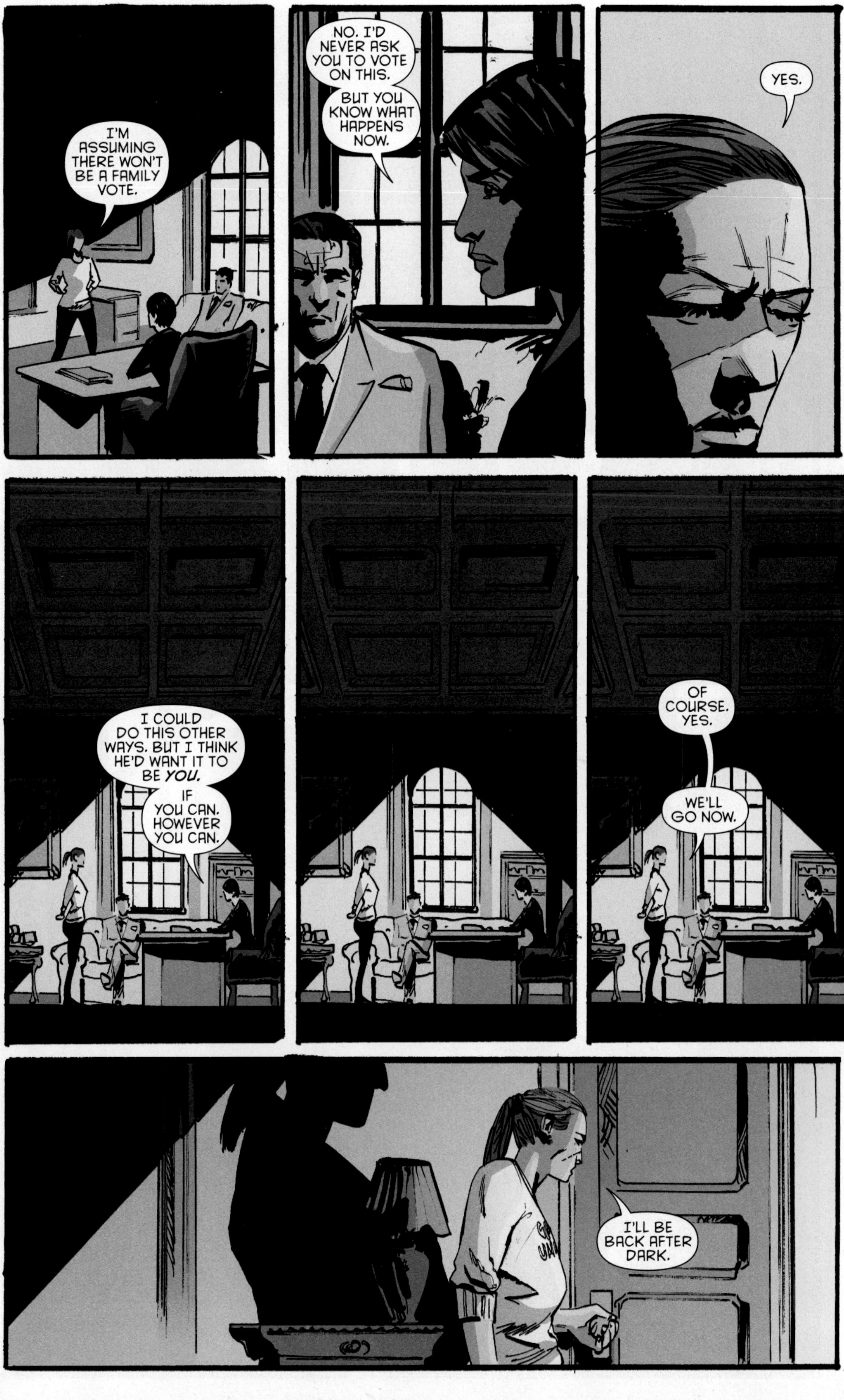
I'M ASSUMING THERE WON'T BE A FAMILY VOTE.
NO. I'D NEVER ASK YOU TO VOTE ON THIS.
BUT YOU KNOW WHAT HAPPENS NOW.
YES.
I COULD DO THIS OTHER WAYS. BUT I THINK HE'D WANT IT TO BE *YOU.*
IF YOU CAN. HOWEVER YOU CAN.
OF COURSE. YES.
WE'LL GO NOW.
I'LL BE BACK AFTER DARK.

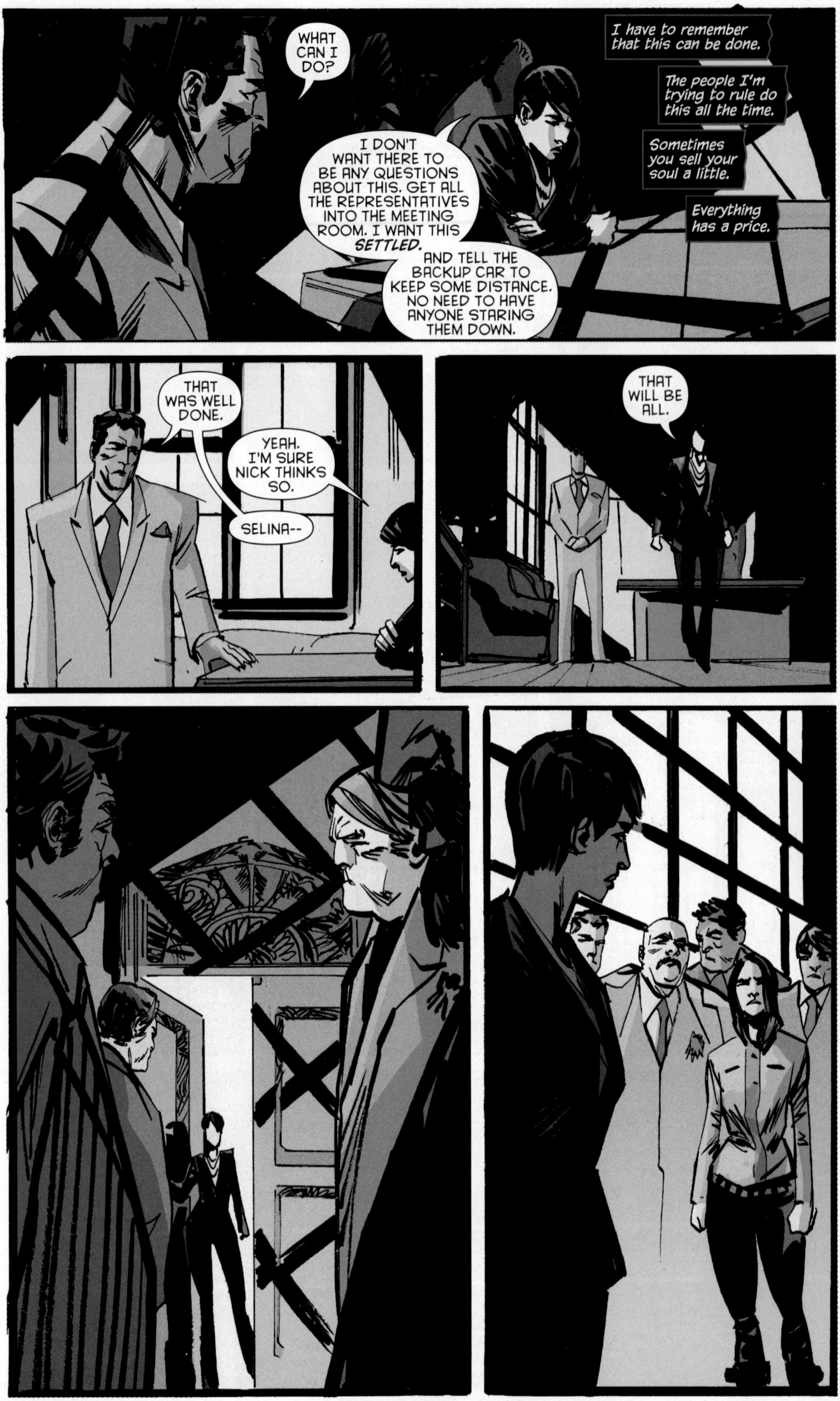
WHAT CAN I DO?
I have to remember that this can be done.
The people I'm trying to rule do this all the time.
Sometimes you sell your soul a little.
Everything has a price.
I DON'T WANT THERE TO BE ANY QUESTIONS ABOUT THIS. GET ALL THE REPRESENTATIVES INTO THE MEETING ROOM. I WANT THIS SETTLED.
AND TELL THE BACKUP CAR TO KEEP SOME DISTANCE. NO NEED TO HAVE ANYONE STARING THEM DOWN.
THAT WAS WELL DONE.
YEAH. I'M SURE NICK THINKS SO.
SELINA--
THAT WILL BE ALL.

THIS IS WHAT'S HAPPENED.

"NICK CALABRESE WILL BE SILENCED FOR WHAT HE DID.

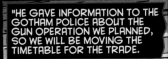
"HE GAVE INFORMATION TO THE GOTHAM POLICE ABOUT THE GUN OPERATION WE PLANNED, SO WE WILL BE MOVING THE TIMETABLE FOR THE TRADE.

"THANKFULLY, HE WAS DISCOVERED BEFORE HE COULD TELL THEM ANYTHING ELSE. WITHOUT OTHER WITNESSES, THE TRAIL DRIES UP.

"I TRUST THAT YOU'LL CHECK YOUR OWN HOUSES AND MAKE SURE ANY TRAIL DOES DRY UP.

"I ASSURE YOU, THEY CAN BE *ANYWHERE*.

"AS YOU SEE, THE HASIGAWA REPRESENTATIVE IS HERE TO FINALIZE THE DETAILS.

WE APPRECIATE THEIR SHOW OF FAITH.

AND I TRUST WE'VE OFFERED ONE TO ALL OF YOU.

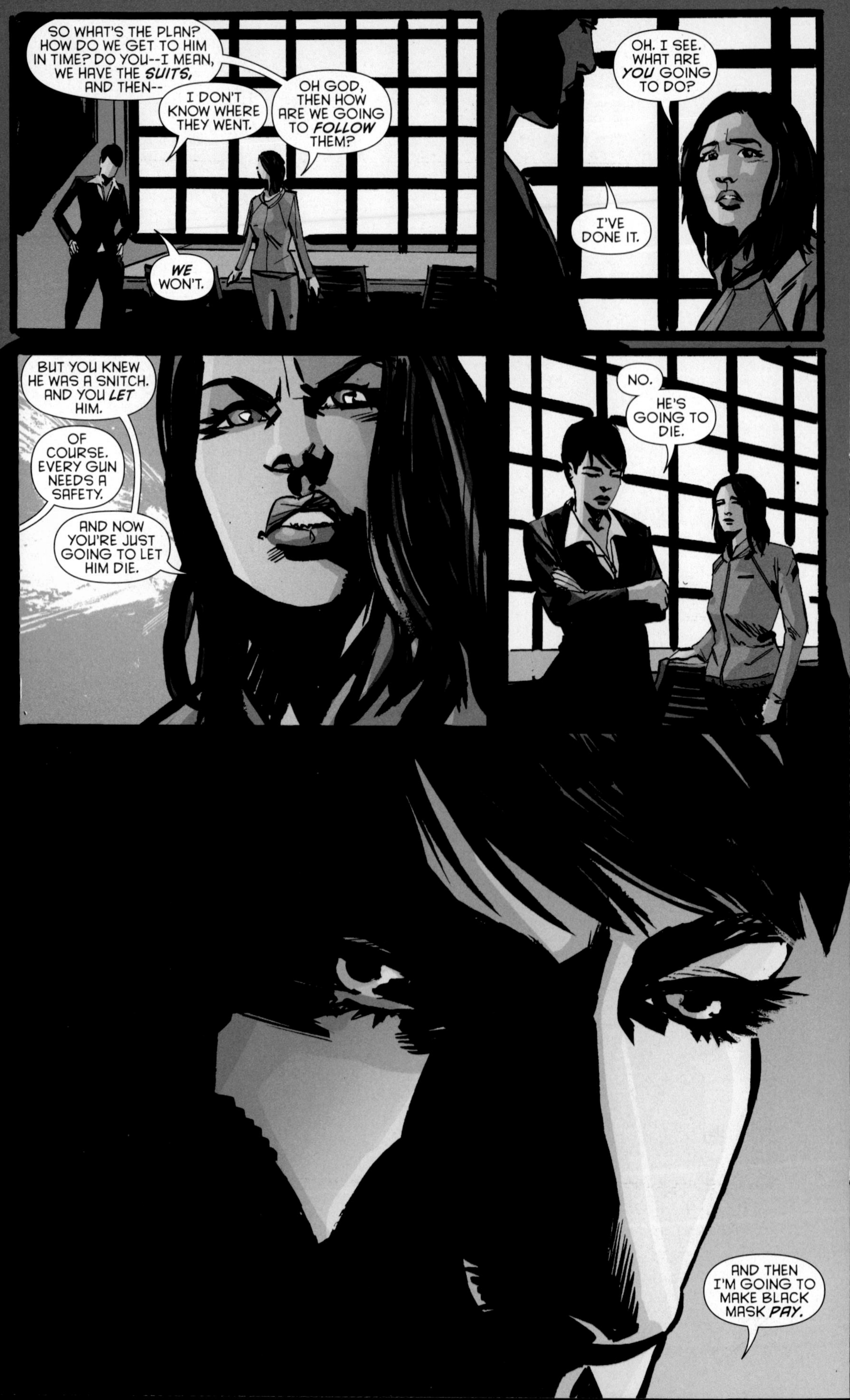
SO WHAT'S THE PLAN? HOW DO WE GET TO HIM IN TIME? DO YOU--I MEAN, WE HAVE THE *SUITS,* AND THEN--
I DON'T KNOW WHERE THEY WENT.
OH GOD, THEN HOW ARE WE GOING TO *FOLLOW* THEM?
WE WON'T.
OH. I SEE. WHAT ARE *YOU* GOING TO DO?
I'VE DONE IT.
BUT YOU KNEW HE WAS A SNITCH. AND YOU *LET* HIM.
OF COURSE. EVERY GUN NEEDS A SAFETY.
AND NOW YOU'RE JUST GOING TO LET HIM DIE.
NO.
HE'S GOING TO DIE.
AND THEN I'M GOING TO MAKE BLACK MASK *PAY.*

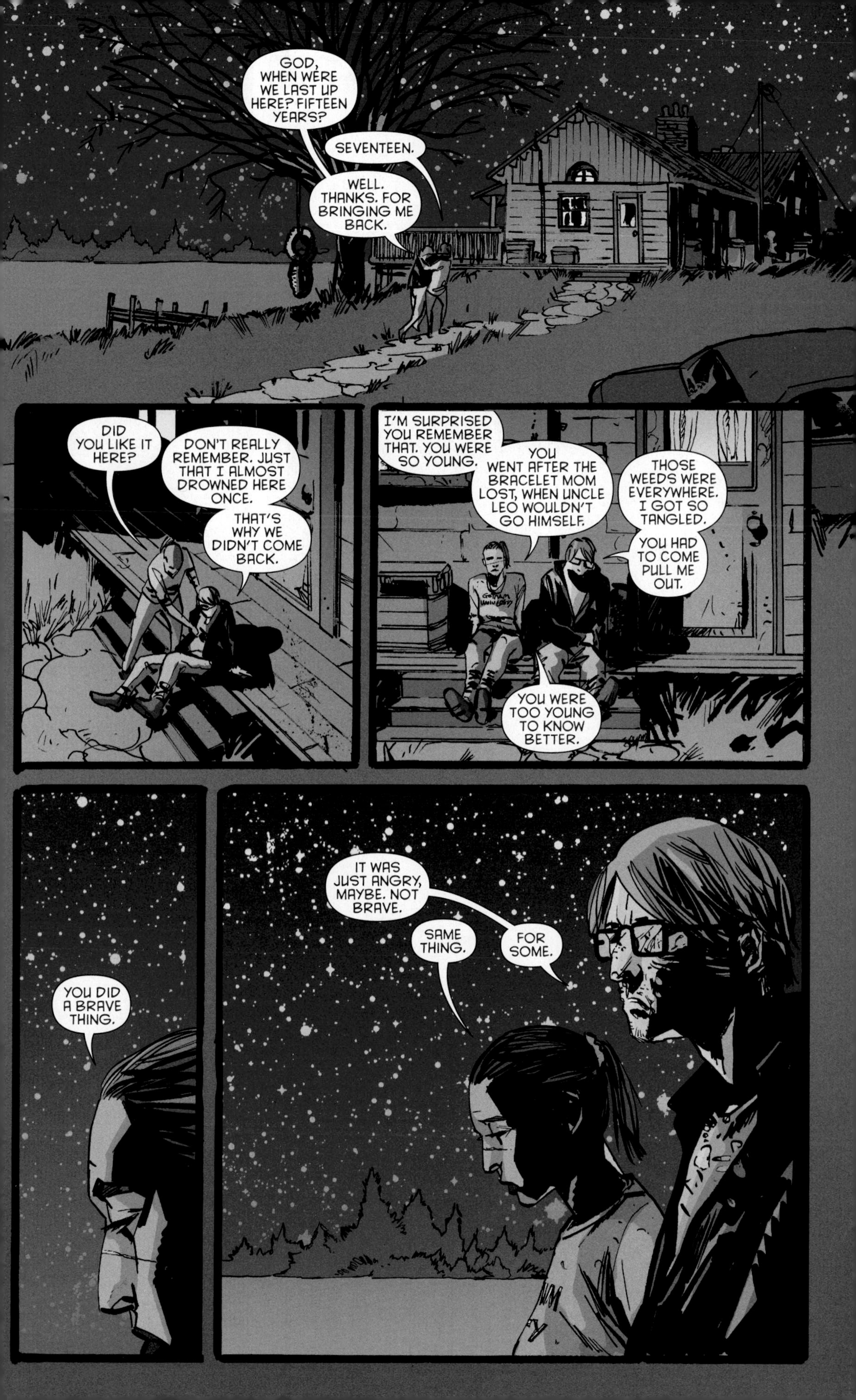
GOD, WHEN WERE WE LAST UP HERE? FIFTEEN YEARS?
SEVENTEEN.
WELL. THANKS. FOR BRINGING ME BACK.
DID YOU LIKE IT HERE?
DON'T REALLY REMEMBER. JUST THAT I ALMOST DROWNED HERE ONCE.
THAT'S WHY WE DIDN'T COME BACK.
I'M SURPRISED YOU REMEMBER THAT. YOU WERE SO YOUNG.
YOU WENT AFTER THE BRACELET MOM LOST, WHEN UNCLE LEO WOULDN'T GO HIMSELF.
THOSE WEEDS WERE EVERYWHERE. I GOT SO TANGLED.
YOU HAD TO COME PULL ME OUT.
YOU WERE TOO YOUNG TO KNOW BETTER.
YOU DID A BRAVE THING.
IT WAS JUST ANGRY, MAYBE. NOT BRAVE.
SAME THING.
FOR SOME.

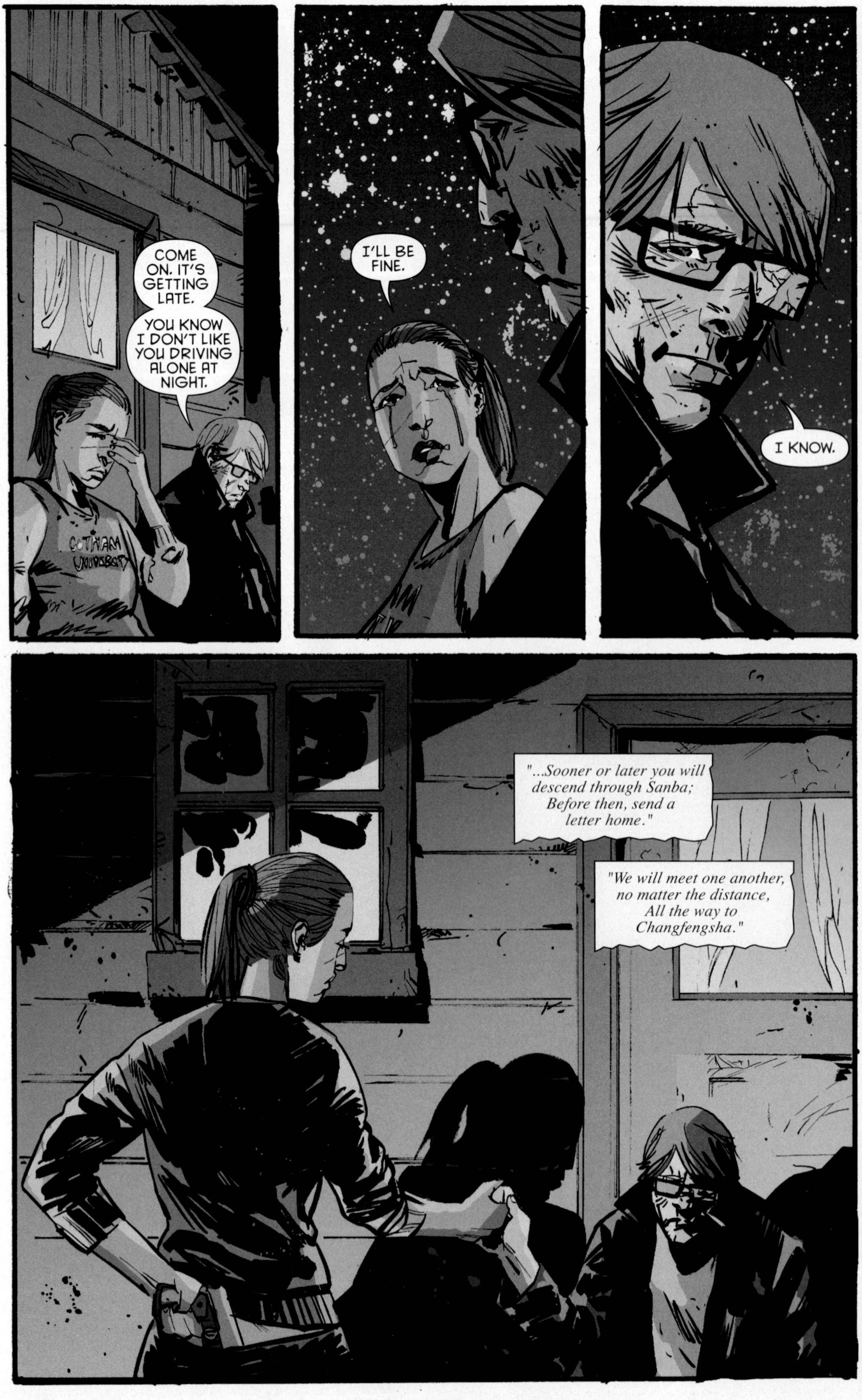
COME ON. IT'S GETTING LATE.
YOU KNOW I DON'T LIKE YOU DRIVING ALONE AT NIGHT.
I'LL BE FINE.
I KNOW.
"...Sooner or later you will descend through Sanba; Before then, send a letter home."
"We will meet one another, no matter the distance, All the way to Changfengsha."

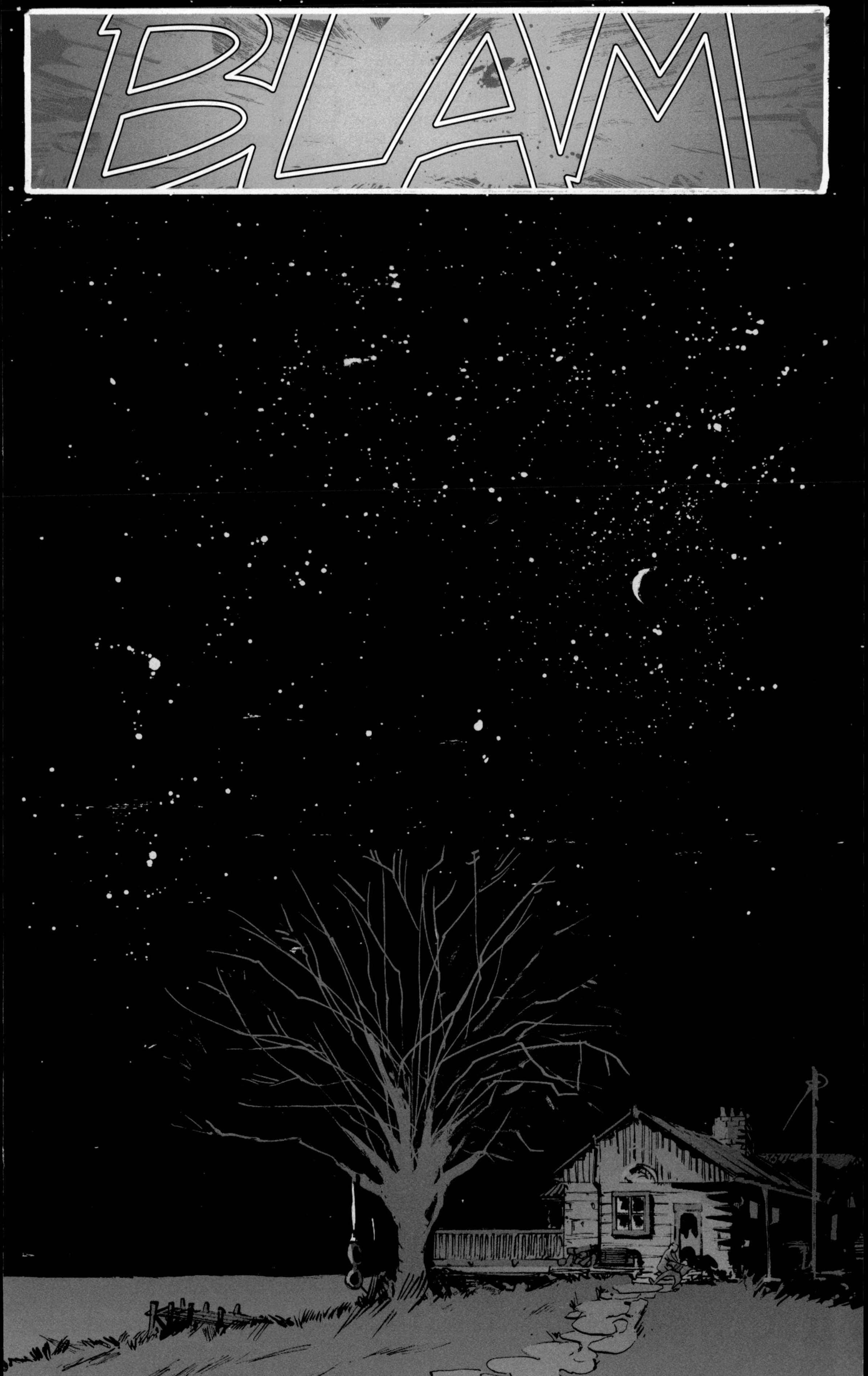
BLAM

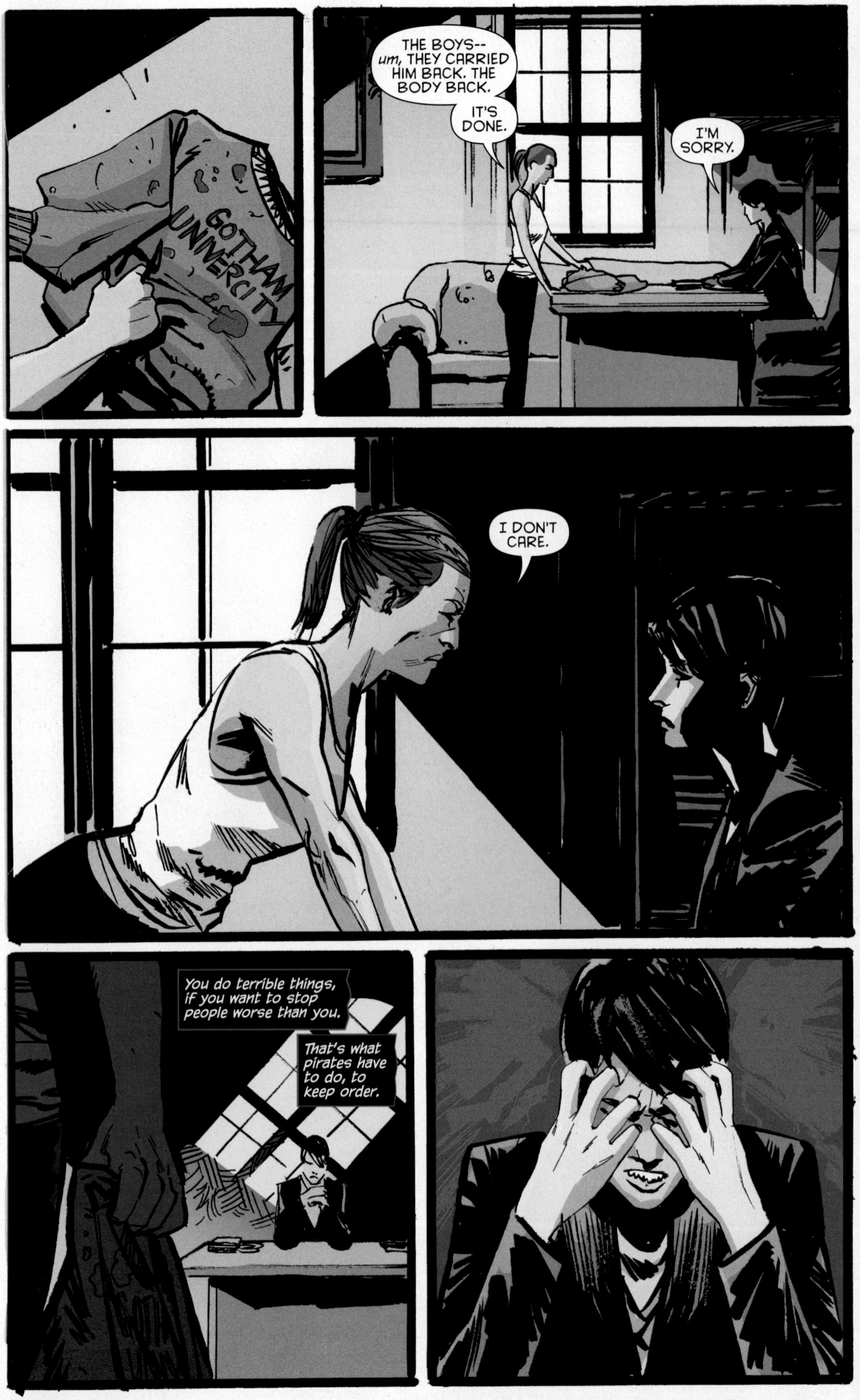
GOTHAM UNIVERCITY
THE BOYS-- *um,* THEY CARRIED HIM BACK. THE BODY BACK.
IT'S DONE.
I'M SORRY.
I DON'T CARE.
You do terrible things, if you want to stop people worse than you.
That's what pirates have to do, to keep order.

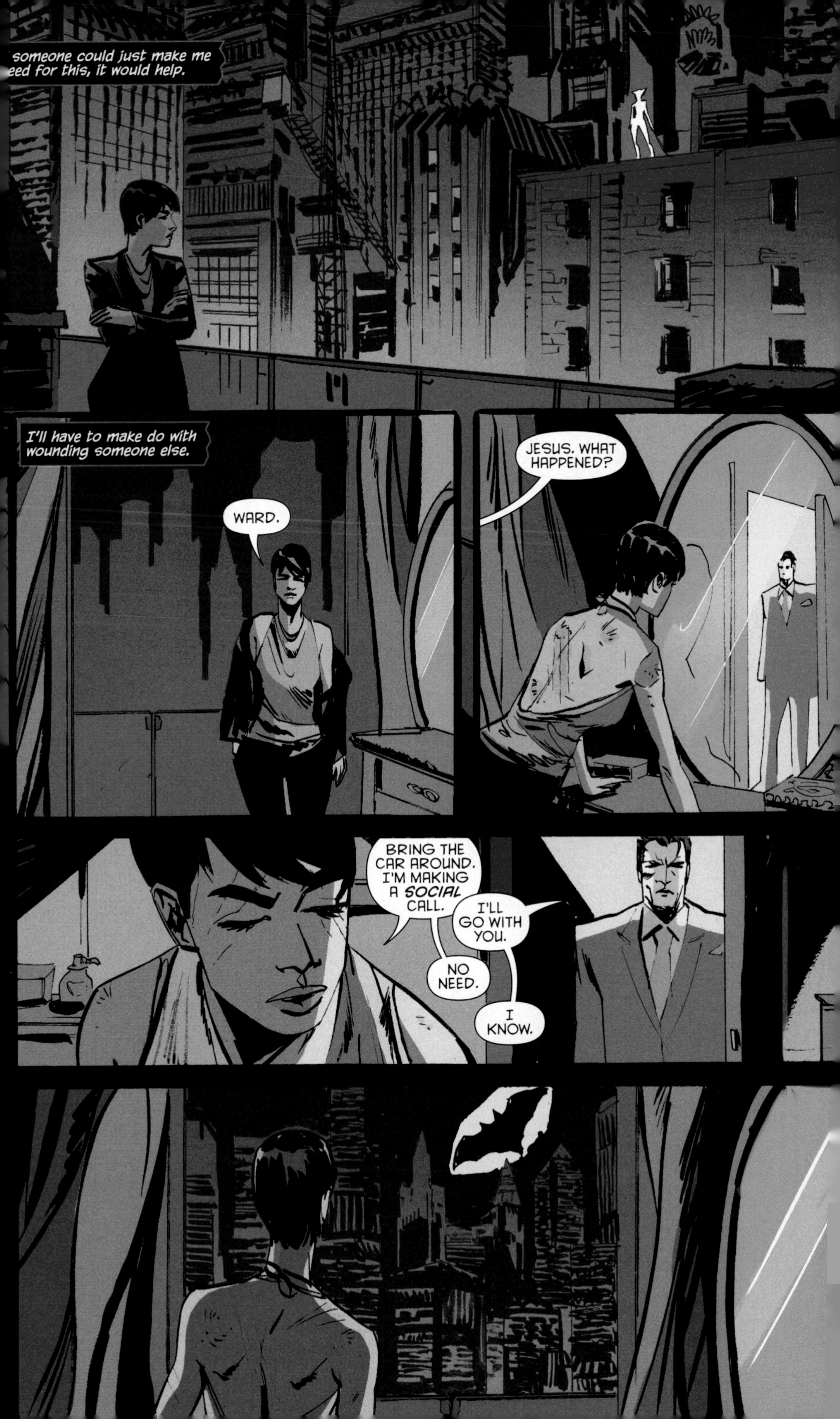
someone could just make me
eed for this, it would help.
I'll have to make do with wounding someone else.
WARD.
JESUS. WHAT HAPPENED?
BRING THE CAR AROUND. I'M MAKING A SOCIAL CALL.
I'LL GO WITH YOU.
NO NEED.
I KNOW.

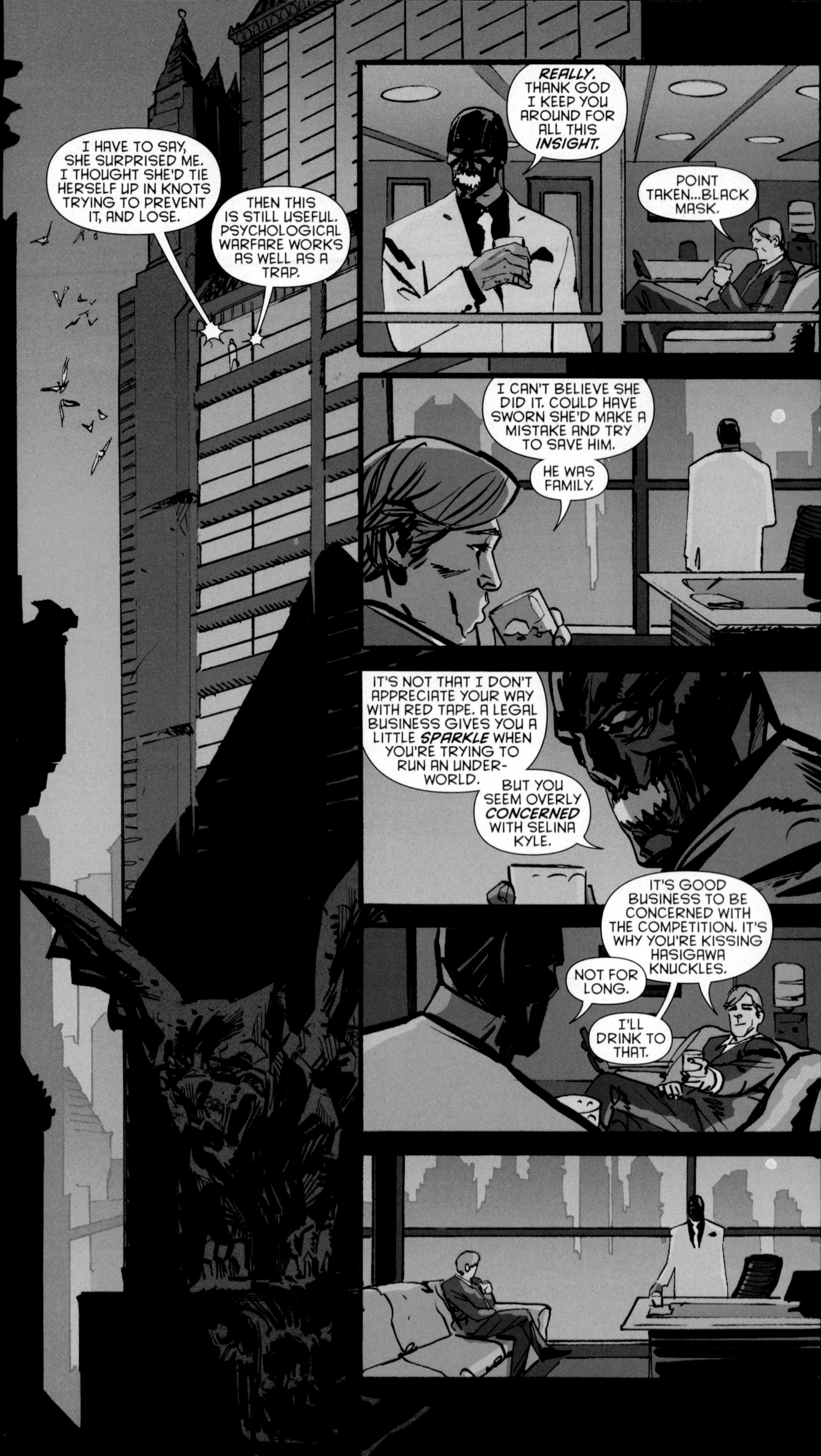
I HAVE TO SAY, SHE SURPRISED ME. I THOUGHT SHE'D TIE HERSELF UP IN KNOTS TRYING TO PREVENT IT, AND LOSE.
THEN THIS IS STILL USEFUL. PSYCHOLOGICAL WARFARE WORKS AS WELL AS A TRAP.
REALLY. THANK GOD I KEEP YOU AROUND FOR ALL THIS INSIGHT.
POINT TAKEN...BLACK MASK.
I CAN'T BELIEVE SHE DID IT. COULD HAVE SWORN SHE'D MAKE A MISTAKE AND TRY TO SAVE HIM.
HE WAS FAMILY.
IT'S NOT THAT I DON'T APPRECIATE YOUR WAY WITH RED TAPE. A LEGAL BUSINESS GIVES YOU A LITTLE SPARKLE WHEN YOU'RE TRYING TO RUN AN UNDER-WORLD.
BUT YOU SEEM OVERLY CONCERNED WITH SELINA KYLE.
IT'S GOOD BUSINESS TO BE CONCERNED WITH THE COMPETITION. IT'S WHY YOU'RE KISSING HASIGAWA KNUCKLES.
NOT FOR LONG.
I'LL DRINK TO THAT.

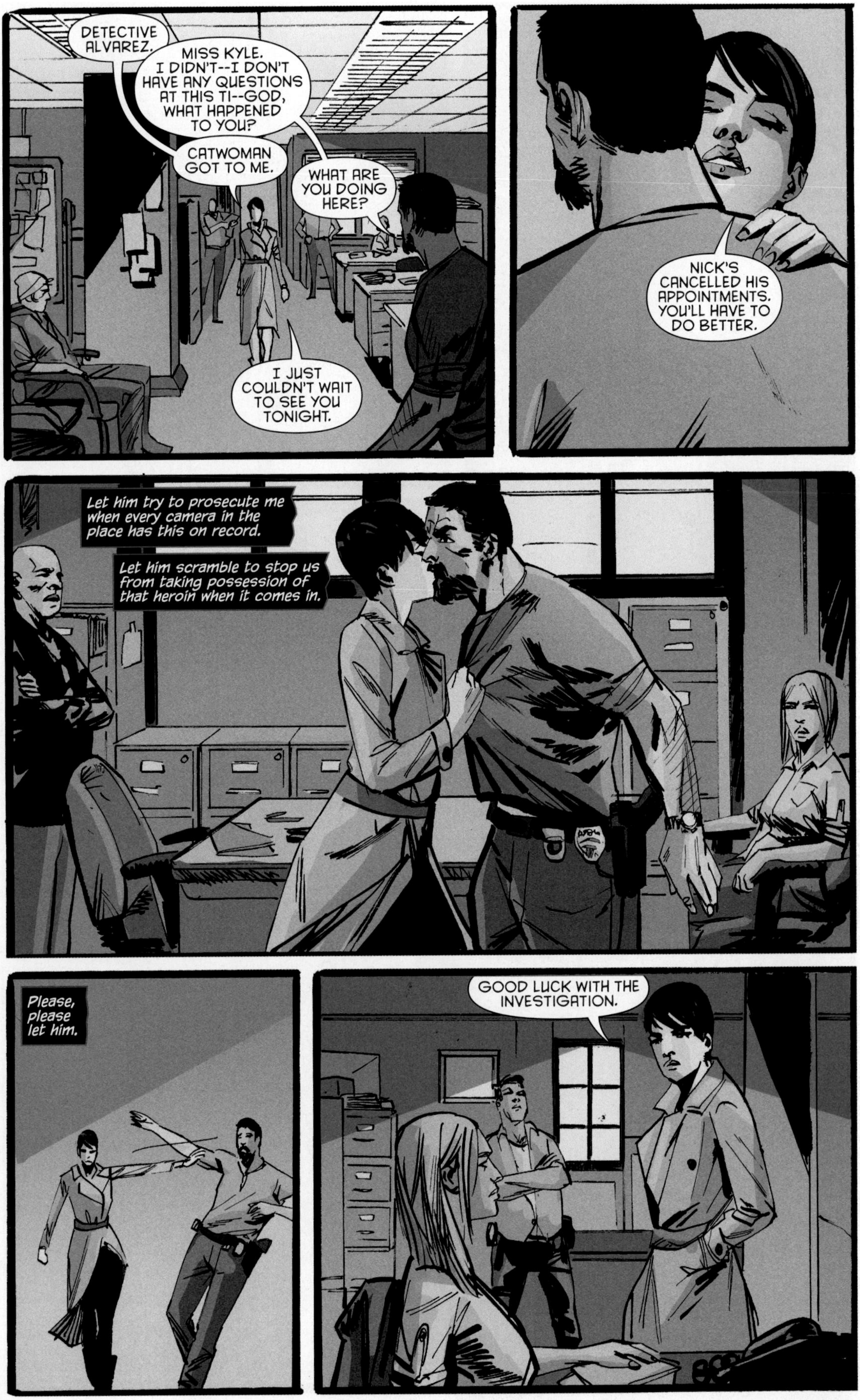
DETECTIVE ALVAREZ.
MISS KYLE. I DIDN'T--I DON'T HAVE ANY QUESTIONS AT THIS TI--GOD, WHAT HAPPENED TO YOU?
CATWOMAN GOT TO ME.
WHAT ARE YOU DOING HERE?
I JUST COULDN'T WAIT TO SEE YOU TONIGHT.
NICK'S CANCELLED HIS APPOINTMENTS. YOU'LL HAVE TO DO BETTER.
Let him try to prosecute me when every camera in the place has this on record.
Let him scramble to stop us from taking possession of that heroin when it comes in.
Please, please let him.
GOOD LUCK WITH THE INVESTIGATION.

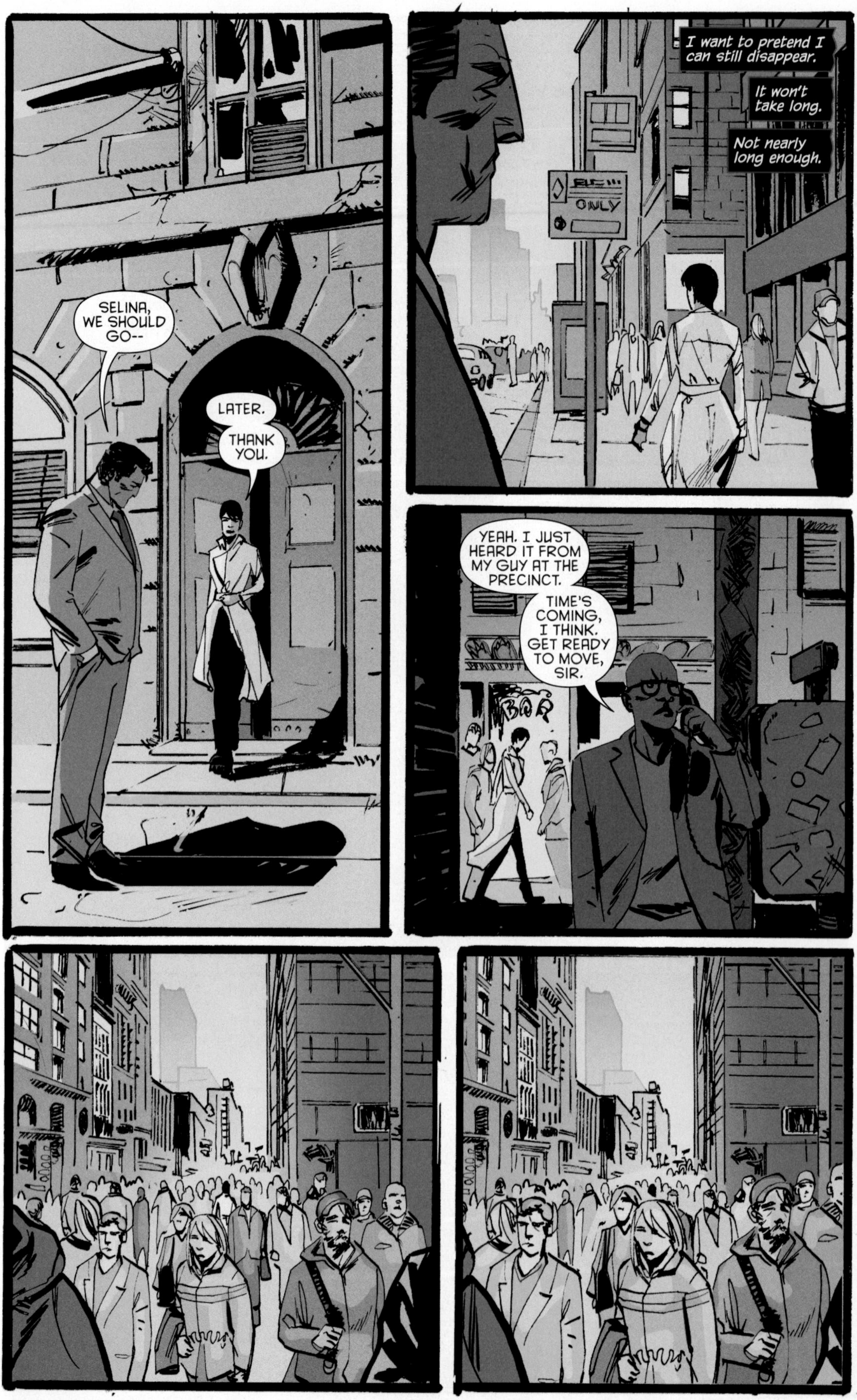
SELINA, WE SHOULD GO--
LATER.
THANK YOU.
I want to pretend I can still disappear.
It won't take long.
Not nearly long enough.
ONLY
YEAH. I JUST HEARD IT FROM MY GUY AT THE PRECINCT.
TIME'S COMING, I THINK. GET READY TO MOVE, SIR.

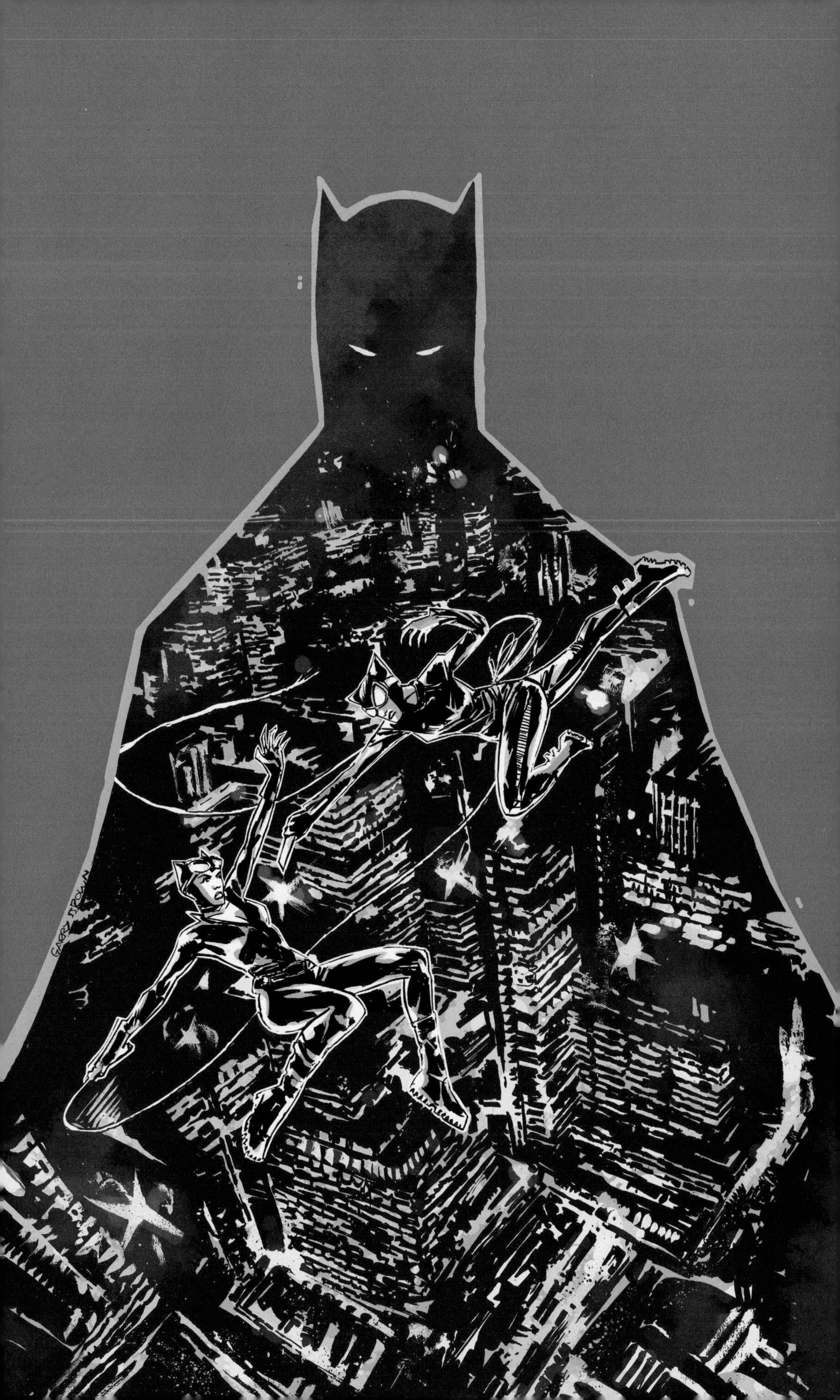

SHOSEN

N MCCREA artists cover art by GARRY BROWN

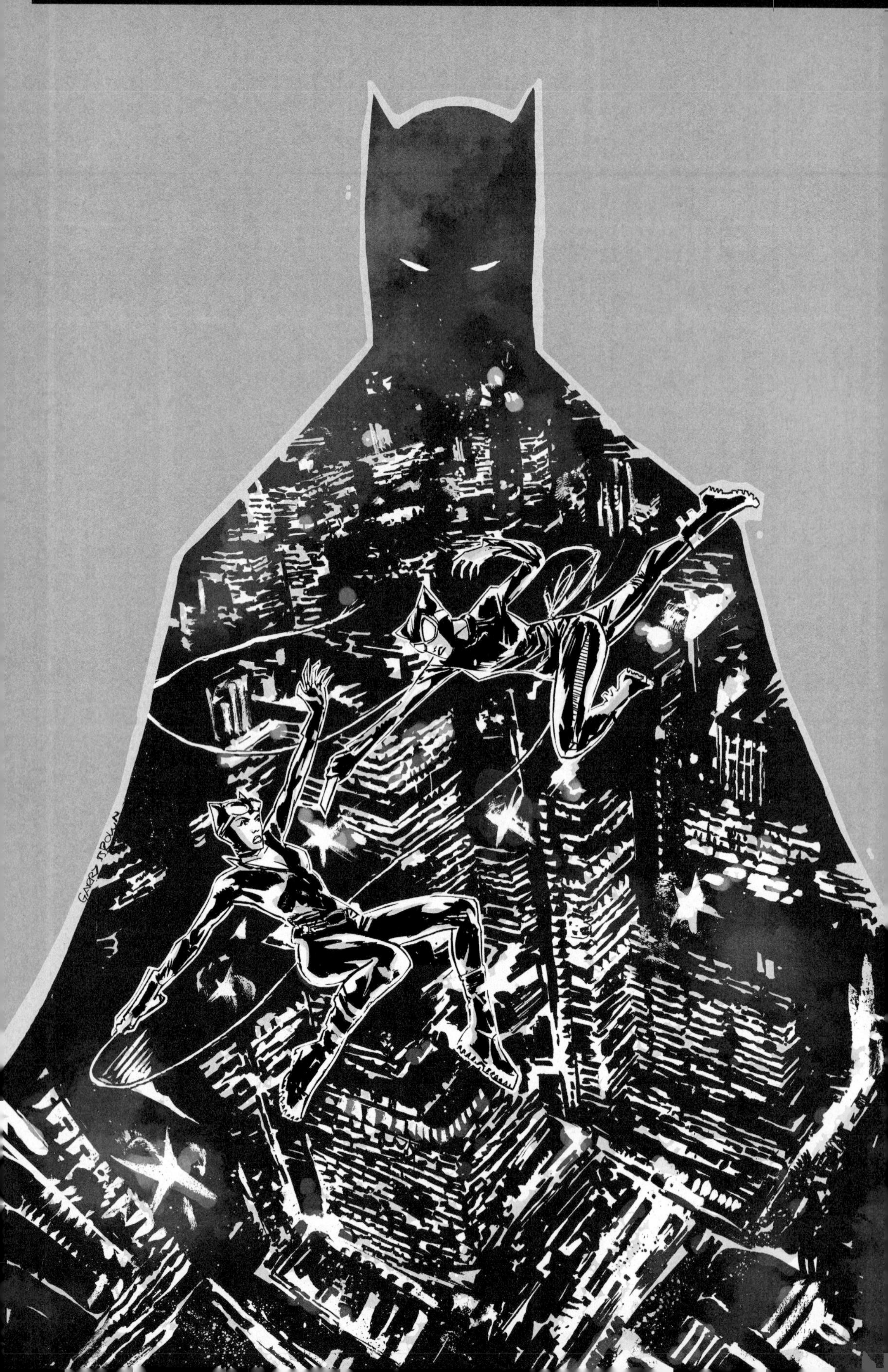
GARRY BROWN

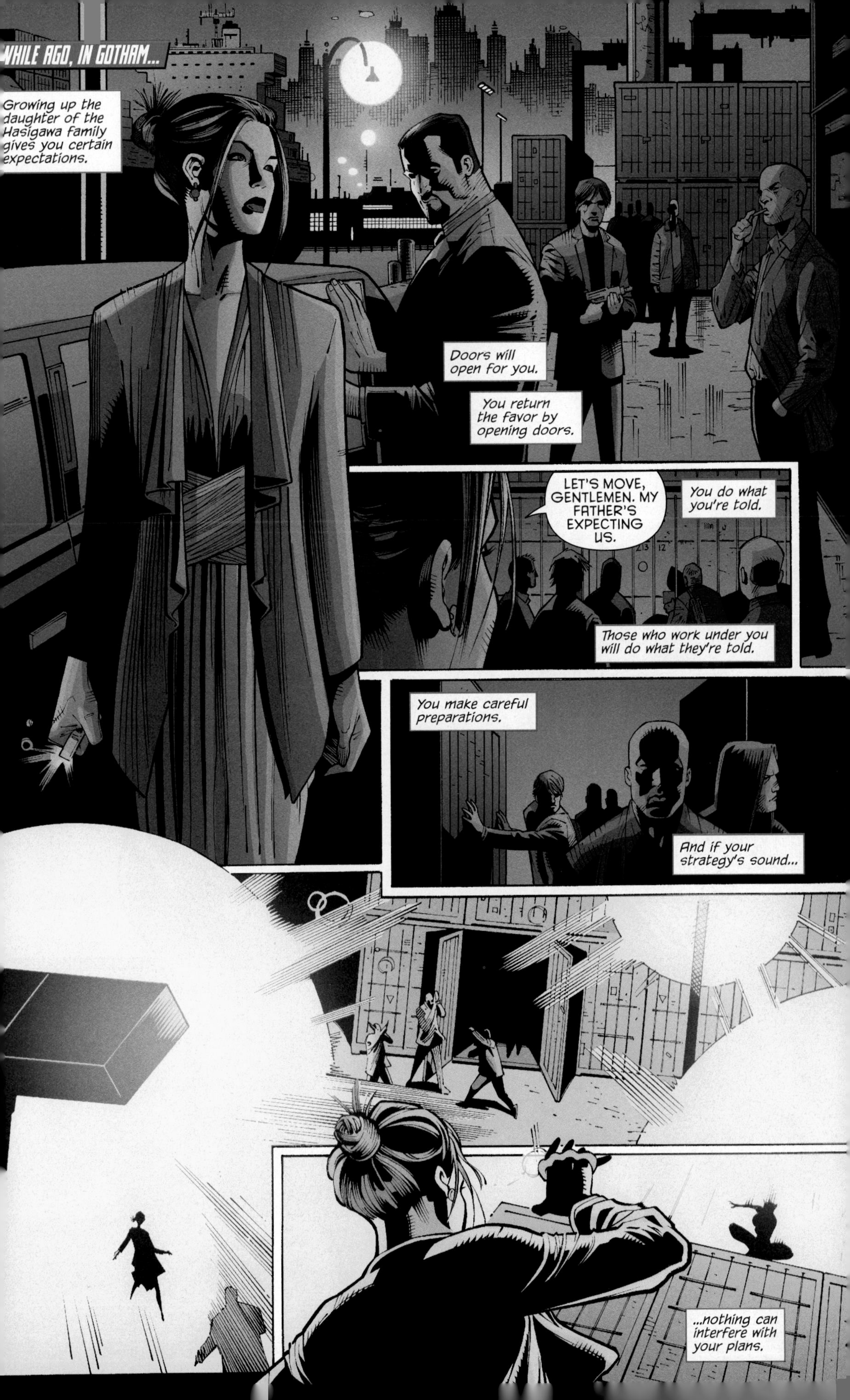

WHILE AGO, IN GOTHAM...
Growing up the daughter of the Hasigawa family gives you certain expectations.
Doors will open for you.
You return the favor by opening doors.
LET'S MOVE, GENTLEMEN. MY FATHER'S EXPECTING US.
You do what you're told.
Those who work under you will do what they're told.
You make careful preparations.
And if your strategy's sound...
...nothing can interfere with your plans.

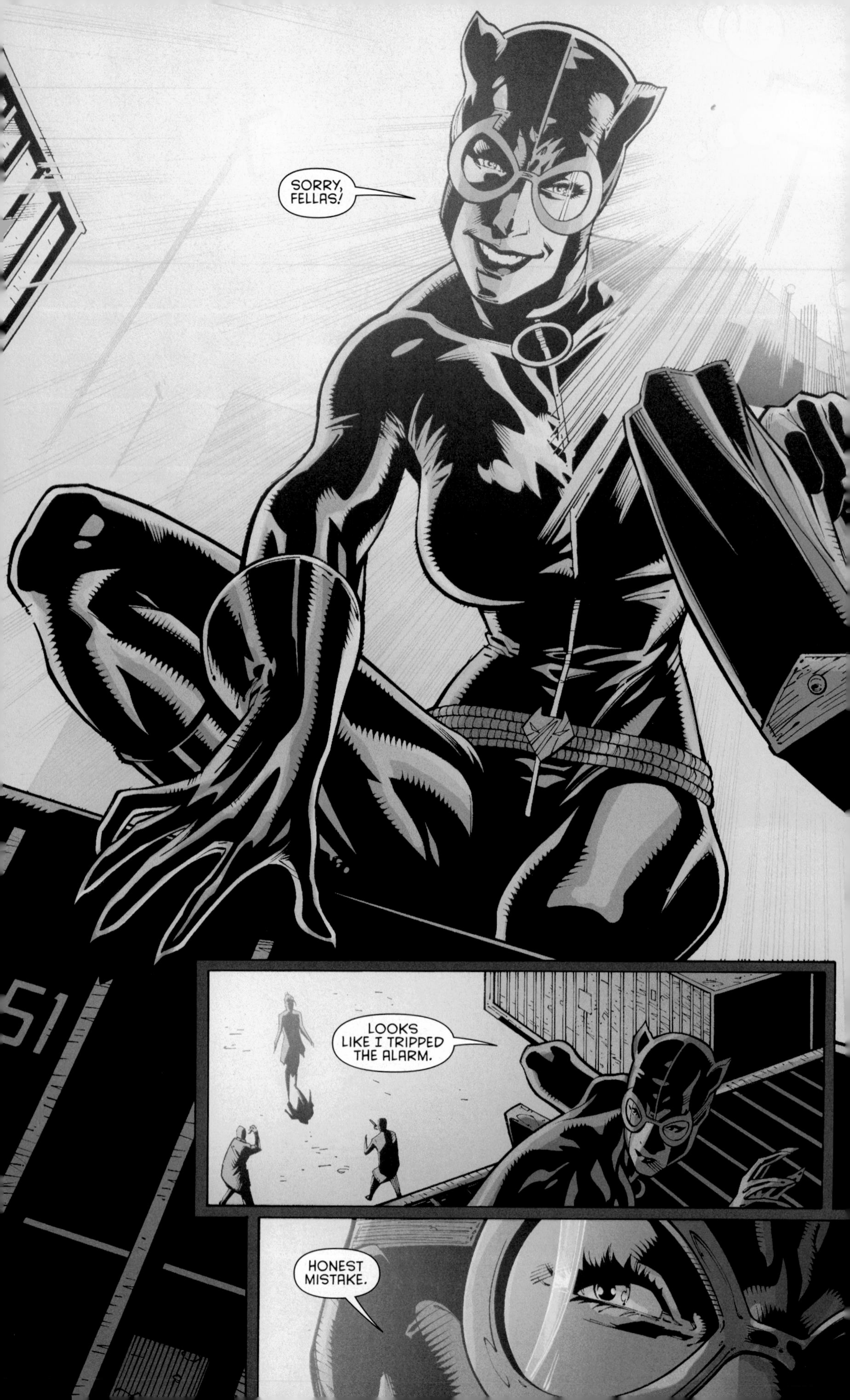
SORRY, FELLAS!
LOOKS LIKE I TRIPPED THE ALARM.
HONEST MISTAKE.

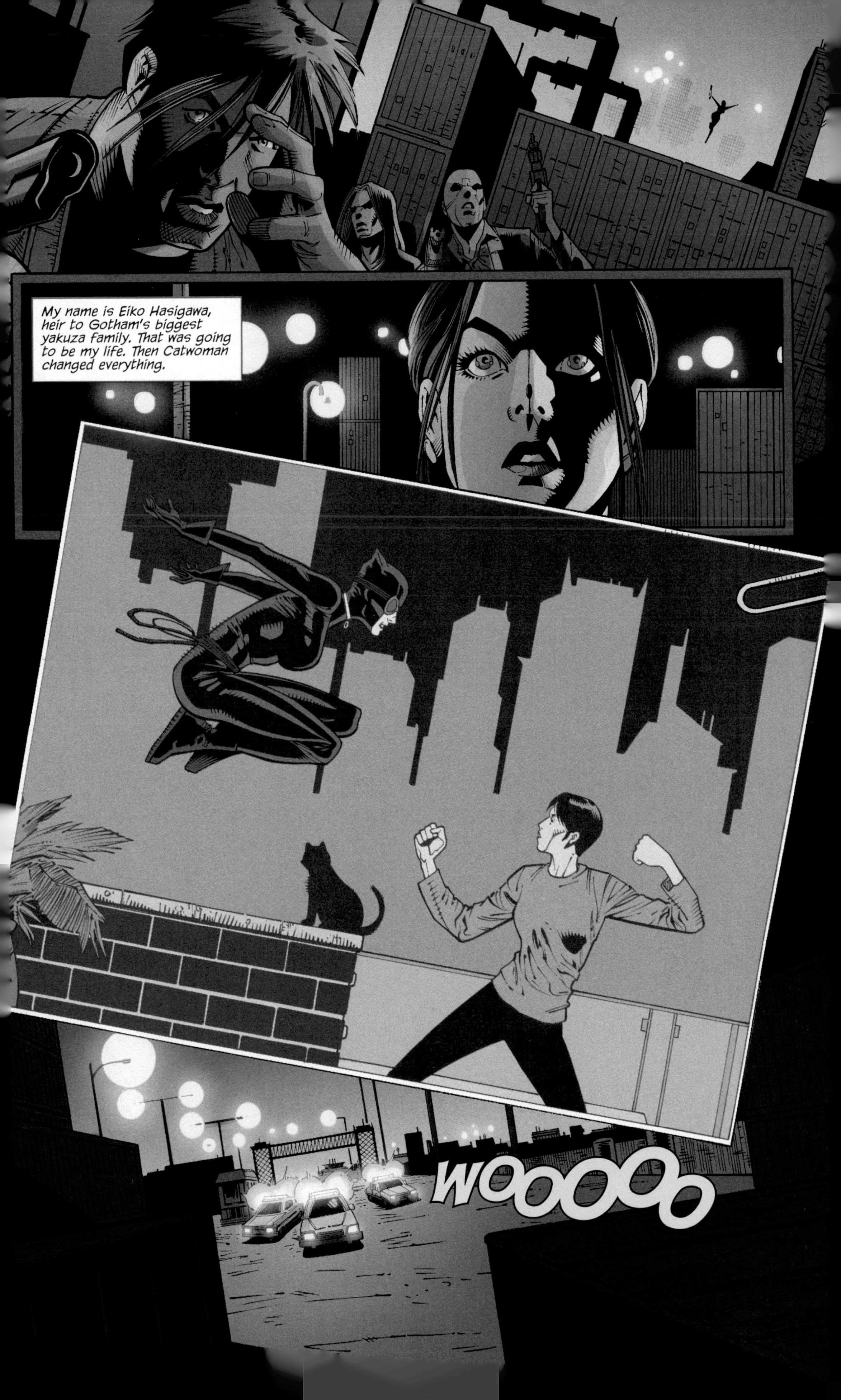
My name is Eiko Hasigawa, heir to Gotham's biggest yakuza family. That was going to be my life. Then Catwoman changed everything.
WOOOOO

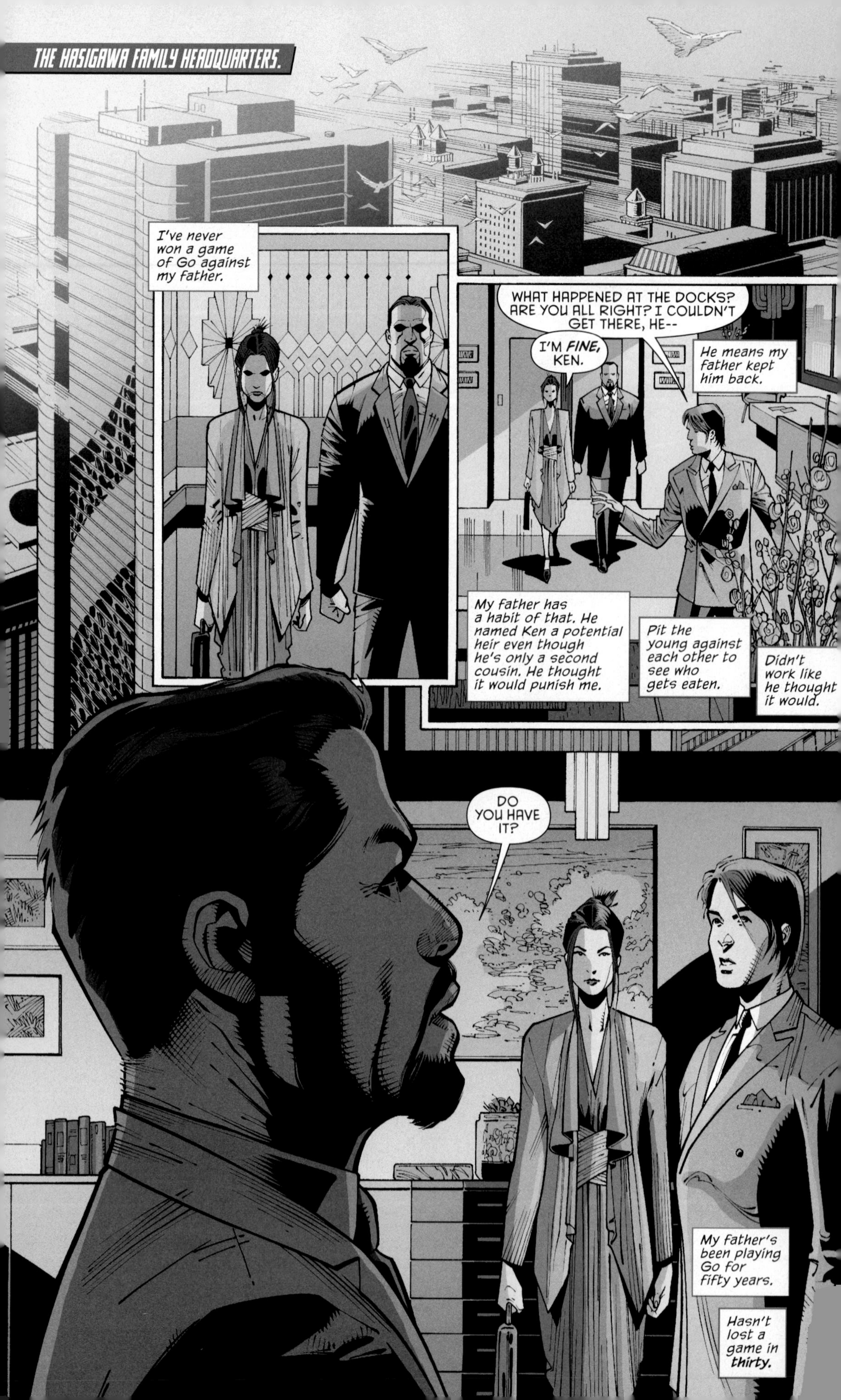
THE HASIGAWA FAMILY HEADQUARTERS.
I've never won a game of Go against my father.
WHAT HAPPENED AT THE DOCKS? ARE YOU ALL RIGHT? I COULDN'T GET THERE, HE--
I'M FINE, KEN.
He means my father kept him back.
My father has a habit of that. He named Ken a potential heir even though he's only a second cousin. He thought it would punish me.
Pit the young against each other to see who gets eaten.
Didn't work like he thought it would.
DO YOU HAVE IT?
My father's been playing Go for fifty years.
Hasn't lost a game in thirty.

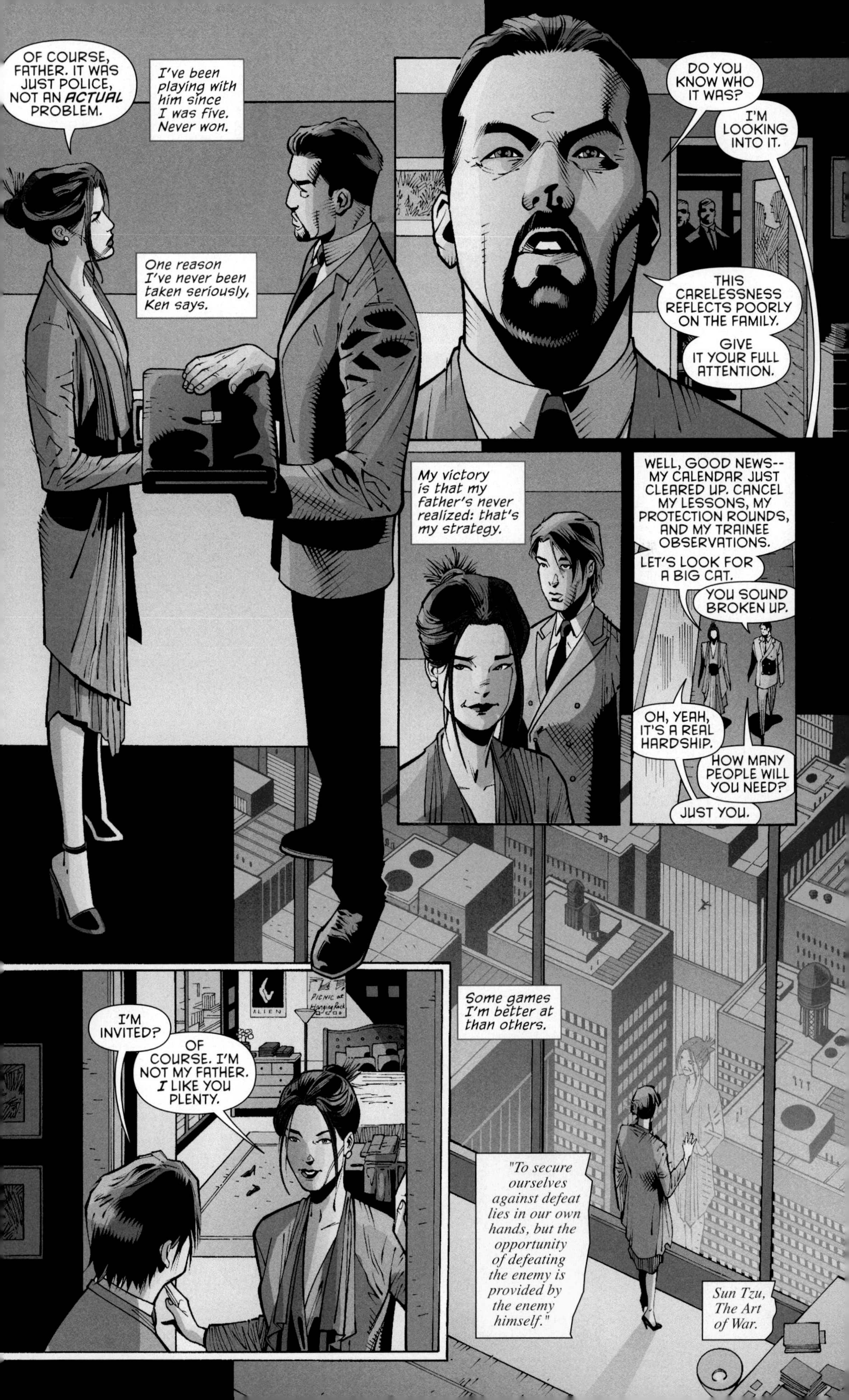
OF COURSE, FATHER. IT WAS JUST POLICE, NOT AN ACTUAL PROBLEM.
I've been playing with him since I was five. Never won.
One reason I've never been taken seriously, Ken says.
DO YOU KNOW WHO IT WAS?
I'M LOOKING INTO IT.
THIS CARELESSNESS REFLECTS POORLY ON THE FAMILY.
GIVE IT YOUR FULL ATTENTION.
My victory is that my father's never realized: that's my strategy.
WELL, GOOD NEWS-- MY CALENDAR JUST CLEARED UP. CANCEL MY LESSONS, MY PROTECTION ROUNDS, AND MY TRAINEE OBSERVATIONS.
LET'S LOOK FOR A BIG CAT.
YOU SOUND BROKEN UP.
OH, YEAH, IT'S A REAL HARDSHIP.
HOW MANY PEOPLE WILL YOU NEED?
JUST YOU.
I'M INVITED?
OF COURSE. I'M NOT MY FATHER. I LIKE YOU PLENTY.
ALIEN
PICNIC at Hanging Rock
Some games I'm better at than others.
"To secure ourselves against defeat lies in our own hands, but the opportunity of defeating the enemy is provided by the enemy himself."
Sun Tzu, The Art of War.

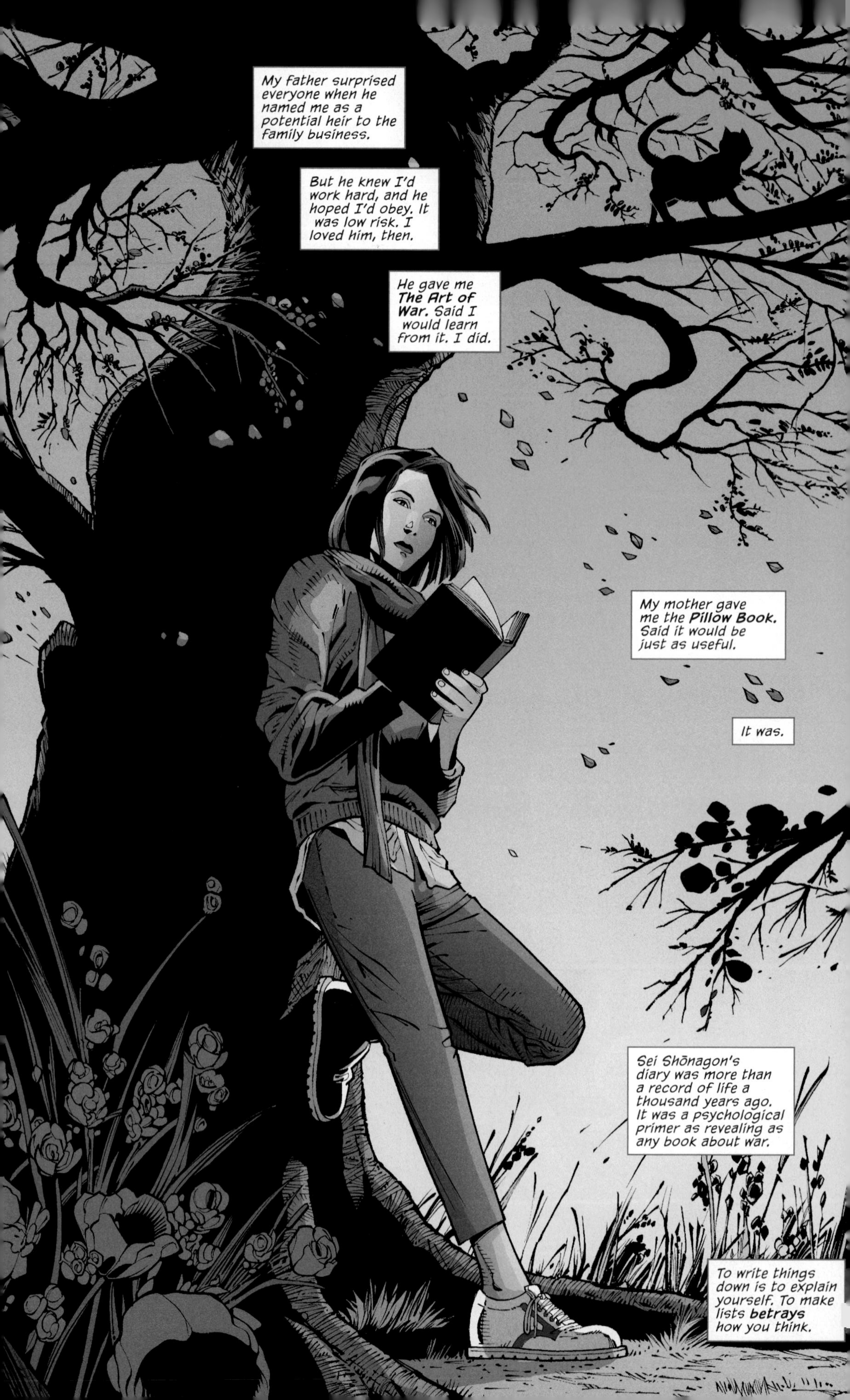
My father surprised everyone when he named me as a potential heir to the family business.
But he knew I'd work hard, and he hoped I'd obey. It was low risk. I loved him, then.
He gave me **The Art of War.** Said I would learn from it. I did.
My mother gave me the **Pillow Book.** Said it would be just as useful.
It was.
Sei Shōnagon's diary was more than a record of life a thousand years ago. It was a psychological primer as revealing as any book about war.
To write things down is to explain yourself. To make lists **betrays** how you think.

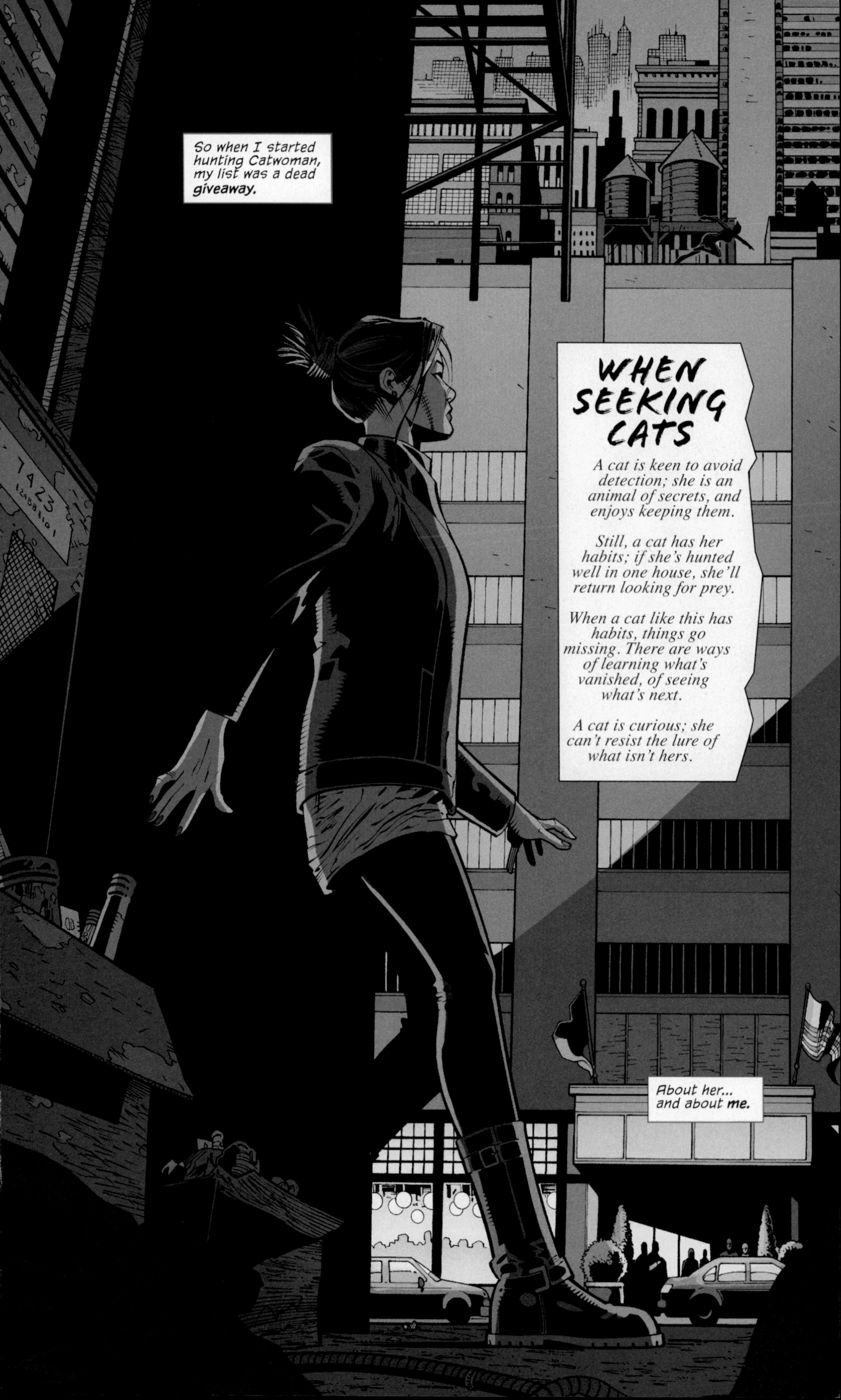

So when I started hunting Catwoman, my list was a dead giveaway.
WHEN SEEKING CATS
A cat is keen to avoid detection; she is an animal of secrets, and enjoys keeping them.
Still, a cat has her habits; if she's hunted well in one house, she'll return looking for prey.
When a cat like this has habits, things go missing. There are ways of learning what's vanished, of seeing what's next.
A cat is curious; she can't resist the lure of what isn't hers.
About her... and about me.

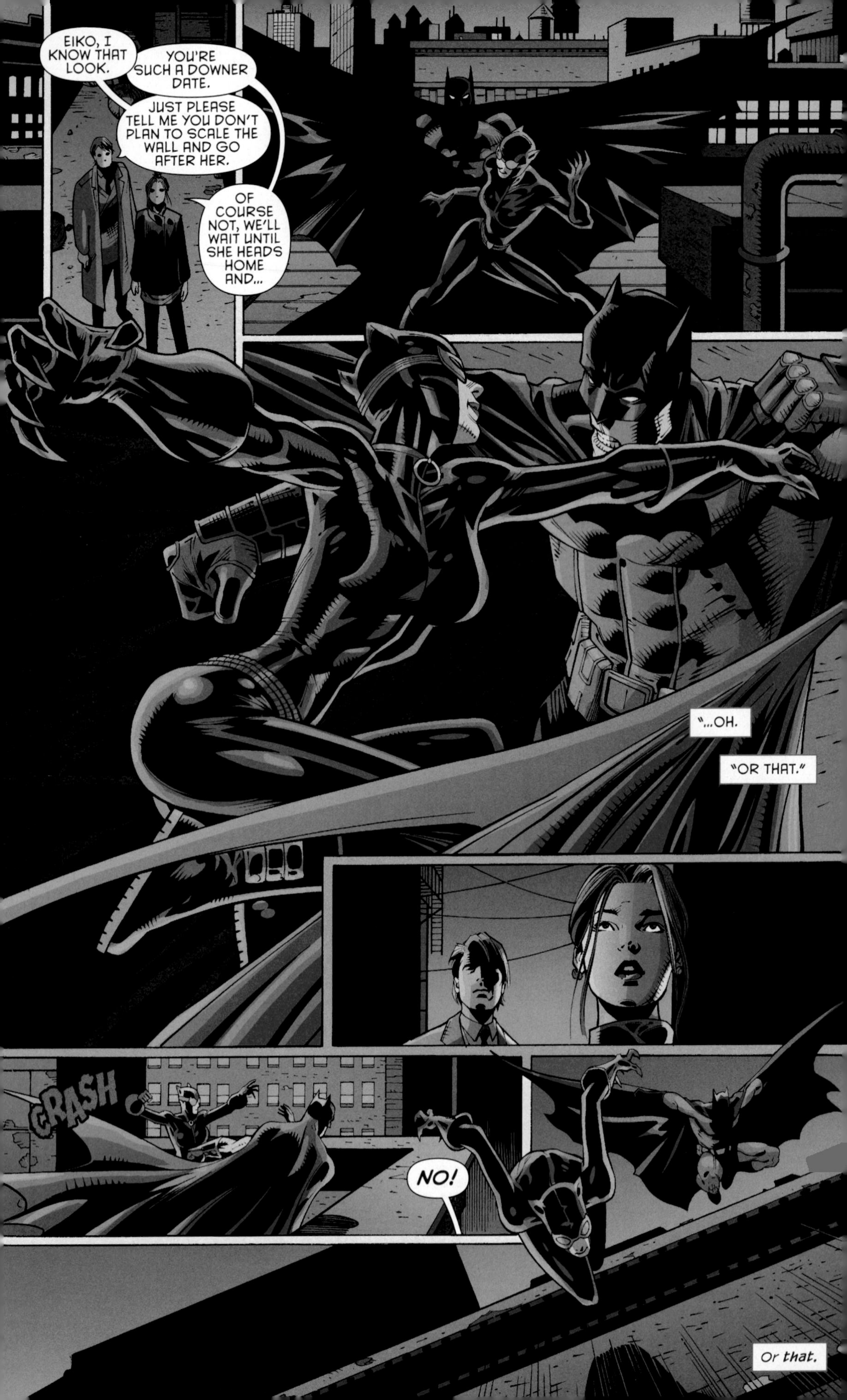
EIKO, I KNOW THAT LOOK.
YOU'RE SUCH A DOWNER DATE.
JUST PLEASE TELL ME YOU DON'T PLAN TO SCALE THE WALL AND GO AFTER HER.
OF COURSE NOT, WE'LL WAIT UNTIL SHE HEADS HOME AND...
"...OH.
"OR THAT."
CRASH
NO!
Or that.

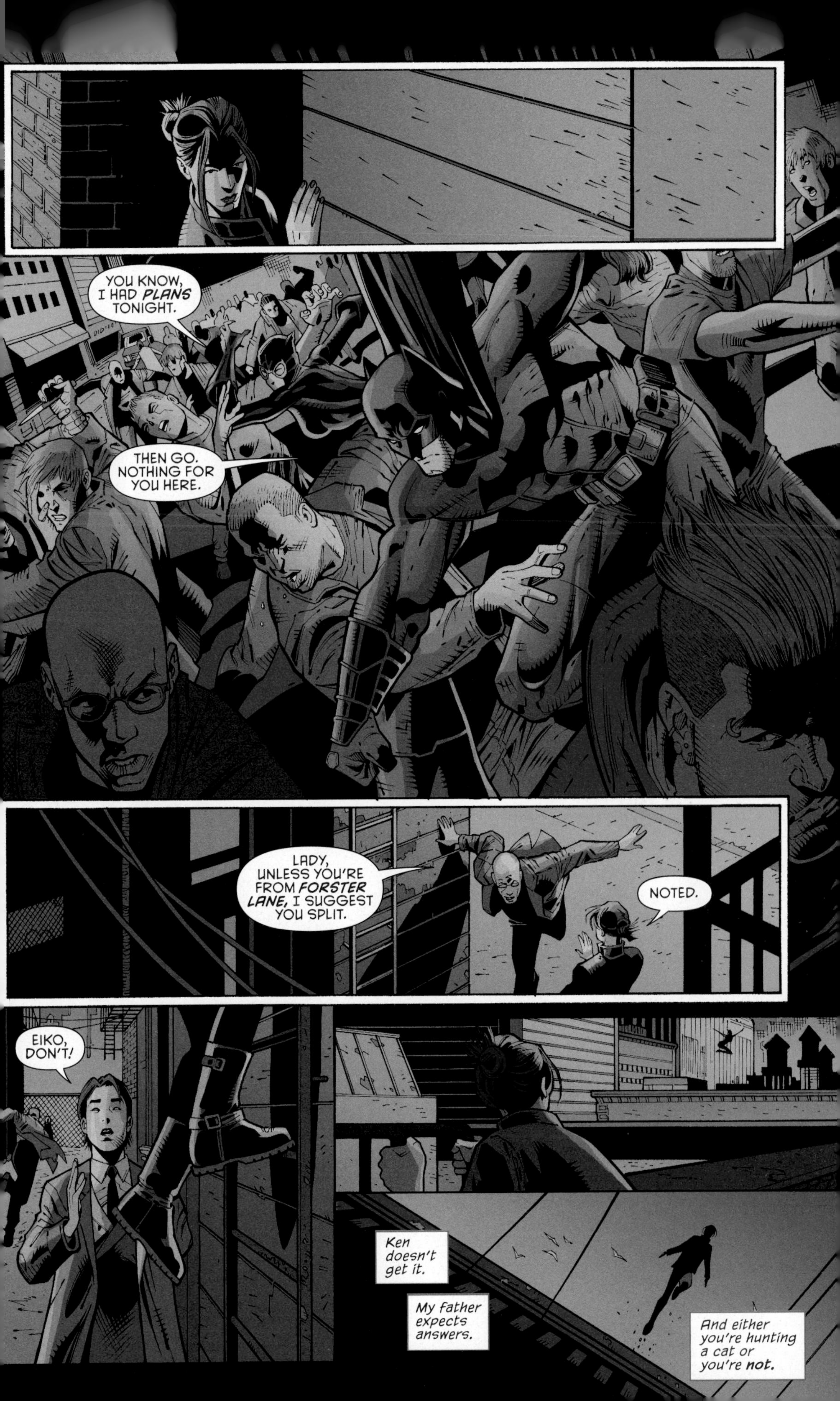

YOU KNOW, I HAD PLANS TONIGHT.
THEN GO. NOTHING FOR YOU HERE.
LADY, UNLESS YOU'RE FROM FORSTER LANE, I SUGGEST YOU SPLIT.
NOTED.
EIKO, DON'T!
Ken doesn't get it.
My father expects answers.
And either you're hunting a cat or you're not.

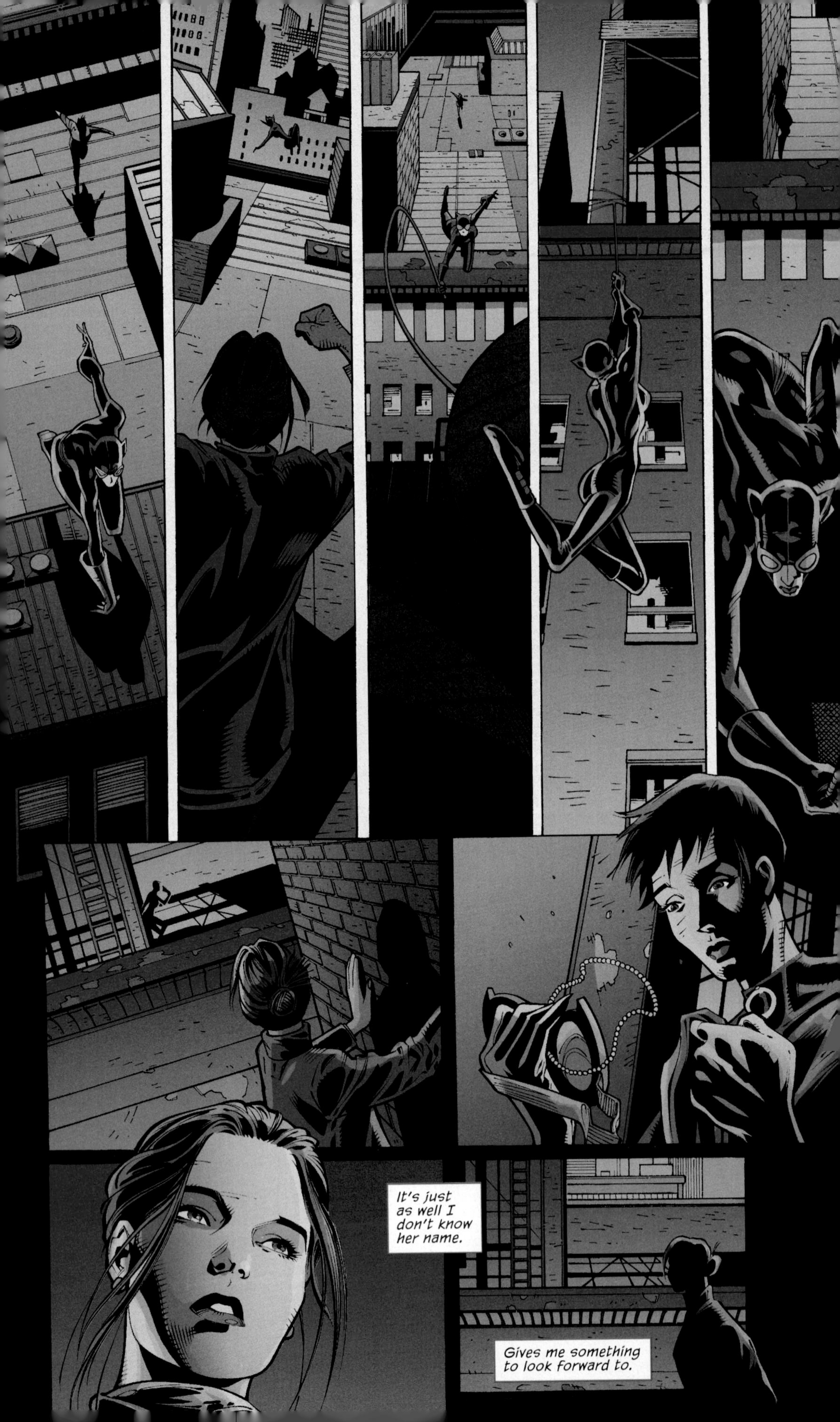
It's just as well I don't know her name.
Gives me something to look forward to.

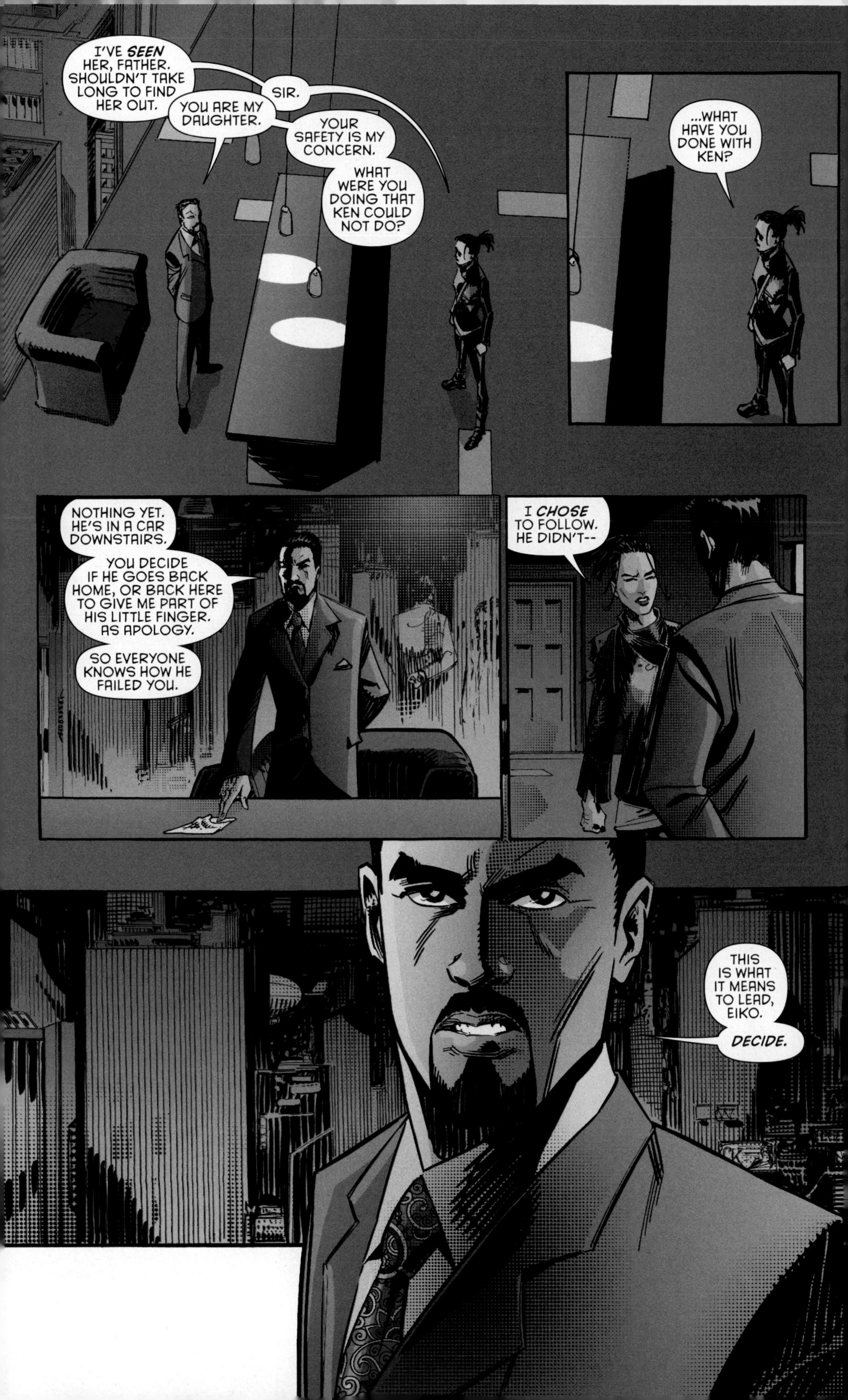
I'VE SEEN HER, FATHER. SHOULDN'T TAKE LONG TO FIND HER OUT.
SIR.
YOU ARE MY DAUGHTER.
YOUR SAFETY IS MY CONCERN.
WHAT WERE YOU DOING THAT KEN COULD NOT DO?
...WHAT HAVE YOU DONE WITH KEN?
NOTHING YET. HE'S IN A CAR DOWNSTAIRS.
YOU DECIDE IF HE GOES BACK HOME, OR BACK HERE TO GIVE ME PART OF HIS LITTLE FINGER. AS APOLOGY.
SO EVERYONE KNOWS HOW HE FAILED YOU.
I CHOSE TO FOLLOW. HE DIDN'T--
THIS IS WHAT IT MEANS TO LEAD, EIKO.
DECIDE.

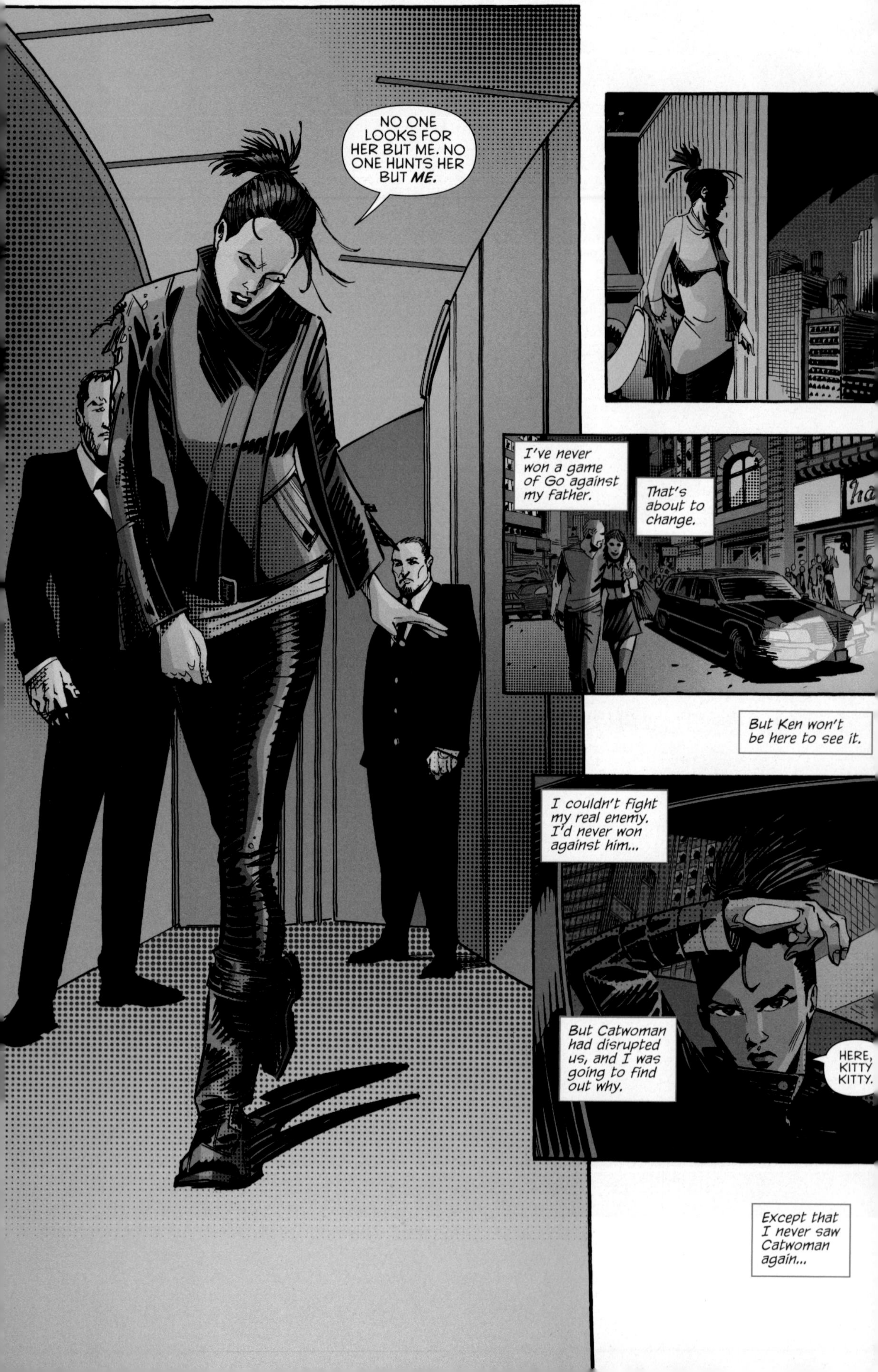
NO ONE LOOKS FOR HER BUT ME. NO ONE HUNTS HER BUT *ME.*
I've never won a game of Go against my father.
That's about to change.
But Ken won't be here to see it.
I couldn't fight my real enemy. I'd never won against him...
But Catwoman had disrupted us, and I was going to find out why.
HERE, KITTY KITTY.
Except that I never saw Catwoman again...

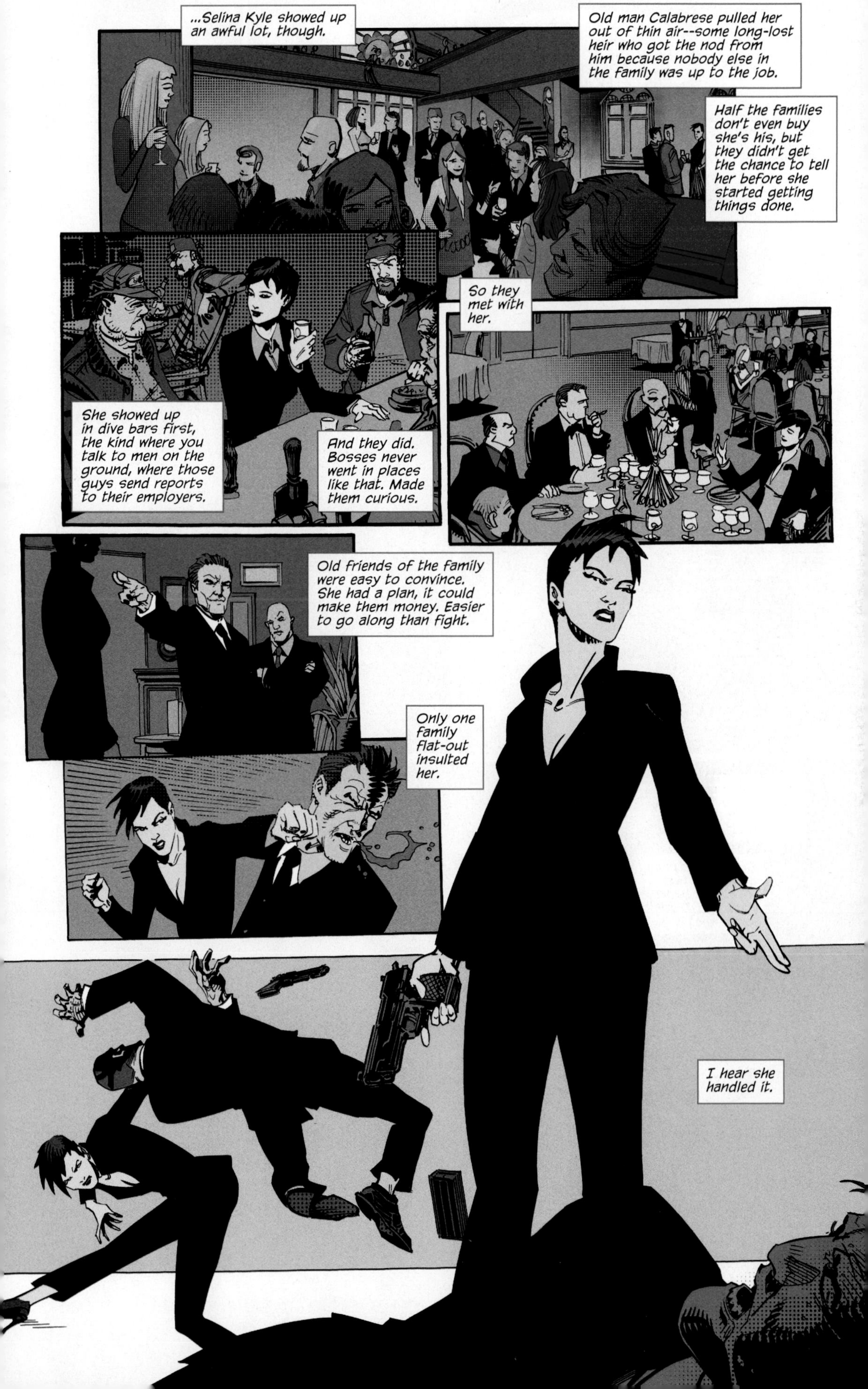
...Selina Kyle showed up an awful lot, though.
Old man Calabrese pulled her out of thin air--some long-lost heir who got the nod from him because nobody else in the family was up to the job.
Half the families don't even buy she's his, but they didn't get the chance to tell her before she started getting things done.
She showed up in dive bars first, the kind where you talk to men on the ground, where those guys send reports to their employers.
And they did. Bosses never went in places like that. Made them curious.
So they met with her.
Old friends of the family were easy to convince. She had a plan, it could make them money. Easier to go along than fight.
Only one family flat-out insulted her.
I hear she handled it.

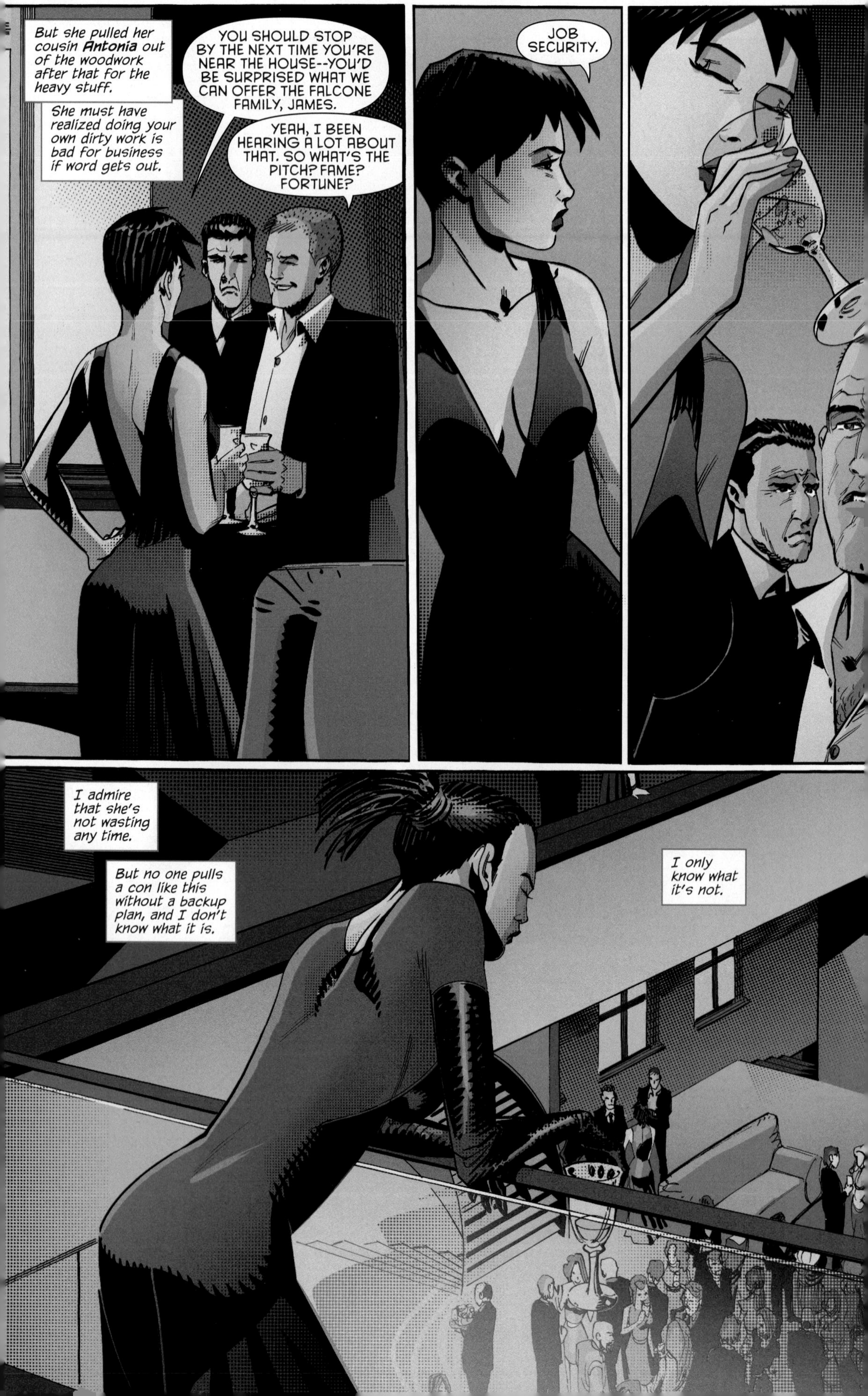
But she pulled her cousin **Antonia** out of the woodwork after that for the heavy stuff.
She must have realized doing your own dirty work is bad for business if word gets out.
YOU SHOULD STOP BY THE NEXT TIME YOU'RE NEAR THE HOUSE--YOU'D BE SURPRISED WHAT WE CAN OFFER THE FALCONE FAMILY, JAMES.
YEAH, I BEEN HEARING A LOT ABOUT THAT. SO WHAT'S THE PITCH? FAME? FORTUNE?
JOB SECURITY.
I admire that she's not wasting any time.
But no one pulls a con like this without a backup plan, and I don't know what it is.
I only know what it's not.

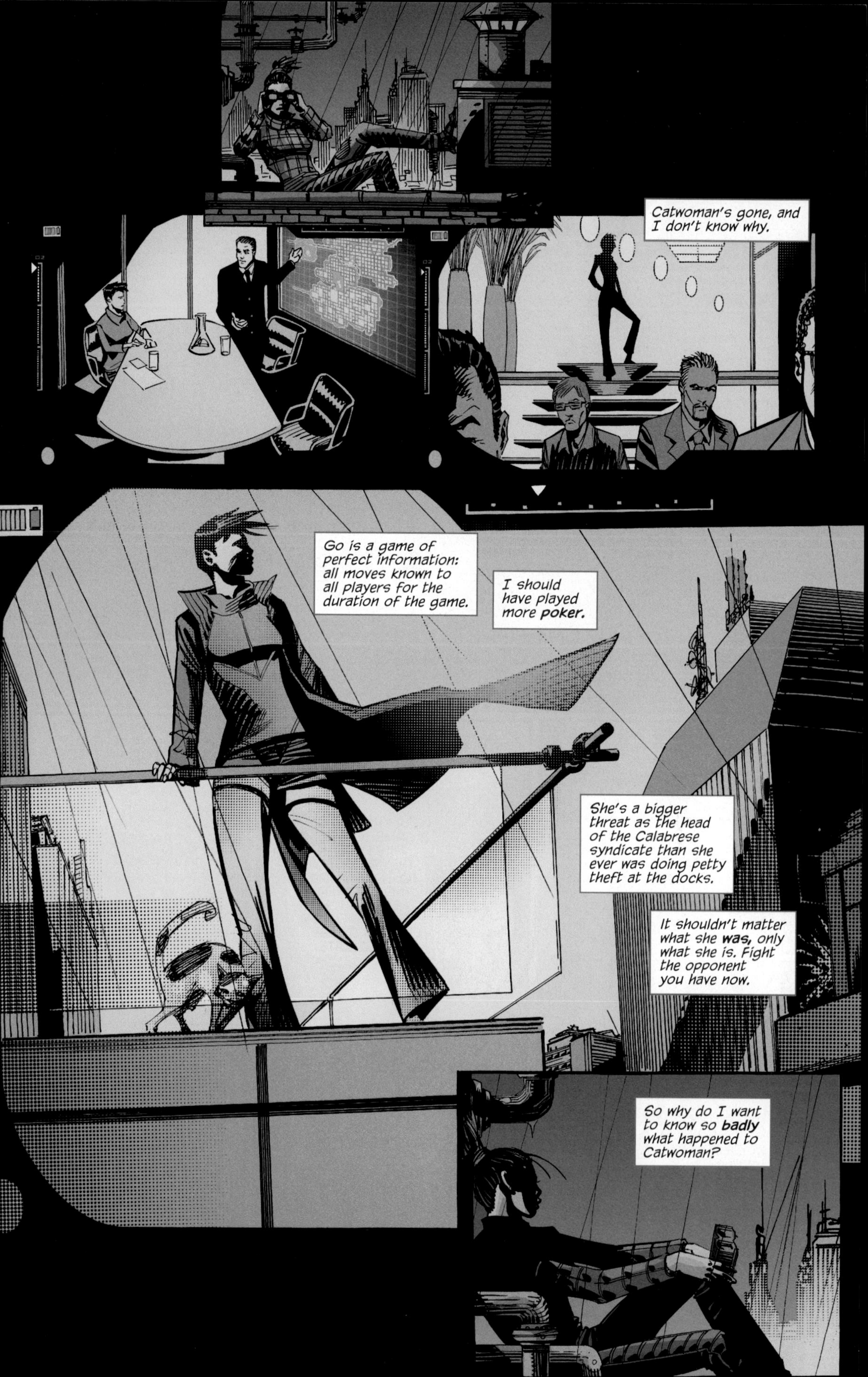

Catwoman's gone, and I don't know why.
Go is a game of perfect information: all moves known to all players for the duration of the game.
I should have played more **poker.**
She's a bigger threat as the head of the Calabrese syndicate than she ever was doing petty theft at the docks.
It shouldn't matter what she **was,** only what she is. Fight the opponent you have now.
So why do I want to know so **badly** what happened to Catwoman?

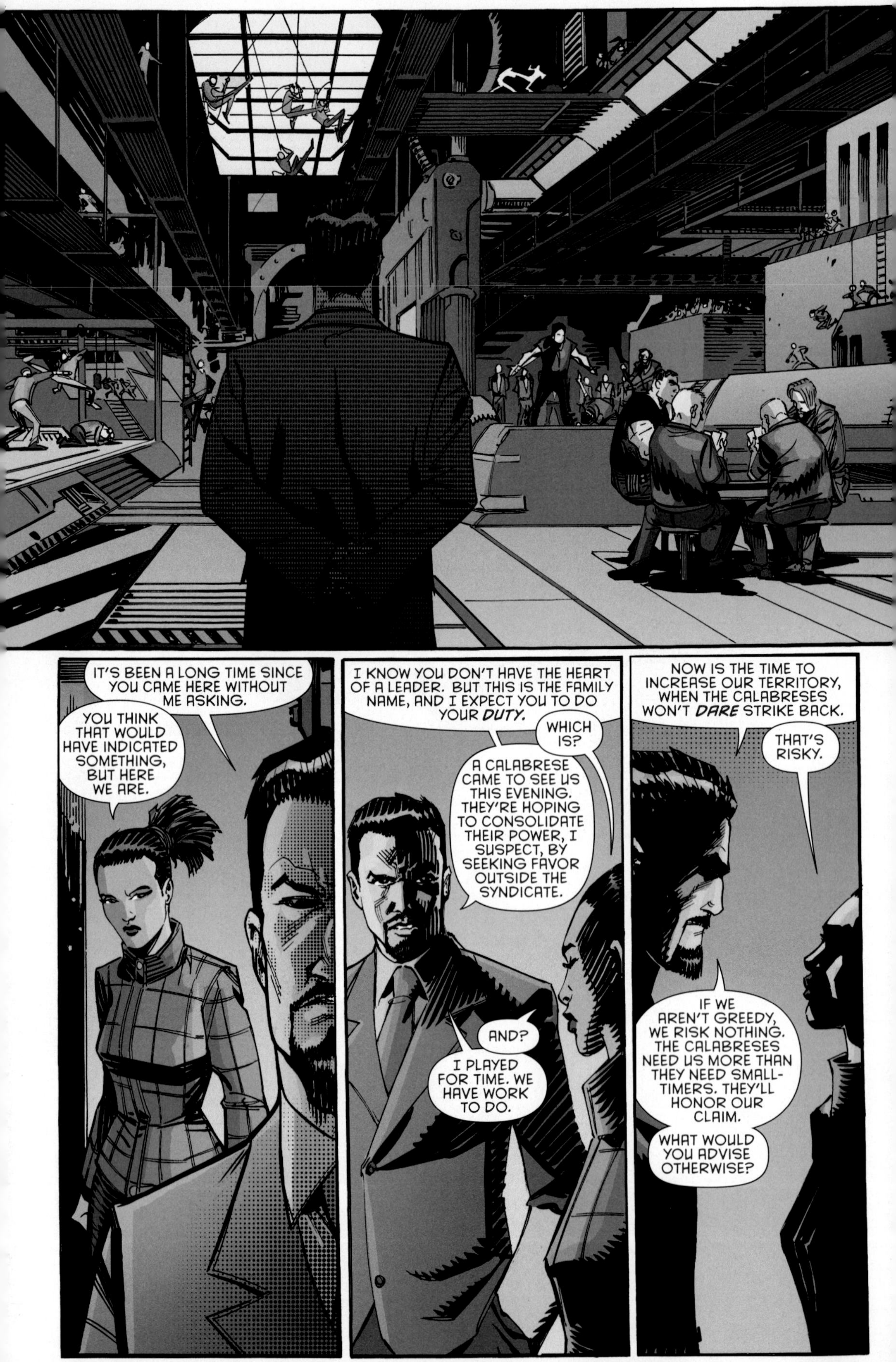
IT'S BEEN A LONG TIME SINCE YOU CAME HERE WITHOUT ME ASKING.
YOU THINK THAT WOULD HAVE INDICATED SOMETHING, BUT HERE WE ARE.
I KNOW YOU DON'T HAVE THE HEART OF A LEADER. BUT THIS IS THE FAMILY NAME, AND I EXPECT YOU TO DO YOUR DUTY.
WHICH IS?
A CALABRESE CAME TO SEE US THIS EVENING. THEY'RE HOPING TO CONSOLIDATE THEIR POWER, I SUSPECT, BY SEEKING FAVOR OUTSIDE THE SYNDICATE.
AND?
I PLAYED FOR TIME. WE HAVE WORK TO DO.
NOW IS THE TIME TO INCREASE OUR TERRITORY, WHEN THE CALABRESES WON'T DARE STRIKE BACK.
THAT'S RISKY.
IF WE AREN'T GREEDY, WE RISK NOTHING. THE CALABRESES NEED US MORE THAN THEY NEED SMALL-TIMERS. THEY'LL HONOR OUR CLAIM.
WHAT WOULD YOU ADVISE OTHERWISE?

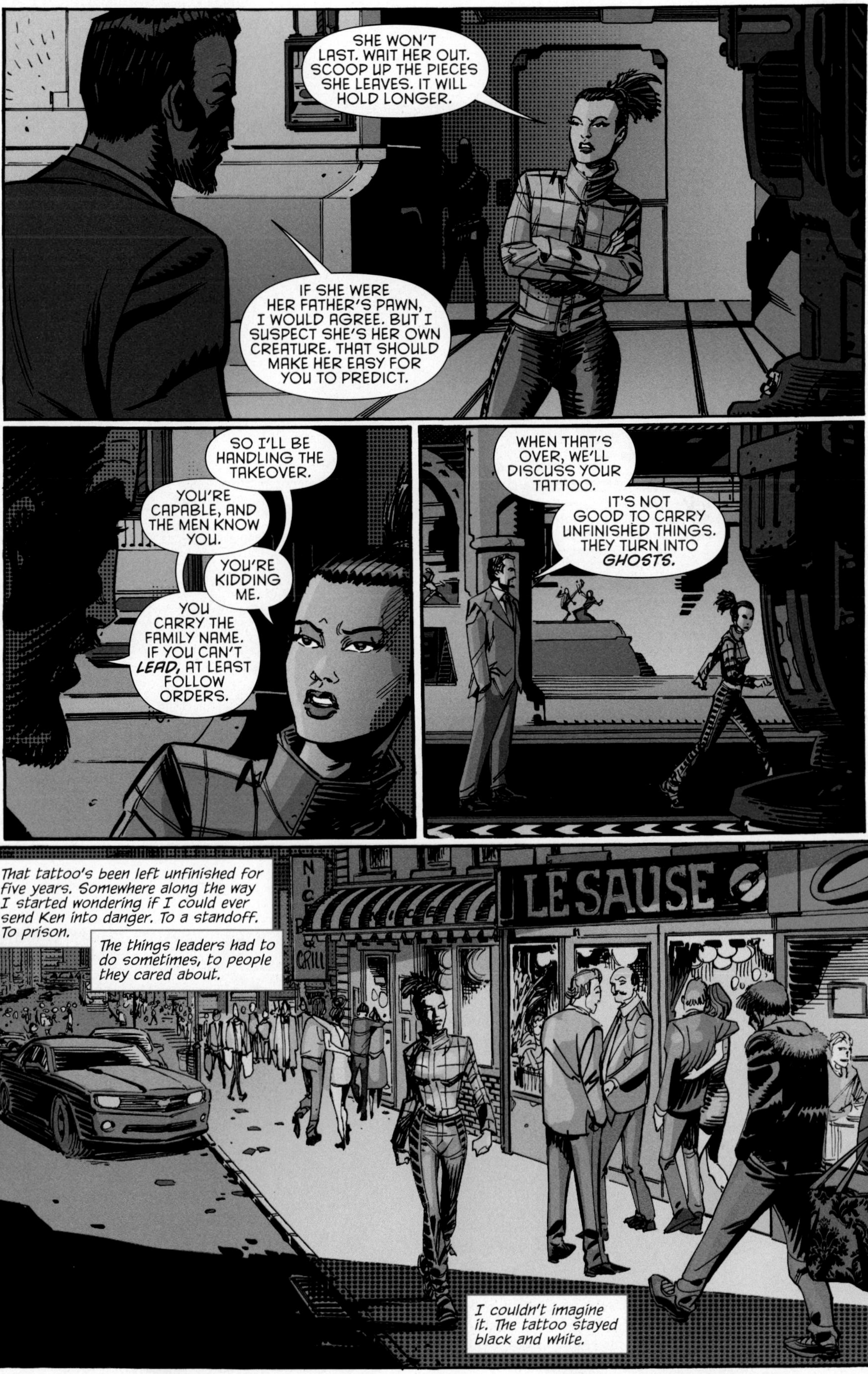
SHE WON'T LAST. WAIT HER OUT. SCOOP UP THE PIECES SHE LEAVES. IT WILL HOLD LONGER.
IF SHE WERE HER FATHER'S PAWN, I WOULD AGREE. BUT I SUSPECT SHE'S HER OWN CREATURE. THAT SHOULD MAKE HER EASY FOR YOU TO PREDICT.
SO I'LL BE HANDLING THE TAKEOVER.
YOU'RE CAPABLE, AND THE MEN KNOW YOU.
YOU'RE KIDDING ME.
YOU CARRY THE FAMILY NAME. IF YOU CAN'T LEAD, AT LEAST FOLLOW ORDERS.
WHEN THAT'S OVER, WE'LL DISCUSS YOUR TATTOO.
IT'S NOT GOOD TO CARRY UNFINISHED THINGS. THEY TURN INTO GHOSTS.
That tattoo's been left unfinished for five years. Somewhere along the way I started wondering if I could ever send Ken into danger. To a standoff. To prison.
The things leaders had to do sometimes, to people they cared about.
LE SAUSE
I couldn't imagine it. The tattoo stayed black and white.

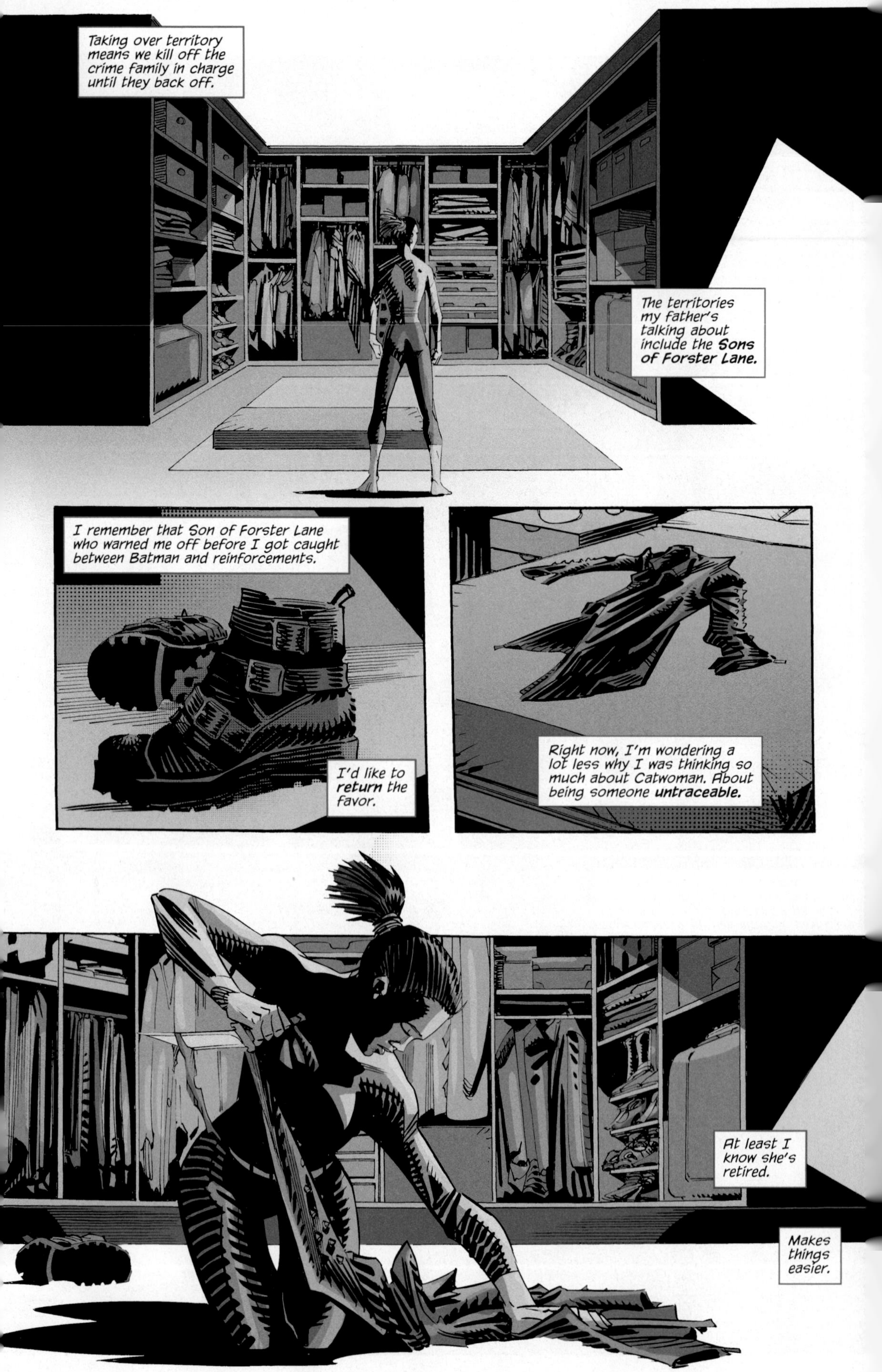
Taking over territory means we kill off the crime family in charge until they back off.
The territories my father's talking about include the Sons of Forster Lane.
I remember that Son of Forster Lane who warned me off before I got caught between Batman and reinforcements.
I'd like to return the favor.
Right now, I'm wondering a lot less why I was thinking so much about Catwoman. About being someone untraceable.
At least I know she's retired.
Makes things easier.

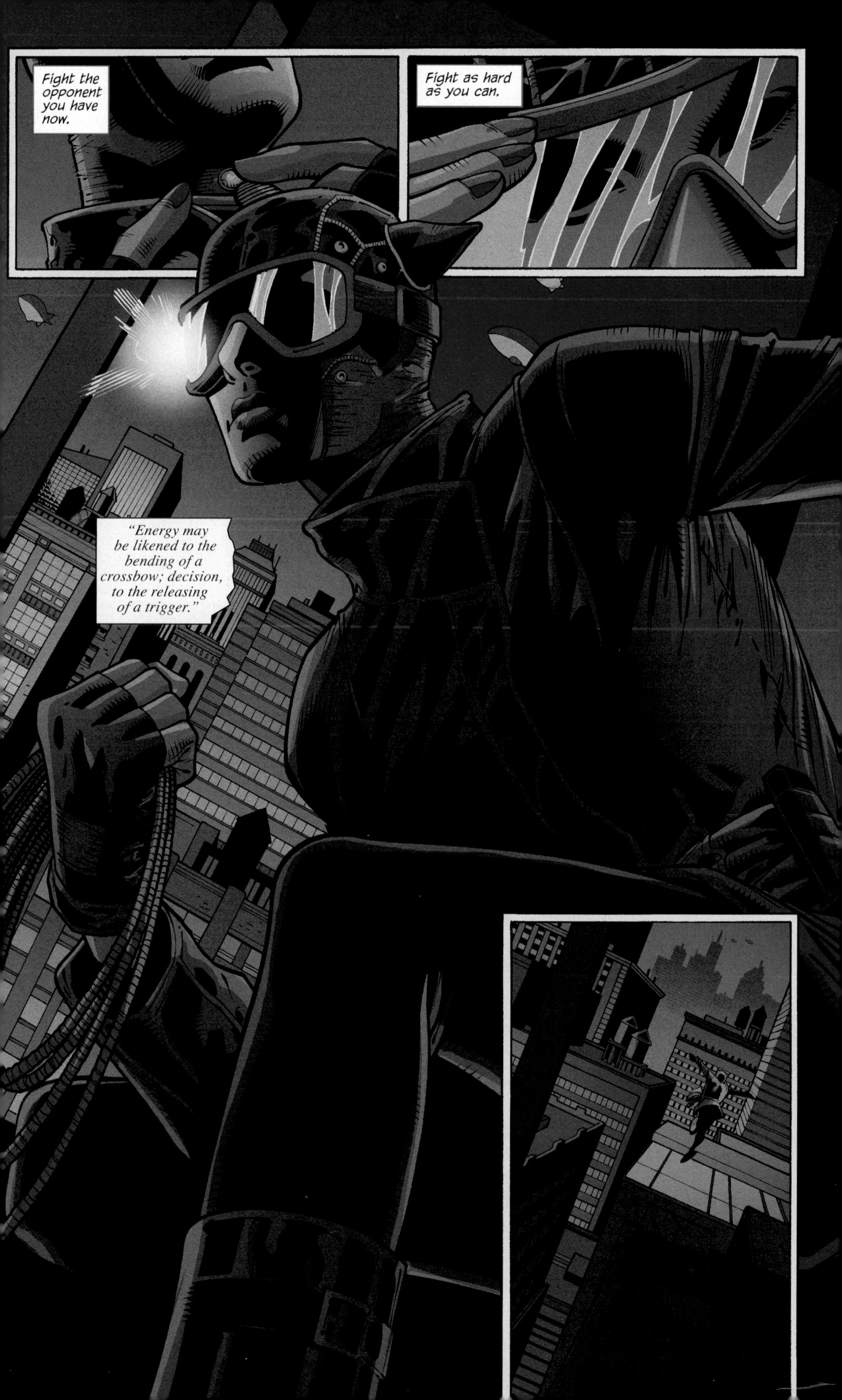
Fight the opponent you have now.
Fight as hard as you can.
"Energy may be likened to the bending of a crossbow; decision, to the releasing of a trigger."

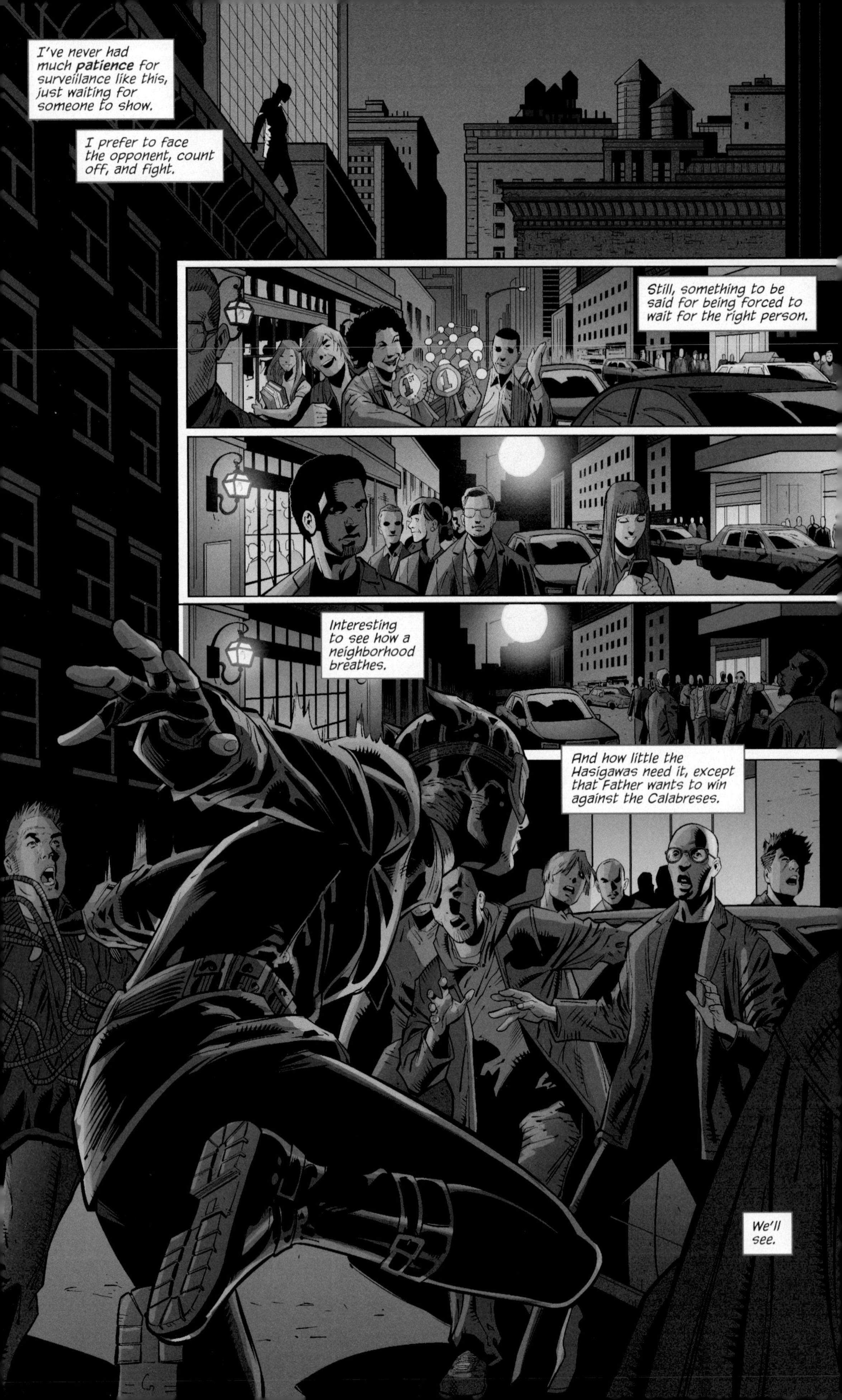
I've never had much patience for surveillance like this, just waiting for someone to show.
I prefer to face the opponent, count off, and fight.
Still, something to be said for being forced to wait for the right person.
Interesting to see how a neighborhood breathes.
And how little the Hasigawas need it, except that Father wants to win against the Calabreses.
We'll see.

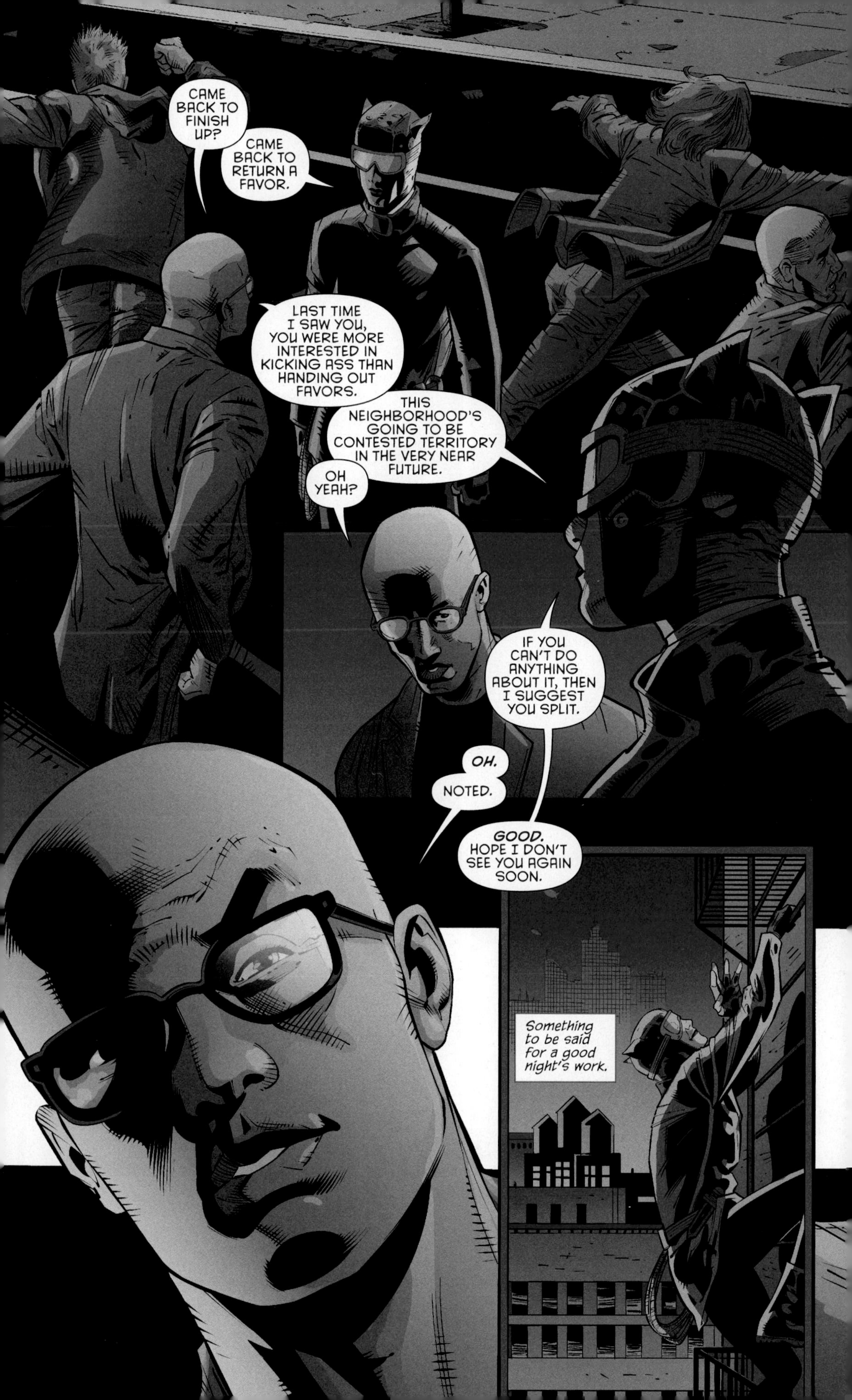
CAME BACK TO FINISH UP?
CAME BACK TO RETURN A FAVOR.
LAST TIME I SAW YOU, YOU WERE MORE INTERESTED IN KICKING ASS THAN HANDING OUT FAVORS.
THIS NEIGHBORHOOD'S GOING TO BE CONTESTED TERRITORY IN THE VERY NEAR FUTURE.
OH YEAH?
IF YOU CAN'T DO ANYTHING ABOUT IT, THEN I SUGGEST YOU SPLIT.
OH.
NOTED.
GOOD. HOPE I DON'T SEE YOU AGAIN SOON.
Something to be said for a good night's work.

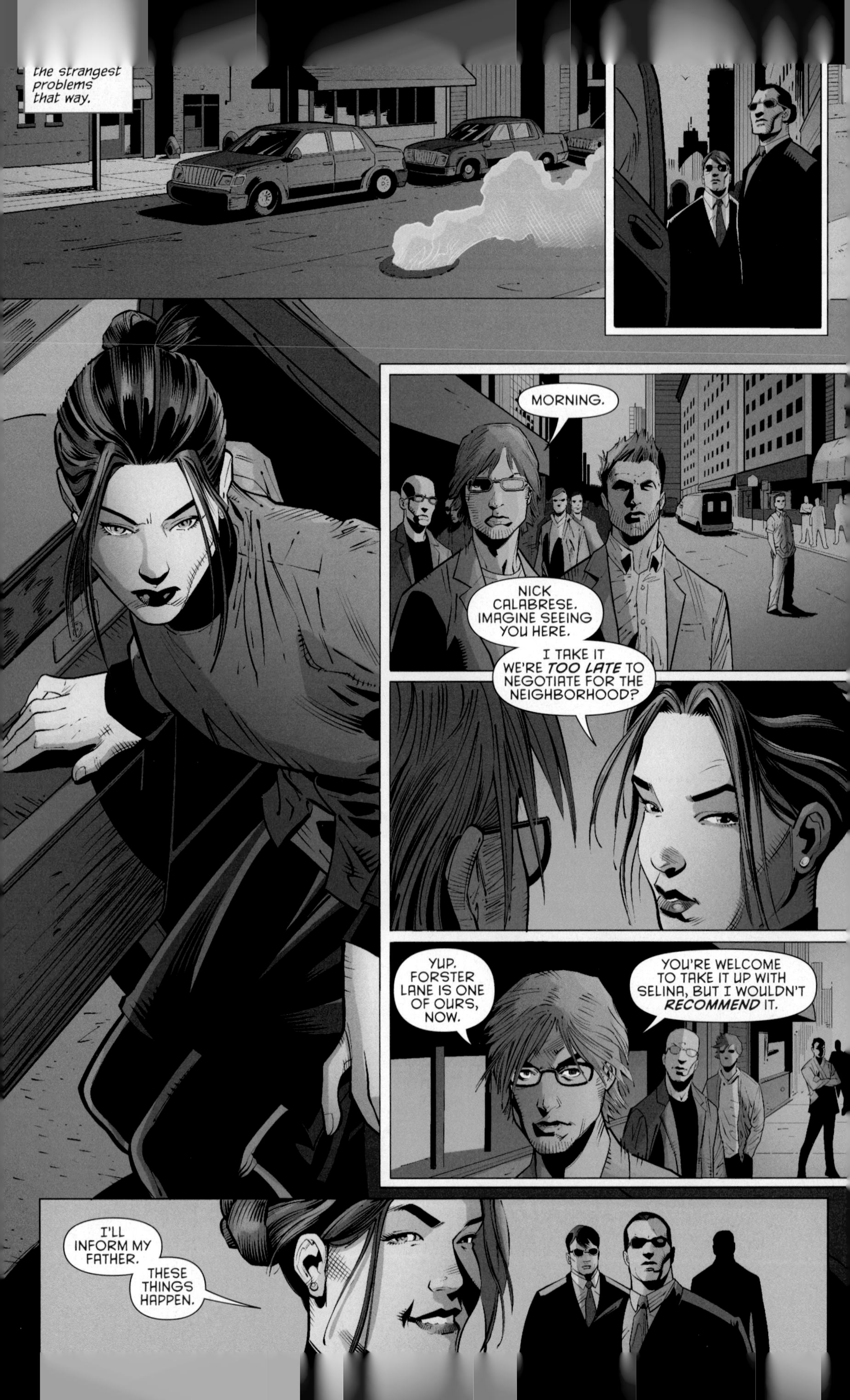
the strangest problems that way.
MORNING.
NICK CALABRESE. IMAGINE SEEING YOU HERE.
I TAKE IT WE'RE *TOO LATE* TO NEGOTIATE FOR THE NEIGHBORHOOD?
YUP. FORSTER LANE IS ONE OF OURS, NOW.
YOU'RE WELCOME TO TAKE IT UP WITH SELINA, BUT I WOULDN'T *RECOMMEND* IT.
I'LL INFORM MY FATHER.
THESE THINGS HAPPEN.

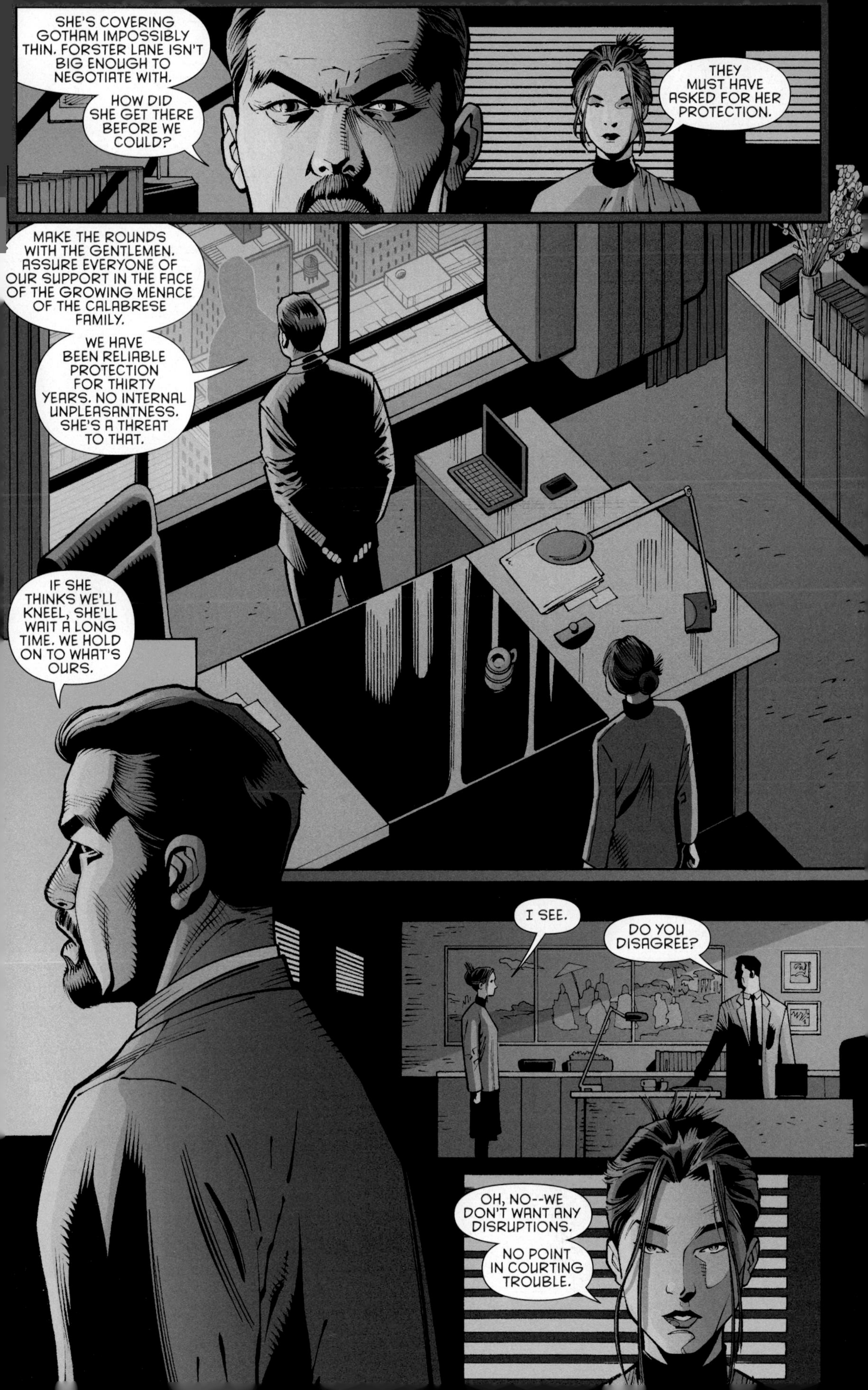
SHE'S COVERING GOTHAM IMPOSSIBLY THIN. FORSTER LANE ISN'T BIG ENOUGH TO NEGOTIATE WITH.
HOW DID SHE GET THERE BEFORE WE COULD?
THEY MUST HAVE ASKED FOR HER PROTECTION.
MAKE THE ROUNDS WITH THE GENTLEMEN. ASSURE EVERYONE OF OUR SUPPORT IN THE FACE OF THE GROWING MENACE OF THE CALABRESE FAMILY.
WE HAVE BEEN RELIABLE PROTECTION FOR THIRTY YEARS. NO INTERNAL UNPLEASANTNESS. SHE'S A THREAT TO THAT.
IF SHE THINKS WE'LL KNEEL, SHE'LL WAIT A LONG TIME. WE HOLD ON TO WHAT'S OURS.
I SEE.
DO YOU DISAGREE?
OH, NO--WE DON'T WANT ANY DISRUPTIONS.
NO POINT IN COURTING TROUBLE.

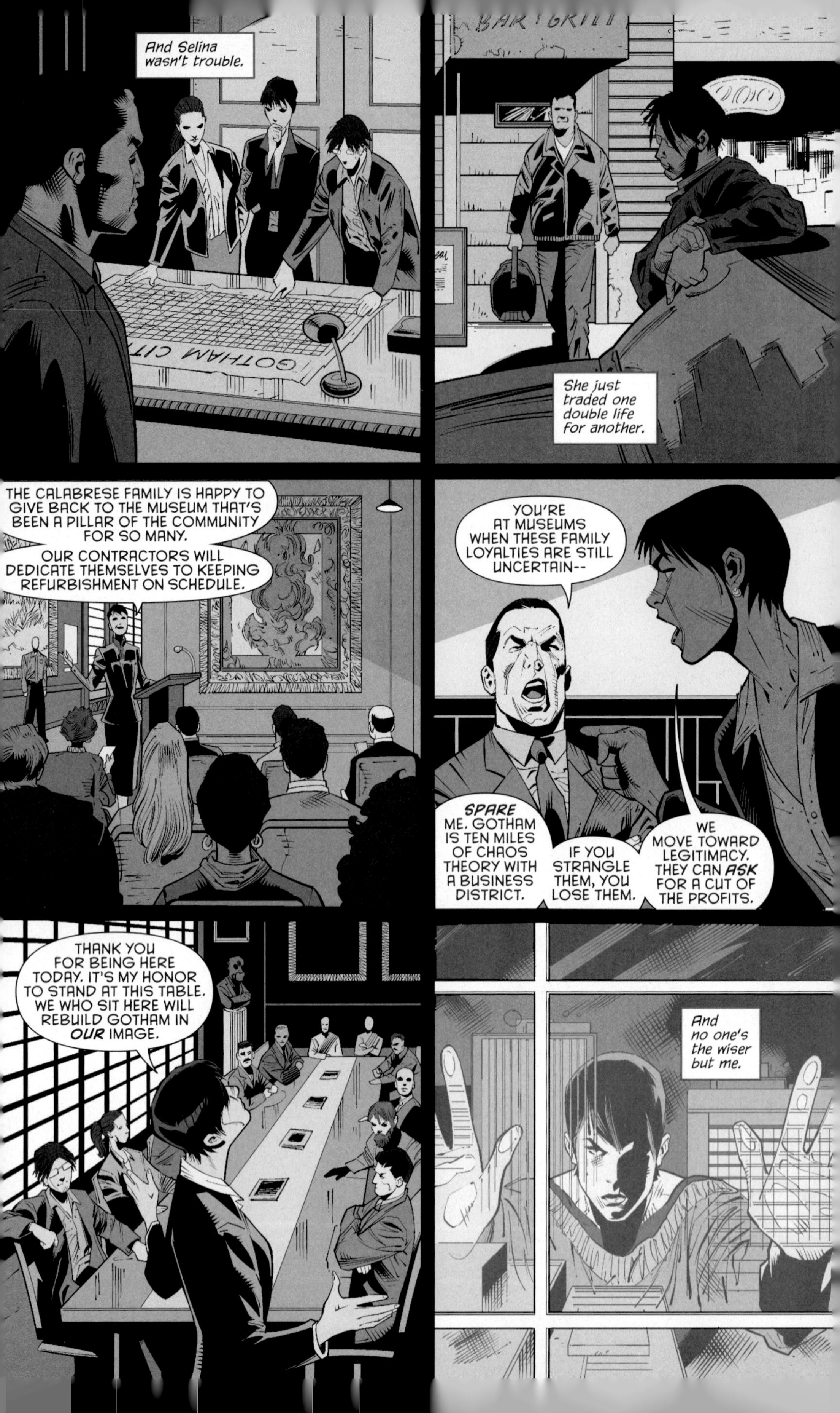
And Selina wasn't trouble.
BAR · GRILL
She just traded one double life for another.
THE CALABRESE FAMILY IS HAPPY TO GIVE BACK TO THE MUSEUM THAT'S BEEN A PILLAR OF THE COMMUNITY FOR SO MANY.
OUR CONTRACTORS WILL DEDICATE THEMSELVES TO KEEPING REFURBISHMENT ON SCHEDULE.
YOU'RE AT MUSEUMS WHEN THESE FAMILY LOYALTIES ARE STILL UNCERTAIN--
SPARE ME. GOTHAM IS TEN MILES OF CHAOS THEORY WITH A BUSINESS DISTRICT.
IF YOU STRANGLE THEM, YOU LOSE THEM.
WE MOVE TOWARD LEGITIMACY. THEY CAN ASK FOR A CUT OF THE PROFITS.
THANK YOU FOR BEING HERE TODAY. IT'S MY HONOR TO STAND AT THIS TABLE. WE WHO SIT HERE WILL REBUILD GOTHAM IN OUR IMAGE.
And no one's the wiser but me.

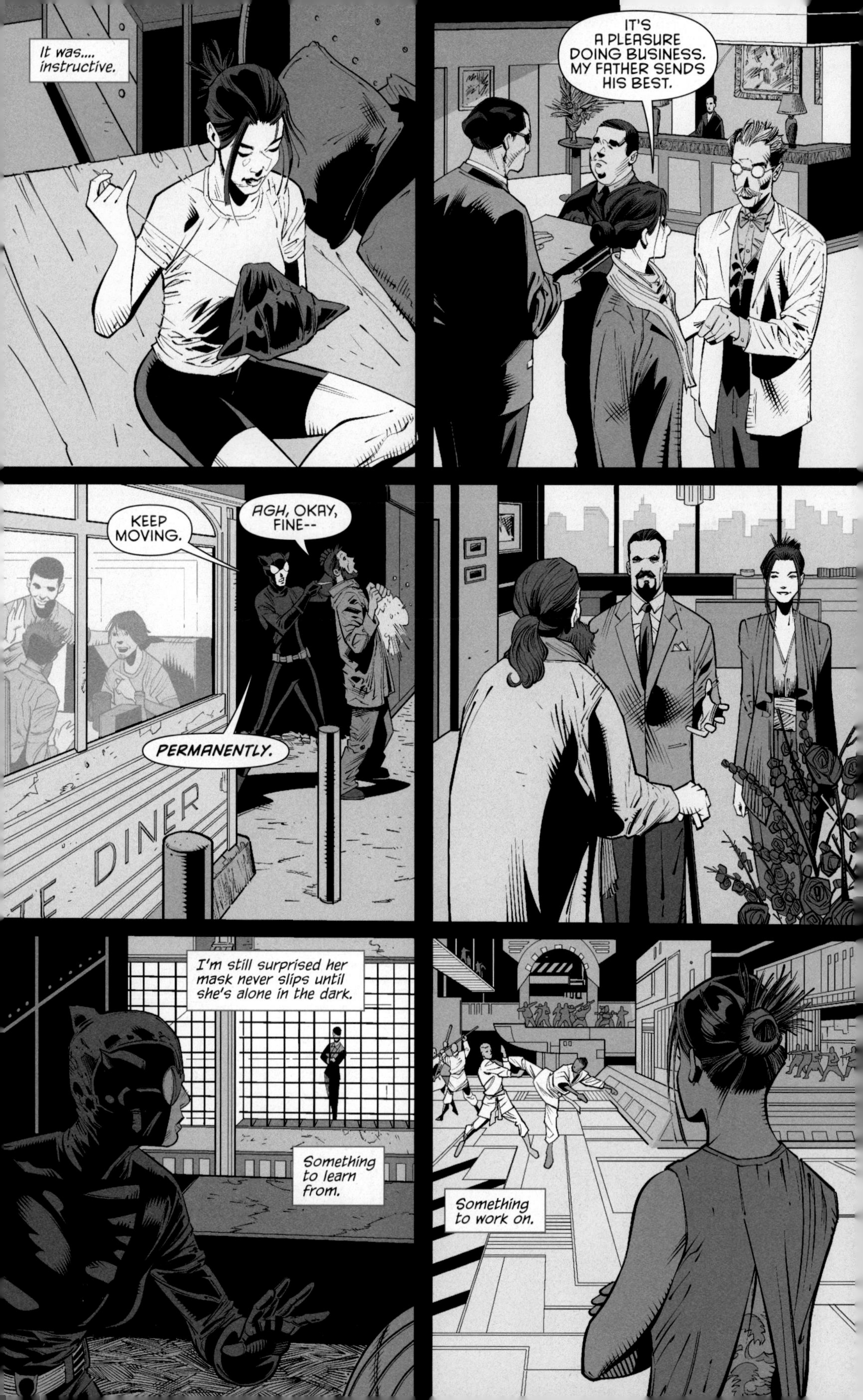
It was.... instructive.
IT'S A PLEASURE DOING BUSINESS. MY FATHER SENDS HIS BEST.
KEEP MOVING.
AGH, OKAY, FINE--
PERMANENTLY.
DINER
I'm still surprised her mask never slips until she's alone in the dark.
Something to learn from.
Something to work on.

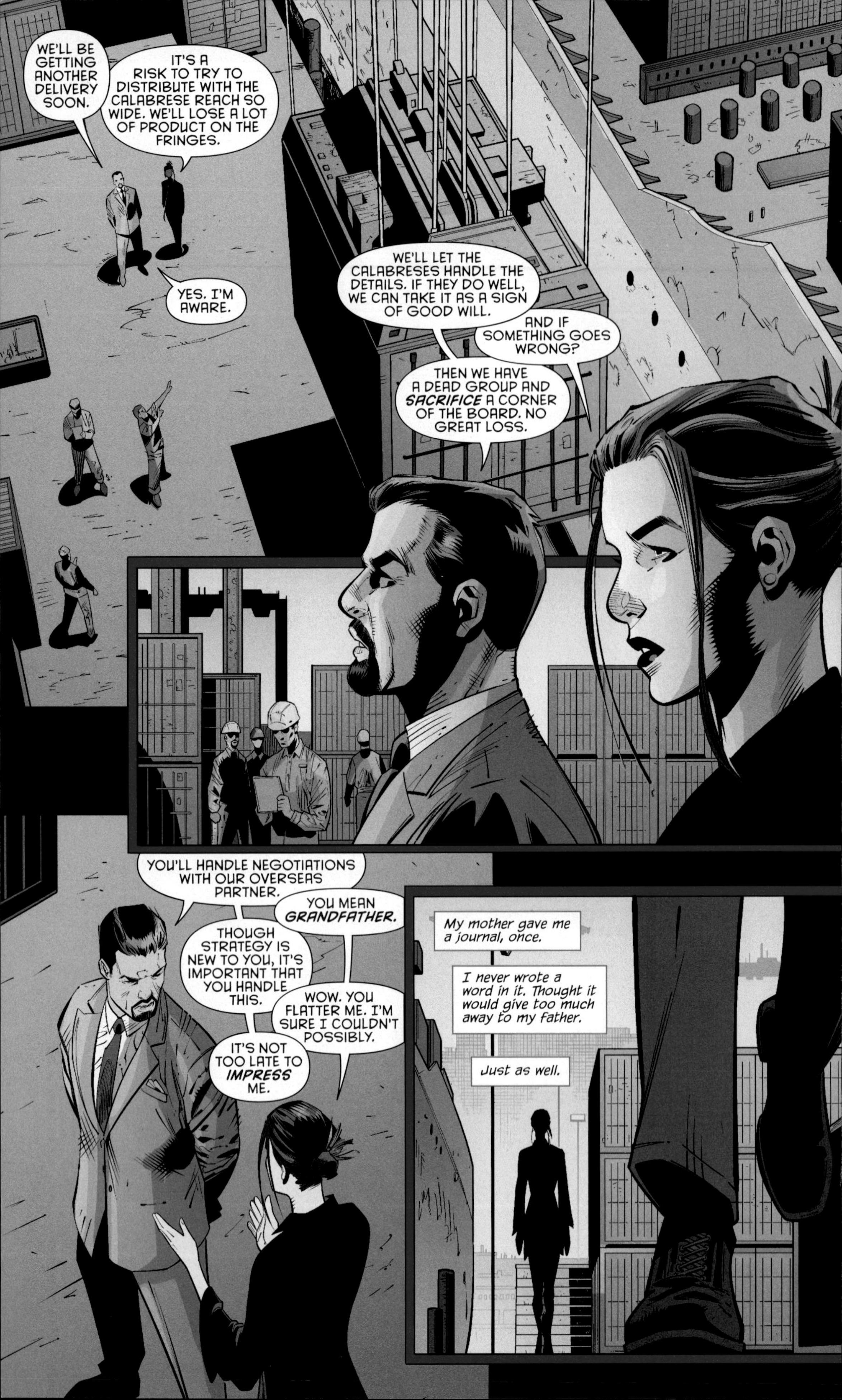
WE'LL BE GETTING ANOTHER DELIVERY SOON.
IT'S A RISK TO TRY TO DISTRIBUTE WITH THE CALABRESE REACH SO WIDE. WE'LL LOSE A LOT OF PRODUCT ON THE FRINGES.
YES. I'M AWARE.
WE'LL LET THE CALABRESES HANDLE THE DETAILS. IF THEY DO WELL, WE CAN TAKE IT AS A SIGN OF GOOD WILL.
AND IF SOMETHING GOES WRONG?
THEN WE HAVE A DEAD GROUP AND SACRIFICE A CORNER OF THE BOARD. NO GREAT LOSS.
YOU'LL HANDLE NEGOTIATIONS WITH OUR OVERSEAS PARTNER.
YOU MEAN GRANDFATHER.
THOUGH STRATEGY IS NEW TO YOU, IT'S IMPORTANT THAT YOU HANDLE THIS.
WOW. YOU FLATTER ME. I'M SURE I COULDN'T POSSIBLY.
IT'S NOT TOO LATE TO IMPRESS ME.
My mother gave me a journal, once.
I never wrote a word in it. Thought it would give too much away to my father.
Just as well.

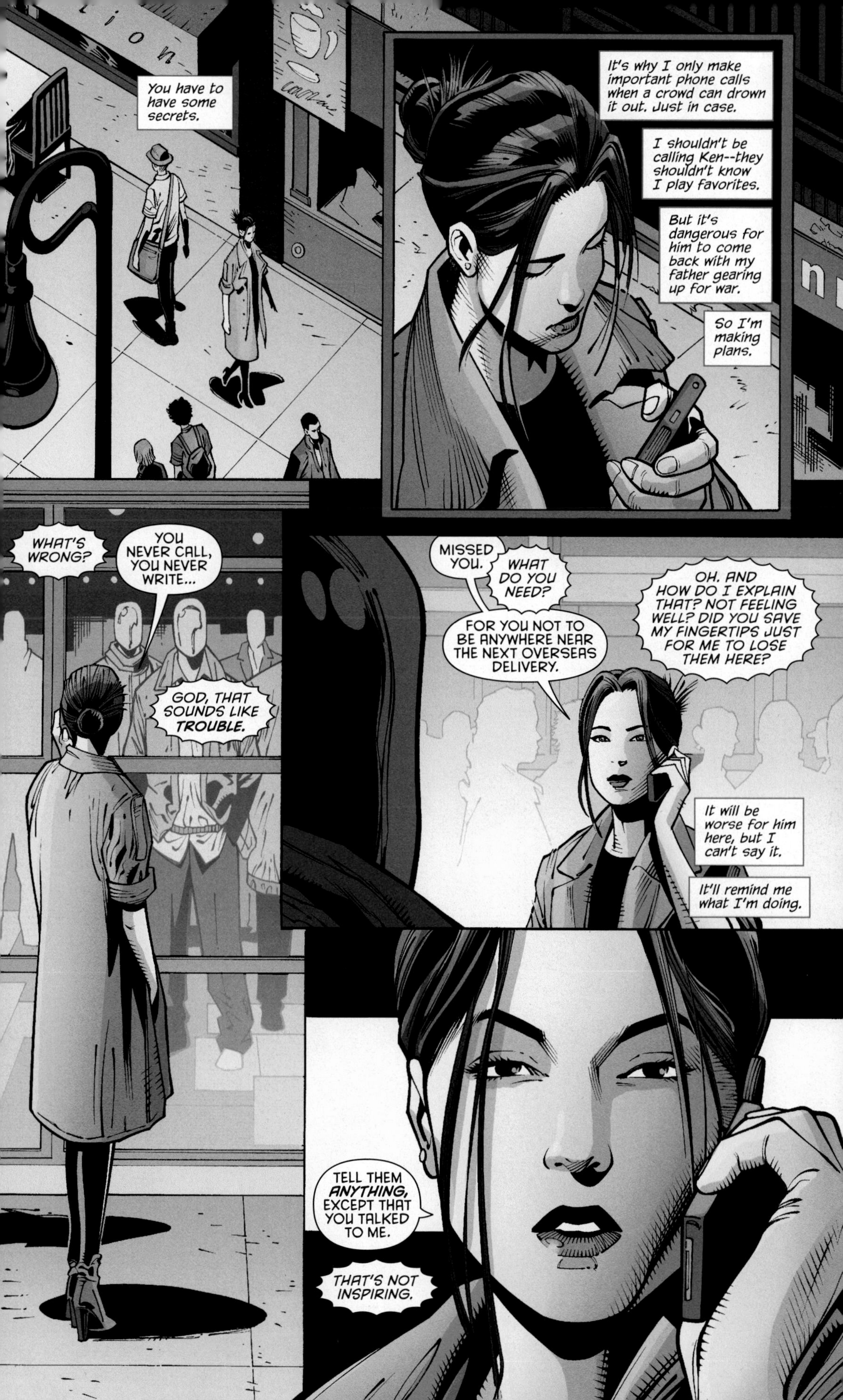
You have to have some secrets.
It's why I only make important phone calls when a crowd can drown it out. Just in case.
I shouldn't be calling Ken--they shouldn't know I play favorites.
But it's dangerous for him to come back with my father gearing up for war.
So I'm making plans.
WHAT'S WRONG?
YOU NEVER CALL, YOU NEVER WRITE...
GOD, THAT SOUNDS LIKE TROUBLE.
MISSED YOU.
WHAT DO YOU NEED?
FOR YOU NOT TO BE ANYWHERE NEAR THE NEXT OVERSEAS DELIVERY.
OH. AND HOW DO I EXPLAIN THAT? NOT FEELING WELL? DID YOU SAVE MY FINGERTIPS JUST FOR ME TO LOSE THEM HERE?
It will be worse for him here, but I can't say it.
It'll remind me what I'm doing.
TELL THEM ANYTHING, EXCEPT THAT YOU TALKED TO ME.
THAT'S NOT INSPIRING.

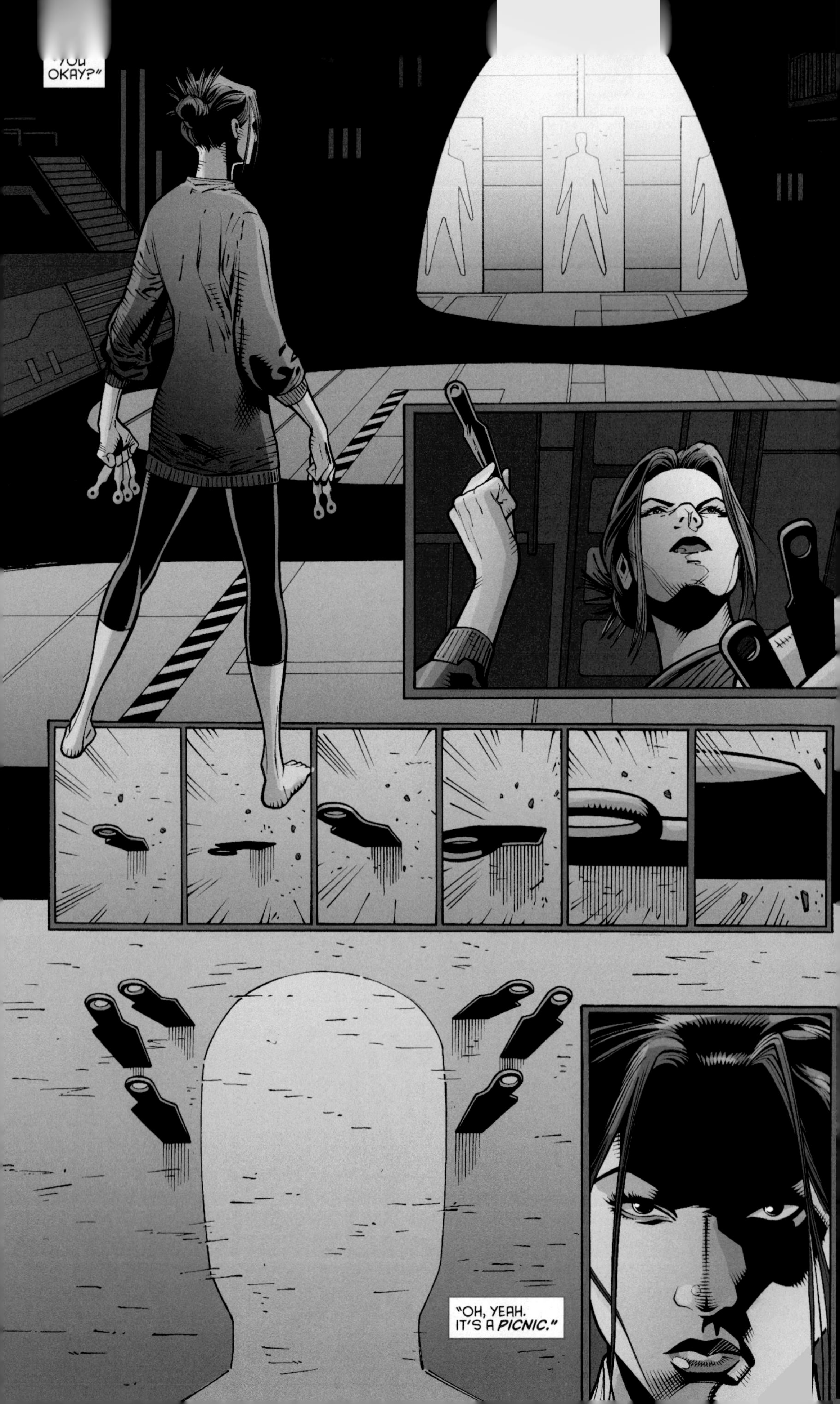
"YOU OKAY?"
"OH, YEAH. IT'S A PICNIC."

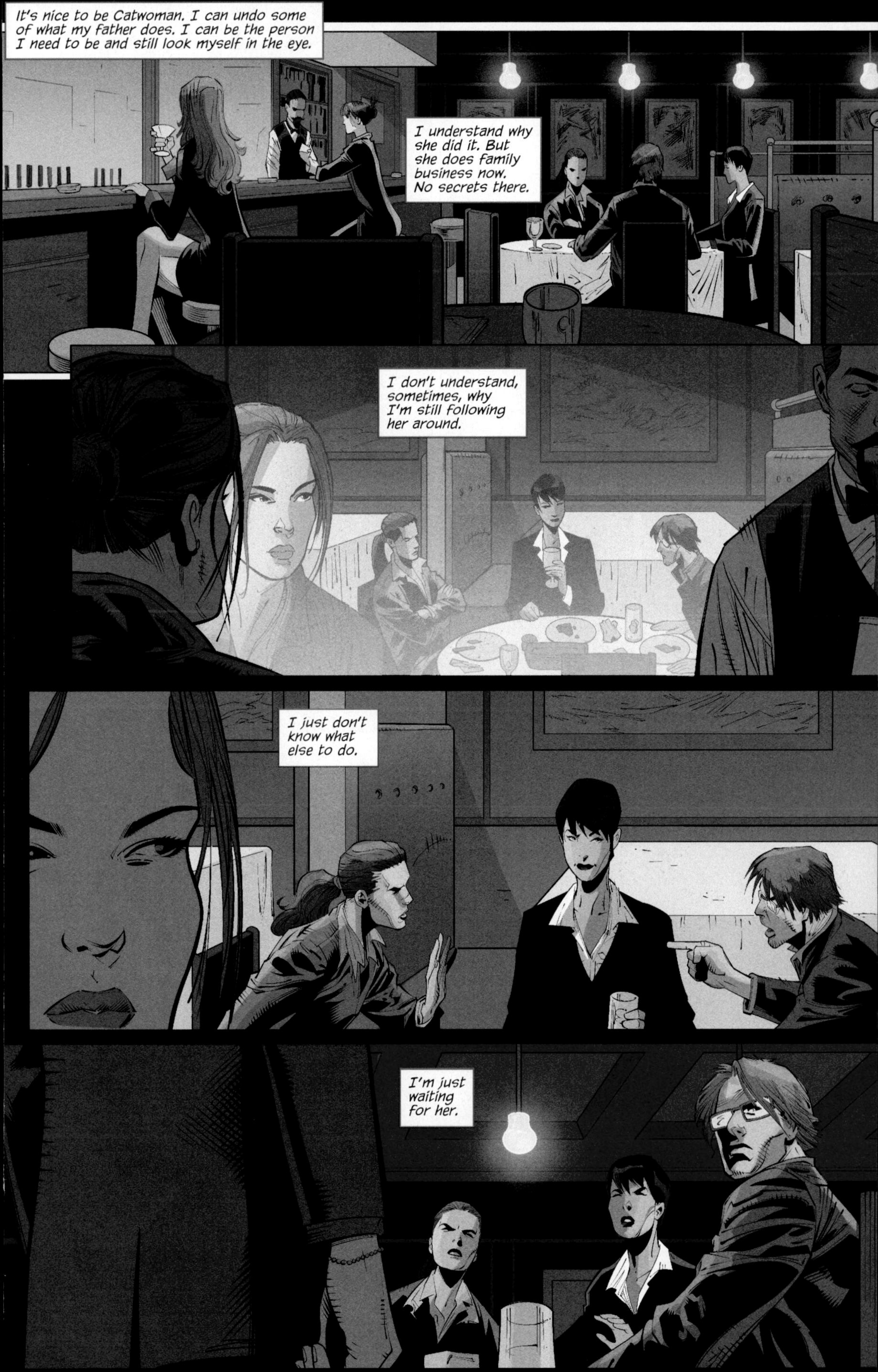
It's nice to be Catwoman. I can undo some of what my father does. I can be the person I need to be and still look myself in the eye.
I understand why she did it. But she does family business now. No secrets there.
I don't understand, sometimes, why I'm still following her around.
I just don't know what else to do.
I'm just waiting for her.

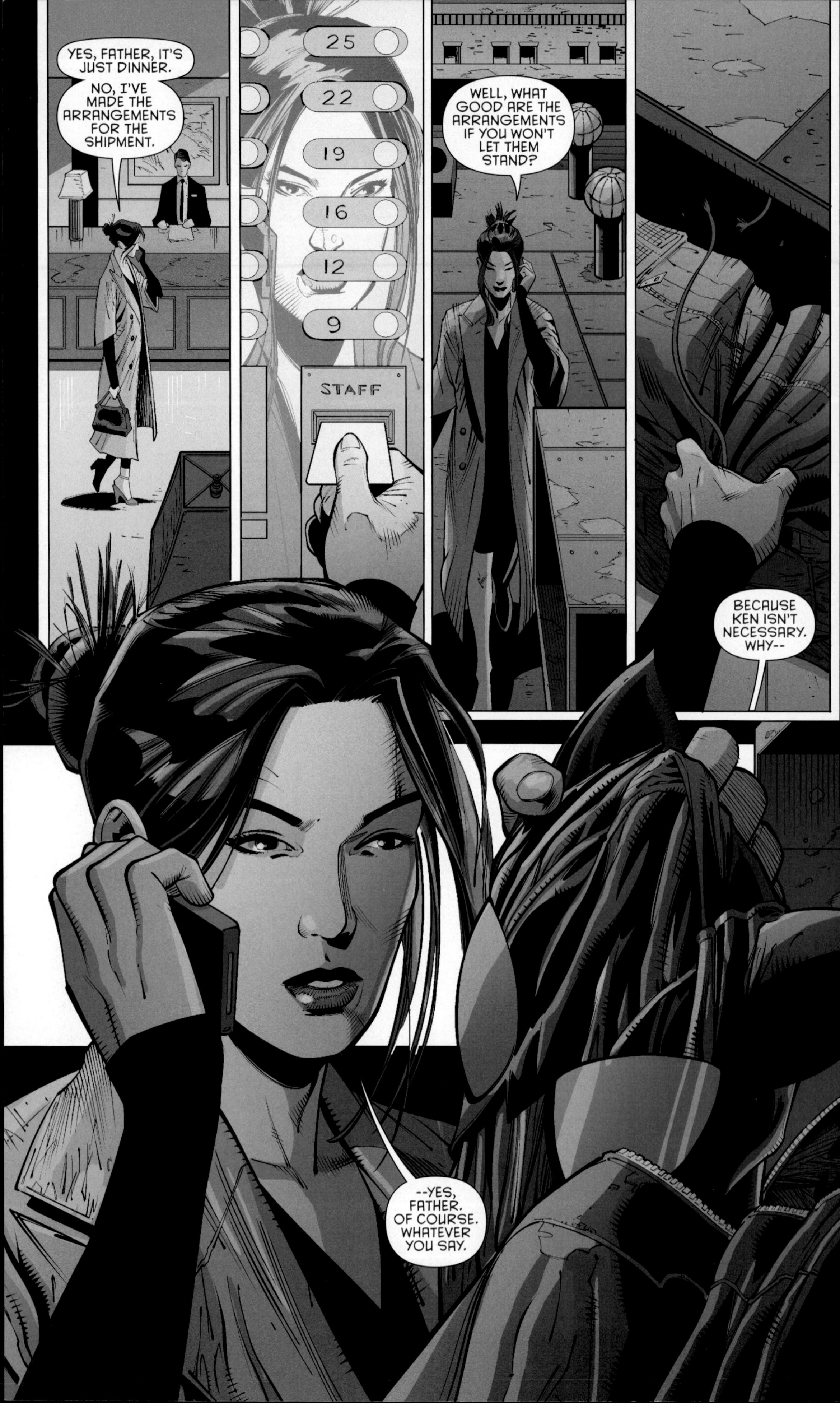
YES, FATHER, IT'S JUST DINNER.
NO, I'VE MADE THE ARRANGEMENTS FOR THE SHIPMENT.
25
22
19
16
12
9
STAFF
WELL, WHAT GOOD ARE THE ARRANGEMENTS IF YOU WON'T LET THEM STAND?
BECAUSE KEN ISN'T NECESSARY. WHY--
--YES, FATHER. OF COURSE. WHATEVER YOU SAY.

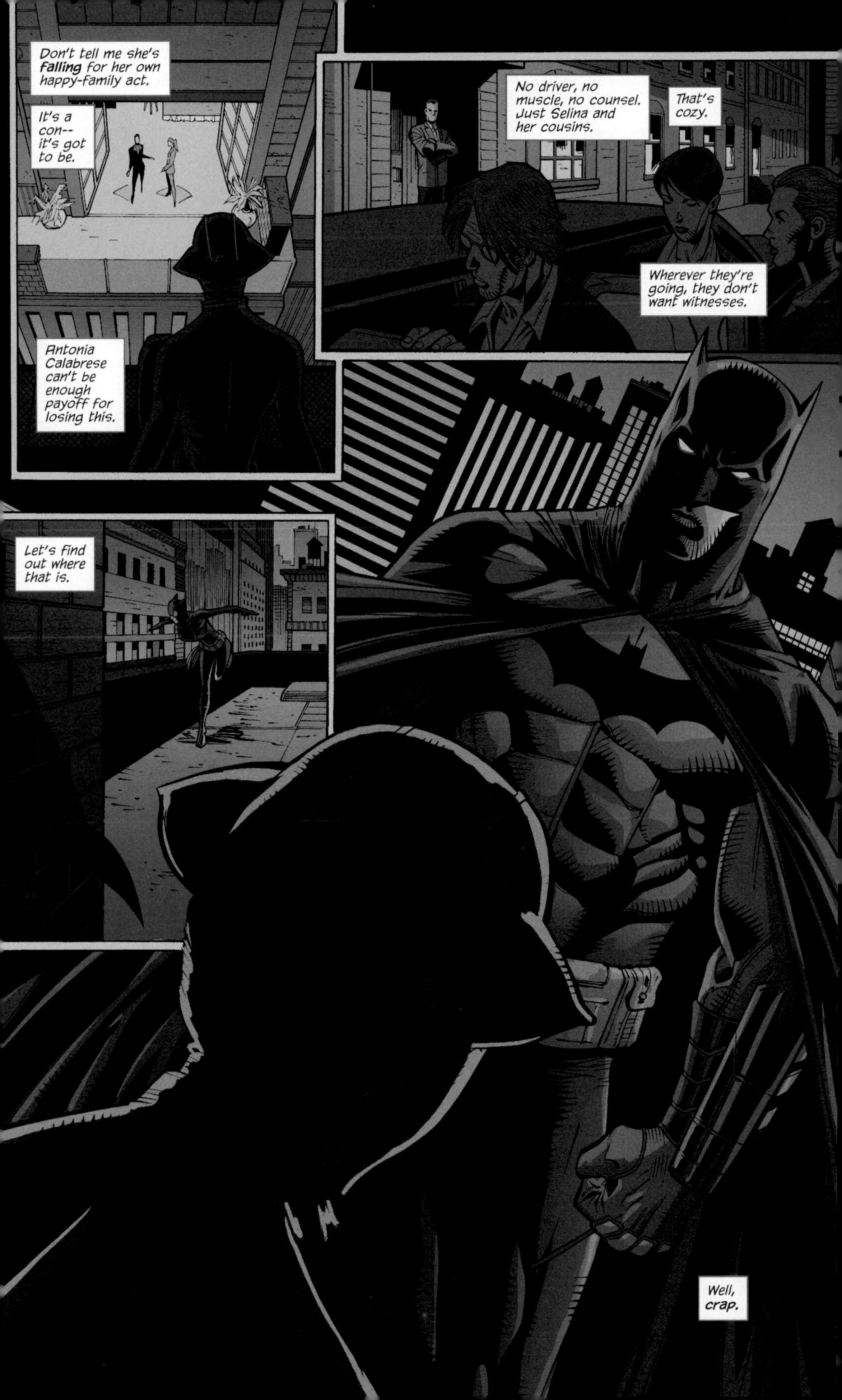
Don't tell me she's **falling** for her own happy-family act.
It's a con--it's got to be.
Antonia Calabrese can't be enough payoff for losing this.
No driver, no muscle, no counsel. Just Selina and her cousins.
That's cozy.
Wherever they're going, they don't want witnesses.
Let's find out where that is.
Well, crap.

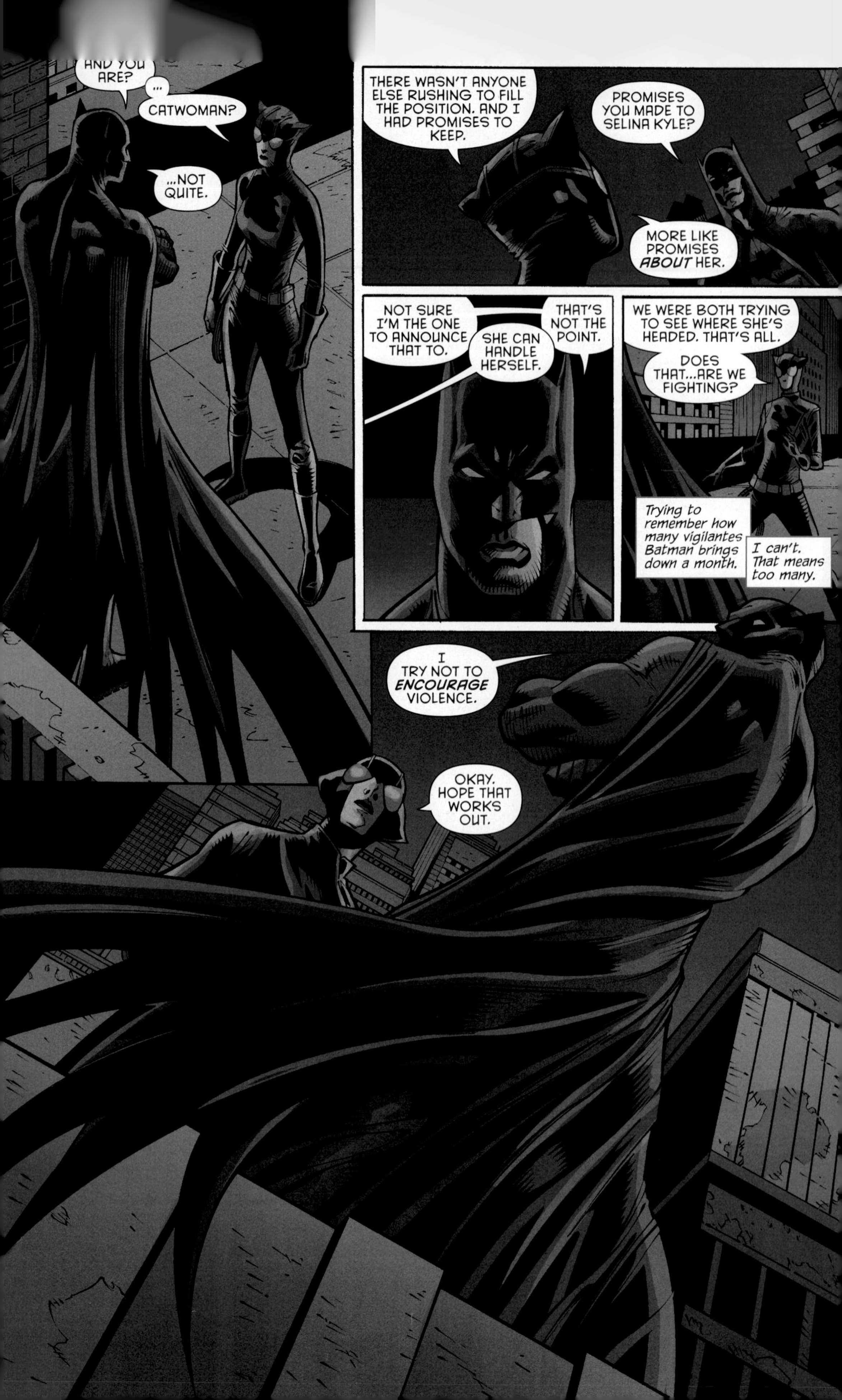
AND YOU ARE?
...
CATWOMAN?
...NOT QUITE.
THERE WASN'T ANYONE ELSE RUSHING TO FILL THE POSITION. AND I HAD PROMISES TO KEEP.
PROMISES YOU MADE TO SELINA KYLE?
MORE LIKE PROMISES ABOUT HER.
NOT SURE I'M THE ONE TO ANNOUNCE THAT TO.
SHE CAN HANDLE HERSELF.
THAT'S NOT THE POINT.
WE WERE BOTH TRYING TO SEE WHERE SHE'S HEADED. THAT'S ALL.
DOES THAT...ARE WE FIGHTING?
Trying to remember how many vigilantes Batman brings down a month.
I can't. That means too many.
I TRY NOT TO ENCOURAGE VIOLENCE.
OKAY. HOPE THAT WORKS OUT.

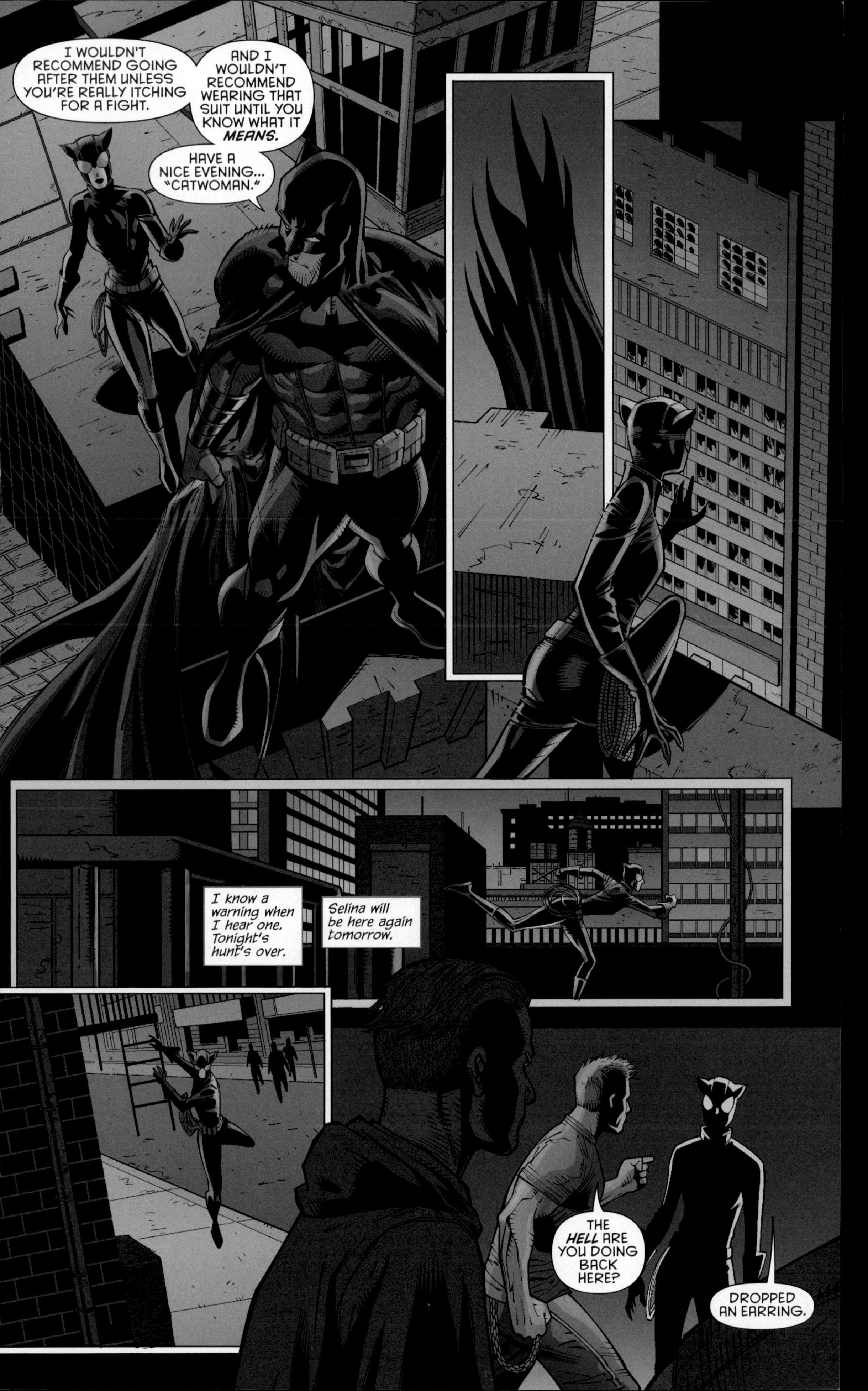

I WOULDN'T RECOMMEND GOING AFTER THEM UNLESS YOU'RE REALLY ITCHING FOR A FIGHT.
AND I WOULDN'T RECOMMEND WEARING THAT SUIT UNTIL YOU KNOW WHAT IT *MEANS.*
HAVE A NICE EVENING... "CATWOMAN."
I know a warning when I hear one. Tonight's hunt's over.
Selina will be here again tomorrow.
THE *HELL* ARE YOU DOING BACK HERE?
DROPPED AN EARRING.

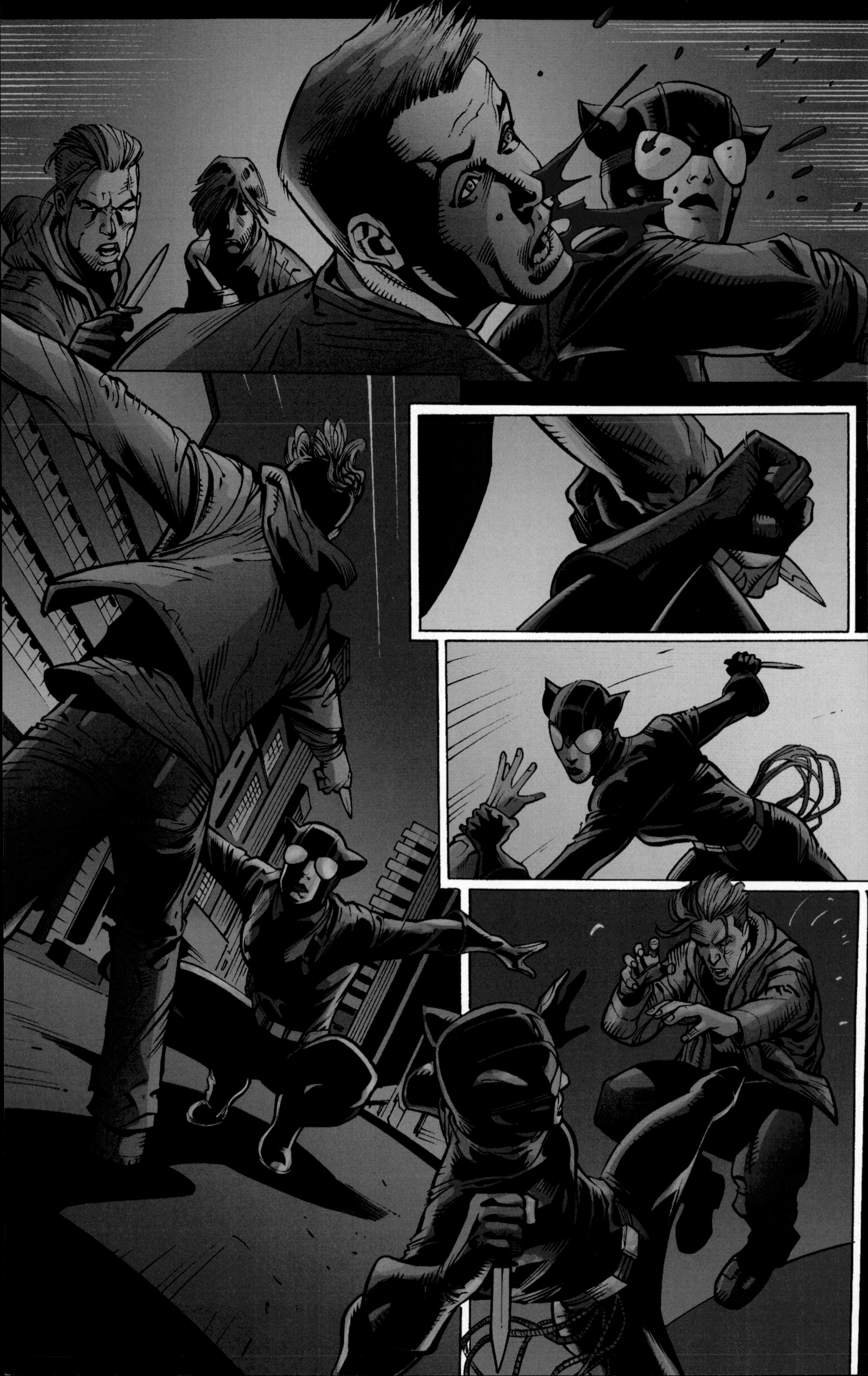

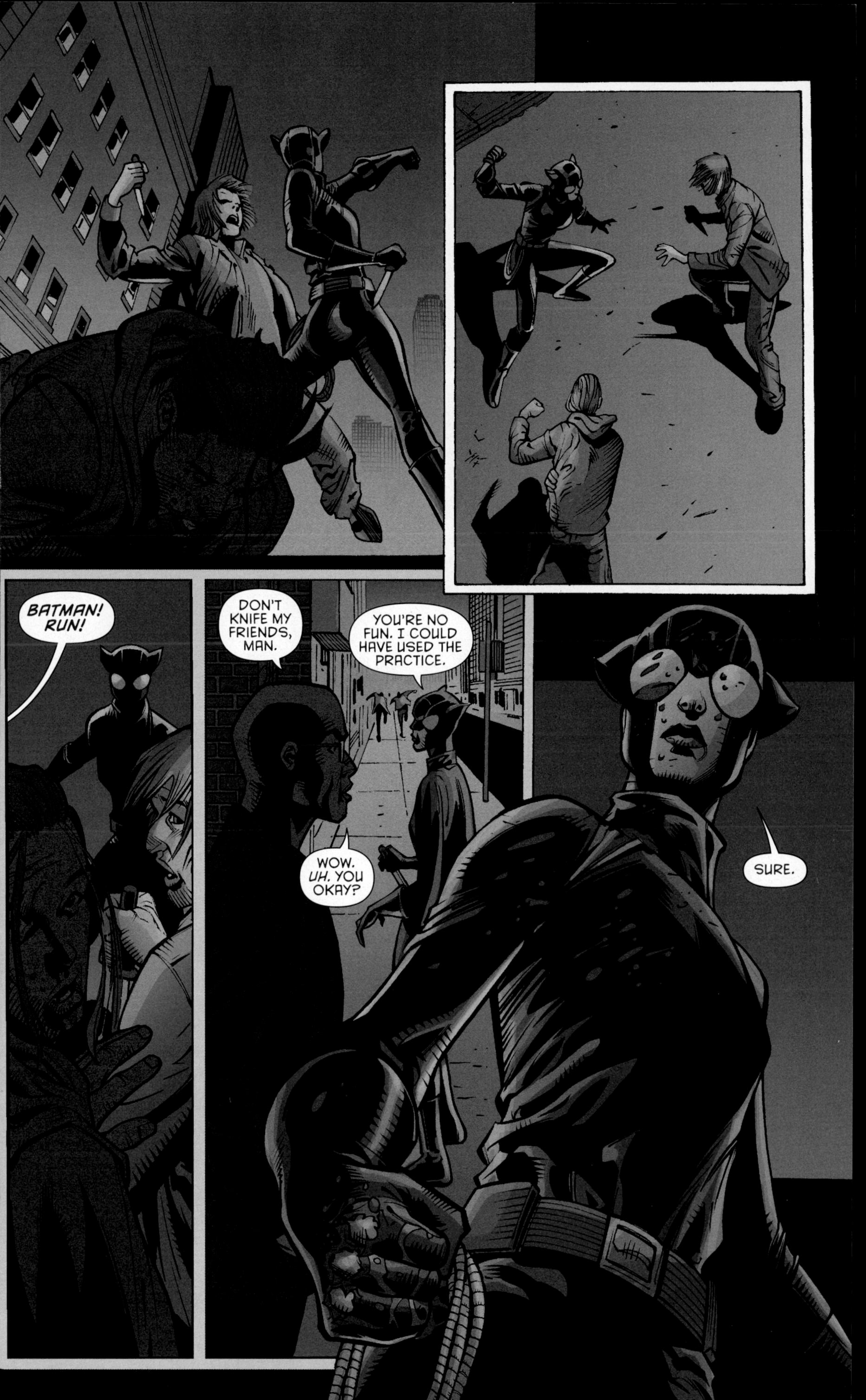
BATMAN! RUN!
DON'T KNIFE MY FRIENDS, MAN.
YOU'RE NO FUN. I COULD HAVE USED THE PRACTICE.
WOW. UH. YOU OKAY?
SURE.

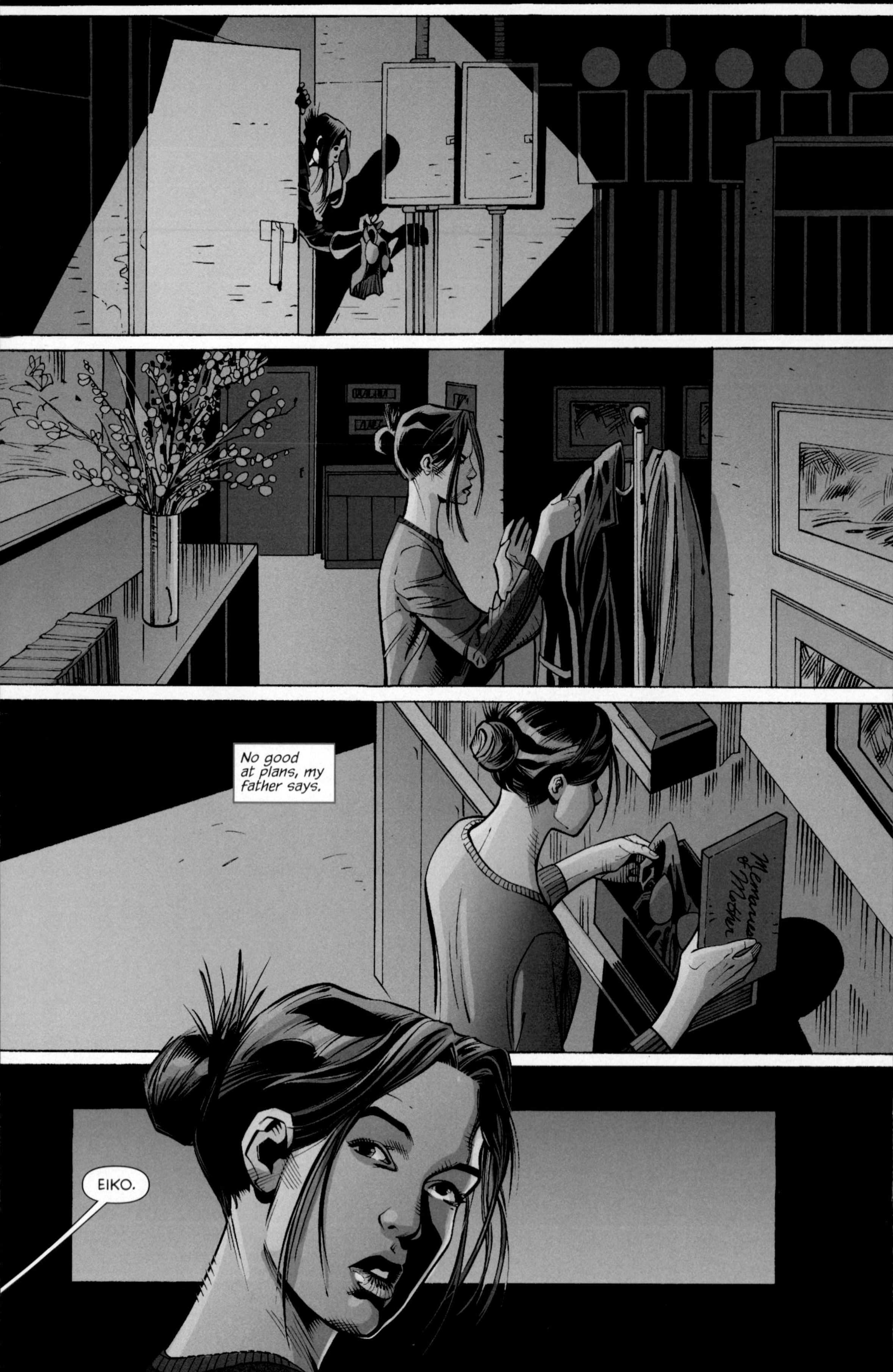
No good at plans, my father says.
EIKO.

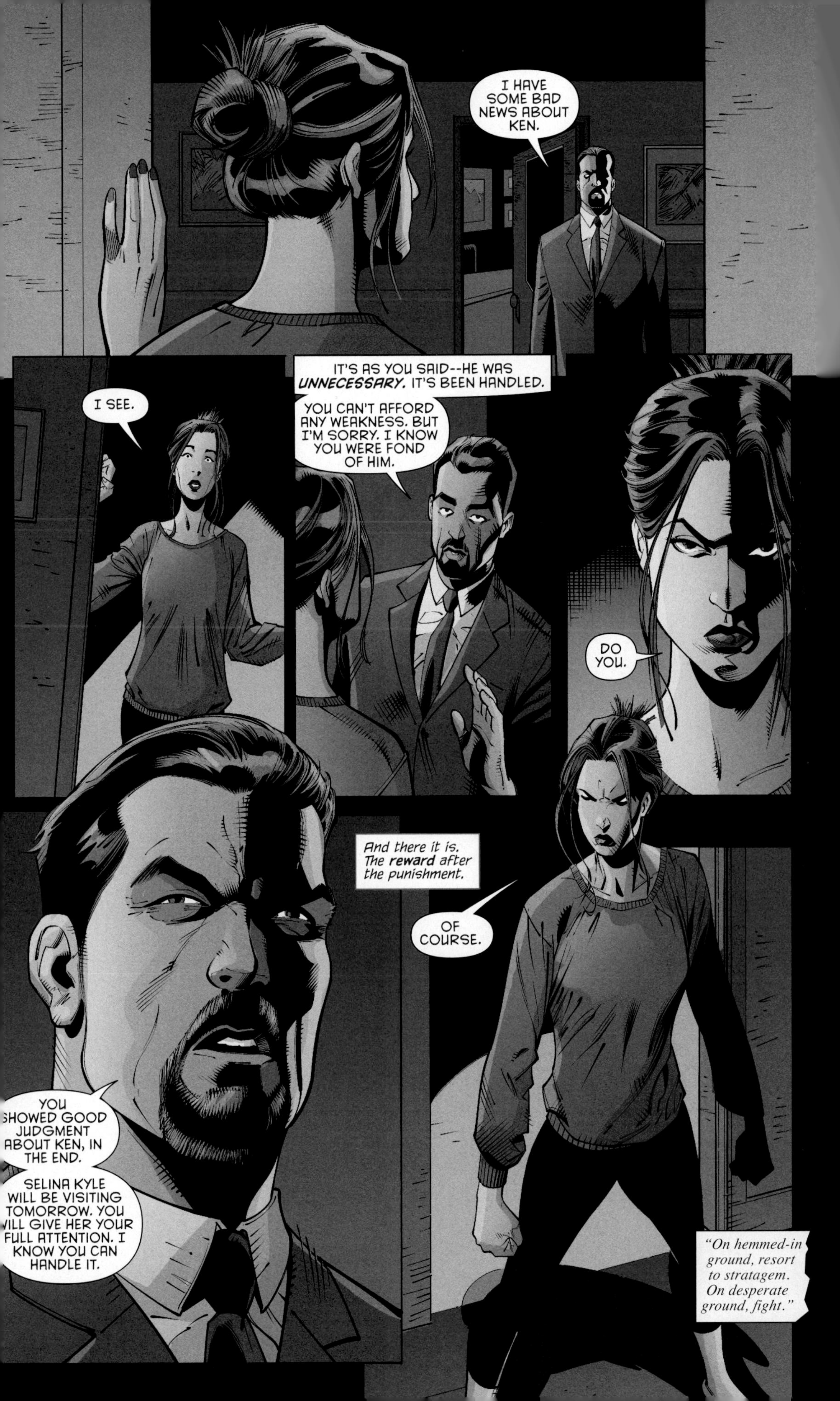
I HAVE SOME BAD NEWS ABOUT KEN.
I SEE.
IT'S AS YOU SAID--HE WAS *UNNECESSARY.* IT'S BEEN HANDLED.
YOU CAN'T AFFORD ANY WEAKNESS. BUT I'M SORRY. I KNOW YOU WERE FOND OF HIM.
DO YOU.
YOU SHOWED GOOD JUDGMENT ABOUT KEN, IN THE END.
SELINA KYLE WILL BE VISITING TOMORROW. YOU WILL GIVE HER YOUR FULL ATTENTION. I KNOW YOU CAN HANDLE IT.
And there it is. The **reward** after the punishment.
OF COURSE.
"On hemmed-in ground, resort to stratagem. On desperate ground, fight."

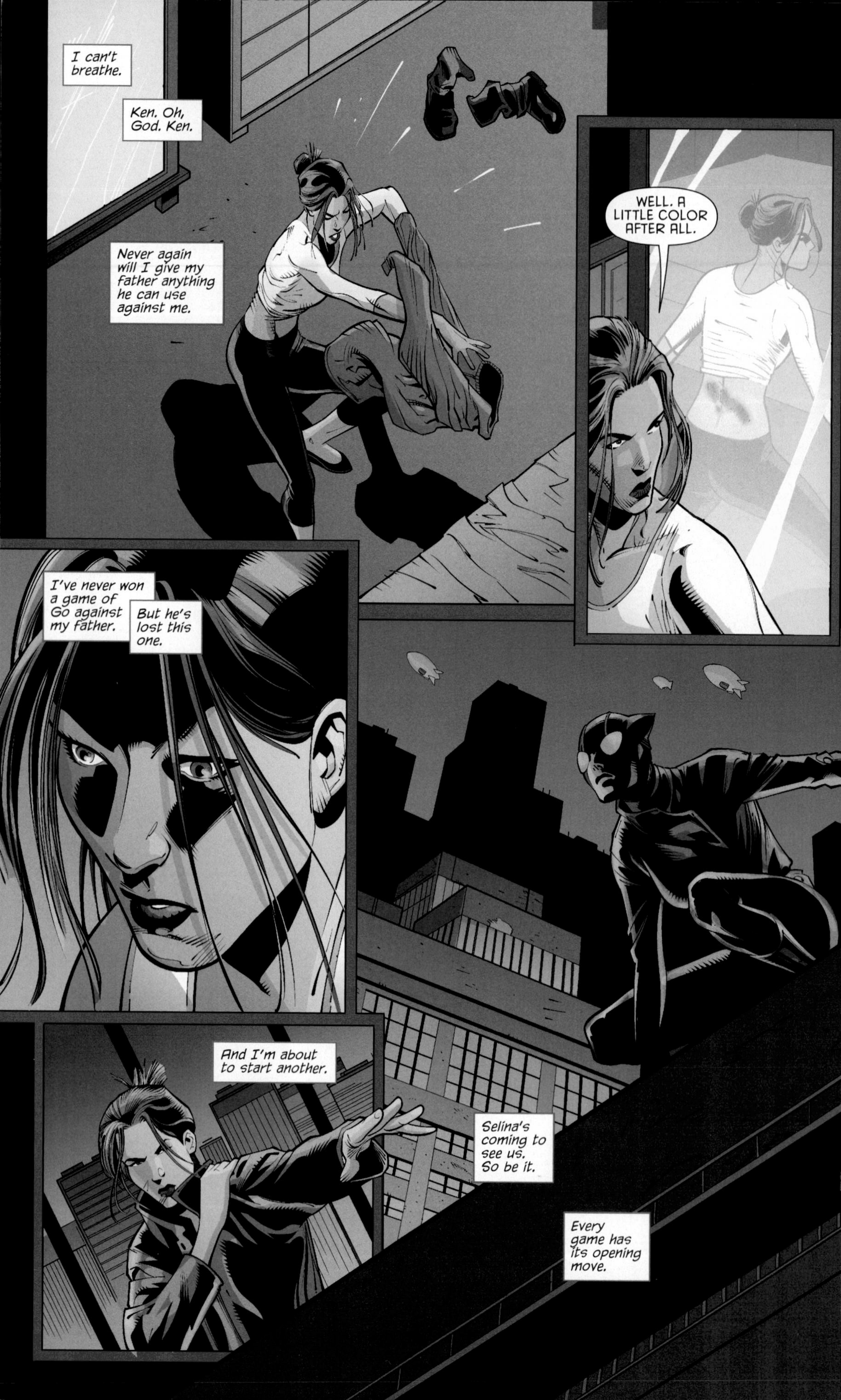
I can't breathe.
Ken. Oh, God. Ken.
Never again will I give my father anything he can use against me.
WELL. A LITTLE COLOR AFTER ALL.
I've never won a game of Go against my father.
But he's lost this one.
And I'm about to start another.
Selina's coming to see us. So be it.
Every game has its opening move.

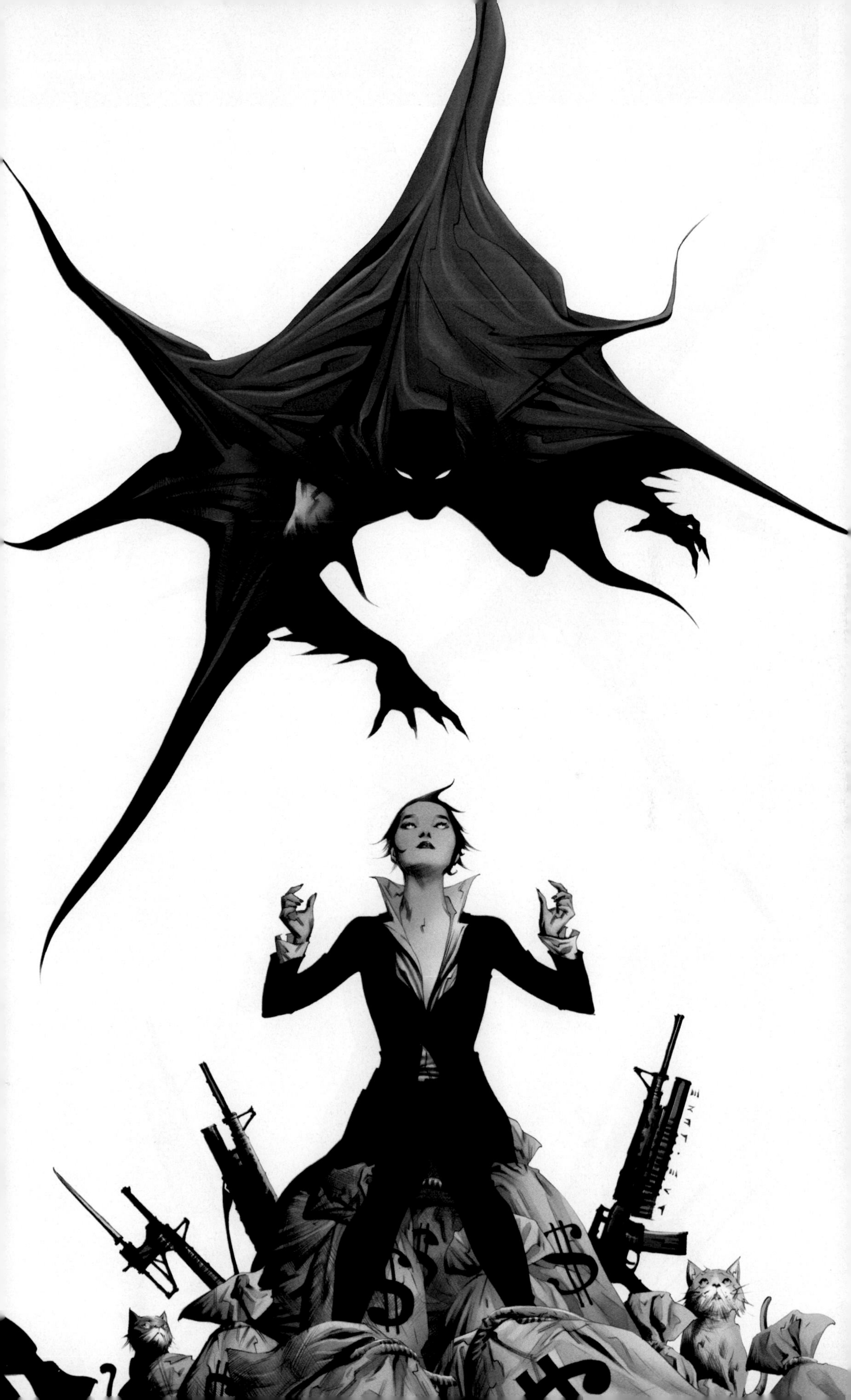

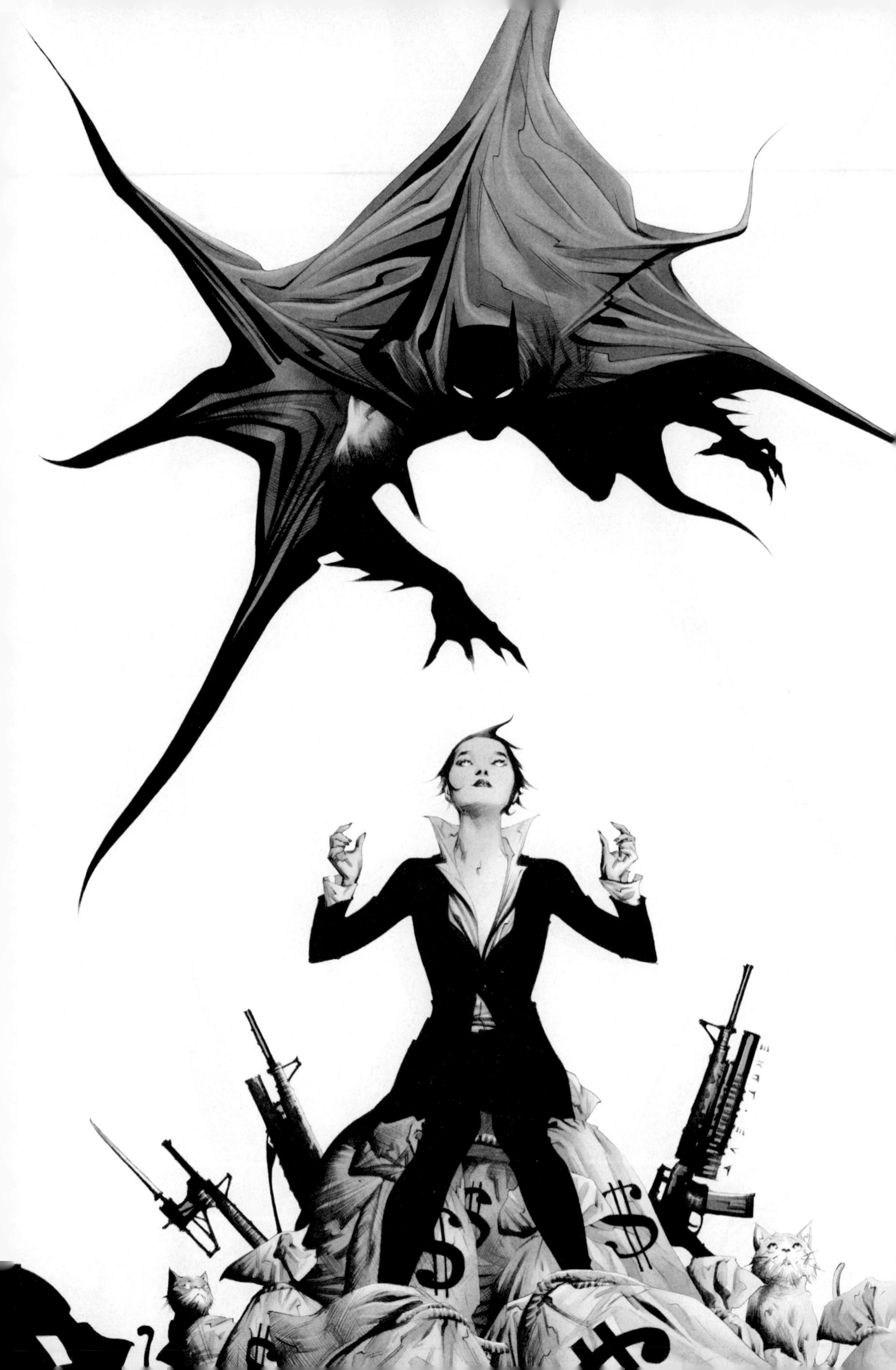

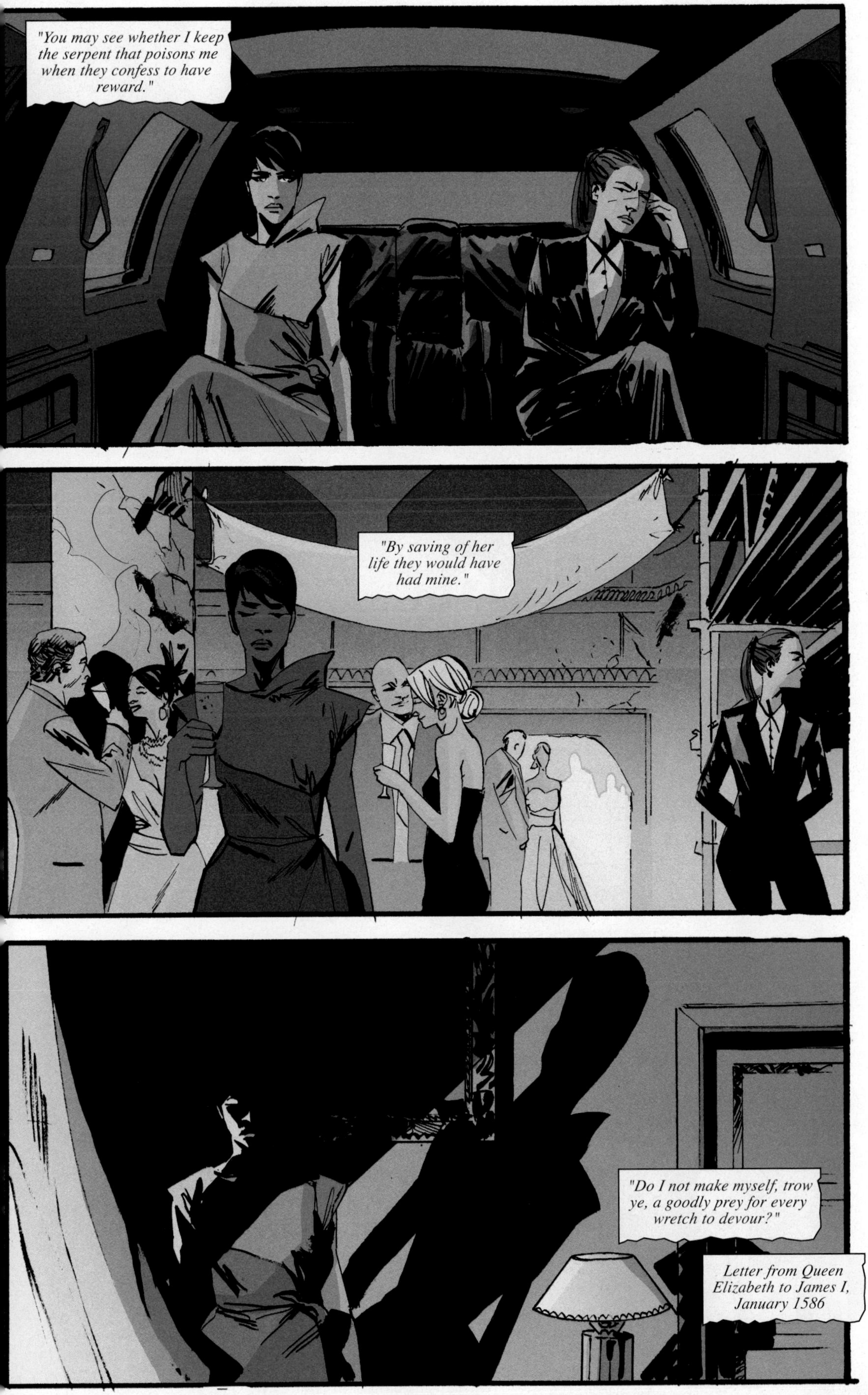
"You may see whether I keep the serpent that poisons me when they confess to have reward."
"By saving of her life they would have had mine."
"Do I not make myself, trow ye, a goodly prey for every wretch to devour?"
Letter from Queen Elizabeth to James I, January 1586

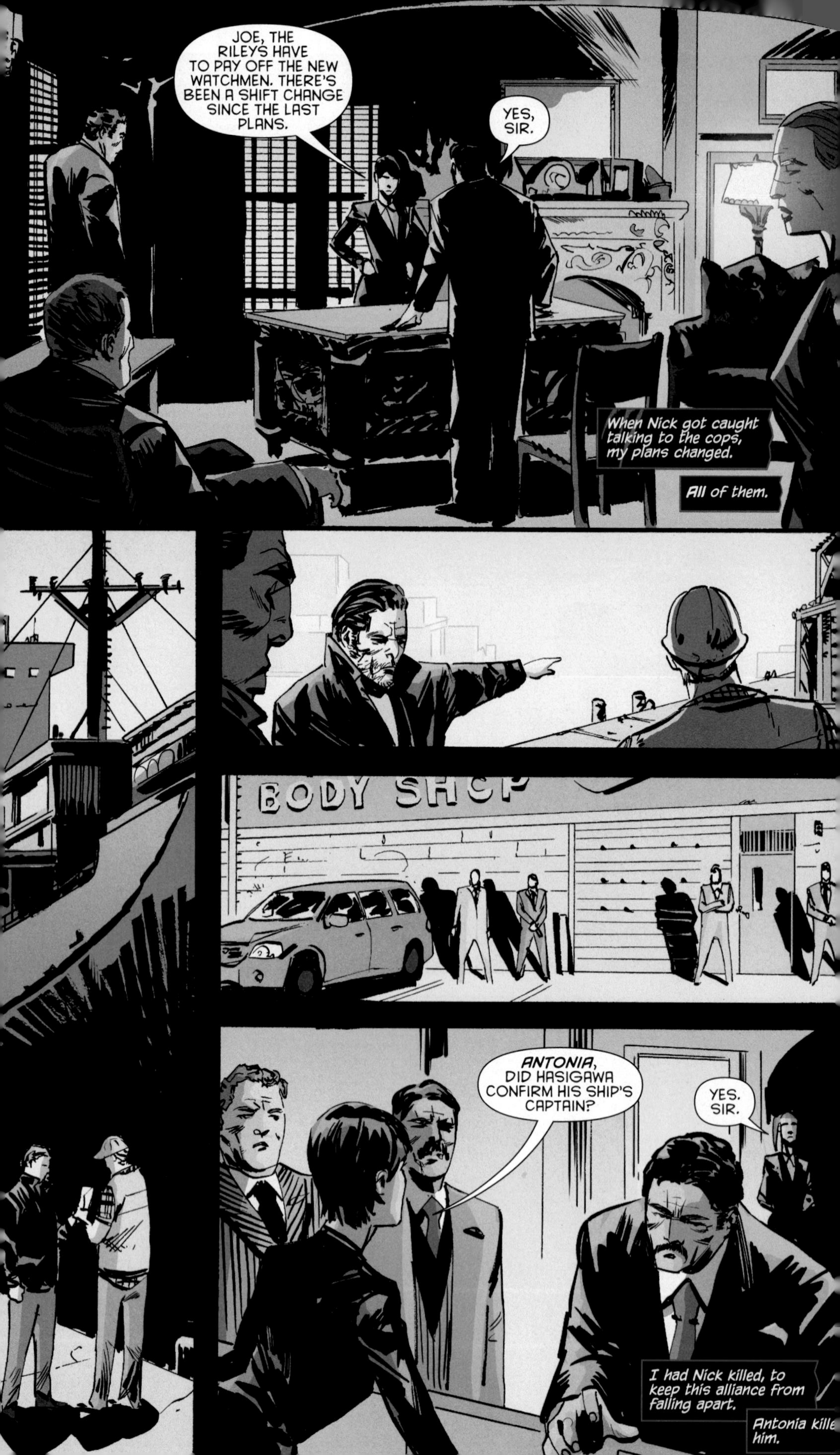

JOE, THE RILEYS HAVE TO PAY OFF THE NEW WATCHMEN. THERE'S BEEN A SHIFT CHANGE SINCE THE LAST PLANS.
YES, SIR.
When Nick got caught talking to the cops, my plans changed.
All of them.
BODY SHOP
ANTONIA, DID HASIGAWA CONFIRM HIS SHIP'S CAPTAIN?
YES. SIR.
I had Nick killed, to keep this alliance from falling apart.
Antonia kille him.

And things fell apart another way.

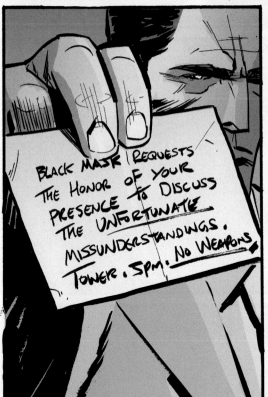

BLACK MASK REQUESTS THE HONOR OF YOUR PRESENCE TO DISCUSS THE UNFORTUNATE MISSUNDERSTANDINGS. TOWER. 5PM. NO WEAPONS

HAND LETTERED. I'M MOVING UP IN THE WORLD.

HE COULD HAVE ADDED "*IT'S A TRAP*," BUT IT SEEMS UNNECESSARY.

I'LL TAKE THE CAR.

YOU *CAN'T* BE SERIOUS.

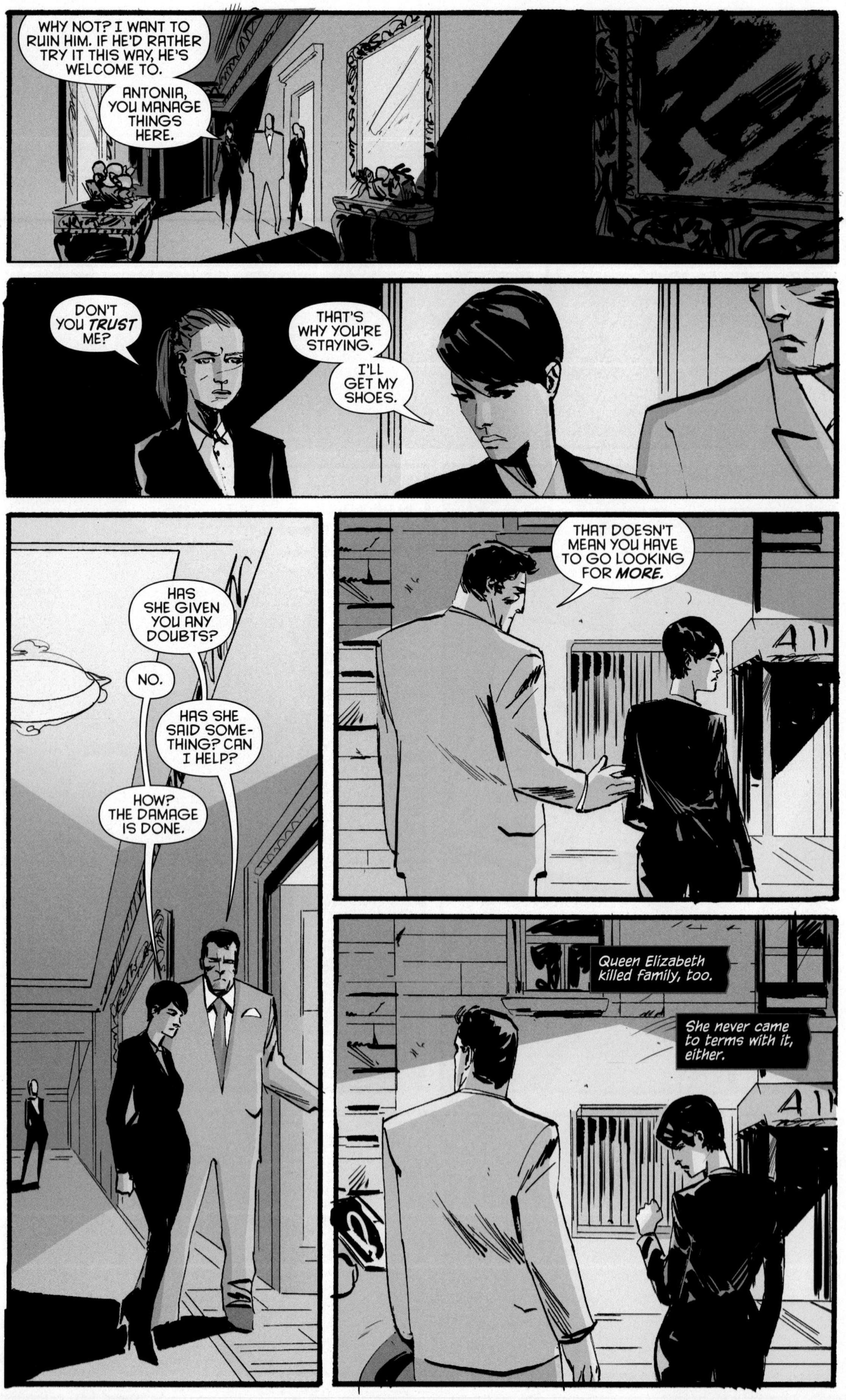
WHY NOT? I WANT TO RUIN HIM. IF HE'D RATHER TRY IT THIS WAY, HE'S WELCOME TO.
ANTONIA, YOU MANAGE THINGS HERE.
DON'T YOU *TRUST* ME?
THAT'S WHY YOU'RE STAYING.
I'LL GET MY SHOES.
HAS SHE GIVEN YOU ANY DOUBTS?
NO.
HAS SHE SAID SOME-THING? CAN I HELP?
HOW? THE DAMAGE IS DONE.
THAT DOESN'T MEAN YOU HAVE TO GO LOOKING FOR *MORE.*
Queen Elizabeth killed family, too.
She never came to terms with it, either.

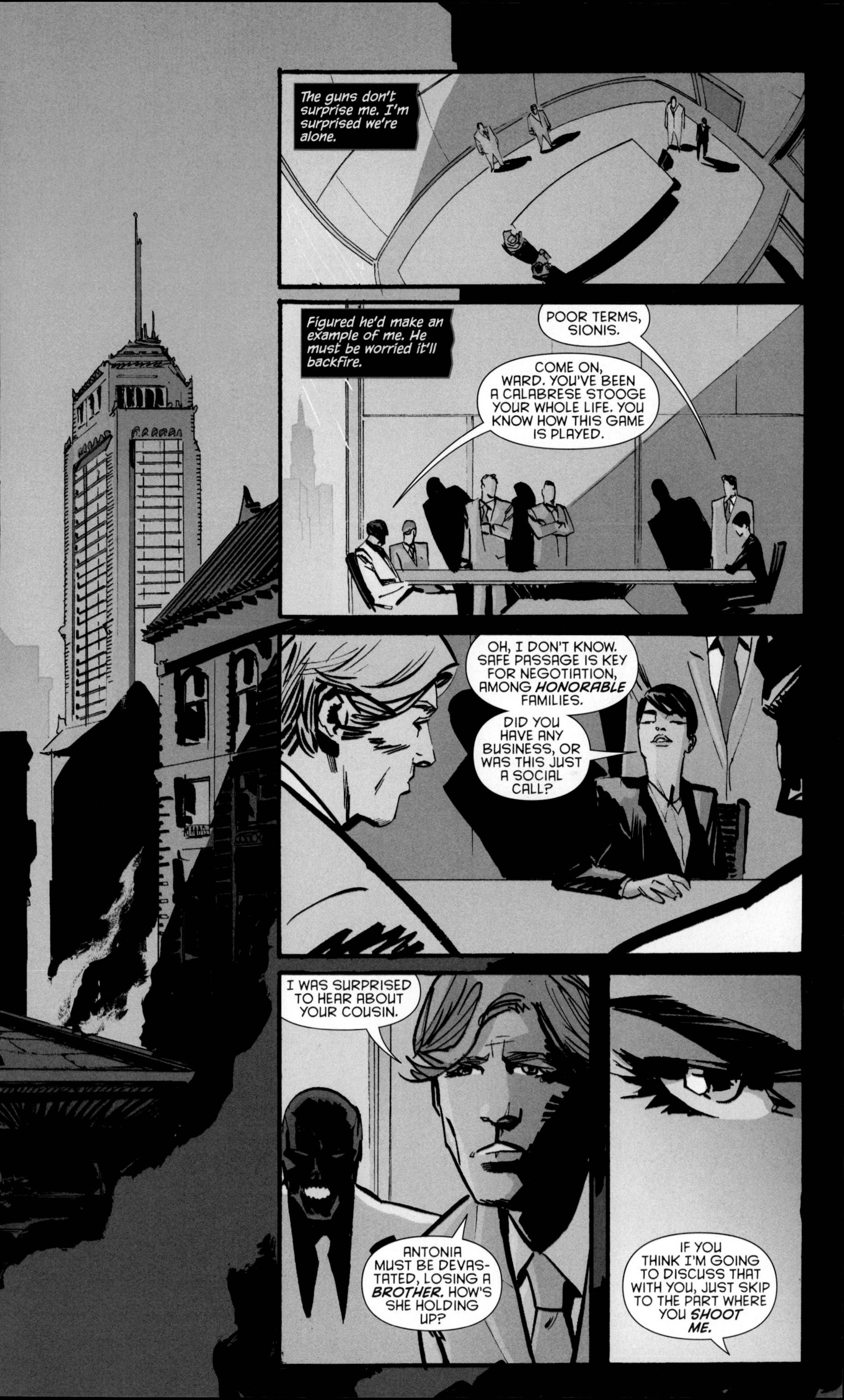

The guns don't surprise me. I'm surprised we're alone.
Figured he'd make an example of me. He must be worried it'll backfire.
POOR TERMS, SIONIS.
COME ON, WARD. YOU'VE BEEN A CALABRESE STOOGE YOUR WHOLE LIFE. YOU KNOW HOW THIS GAME IS PLAYED.
OH, I DON'T KNOW. SAFE PASSAGE IS KEY FOR NEGOTIATION, AMONG HONORABLE FAMILIES.
DID YOU HAVE ANY BUSINESS, OR WAS THIS JUST A SOCIAL CALL?
I WAS SURPRISED TO HEAR ABOUT YOUR COUSIN.
ANTONIA MUST BE DEVAS-TATED, LOSING A BROTHER. HOW'S SHE HOLDING UP?
IF YOU THINK I'M GOING TO DISCUSS THAT WITH YOU, JUST SKIP TO THE PART WHERE YOU SHOOT ME.

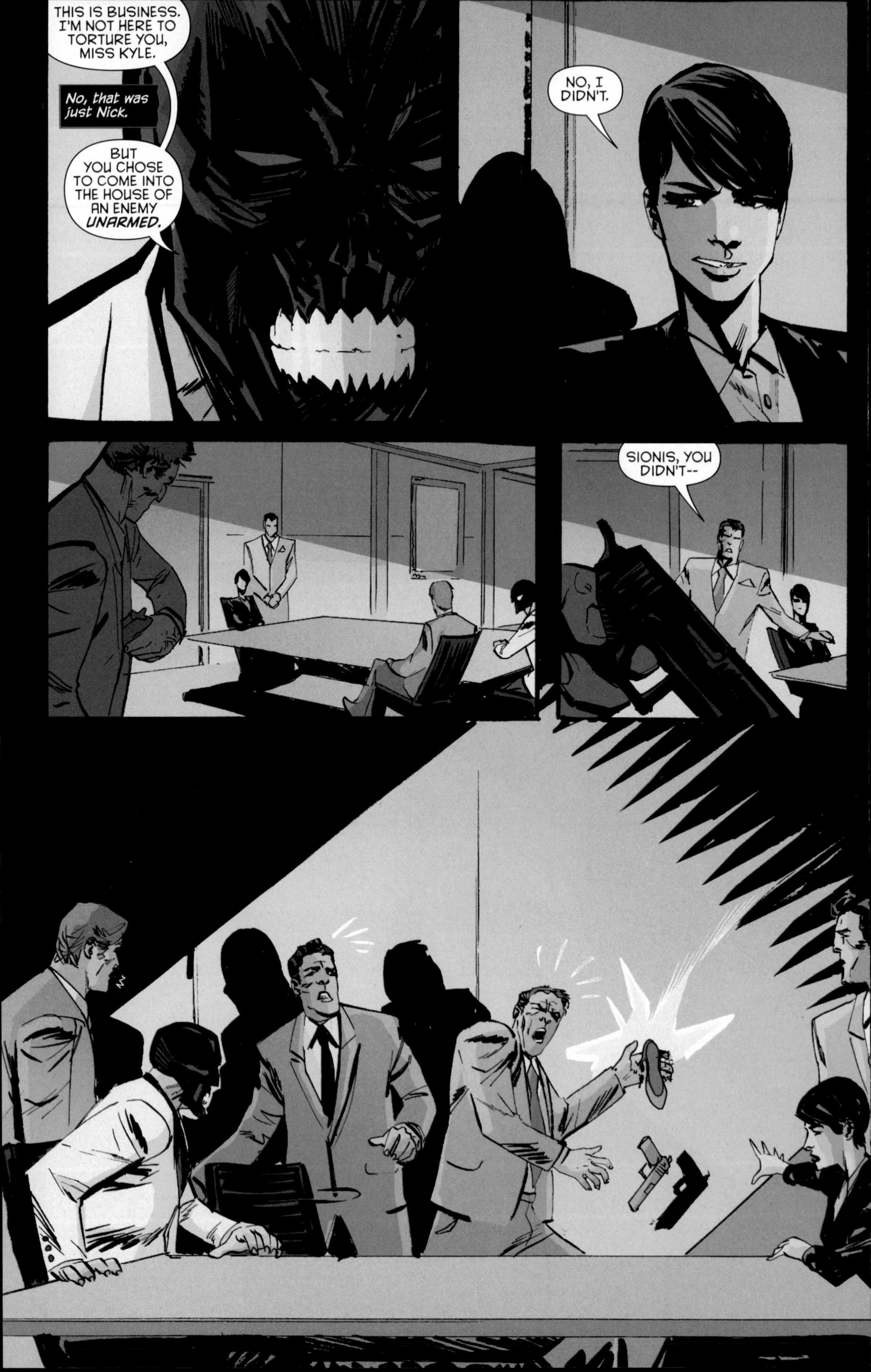
THIS IS BUSINESS. I'M NOT HERE TO TORTURE YOU, MISS KYLE.
No, that was just Nick.
BUT YOU CHOSE TO COME INTO THE HOUSE OF AN ENEMY *UNARMED.*
NO, I DIDN'T.
SIONIS, YOU DIDN'T--

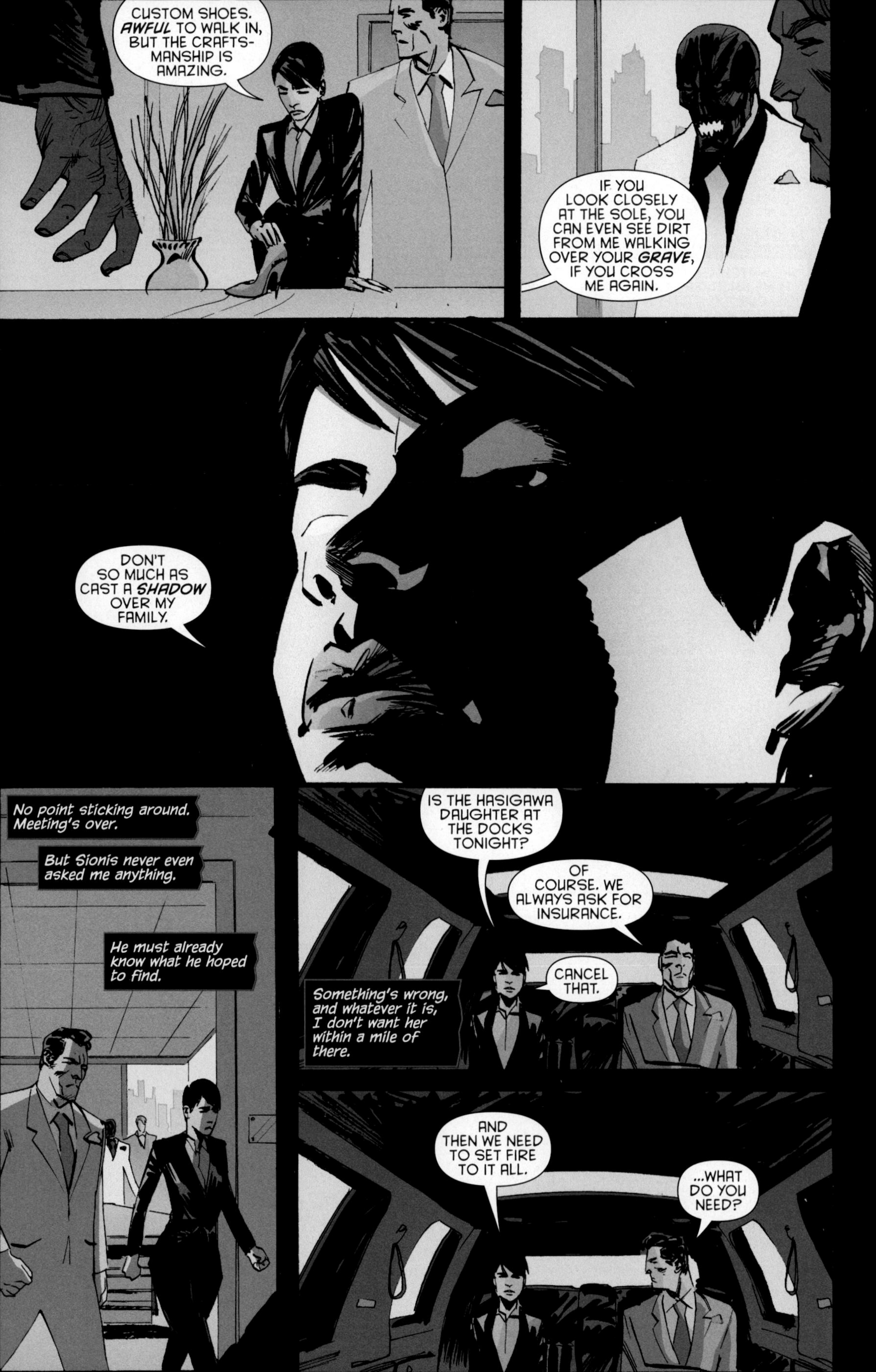
CUSTOM SHOES. AWFUL TO WALK IN, BUT THE CRAFTSMANSHIP IS AMAZING.
IF YOU LOOK CLOSELY AT THE SOLE, YOU CAN EVEN SEE DIRT FROM ME WALKING OVER YOUR GRAVE, IF YOU CROSS ME AGAIN.
DON'T SO MUCH AS CAST A SHADOW OVER MY FAMILY.
No point sticking around. Meeting's over.
But Sionis never even asked me anything.
He must already know what he hoped to find.
IS THE HASIGAWA DAUGHTER AT THE DOCKS TONIGHT?
OF COURSE. WE ALWAYS ASK FOR INSURANCE.
Something's wrong, and whatever it is, I don't want her within a mile of there.
CANCEL THAT.
AND THEN WE NEED TO SET FIRE TO IT ALL.
...WHAT DO YOU NEED?

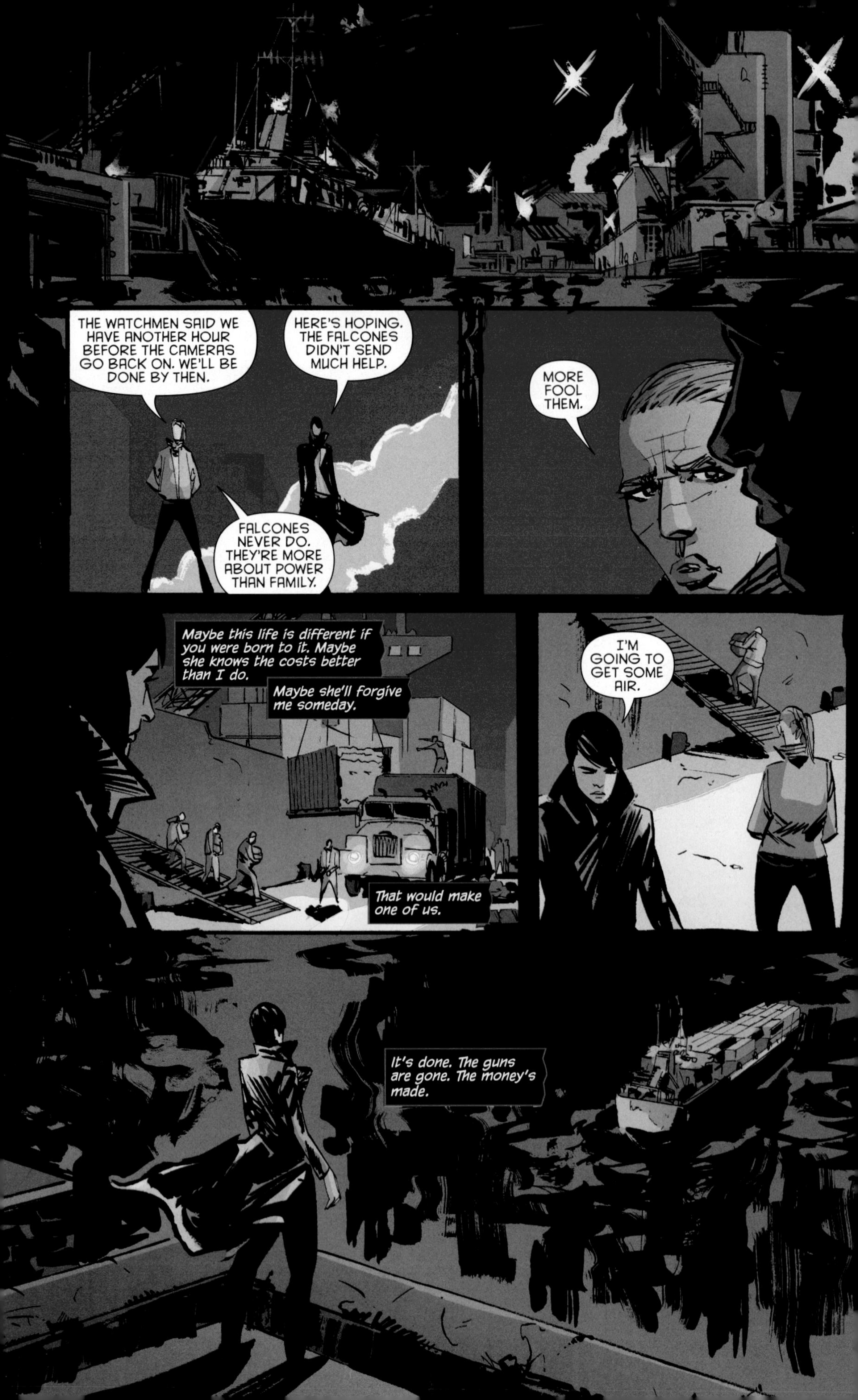
THE WATCHMEN SAID WE HAVE ANOTHER HOUR BEFORE THE CAMERAS GO BACK ON. WE'LL BE DONE BY THEN.
HERE'S HOPING. THE FALCONES DIDN'T SEND MUCH HELP.
FALCONES NEVER DO. THEY'RE MORE ABOUT POWER THAN FAMILY.
MORE FOOL THEM.
Maybe this life is different if you were born to it. Maybe she knows the costs better than I do.
Maybe she'll forgive me someday.
That would make one of us.
I'M GOING TO GET SOME AIR.
It's done. The guns are gone. The money's made.

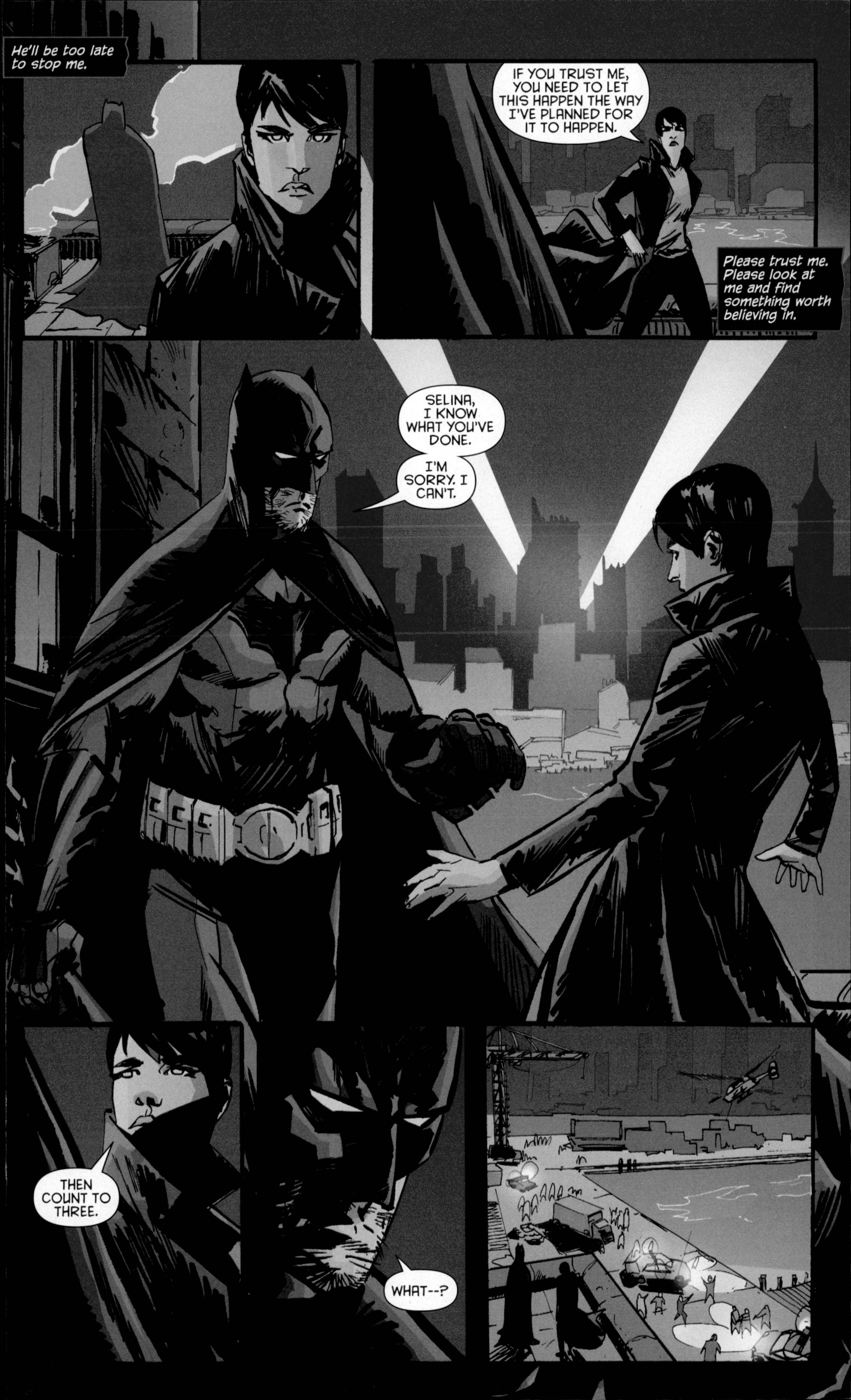
He'll be too late to stop me.
IF YOU TRUST ME, YOU NEED TO LET THIS HAPPEN THE WAY I'VE PLANNED FOR IT TO HAPPEN.
Please trust me. Please look at me and find something worth believing in.
SELINA, I KNOW WHAT YOU'VE DONE.
I'M SORRY. I CAN'T.
THEN COUNT TO THREE.
WHAT--?

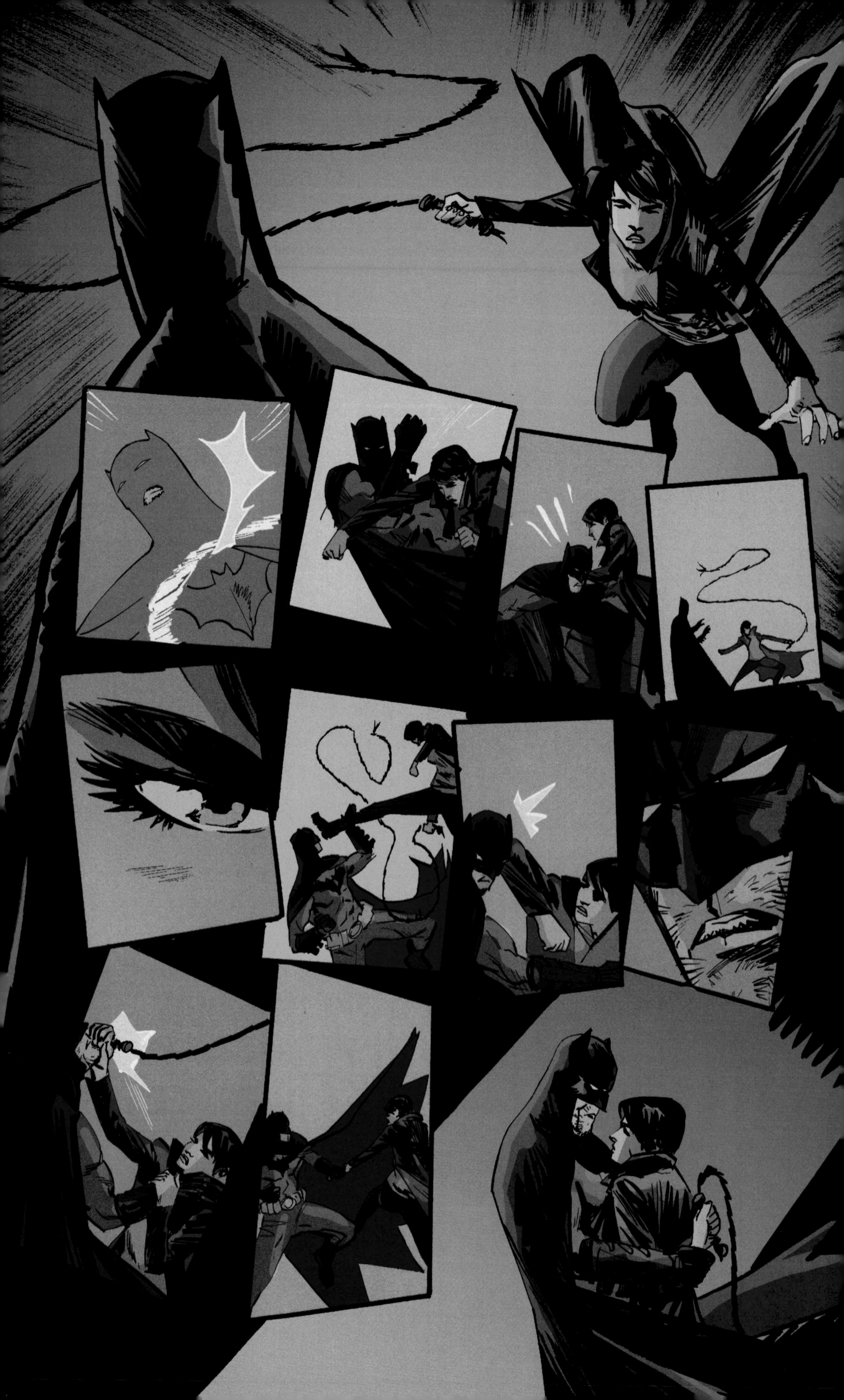

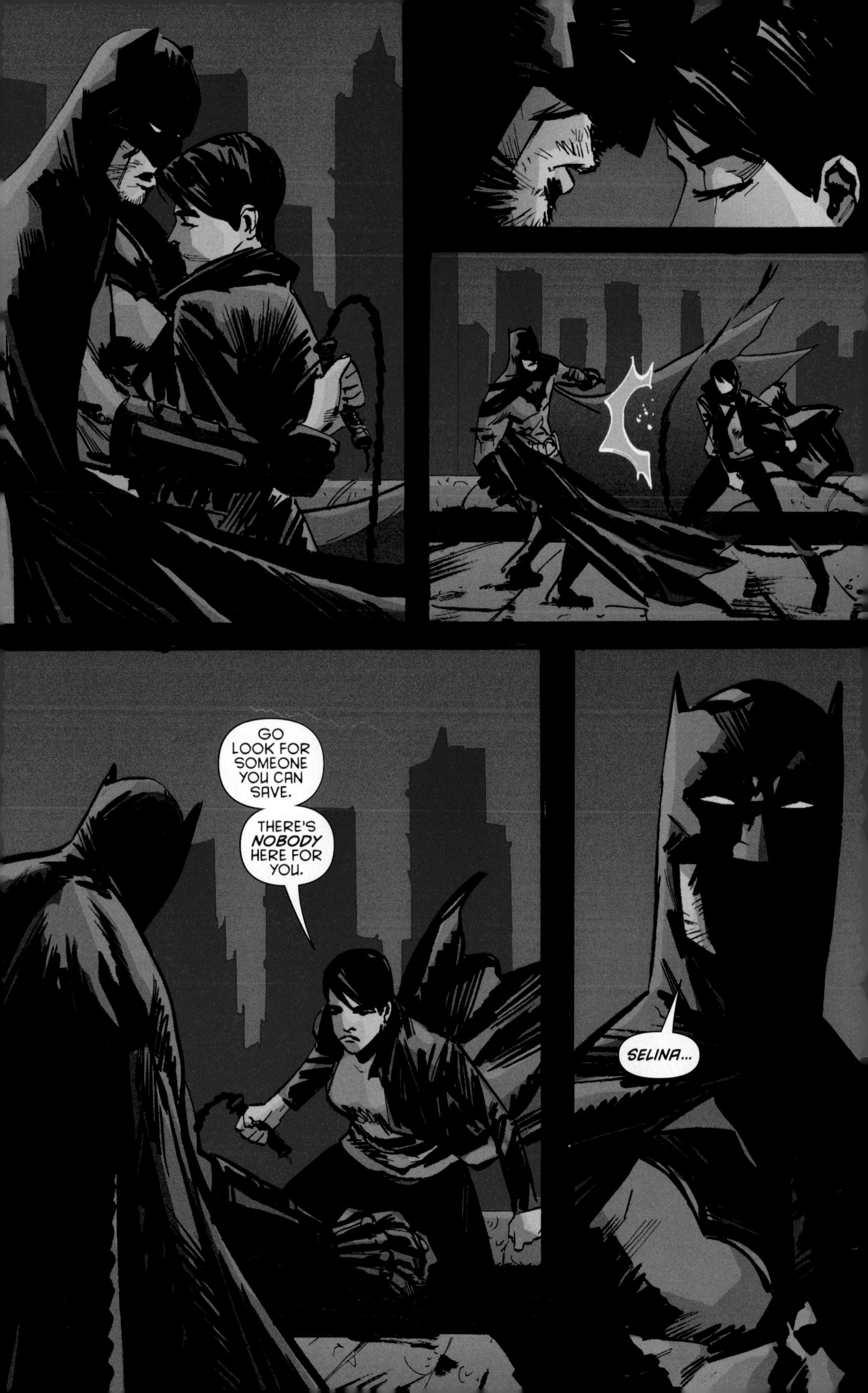
GO LOOK FOR SOMEONE YOU CAN SAVE.
THERE'S NOBODY HERE FOR YOU.
SELINA...

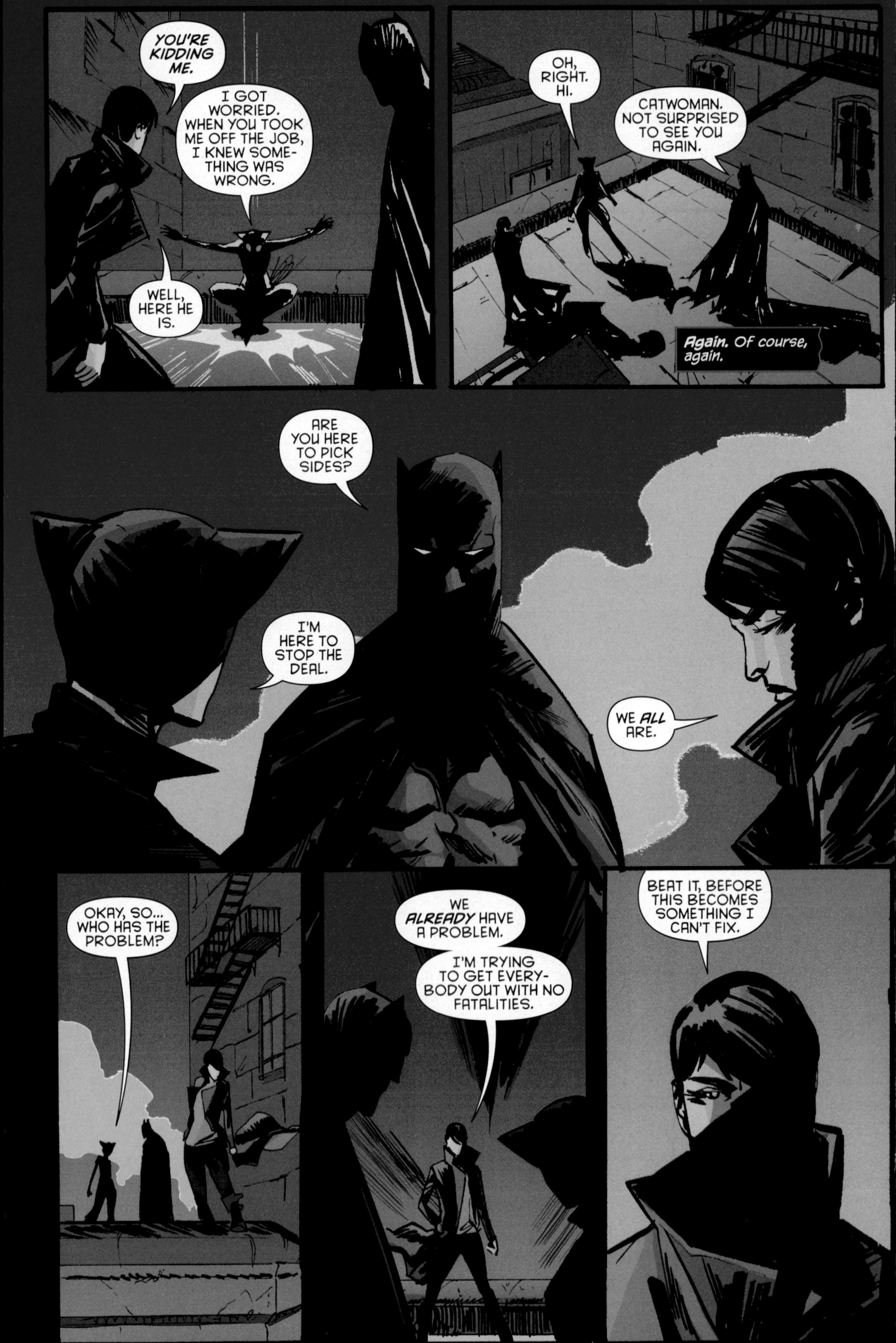
YOU'RE KIDDING ME.
I GOT WORRIED. WHEN YOU TOOK ME OFF THE JOB, I KNEW SOME-THING WAS WRONG.
WELL, HERE HE IS.
OH, RIGHT. HI.
CATWOMAN. NOT SURPRISED TO SEE YOU AGAIN.
Again. Of course, again.
ARE YOU HERE TO PICK SIDES?
I'M HERE TO STOP THE DEAL.
WE ALL ARE.
OKAY, SO... WHO HAS THE PROBLEM?
WE ALREADY HAVE A PROBLEM.
I'M TRYING TO GET EVERY-BODY OUT WITH NO FATALITIES.
BEAT IT, BEFORE THIS BECOMES SOMETHING I CAN'T FIX.

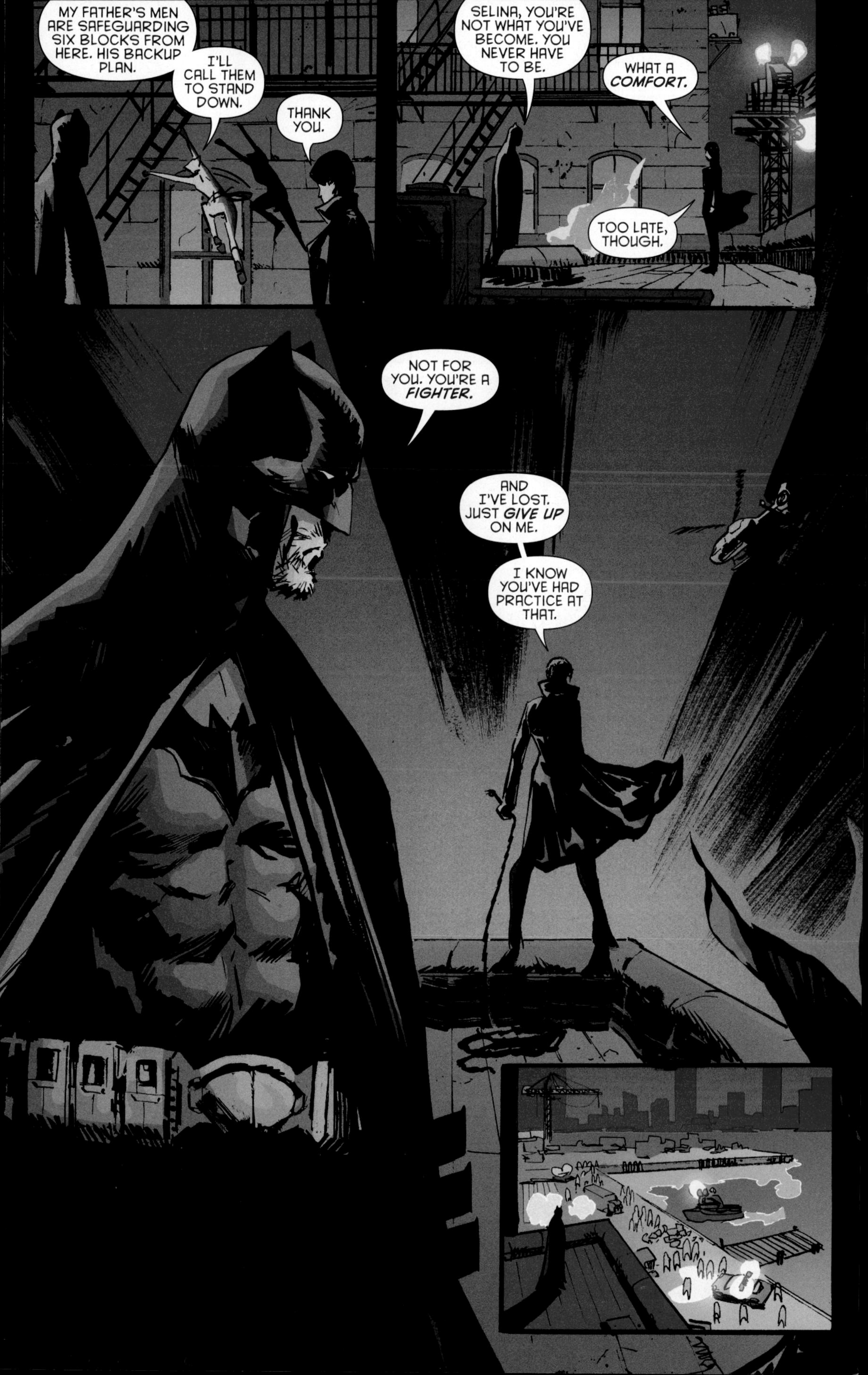
MY FATHER'S MEN ARE SAFEGUARDING SIX BLOCKS FROM HERE. HIS BACKUP PLAN.
I'LL CALL THEM TO STAND DOWN.
THANK YOU.
SELINA, YOU'RE NOT WHAT YOU'VE BECOME. YOU NEVER HAVE TO BE.
WHAT A *COMFORT.*
TOO LATE, THOUGH.
NOT FOR YOU. YOU'RE A *FIGHTER.*
AND I'VE LOST. JUST *GIVE UP* ON ME.
I KNOW YOU'VE HAD PRACTICE AT THAT.

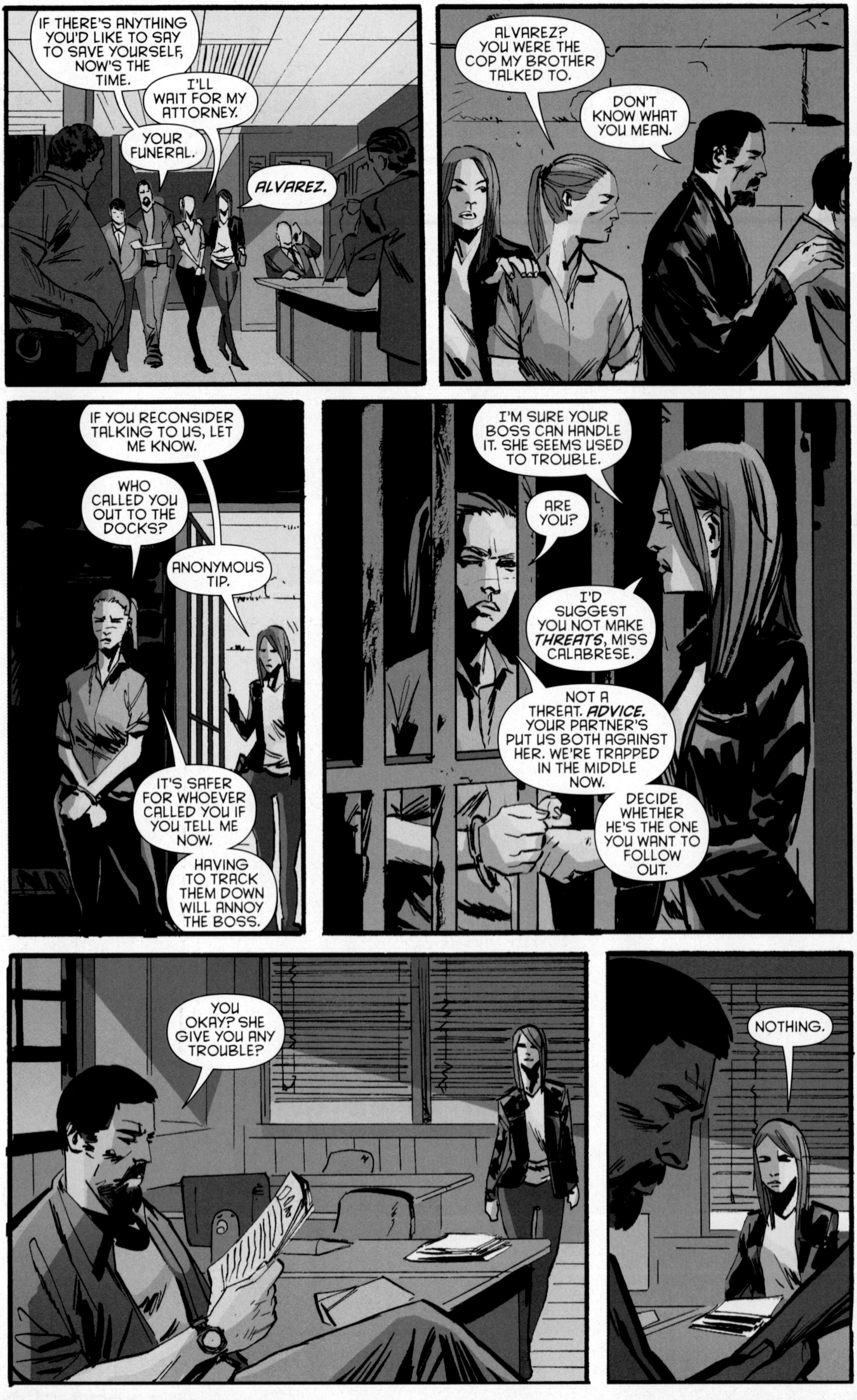
IF THERE'S ANYTHING YOU'D LIKE TO SAY TO SAVE YOURSELF, NOW'S THE TIME.
I'LL WAIT FOR MY ATTORNEY.
YOUR FUNERAL.
ALVAREZ.
ALVAREZ? YOU WERE THE COP MY BROTHER TALKED TO.
DON'T KNOW WHAT YOU MEAN.
IF YOU RECONSIDER TALKING TO US, LET ME KNOW.
WHO CALLED YOU OUT TO THE DOCKS?
ANONYMOUS TIP.
IT'S SAFER FOR WHOEVER CALLED YOU IF YOU TELL ME NOW.
HAVING TO TRACK THEM DOWN WILL ANNOY THE BOSS.
I'M SURE YOUR BOSS CAN HANDLE IT. SHE SEEMS USED TO TROUBLE.
ARE YOU?
I'D SUGGEST YOU NOT MAKE THREATS, MISS CALABRESE.
NOT A THREAT. ADVICE. YOUR PARTNER'S PUT US BOTH AGAINST HER. WE'RE TRAPPED IN THE MIDDLE NOW.
DECIDE WHETHER HE'S THE ONE YOU WANT TO FOLLOW OUT.
YOU OKAY? SHE GIVE YOU ANY TROUBLE?
NOTHING.

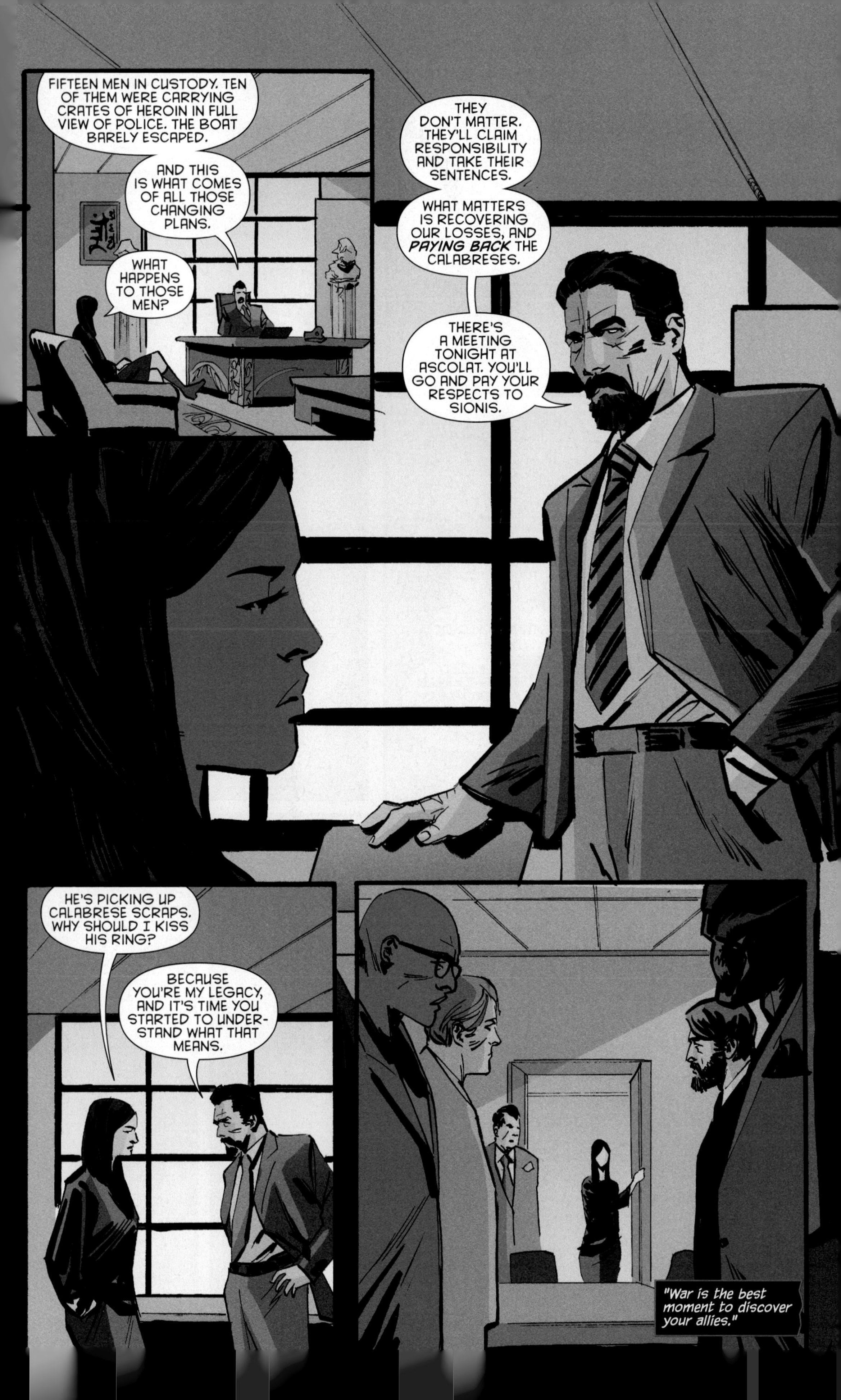
FIFTEEN MEN IN CUSTODY. TEN OF THEM WERE CARRYING CRATES OF HEROIN IN FULL VIEW OF POLICE. THE BOAT BARELY ESCAPED.
AND THIS IS WHAT COMES OF ALL THOSE CHANGING PLANS.
WHAT HAPPENS TO THOSE MEN?
THEY DON'T MATTER. THEY'LL CLAIM RESPONSIBILITY AND TAKE THEIR SENTENCES.
WHAT MATTERS IS RECOVERING OUR LOSSES, AND PAYING BACK THE CALABRESES.
THERE'S A MEETING TONIGHT AT ASCOLAT. YOU'LL GO AND PAY YOUR RESPECTS TO SIONIS.
HE'S PICKING UP CALABRESE SCRAPS. WHY SHOULD I KISS HIS RING?
BECAUSE YOU'RE MY LEGACY, AND IT'S TIME YOU STARTED TO UNDER-STAND WHAT THAT MEANS.
"War is the best moment to discover your allies."

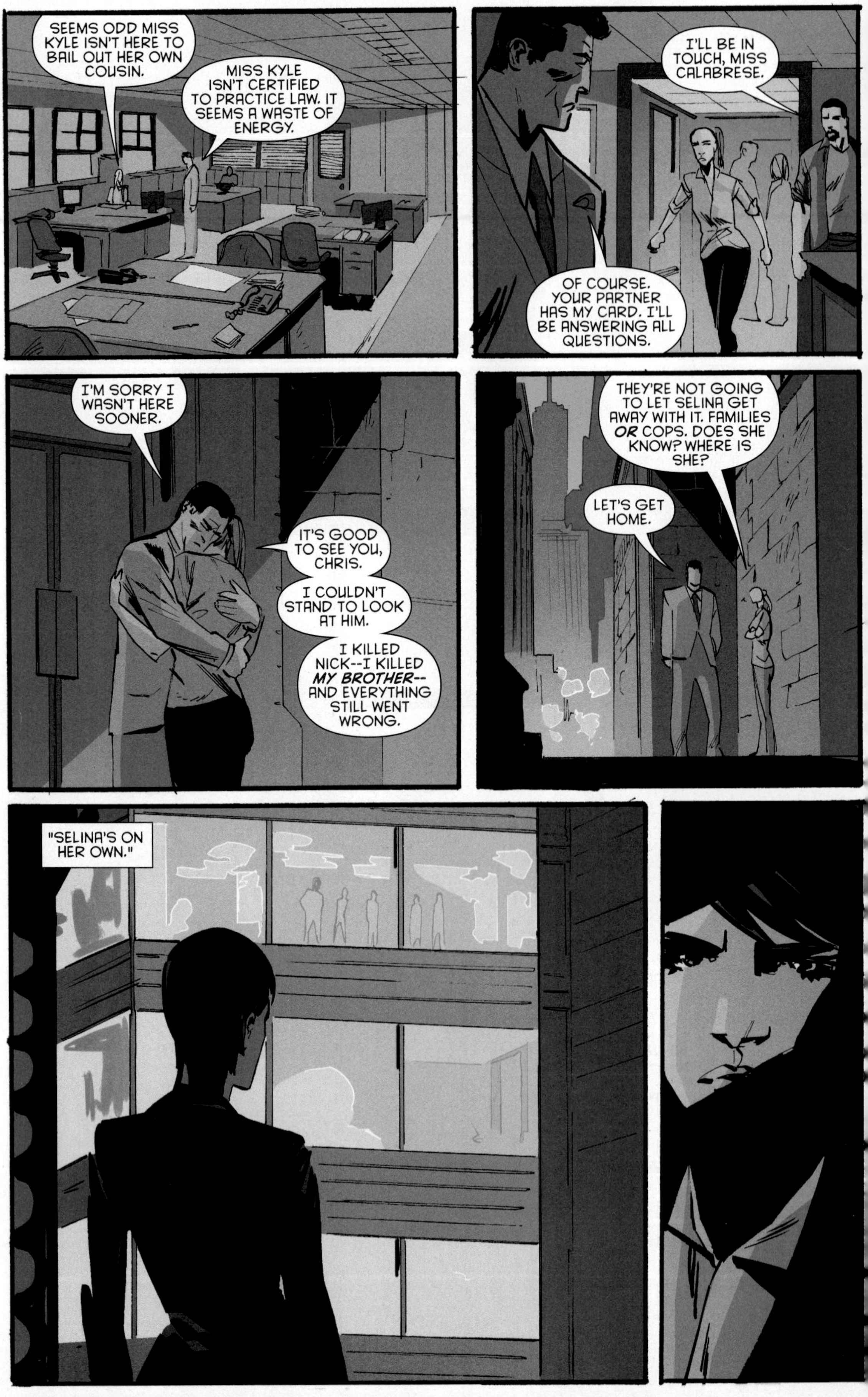
SEEMS ODD MISS KYLE ISN'T HERE TO BAIL OUT HER OWN COUSIN.
MISS KYLE ISN'T CERTIFIED TO PRACTICE LAW. IT SEEMS A WASTE OF ENERGY.
I'LL BE IN TOUCH, MISS CALABRESE.
OF COURSE. YOUR PARTNER HAS MY CARD. I'LL BE ANSWERING ALL QUESTIONS.
I'M SORRY I WASN'T HERE SOONER.
IT'S GOOD TO SEE YOU, CHRIS.
I COULDN'T STAND TO LOOK AT HIM.
I KILLED NICK--I KILLED *MY BROTHER*-- AND EVERYTHING STILL WENT WRONG.
THEY'RE NOT GOING TO LET SELINA GET AWAY WITH IT. FAMILIES *OR* COPS. DOES SHE KNOW? WHERE IS SHE?
LET'S GET HOME.
"SELINA'S ON HER OWN."

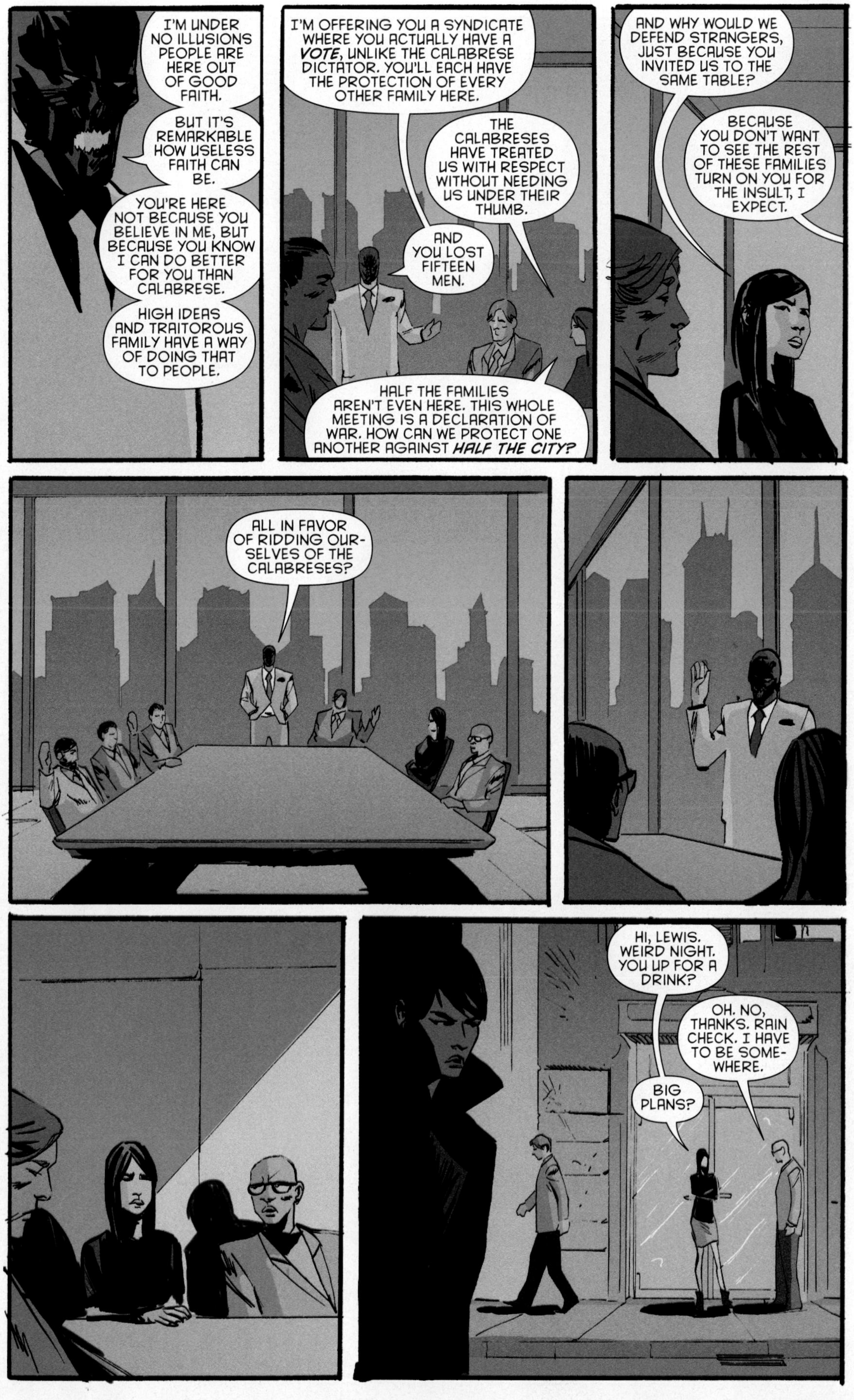
I'M UNDER NO ILLUSIONS PEOPLE ARE HERE OUT OF GOOD FAITH.
BUT IT'S REMARKABLE HOW USELESS FAITH CAN BE.
YOU'RE HERE NOT BECAUSE YOU BELIEVE IN ME, BUT BECAUSE YOU KNOW I CAN DO BETTER FOR YOU THAN CALABRESE.
HIGH IDEAS AND TRAITOROUS FAMILY HAVE A WAY OF DOING THAT TO PEOPLE.
I'M OFFERING YOU A SYNDICATE WHERE YOU ACTUALLY HAVE A VOTE, UNLIKE THE CALABRESE DICTATOR. YOU'LL EACH HAVE THE PROTECTION OF EVERY OTHER FAMILY HERE.
THE CALABRESES HAVE TREATED US WITH RESPECT WITHOUT NEEDING US UNDER THEIR THUMB.
AND YOU LOST FIFTEEN MEN.
HALF THE FAMILIES AREN'T EVEN HERE. THIS WHOLE MEETING IS A DECLARATION OF WAR. HOW CAN WE PROTECT ONE ANOTHER AGAINST HALF THE CITY?
AND WHY WOULD WE DEFEND STRANGERS, JUST BECAUSE YOU INVITED US TO THE SAME TABLE?
BECAUSE YOU DON'T WANT TO SEE THE REST OF THESE FAMILIES TURN ON YOU FOR THE INSULT, I EXPECT.
ALL IN FAVOR OF RIDDING OUR-SELVES OF THE CALABRESES?
HI, LEWIS. WEIRD NIGHT. YOU UP FOR A DRINK?
OH. NO, THANKS. RAIN CHECK. I HAVE TO BE SOME-WHERE.
BIG PLANS?

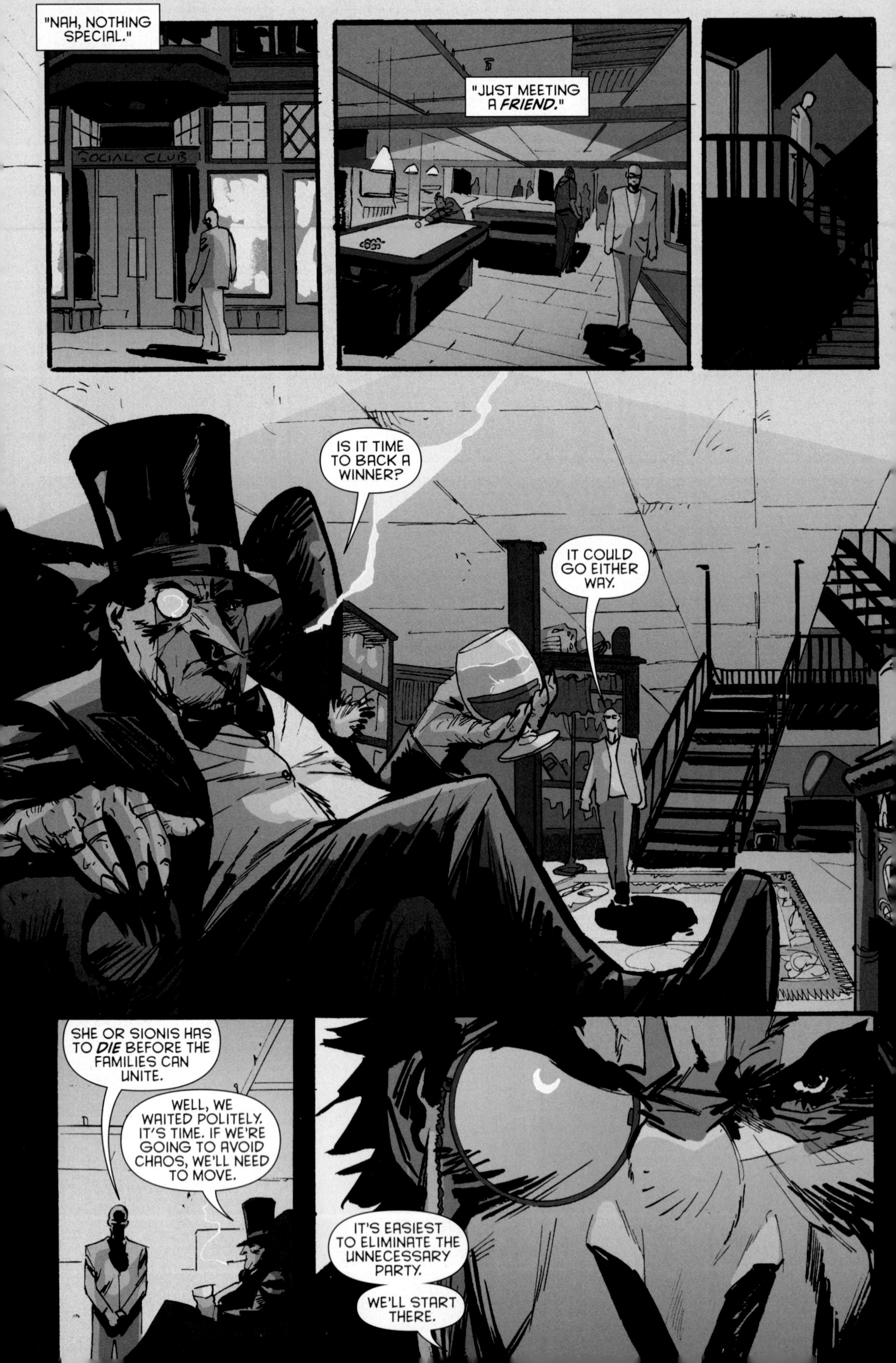
"NAH, NOTHING SPECIAL."
SOCIAL CLUB
"JUST MEETING A *FRIEND.*"
IS IT TIME TO BACK A WINNER?
IT COULD GO EITHER WAY.
SHE OR SIONIS HAS TO *DIE* BEFORE THE FAMILIES CAN UNITE.
WELL, WE WAITED POLITELY. IT'S TIME. IF WE'RE GOING TO AVOID CHAOS, WE'LL NEED TO MOVE.
IT'S EASIEST TO ELIMINATE THE UNNECESSARY PARTY.
WE'LL START THERE.

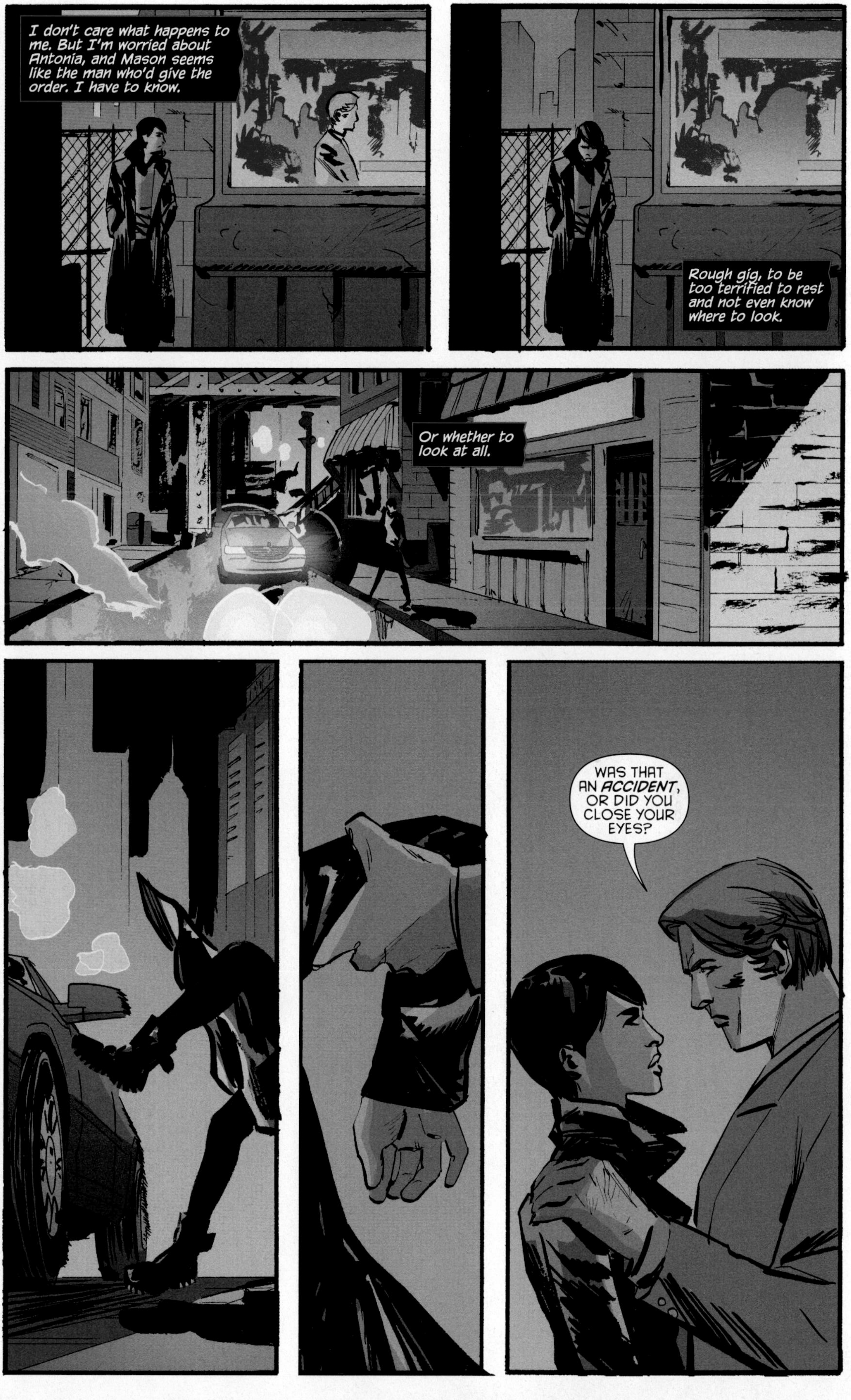
I don't care what happens to me. But I'm worried about Antonia, and Mason seems like the man who'd give the order. I have to know.
Rough gig, to be too terrified to rest and not even know where to look.
Or whether to look at all.
WAS THAT AN ACCIDENT, OR DID YOU CLOSE YOUR EYES?

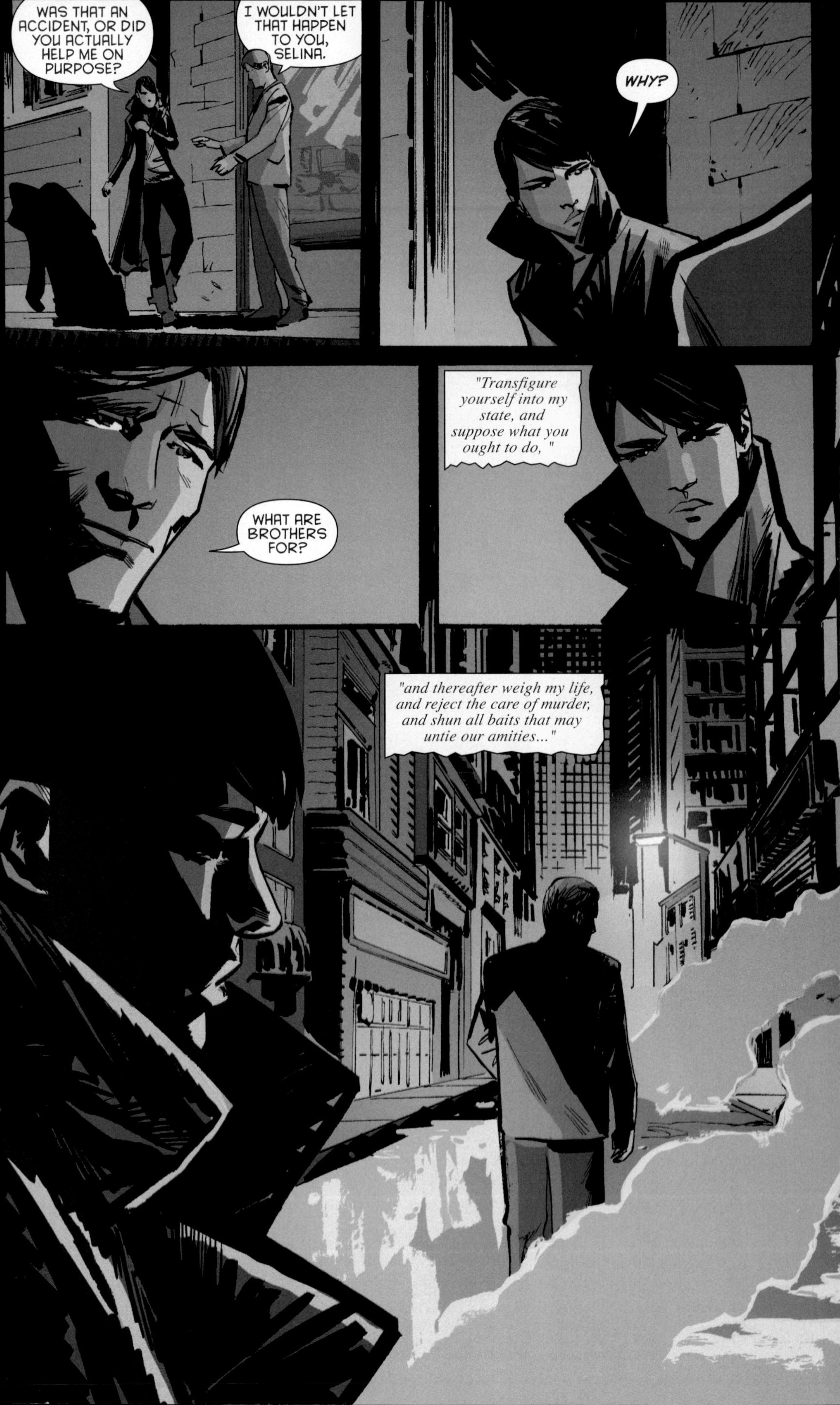
WAS THAT AN ACCIDENT, OR DID YOU ACTUALLY HELP ME ON PURPOSE?
I WOULDN'T LET THAT HAPPEN TO YOU, SELINA.
WHY?
WHAT ARE BROTHERS FOR?
"Transfigure yourself into my state, and suppose what you ought to do, "
"and thereafter weigh my life, and reject the care of murder, and shun all baits that may untie our amities..."

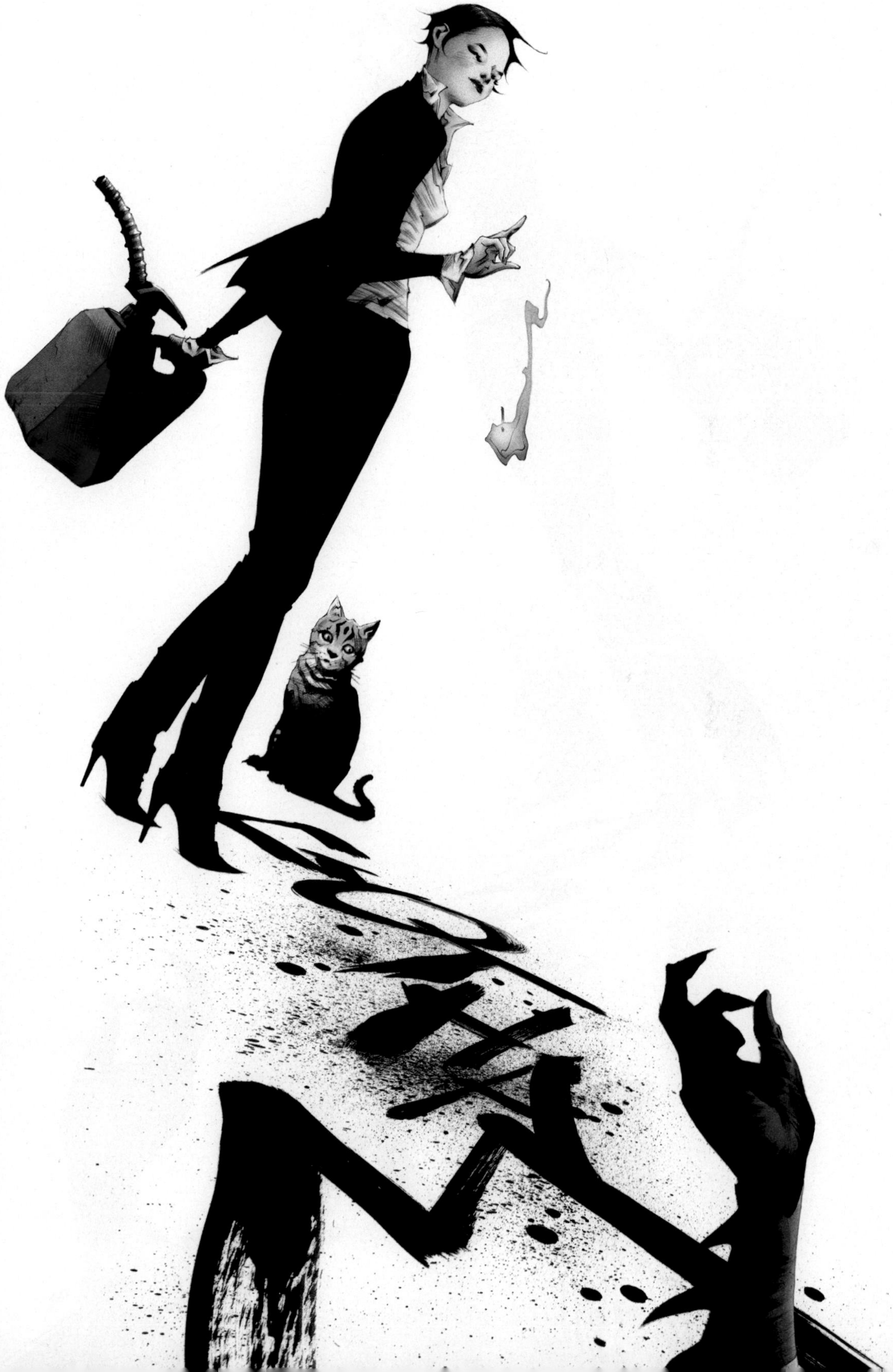

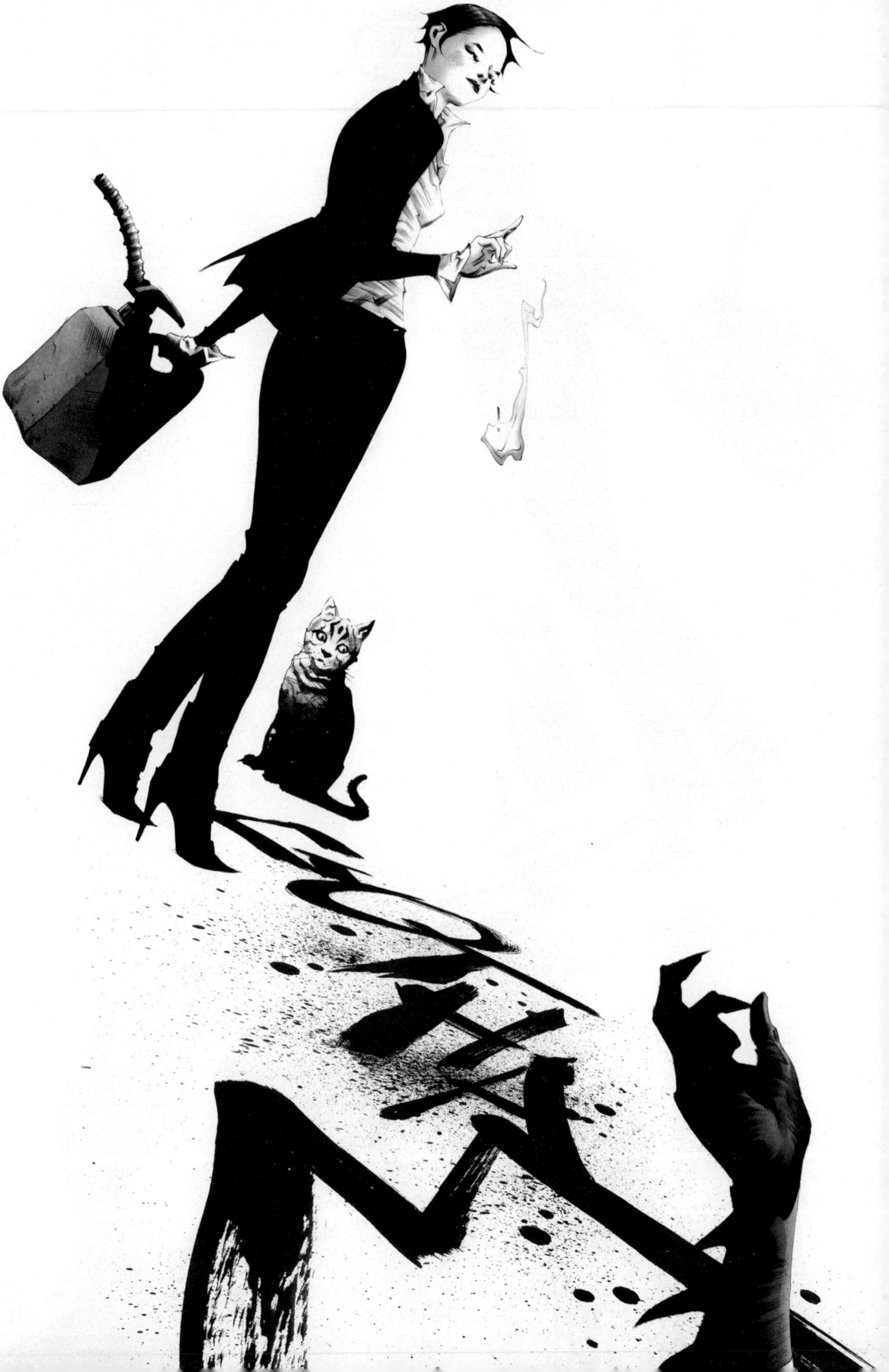

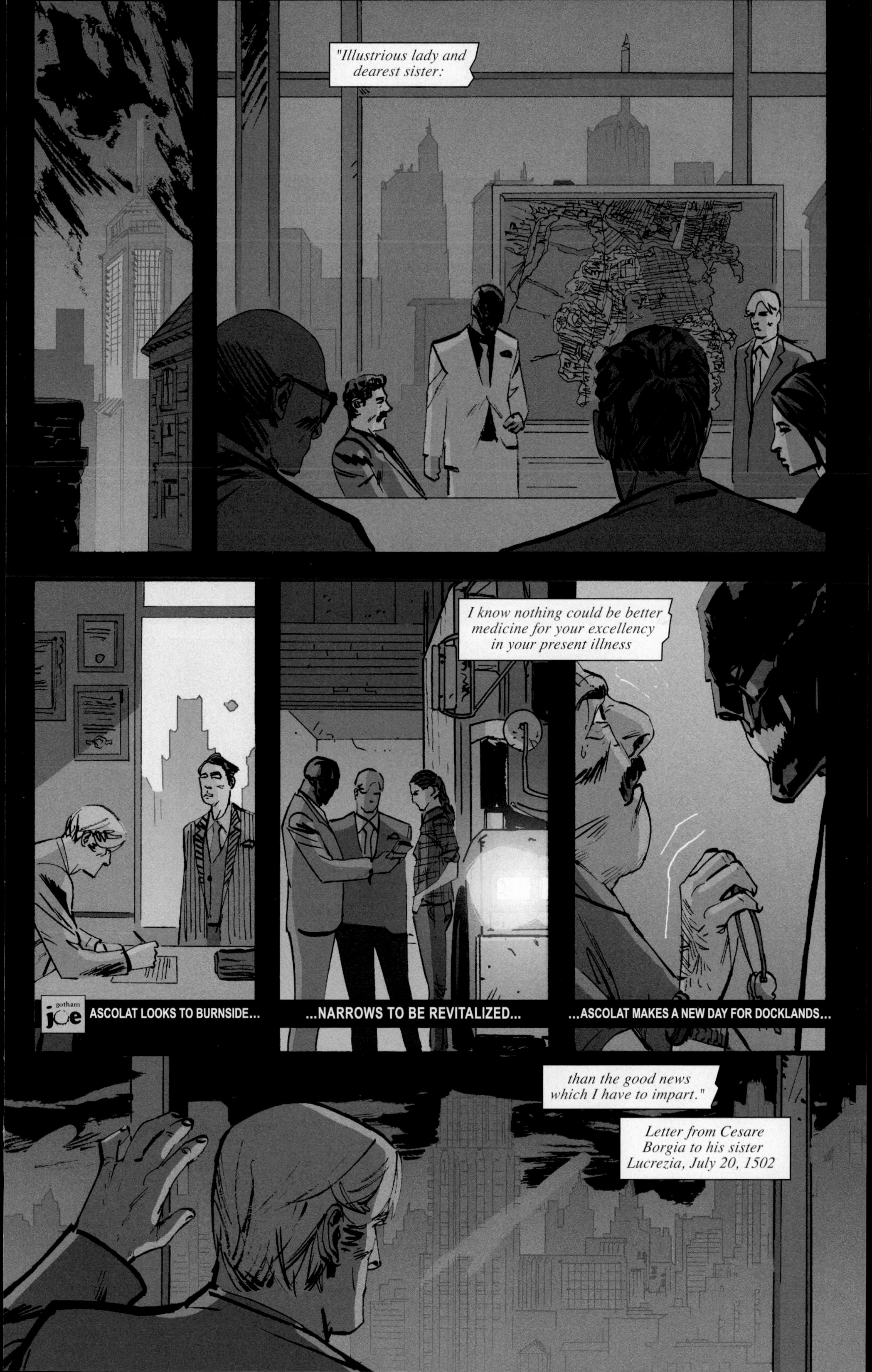
"Illustrious lady and dearest sister:
I know nothing could be better medicine for your excellency in your present illness
gotham joe
ASCOLAT LOOKS TO BURNSIDE...
...NARROWS TO BE REVITALIZED...
...ASCOLAT MAKES A NEW DAY FOR DOCKLANDS...
than the good news which I have to impart."
Letter from Cesare Borgia to his sister Lucrezia, July 20, 1502

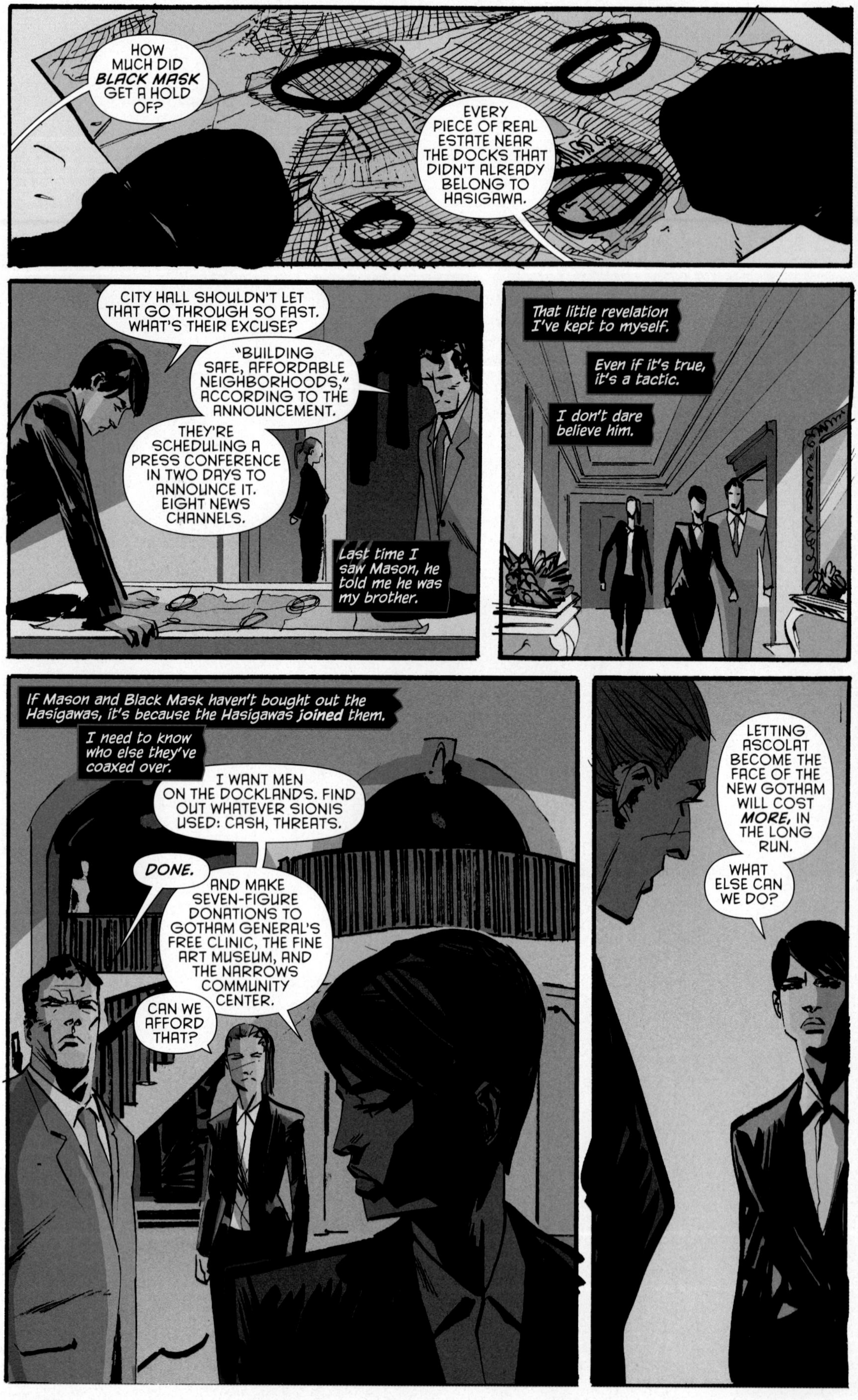
HOW MUCH DID BLACK MASK GET A HOLD OF?
EVERY PIECE OF REAL ESTATE NEAR THE DOCKS THAT DIDN'T ALREADY BELONG TO HASIGAWA.
CITY HALL SHOULDN'T LET THAT GO THROUGH SO FAST. WHAT'S THEIR EXCUSE?
"BUILDING SAFE, AFFORDABLE NEIGHBORHOODS," ACCORDING TO THE ANNOUNCEMENT.
THEY'RE SCHEDULING A PRESS CONFERENCE IN TWO DAYS TO ANNOUNCE IT. EIGHT NEWS CHANNELS.
Last time I saw Mason, he told me he was my brother.
That little revelation I've kept to myself.
Even if it's true, it's a tactic.
I don't dare believe him.
If Mason and Black Mask haven't bought out the Hasigawas, it's because the Hasigawas joined them.
I need to know who else they've coaxed over.
I WANT MEN ON THE DOCKLANDS. FIND OUT WHATEVER SIONIS USED: CASH, THREATS.
DONE.
AND MAKE SEVEN-FIGURE DONATIONS TO GOTHAM GENERAL'S FREE CLINIC, THE FINE ART MUSEUM, AND THE NARROWS COMMUNITY CENTER.
CAN WE AFFORD THAT?
LETTING ASCOLAT BECOME THE FACE OF THE NEW GOTHAM WILL COST MORE, IN THE LONG RUN.
WHAT ELSE CAN WE DO?

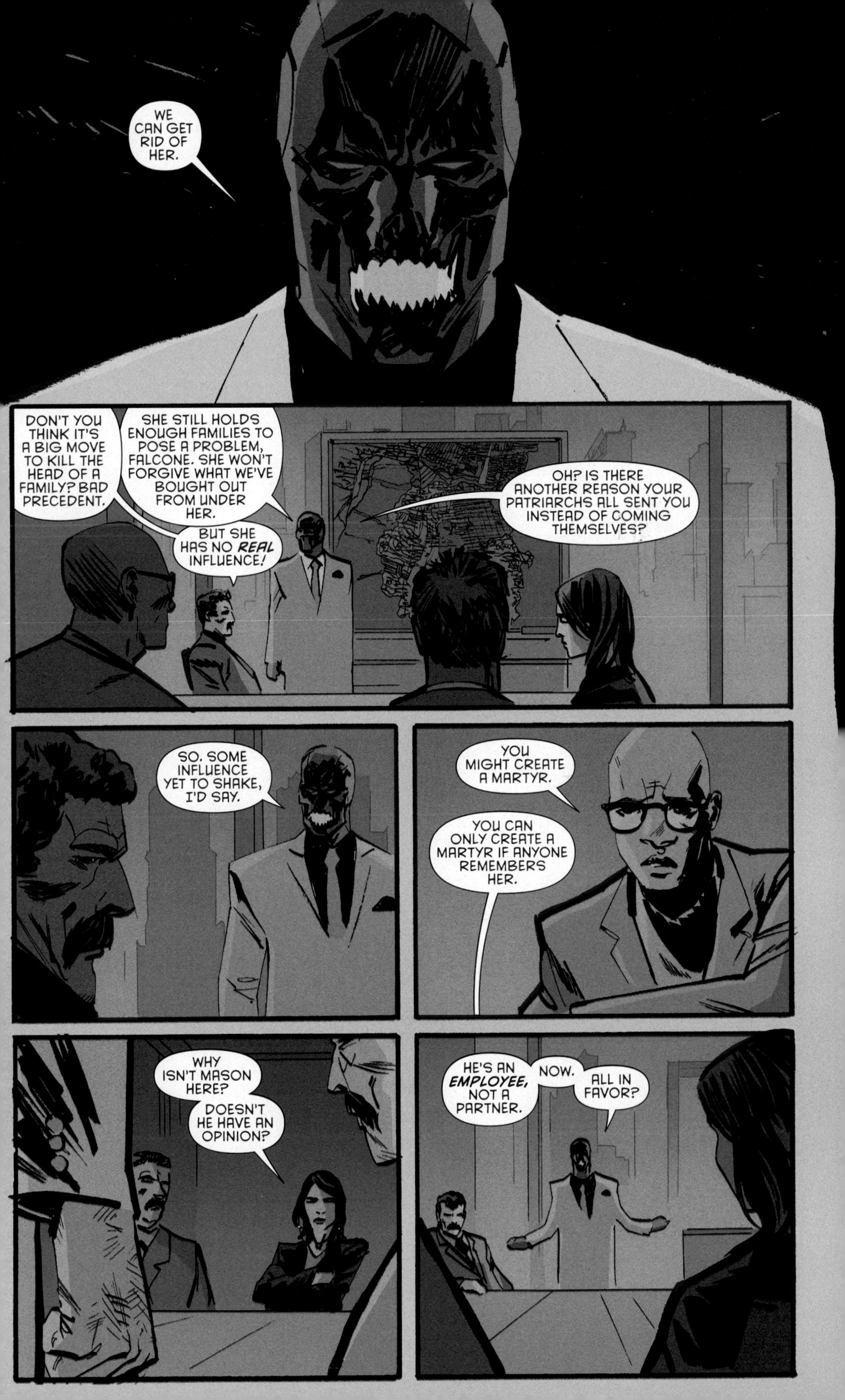
WE CAN GET RID OF HER.
DON'T YOU THINK IT'S A BIG MOVE TO KILL THE HEAD OF A FAMILY? BAD PRECEDENT.
SHE STILL HOLDS ENOUGH FAMILIES TO POSE A PROBLEM, FALCONE. SHE WON'T FORGIVE WHAT WE'VE BOUGHT OUT FROM UNDER HER.
BUT SHE HAS NO REAL INFLUENCE!
OH? IS THERE ANOTHER REASON YOUR PATRIARCHS ALL SENT YOU INSTEAD OF COMING THEMSELVES?
SO. SOME INFLUENCE YET TO SHAKE, I'D SAY.
YOU MIGHT CREATE A MARTYR.
YOU CAN ONLY CREATE A MARTYR IF ANYONE REMEMBERS HER.
WHY ISN'T MASON HERE?
DOESN'T HE HAVE AN OPINION?
HE'S AN EMPLOYEE, NOT A PARTNER.
NOW.
ALL IN FAVOR?

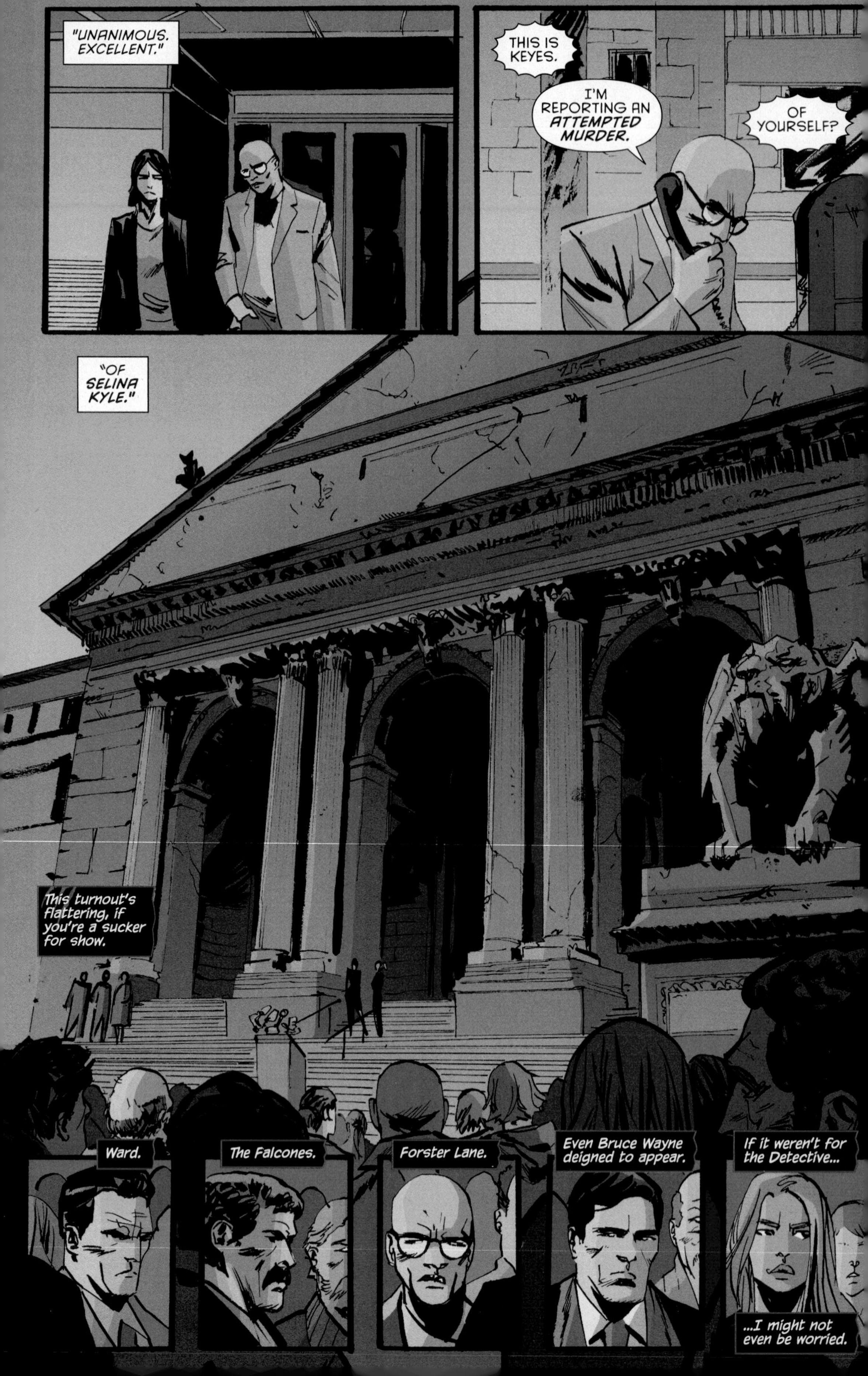
"UNANIMOUS. EXCELLENT."
THIS IS KEYES.
I'M REPORTING AN *ATTEMPTED MURDER.*
OF YOURSELF?
"OF SELINA KYLE."
This turnout's flattering, if you're a sucker for show.
Ward.
The Falcones.
Forster Lane.
Even Bruce Wayne deigned to appear.
If it weren't for the Detective...
...I might not even be worried.

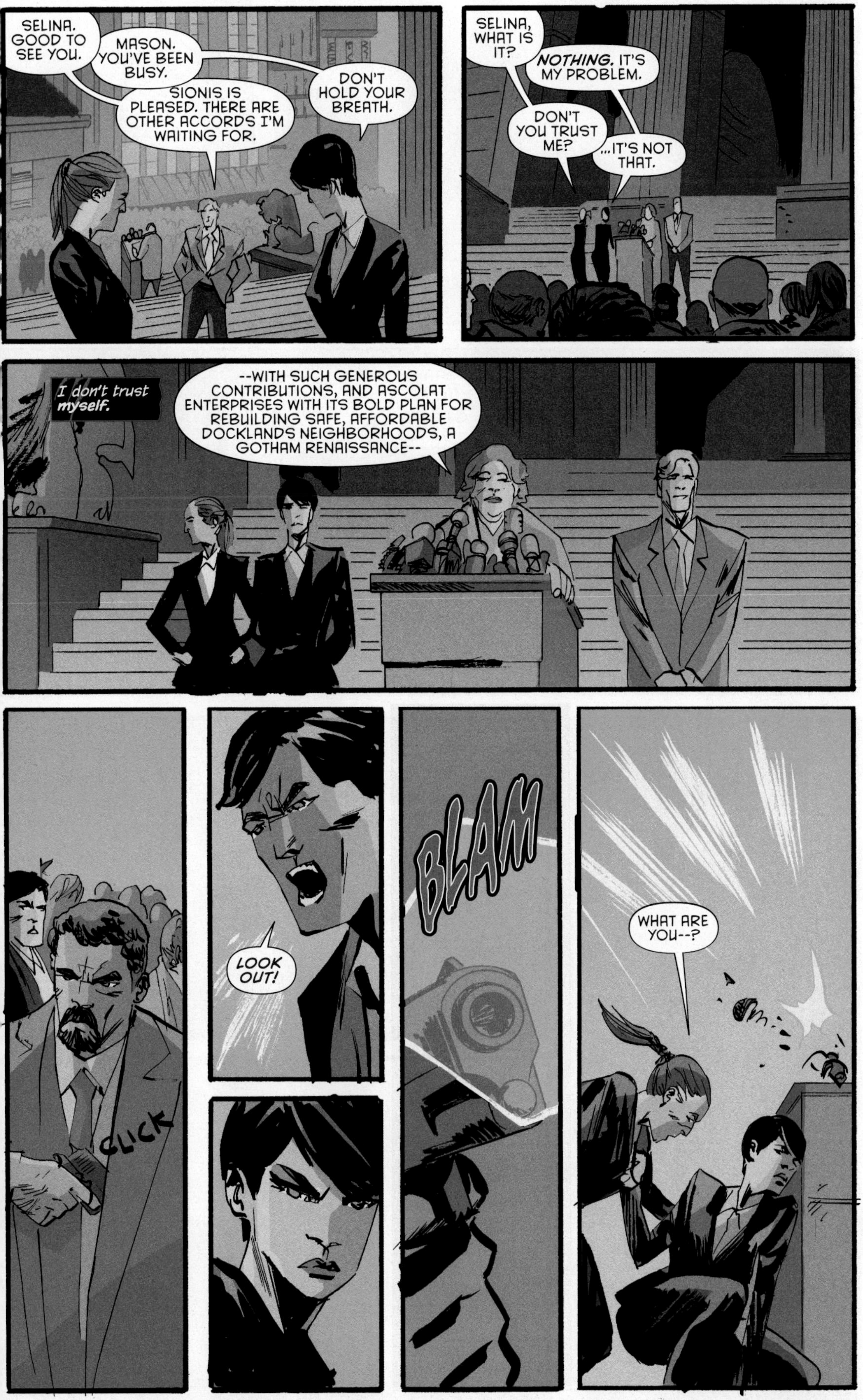
SELINA. GOOD TO SEE YOU.
MASON. YOU'VE BEEN BUSY.
SIONIS IS PLEASED. THERE ARE OTHER ACCORDS I'M WAITING FOR.
DON'T HOLD YOUR BREATH.
SELINA, WHAT IS IT?
NOTHING. IT'S MY PROBLEM.
DON'T YOU TRUST ME?
...IT'S NOT THAT.
I don't trust myself.
--WITH SUCH GENEROUS CONTRIBUTIONS, AND ASCOLAT ENTERPRISES WITH ITS BOLD PLAN FOR REBUILDING SAFE, AFFORDABLE DOCKLANDS NEIGHBORHOODS, A GOTHAM RENAISSANCE--
CLICK
LOOK OUT!
BLAM
WHAT ARE YOU--?

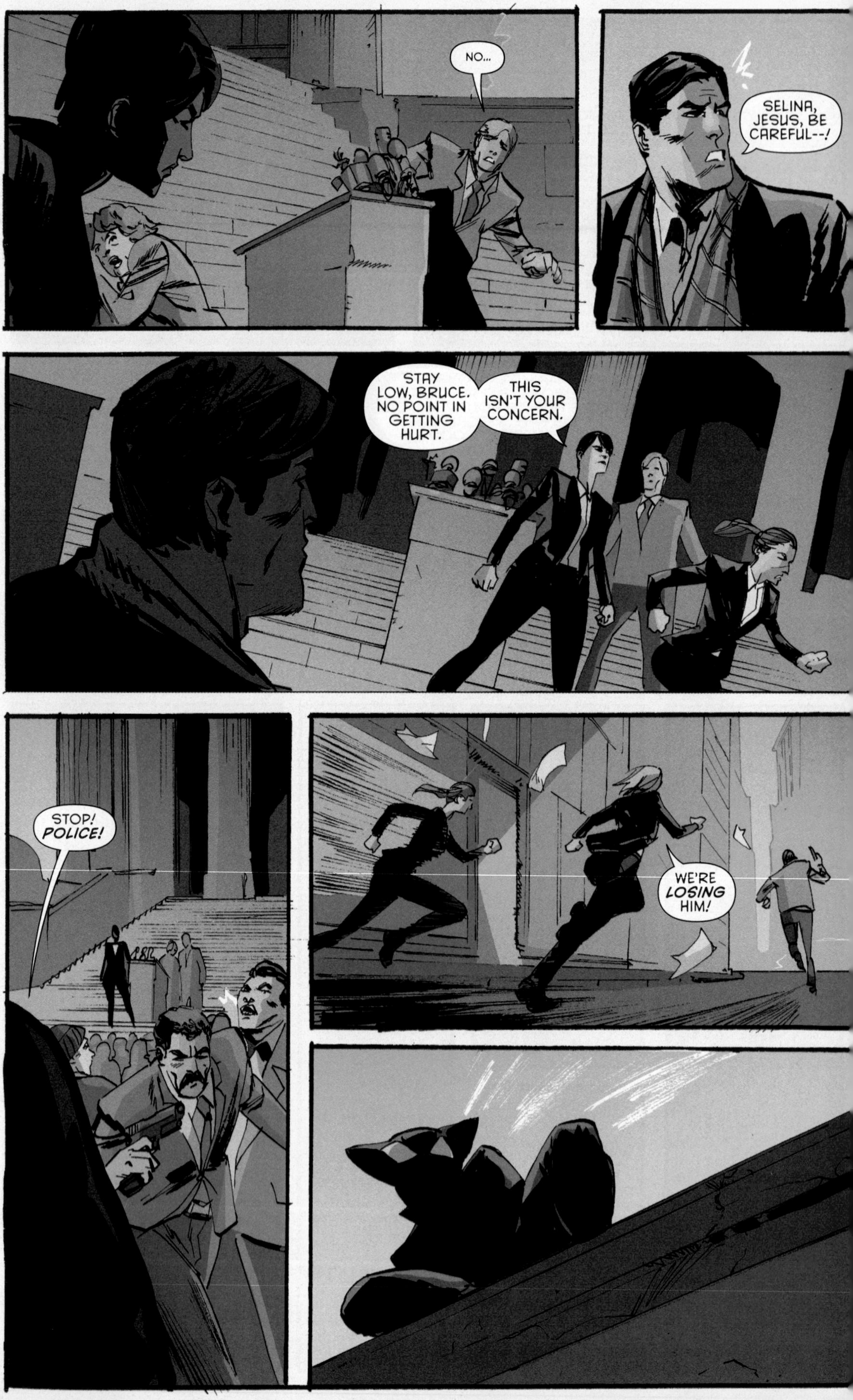
NO...
SELINA, JESUS, BE CAREFUL--!
STAY LOW, BRUCE. NO POINT IN GETTING HURT.
THIS ISN'T YOUR CONCERN.
STOP! POLICE!
WE'RE LOSING HIM!

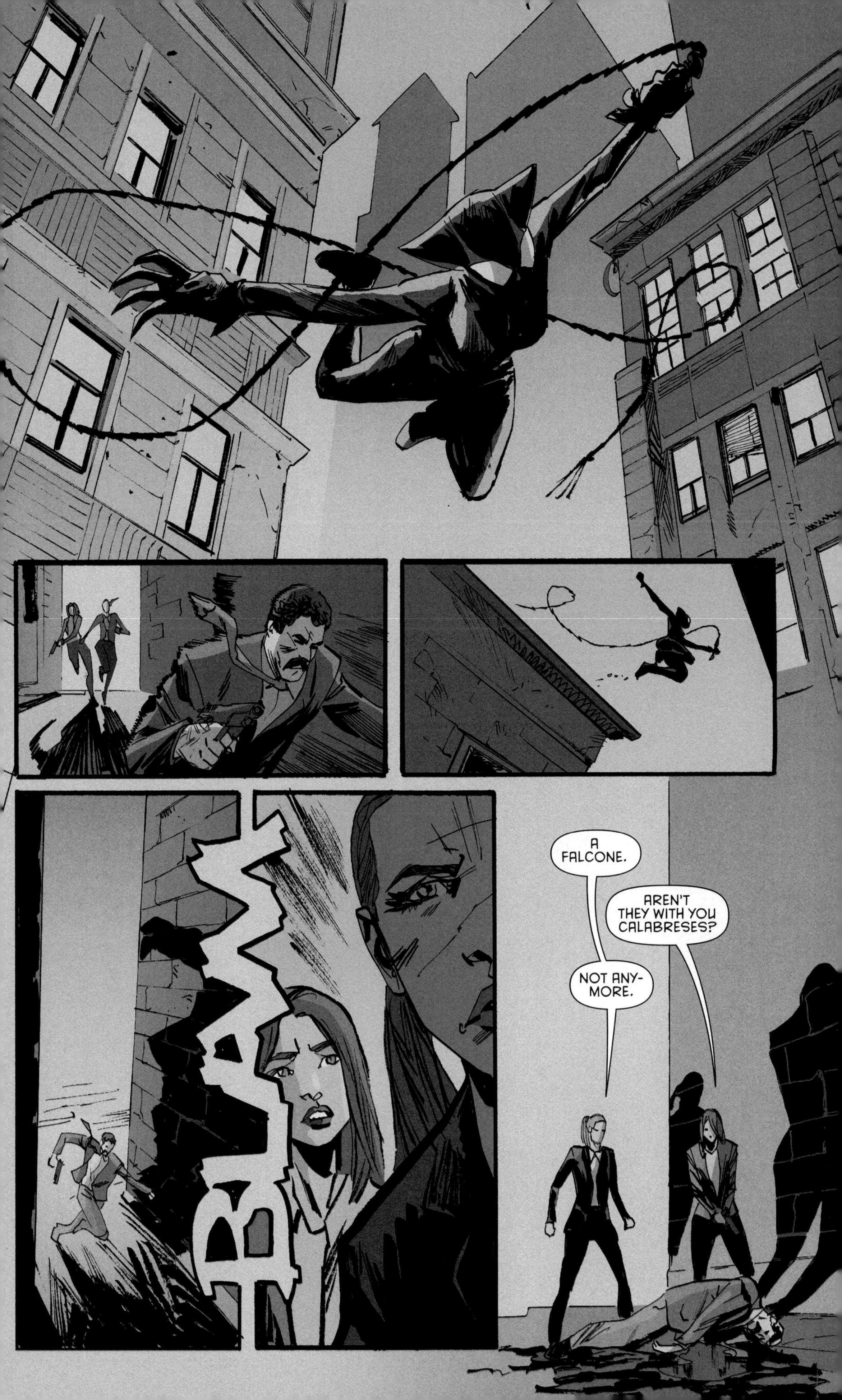
A FALCONE.
AREN'T THEY WITH YOU CALABRESES?
NOT ANY-MORE.

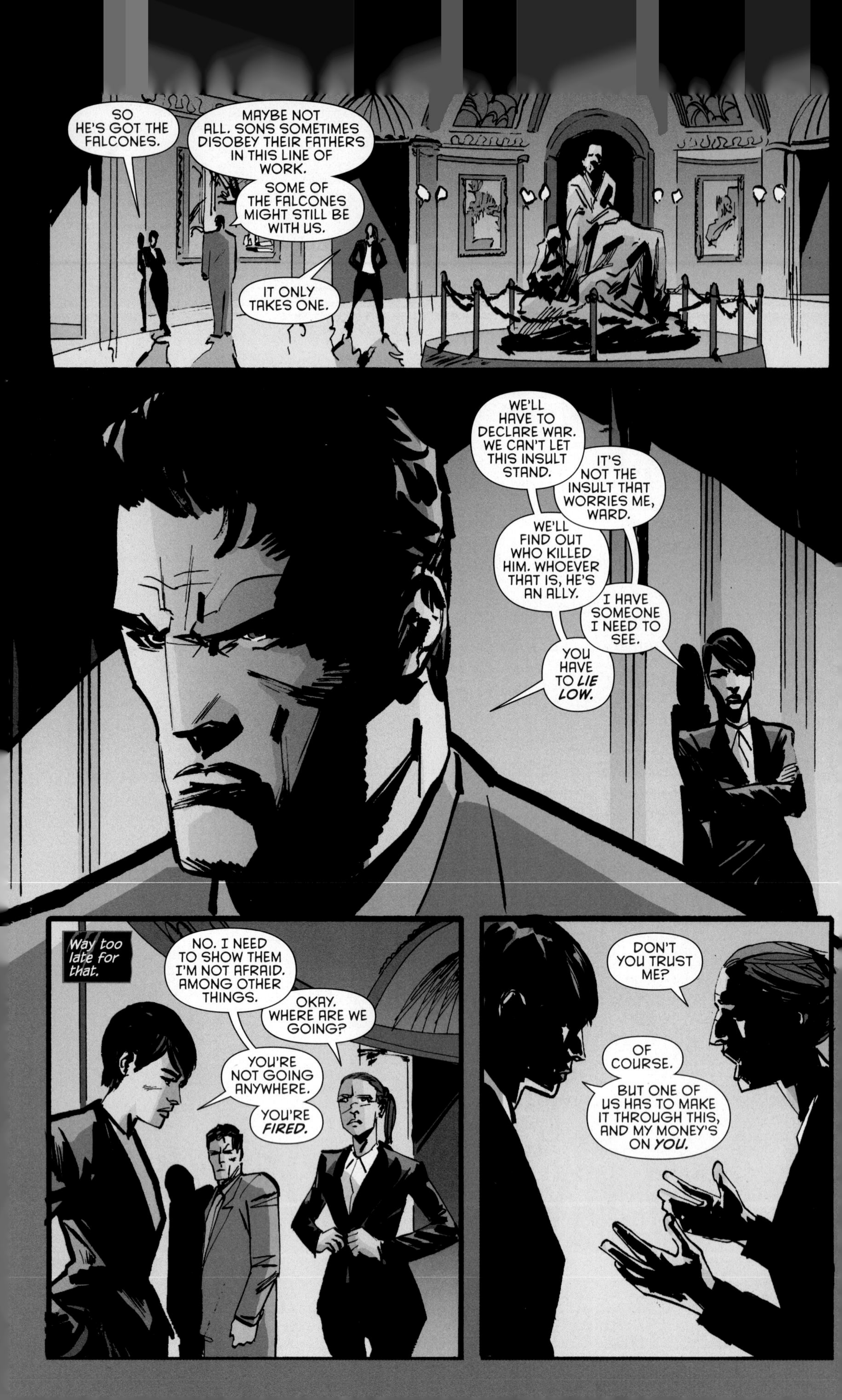

SO HE'S GOT THE FALCONES.
MAYBE NOT ALL. SONS SOMETIMES DISOBEY THEIR FATHERS IN THIS LINE OF WORK.
SOME OF THE FALCONES MIGHT STILL BE WITH US.
IT ONLY TAKES ONE.
WE'LL HAVE TO DECLARE WAR. WE CAN'T LET THIS INSULT STAND.
IT'S NOT THE INSULT THAT WORRIES ME, WARD.
WE'LL FIND OUT WHO KILLED HIM. WHOEVER THAT IS, HE'S AN ALLY.
I HAVE SOMEONE I NEED TO SEE.
YOU HAVE TO *LIE LOW.*
Way too late for that.
NO. I NEED TO SHOW THEM I'M NOT AFRAID. AMONG OTHER THINGS.
OKAY. WHERE ARE WE GOING?
YOU'RE NOT GOING ANYWHERE.
YOU'RE *FIRED.*
DON'T YOU TRUST ME?
OF COURSE.
BUT ONE OF US HAS TO MAKE IT THROUGH THIS, AND MY MONEY'S ON *YOU.*

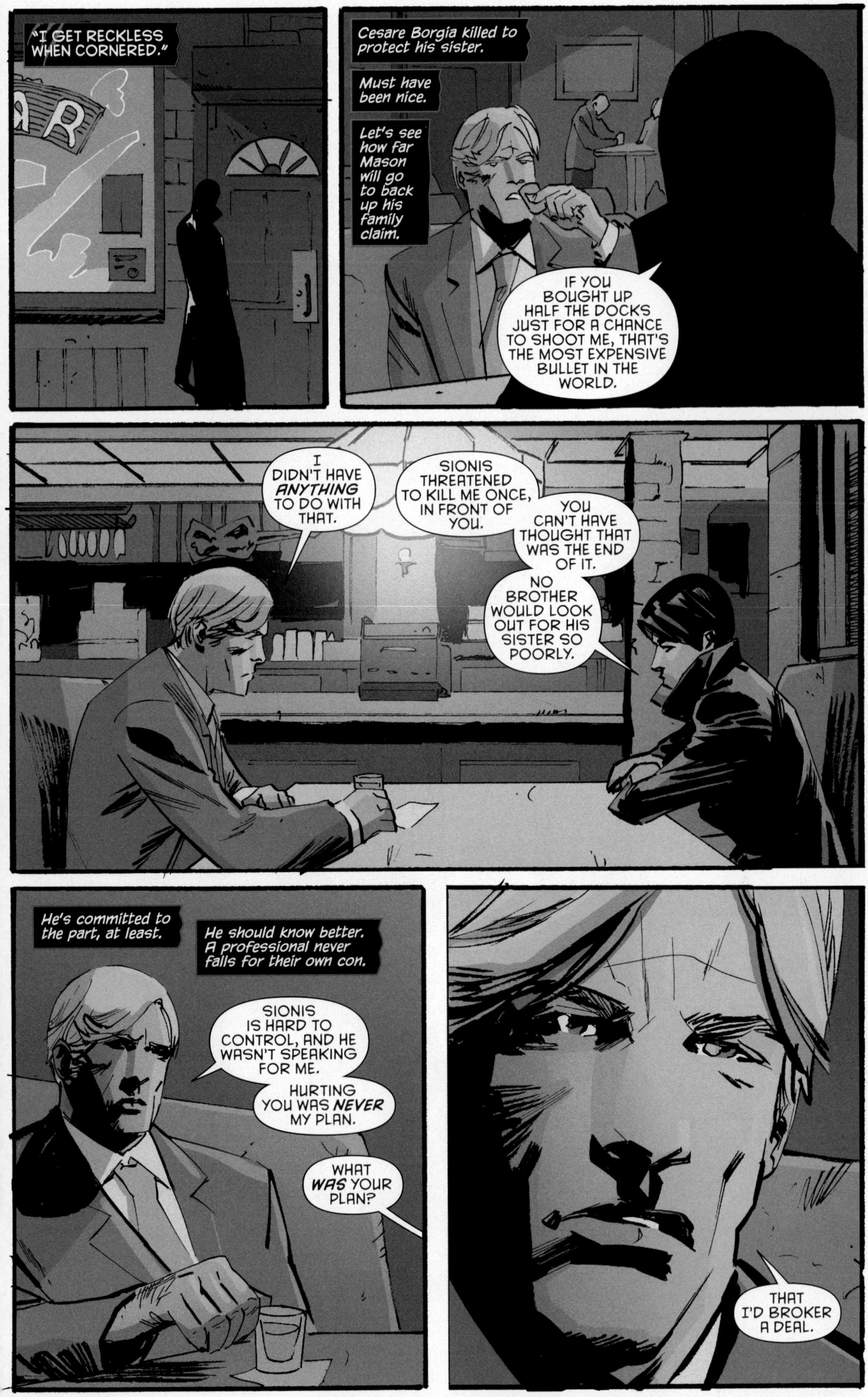
"I GET RECKLESS WHEN CORNERED."
Cesare Borgia killed to protect his sister.
Must have been nice.
Let's see how far Mason will go to back up his family claim.
IF YOU BOUGHT UP HALF THE DOCKS JUST FOR A CHANCE TO SHOOT ME, THAT'S THE MOST EXPENSIVE BULLET IN THE WORLD.
I DIDN'T HAVE ANYTHING TO DO WITH THAT.
SIONIS THREATENED TO KILL ME ONCE, IN FRONT OF YOU.
YOU CAN'T HAVE THOUGHT THAT WAS THE END OF IT.
NO BROTHER WOULD LOOK OUT FOR HIS SISTER SO POORLY.
He's committed to the part, at least.
He should know better. A professional never falls for their own con.
SIONIS IS HARD TO CONTROL, AND HE WASN'T SPEAKING FOR ME.
HURTING YOU WAS NEVER MY PLAN.
WHAT WAS YOUR PLAN?
THAT I'D BROKER A DEAL.

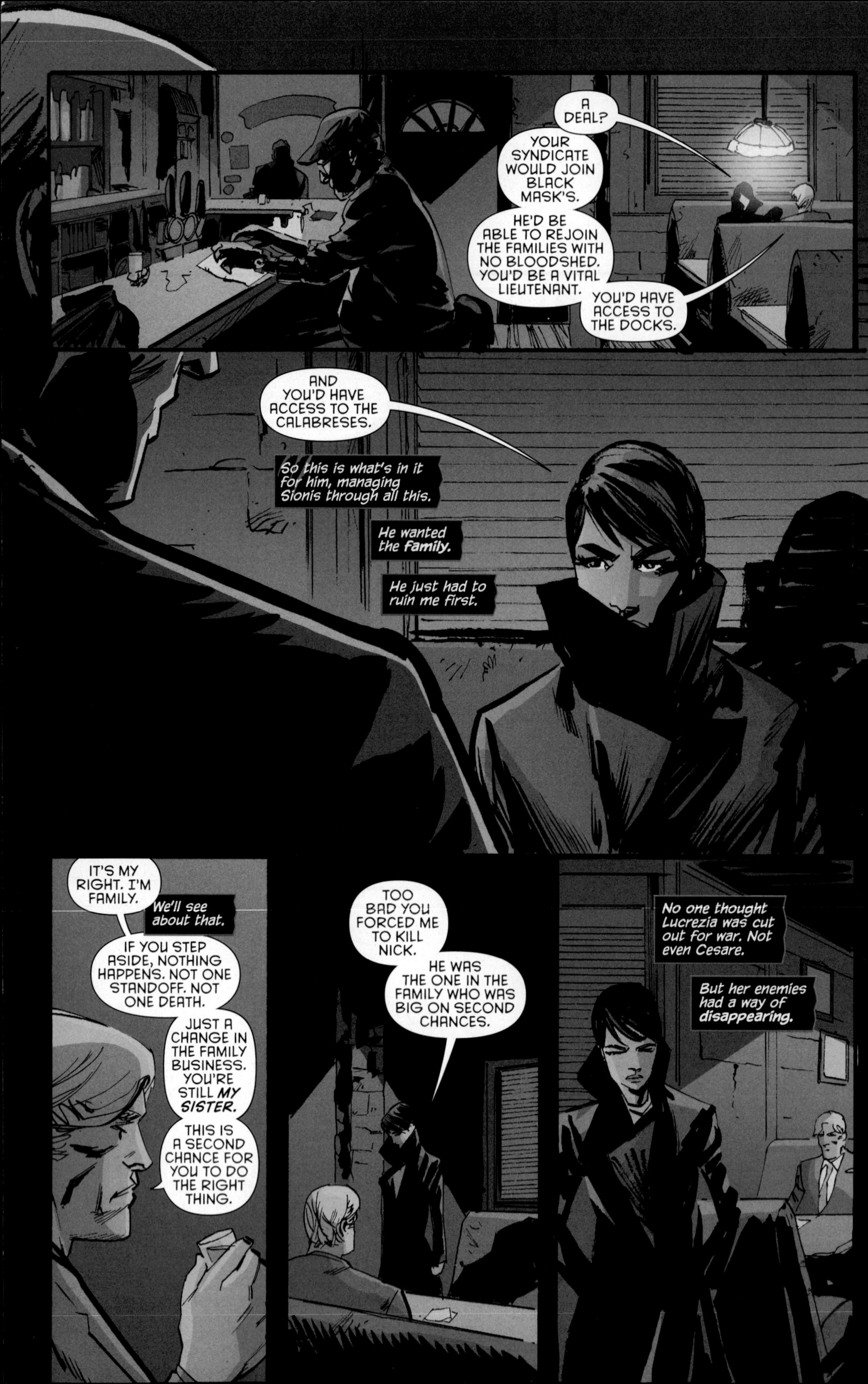
A DEAL?
YOUR SYNDICATE WOULD JOIN BLACK MASK'S.
HE'D BE ABLE TO REJOIN THE FAMILIES WITH NO BLOODSHED. YOU'D BE A VITAL LIEUTENANT.
YOU'D HAVE ACCESS TO THE DOCKS.
AND YOU'D HAVE ACCESS TO THE CALABRESES.
So this is what's in it for him, managing Sionis through all this.
He wanted the family.
He just had to ruin me first.
IT'S MY RIGHT. I'M FAMILY.
We'll see about that.
IF YOU STEP ASIDE, NOTHING HAPPENS. NOT ONE STANDOFF. NOT ONE DEATH.
JUST A CHANGE IN THE FAMILY BUSINESS. YOU'RE STILL MY SISTER.
THIS IS A SECOND CHANCE FOR YOU TO DO THE RIGHT THING.
TOO BAD YOU FORCED ME TO KILL NICK.
HE WAS THE ONE IN THE FAMILY WHO WAS BIG ON SECOND CHANCES.
No one thought Lucrezia was cut out for war. Not even Cesare.
But her enemies had a way of disappearing.

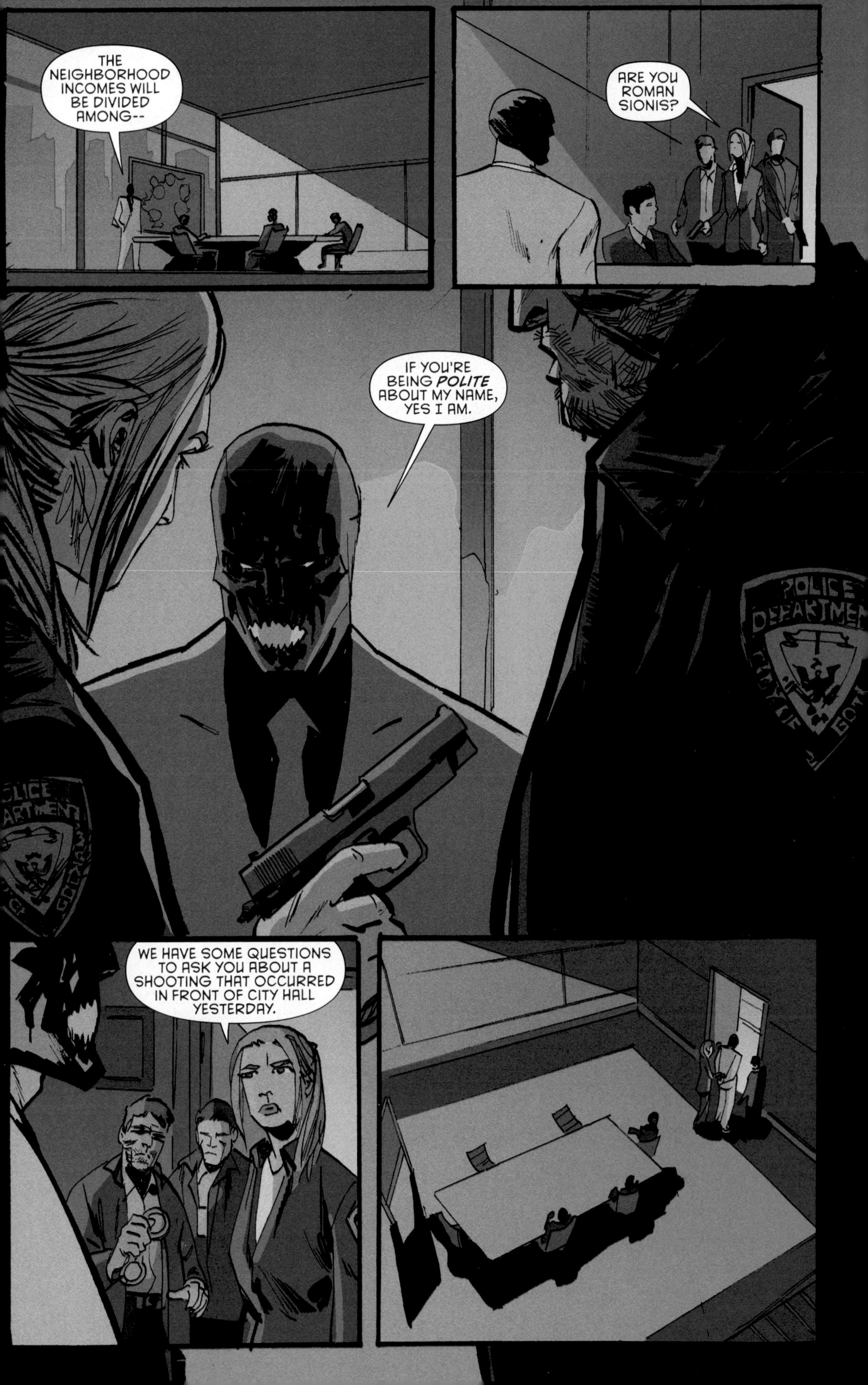
THE NEIGHBORHOOD INCOMES WILL BE DIVIDED AMONG--
ARE YOU ROMAN SIONIS?
IF YOU'RE BEING *POLITE* ABOUT MY NAME, YES I AM.
POLICE DEPARTMENT
WE HAVE SOME QUESTIONS TO ASK YOU ABOUT A SHOOTING THAT OCCURRED IN FRONT OF CITY HALL YESTERDAY.

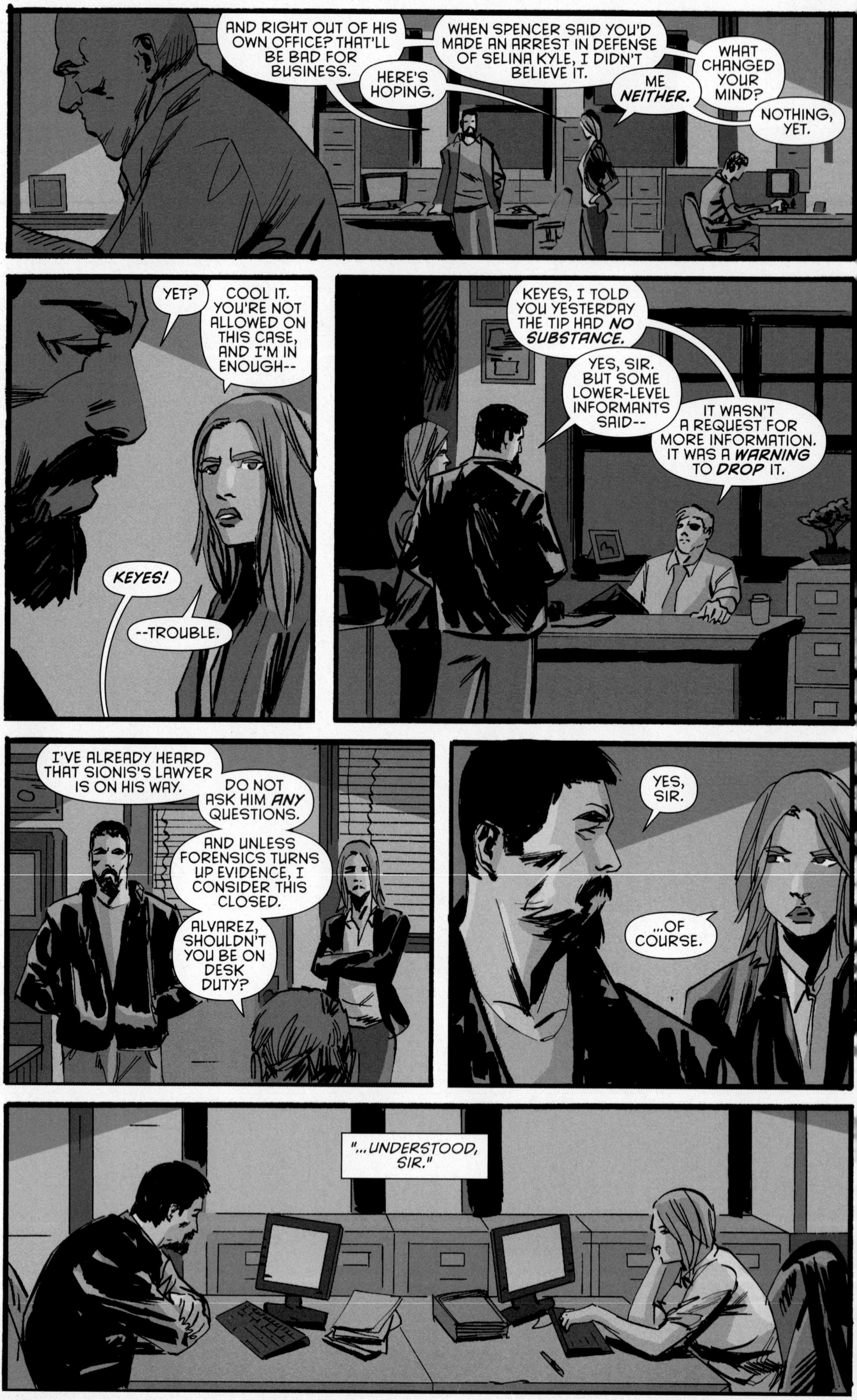
AND RIGHT OUT OF HIS OWN OFFICE? THAT'LL BE BAD FOR BUSINESS.
HERE'S HOPING.
WHEN SPENCER SAID YOU'D MADE AN ARREST IN DEFENSE OF SELINA KYLE, I DIDN'T BELIEVE IT.
ME NEITHER.
WHAT CHANGED YOUR MIND?
NOTHING, YET.
YET?
COOL IT. YOU'RE NOT ALLOWED ON THIS CASE, AND I'M IN ENOUGH--
KEYES!
--TROUBLE.
KEYES, I TOLD YOU YESTERDAY THE TIP HAD NO SUBSTANCE.
YES, SIR. BUT SOME LOWER-LEVEL INFORMANTS SAID--
IT WASN'T A REQUEST FOR MORE INFORMATION. IT WAS A WARNING TO DROP IT.
I'VE ALREADY HEARD THAT SIONIS'S LAWYER IS ON HIS WAY.
DO NOT ASK HIM ANY QUESTIONS.
AND UNLESS FORENSICS TURNS UP EVIDENCE, I CONSIDER THIS CLOSED.
ALVAREZ, SHOULDN'T YOU BE ON DESK DUTY?
YES, SIR.
...OF COURSE.
"...UNDERSTOOD, SIR."

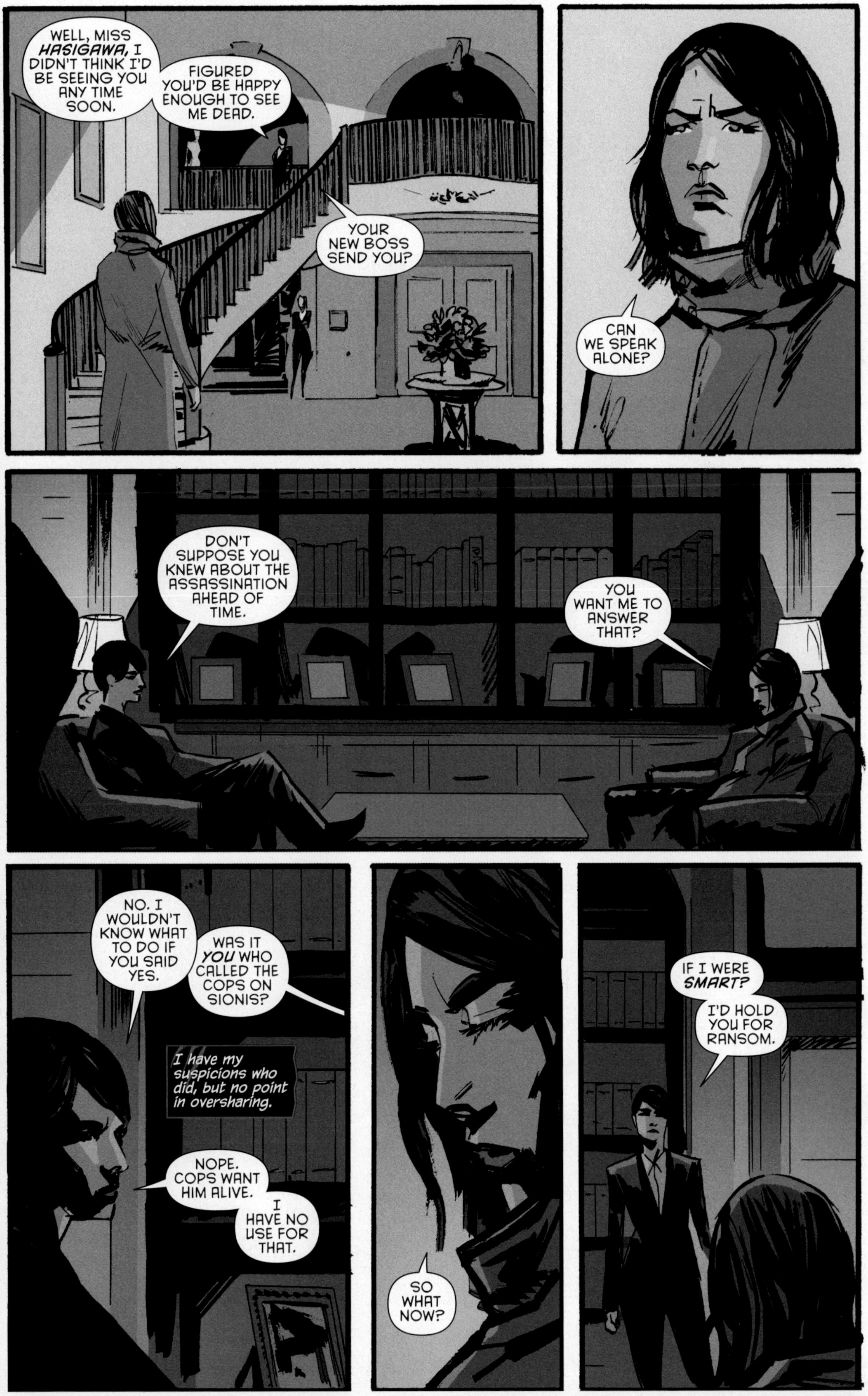
WELL, MISS HASIGAWA, I DIDN'T THINK I'D BE SEEING YOU ANY TIME SOON.
FIGURED YOU'D BE HAPPY ENOUGH TO SEE ME DEAD.
YOUR NEW BOSS SEND YOU?
CAN WE SPEAK ALONE?
DON'T SUPPOSE YOU KNEW ABOUT THE ASSASSINATION AHEAD OF TIME.
YOU WANT ME TO ANSWER THAT?
NO. I WOULDN'T KNOW WHAT TO DO IF YOU SAID YES.
WAS IT YOU WHO CALLED THE COPS ON SIONIS?
I have my suspicions who did, but no point in oversharing.
NOPE. COPS WANT HIM ALIVE.
I HAVE NO USE FOR THAT.
SO WHAT NOW?
IF I WERE SMART?
I'D HOLD YOU FOR RANSOM.

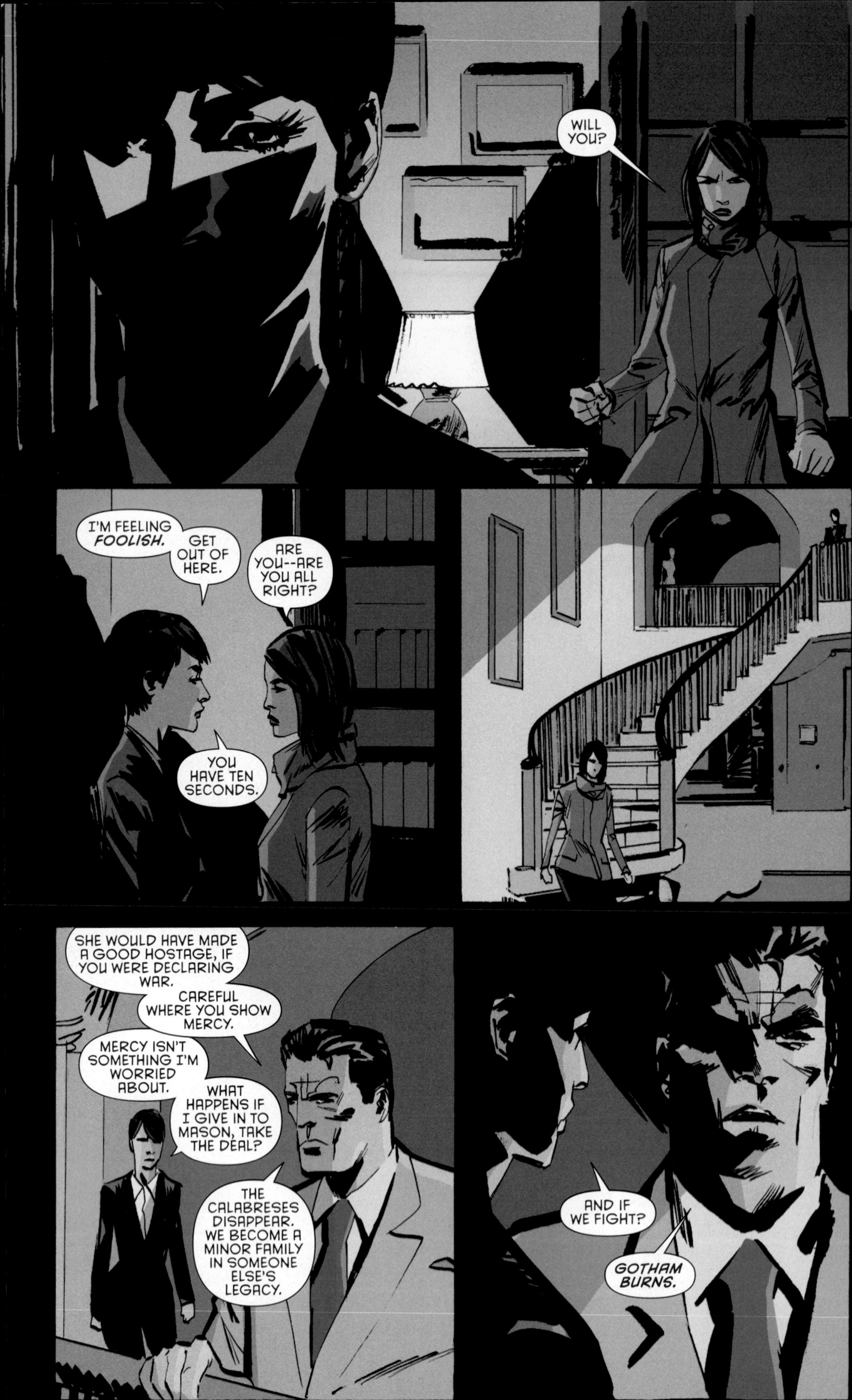
WILL YOU?
I'M FEELING *FOOLISH.*
GET OUT OF HERE.
ARE YOU--ARE YOU ALL RIGHT?
YOU HAVE TEN SECONDS.
SHE WOULD HAVE MADE A GOOD HOSTAGE, IF YOU WERE DECLARING WAR.
CAREFUL WHERE YOU SHOW MERCY.
MERCY ISN'T SOMETHING I'M WORRIED ABOUT.
WHAT HAPPENS IF I GIVE IN TO MASON, TAKE THE DEAL?
THE CALABRESES DISAPPEAR. WE BECOME A MINOR FAMILY IN SOMEONE ELSE'S LEGACY.
AND IF WE FIGHT?
GOTHAM BURNS.

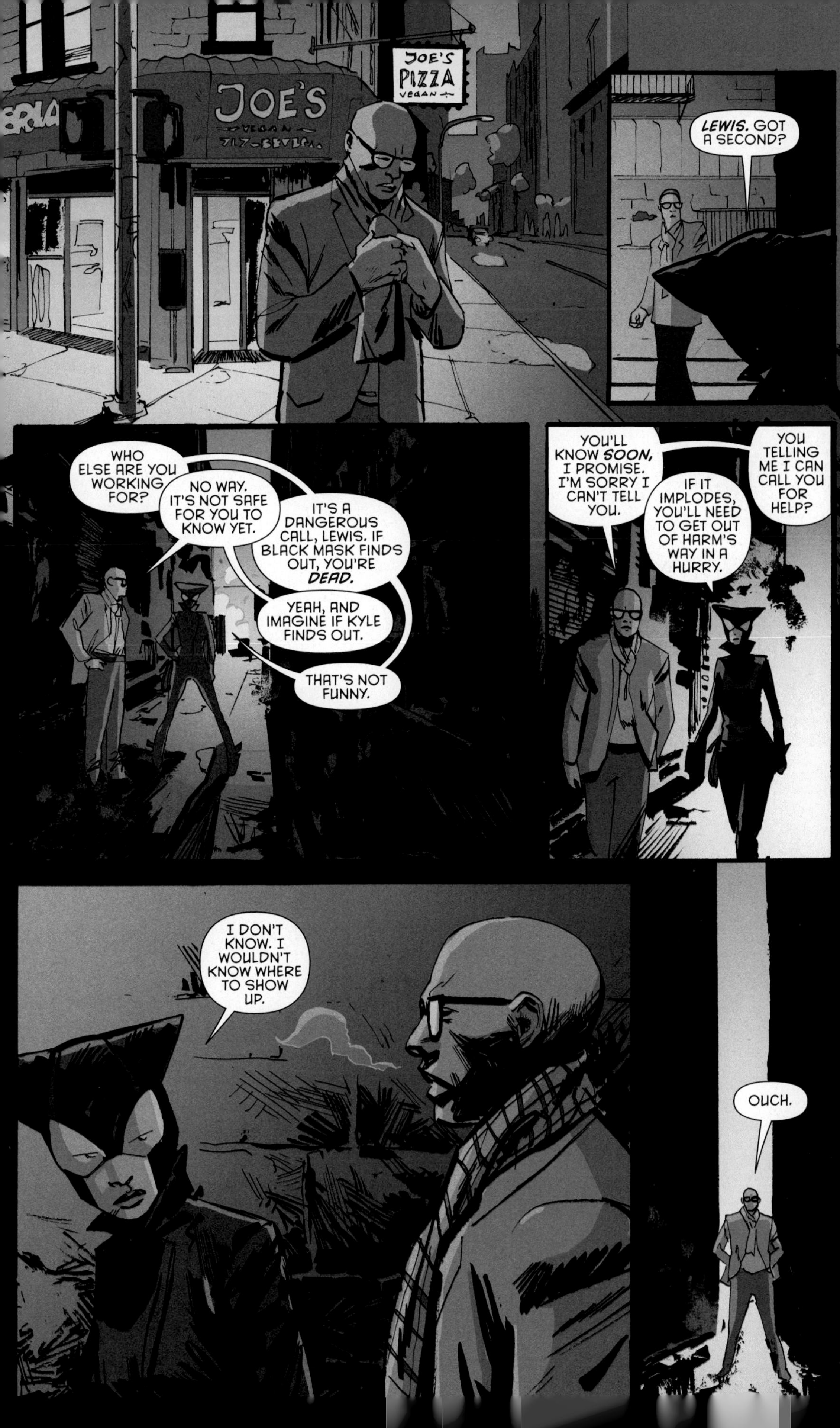
JOE'S PIZZA VEGAN
JOE'S
LEWIS. GOT A SECOND?
WHO ELSE ARE YOU WORKING FOR?
NO WAY. IT'S NOT SAFE FOR YOU TO KNOW YET.
IT'S A DANGEROUS CALL, LEWIS. IF BLACK MASK FINDS OUT, YOU'RE DEAD.
YEAH, AND IMAGINE IF KYLE FINDS OUT.
THAT'S NOT FUNNY.
YOU'LL KNOW SOON, I PROMISE. I'M SORRY I CAN'T TELL YOU.
IF IT IMPLODES, YOU'LL NEED TO GET OUT OF HARM'S WAY IN A HURRY.
YOU TELLING ME I CAN CALL YOU FOR HELP?
I DON'T KNOW. I WOULDN'T KNOW WHERE TO SHOW UP.
OUCH.

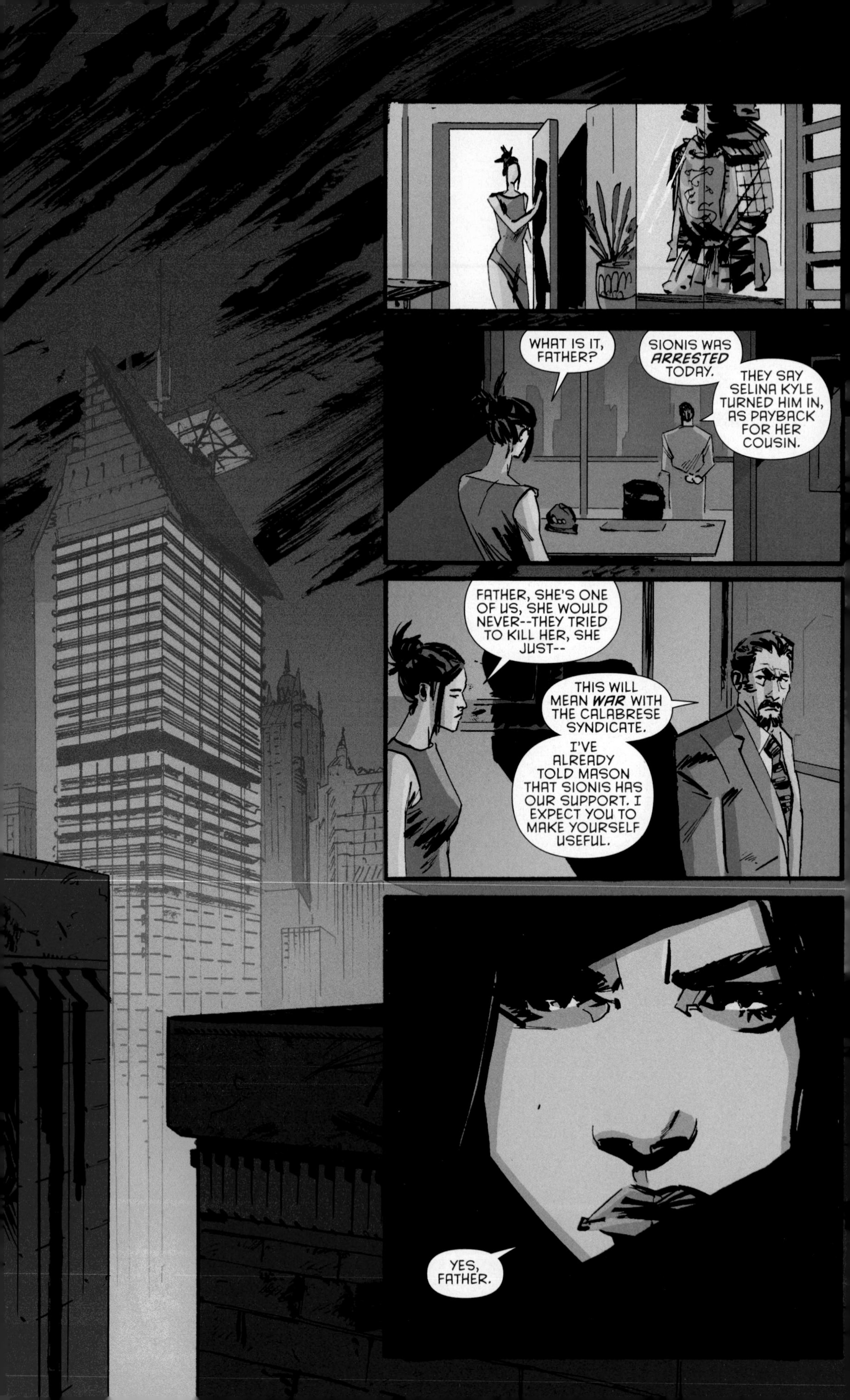
WHAT IS IT, FATHER?
SIONIS WAS ARRESTED TODAY.
THEY SAY SELINA KYLE TURNED HIM IN, AS PAYBACK FOR HER COUSIN.
FATHER, SHE'S ONE OF US, SHE WOULD NEVER--THEY TRIED TO KILL HER, SHE JUST--
THIS WILL MEAN WAR WITH THE CALABRESE SYNDICATE.
I'VE ALREADY TOLD MASON THAT SIONIS HAS OUR SUPPORT. I EXPECT YOU TO MAKE YOURSELF USEFUL.
YES, FATHER.

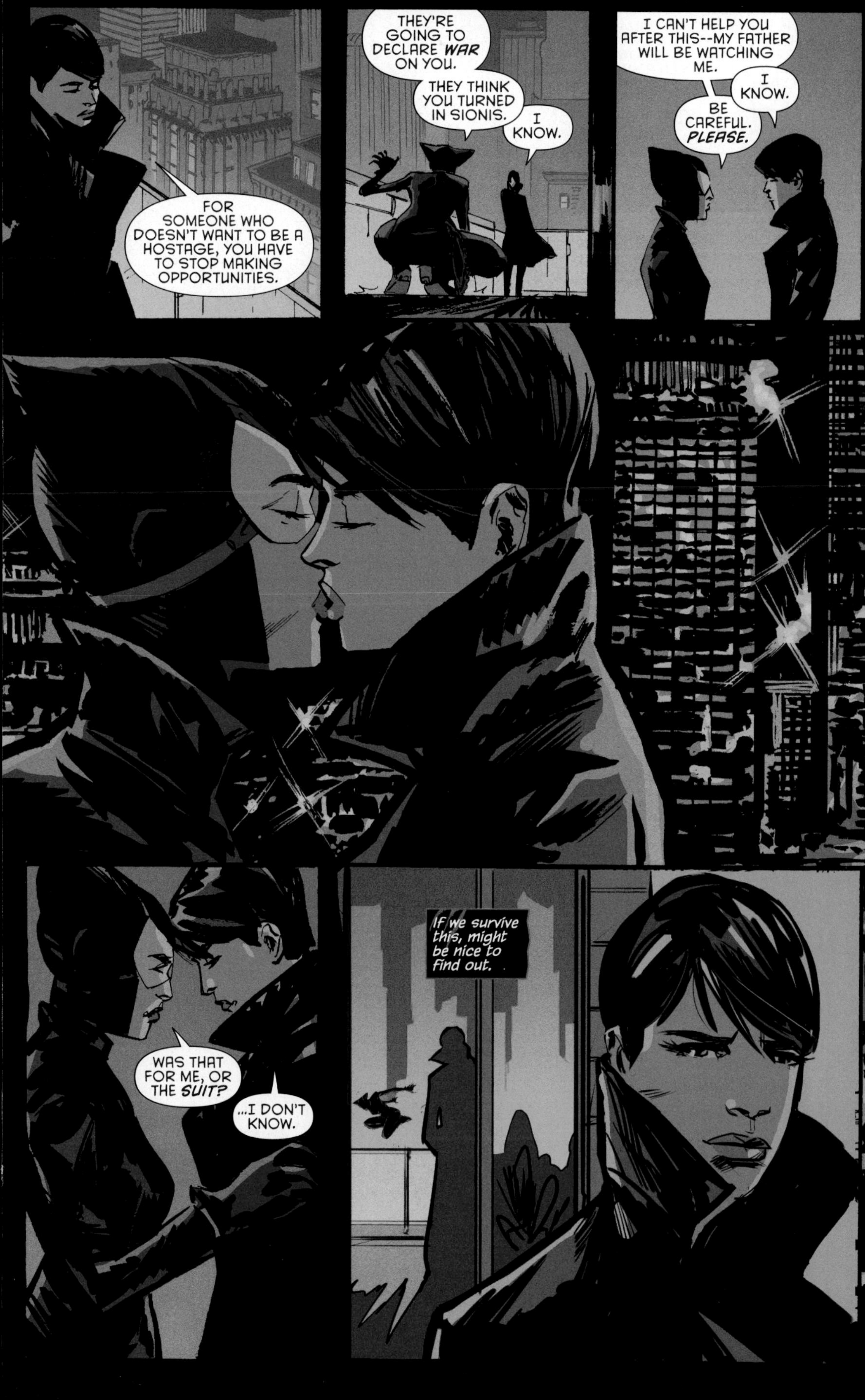

FOR SOMEONE WHO DOESN'T WANT TO BE A HOSTAGE, YOU HAVE TO STOP MAKING OPPORTUNITIES.
THEY'RE GOING TO DECLARE WAR ON YOU.
THEY THINK YOU TURNED IN SIONIS.
I KNOW.
I CAN'T HELP YOU AFTER THIS--MY FATHER WILL BE WATCHING ME.
I KNOW.
BE CAREFUL. PLEASE.
WAS THAT FOR ME, OR THE SUIT?
...I DON'T KNOW.
If we survive this, might be nice to find out.

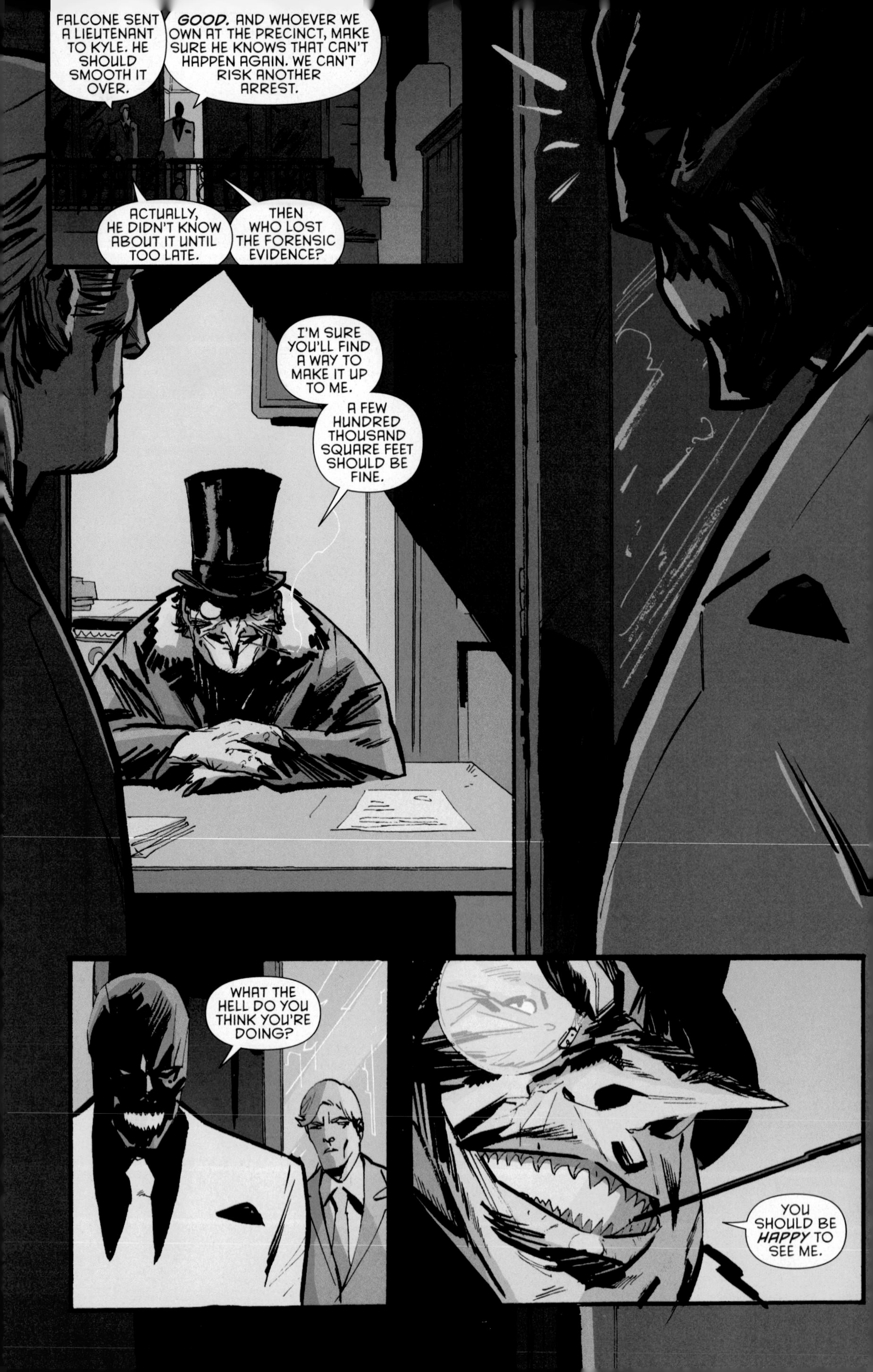
FALCONE SENT A LIEUTENANT TO KYLE. HE SHOULD SMOOTH IT OVER.
GOOD. AND WHOEVER WE OWN AT THE PRECINCT, MAKE SURE HE KNOWS THAT CAN'T HAPPEN AGAIN. WE CAN'T RISK ANOTHER ARREST.
ACTUALLY, HE DIDN'T KNOW ABOUT IT UNTIL TOO LATE.
THEN WHO LOST THE FORENSIC EVIDENCE?
I'M SURE YOU'LL FIND A WAY TO MAKE IT UP TO ME.
A FEW HUNDRED THOUSAND SQUARE FEET SHOULD BE FINE.
WHAT THE HELL DO YOU THINK YOU'RE DOING?
YOU SHOULD BE HAPPY TO SEE ME.

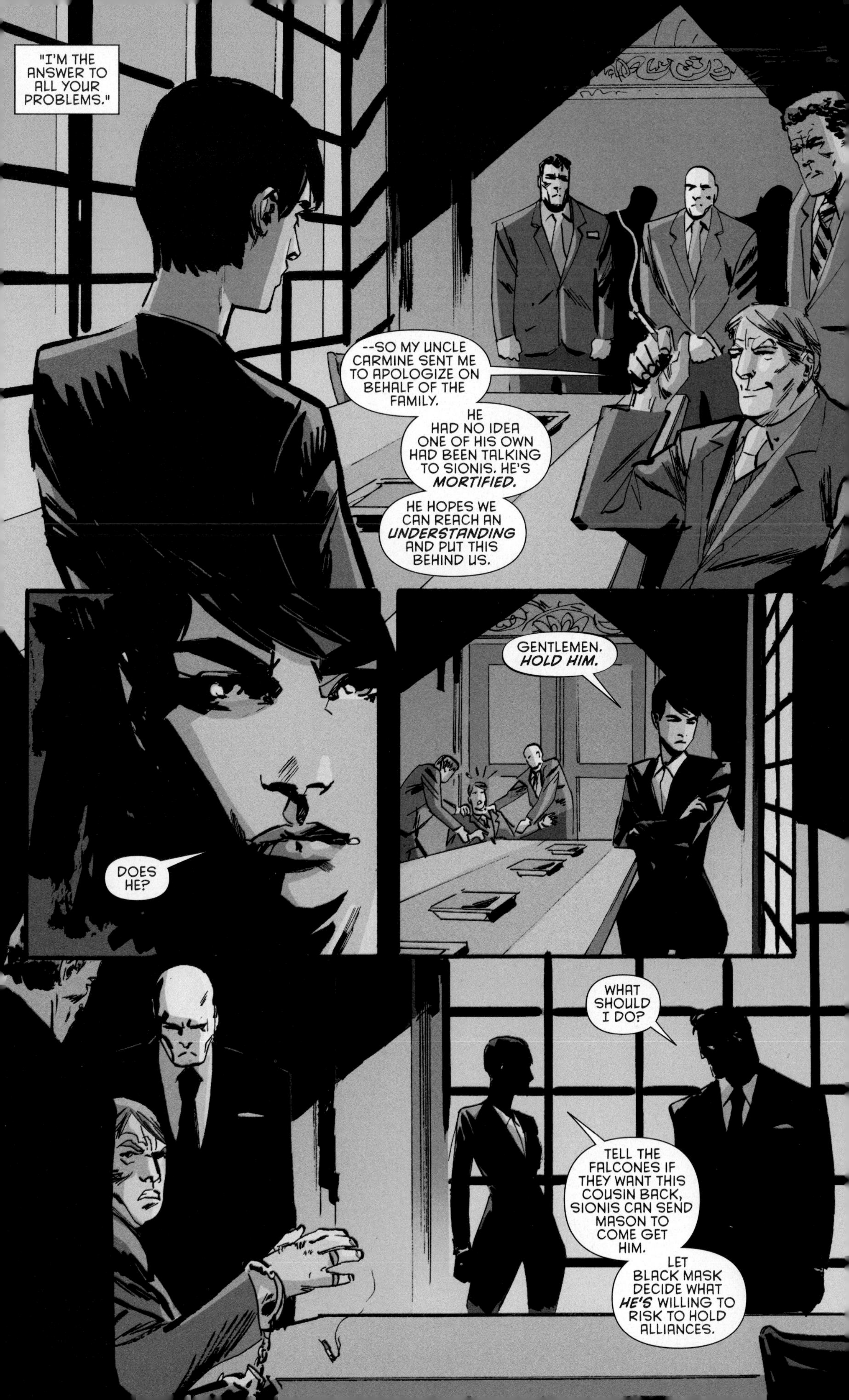
"I'M THE ANSWER TO ALL YOUR PROBLEMS."
--SO MY UNCLE CARMINE SENT ME TO APOLOGIZE ON BEHALF OF THE FAMILY.
HE HAD NO IDEA ONE OF HIS OWN HAD BEEN TALKING TO SIONIS. HE'S MORTIFIED.
HE HOPES WE CAN REACH AN UNDERSTANDING AND PUT THIS BEHIND US.
DOES HE?
GENTLEMEN. HOLD HIM.
WHAT SHOULD I DO?
TELL THE FALCONES IF THEY WANT THIS COUSIN BACK, SIONIS CAN SEND MASON TO COME GET HIM.
LET BLACK MASK DECIDE WHAT HE'S WILLING TO RISK TO HOLD ALLIANCES.

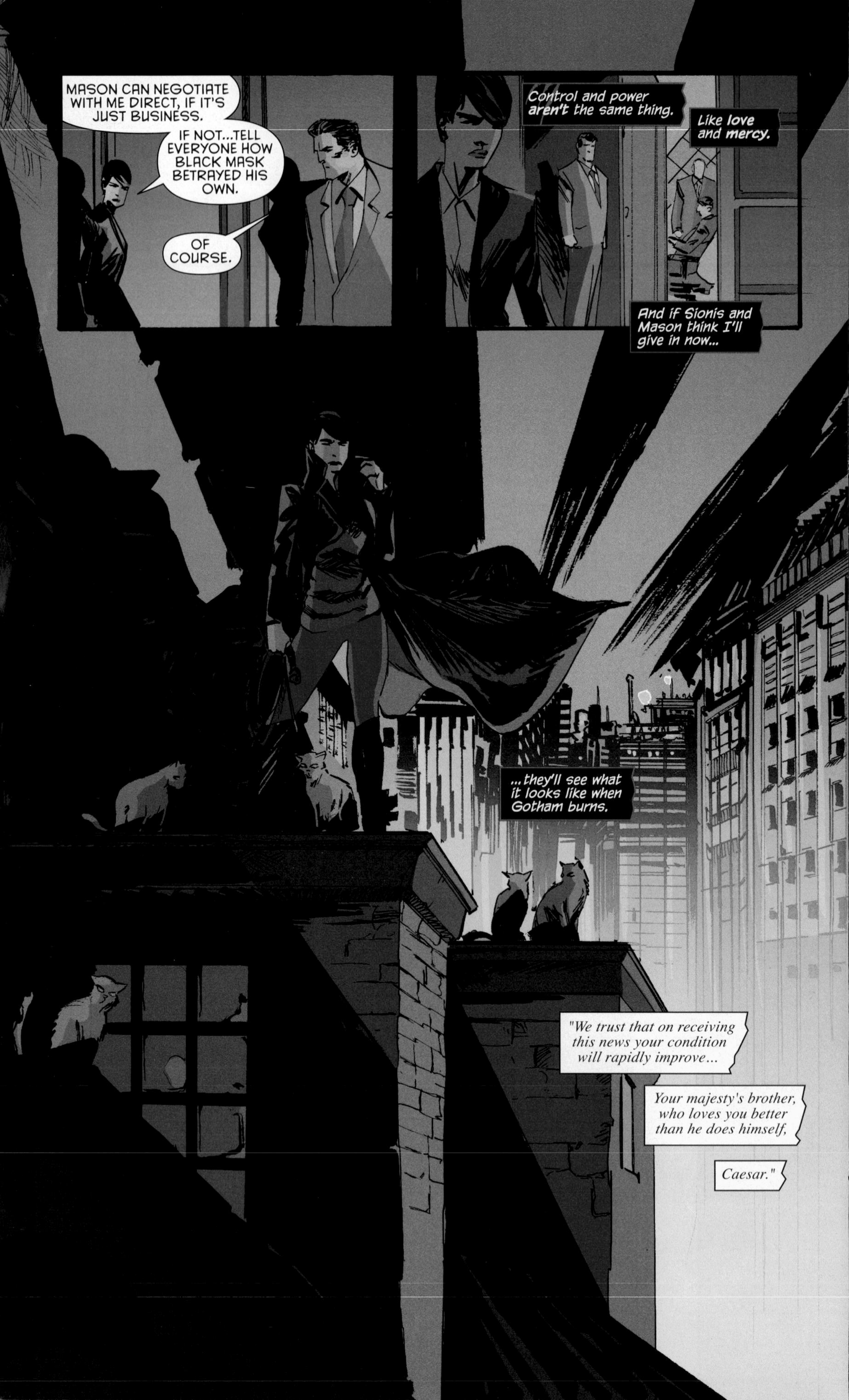

MASON CAN NEGOTIATE WITH ME DIRECT, IF IT'S JUST BUSINESS.
IF NOT...TELL EVERYONE HOW BLACK MASK BETRAYED HIS OWN.
OF COURSE.
Control and power **aren't** the same thing.
Like **love** and **mercy.**
And if Sionis and Mason think I'll give in now...
...they'll see what it looks like when Gotham burns.
"We trust that on receiving this news your condition will rapidly improve...
Your majesty's brother, who loves you better than he does himself,
Caesar."

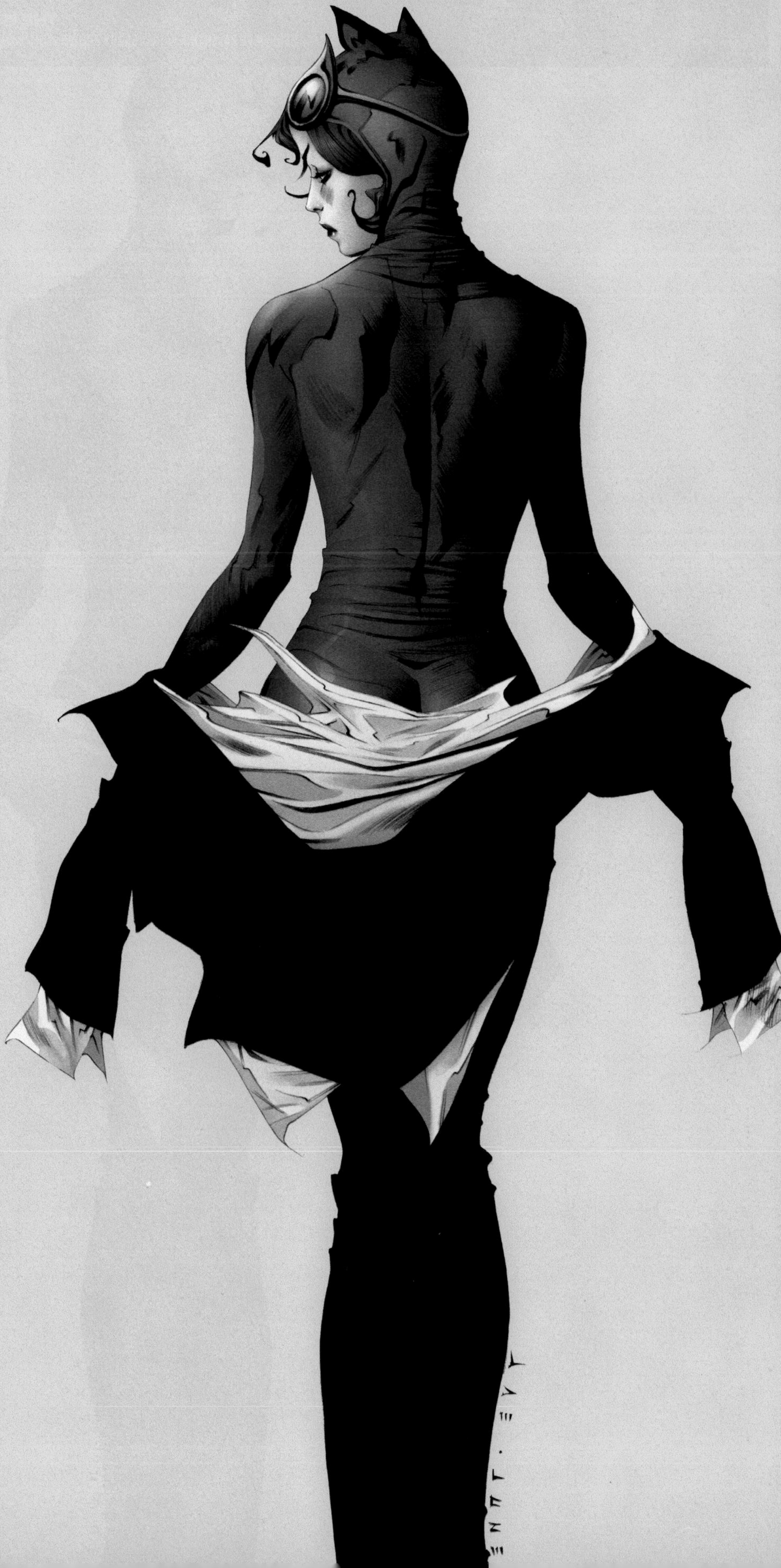

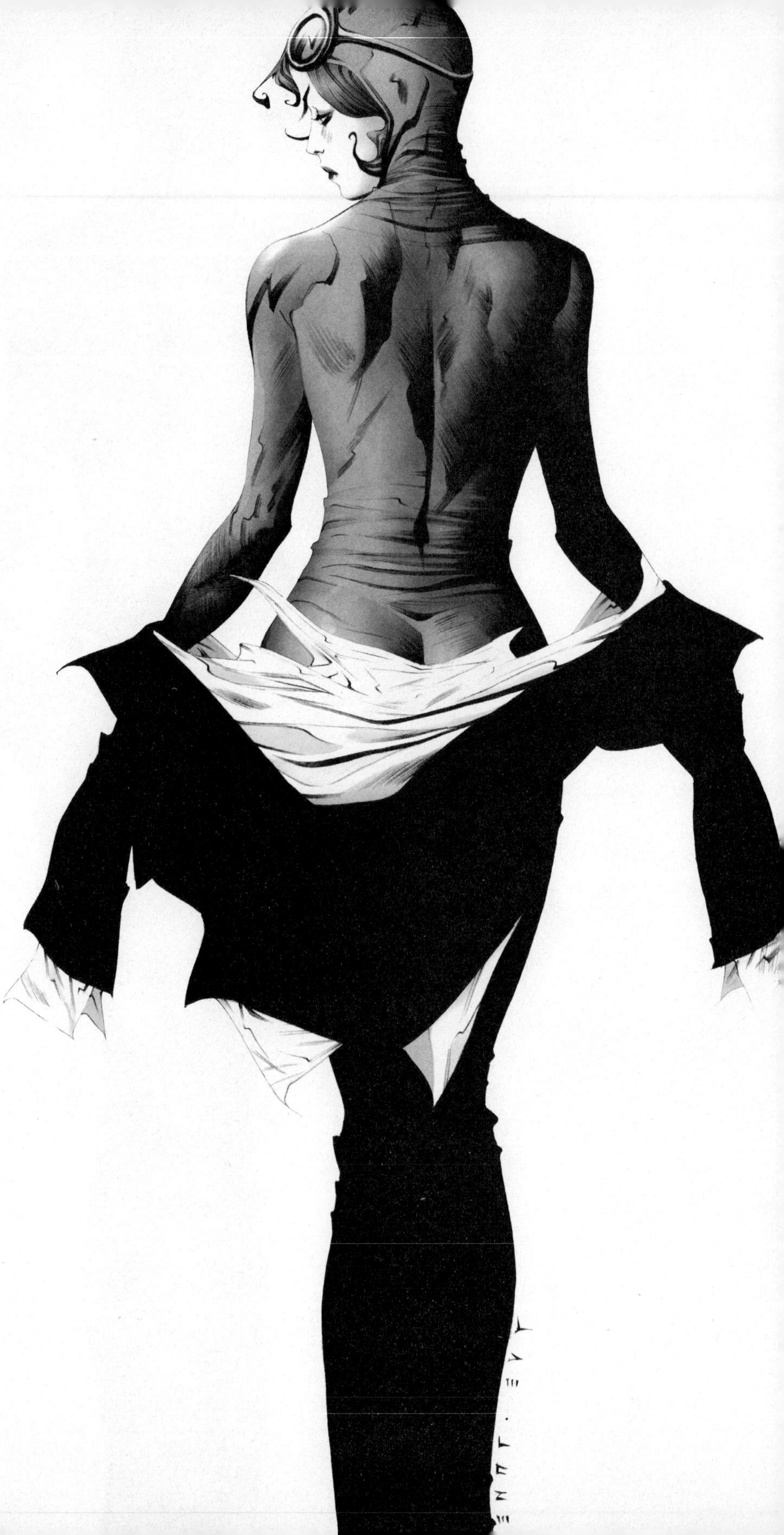

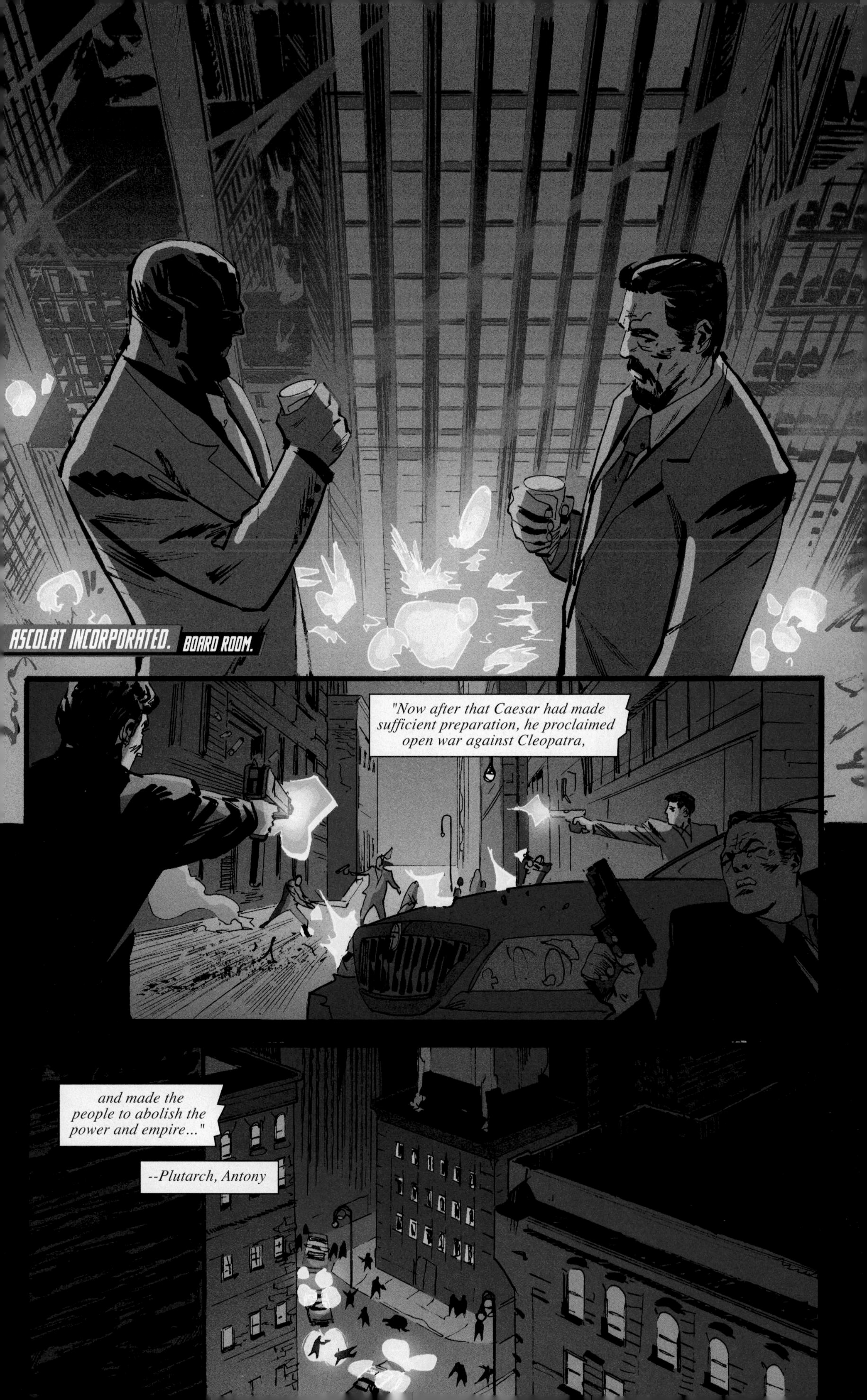
ASCOLAT INCORPORATED. BOARD ROOM.
"Now after that Caesar had made sufficient preparation, he proclaimed open war against Cleopatra,
and made the people to abolish the power and empire..."
--Plutarch, Antony

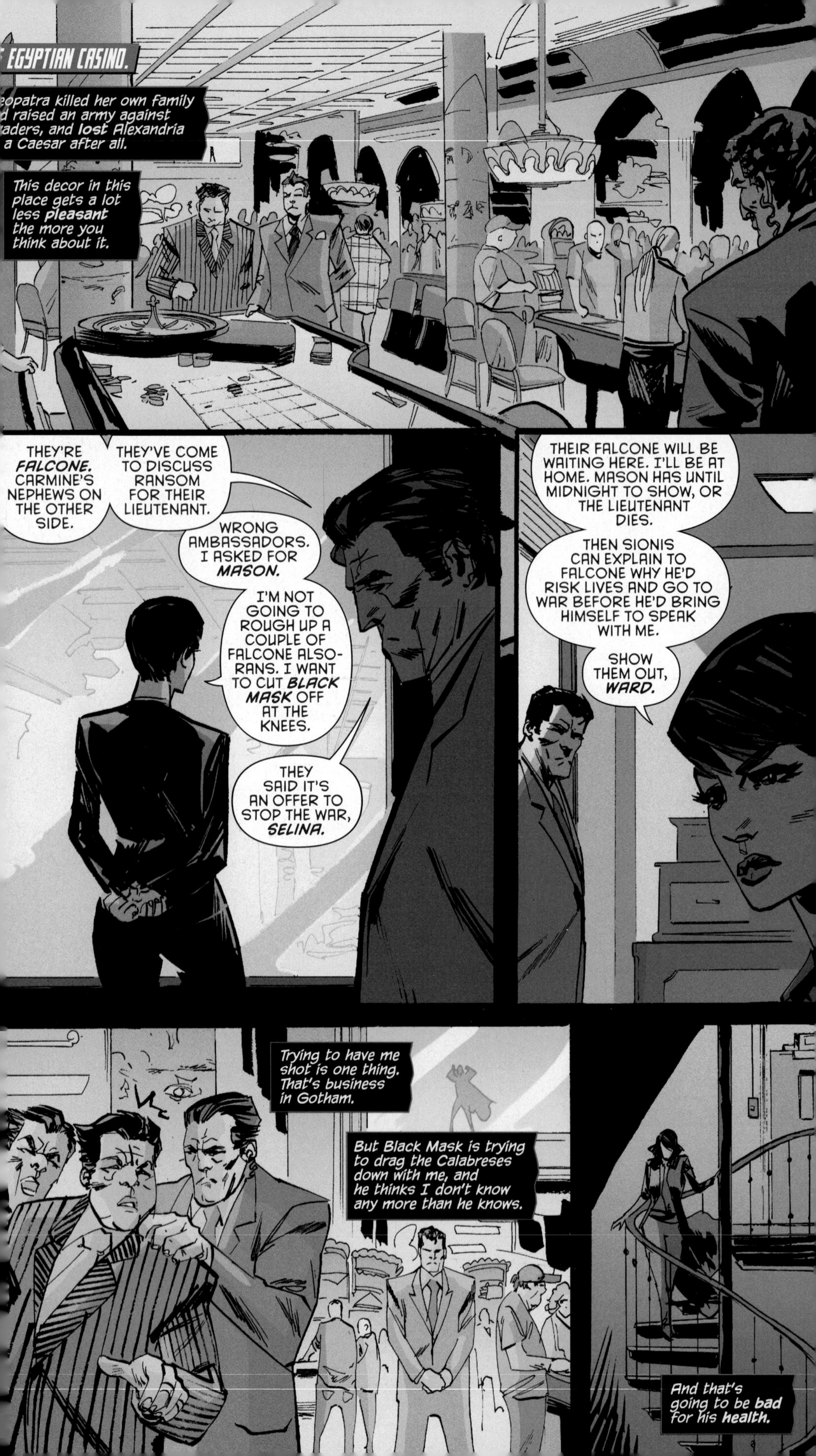

EGYPTIAN CASINO.
eopatra killed her own family
d raised an army against
aders, and lost Alexandria
a Caesar after all.
This decor in this place gets a lot less pleasant the more you think about it.
THEY'RE FALCONE. CARMINE'S NEPHEWS ON THE OTHER SIDE.
THEY'VE COME TO DISCUSS RANSOM FOR THEIR LIEUTENANT.
WRONG AMBASSADORS. I ASKED FOR MASON.
I'M NOT GOING TO ROUGH UP A COUPLE OF FALCONE ALSO-RANS. I WANT TO CUT BLACK MASK OFF AT THE KNEES.
THEY SAID IT'S AN OFFER TO STOP THE WAR, SELINA.
THEIR FALCONE WILL BE WAITING HERE. I'LL BE AT HOME. MASON HAS UNTIL MIDNIGHT TO SHOW, OR THE LIEUTENANT DIES.
THEN SIONIS CAN EXPLAIN TO FALCONE WHY HE'D RISK LIVES AND GO TO WAR BEFORE HE'D BRING HIMSELF TO SPEAK WITH ME.
SHOW THEM OUT, WARD.
Trying to have me shot is one thing. That's business in Gotham.
But Black Mask is trying to drag the Calabreses down with me, and he thinks I don't know any more than he knows.
And that's going to be bad for his health.

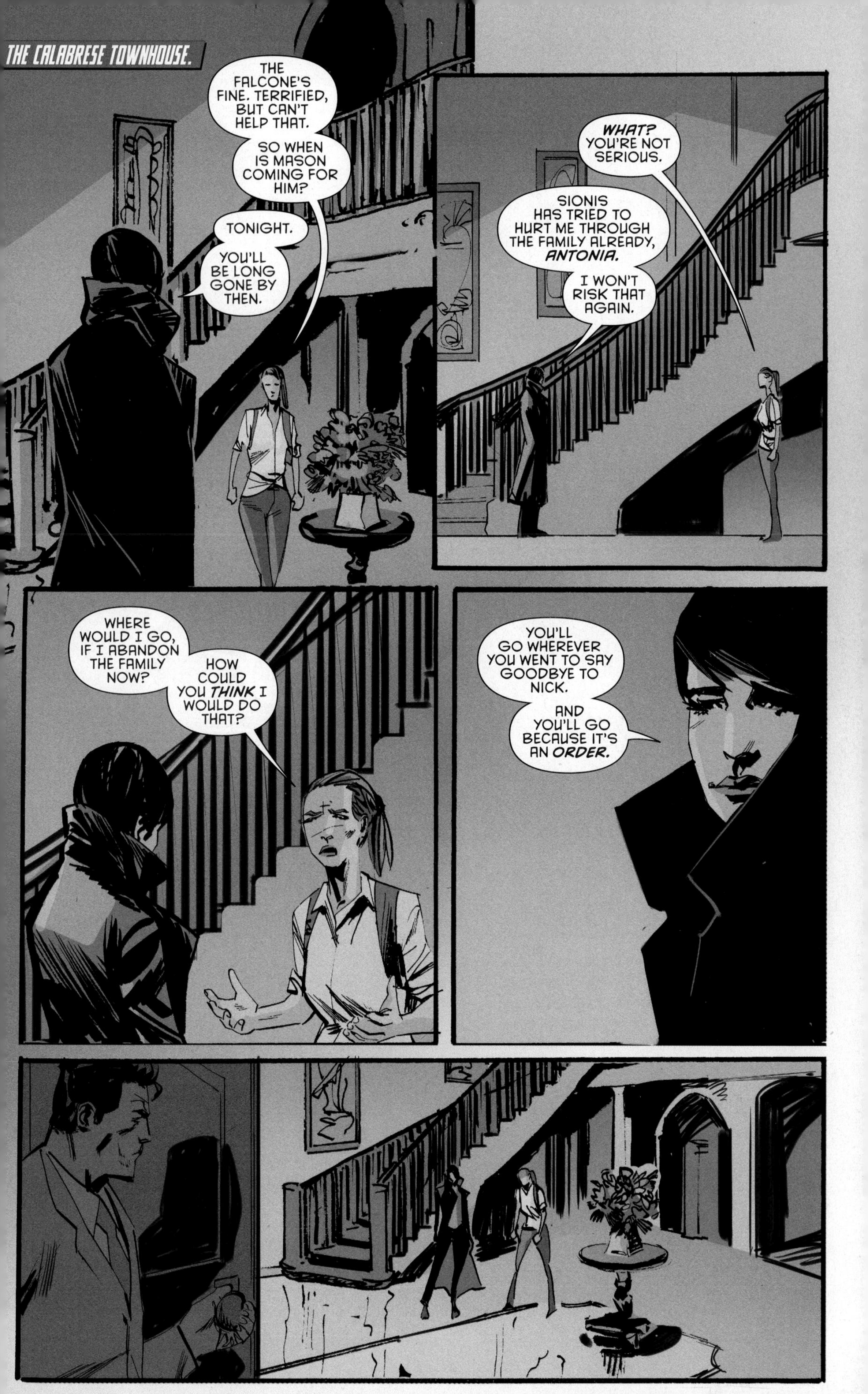
THE CALABRESE TOWNHOUSE.
THE FALCONE'S FINE. TERRIFIED, BUT CAN'T HELP THAT.
SO WHEN IS MASON COMING FOR HIM?
TONIGHT.
YOU'LL BE LONG GONE BY THEN.
WHAT? YOU'RE NOT SERIOUS.
SIONIS HAS TRIED TO HURT ME THROUGH THE FAMILY ALREADY, ANTONIA.
I WON'T RISK THAT AGAIN.
WHERE WOULD I GO, IF I ABANDON THE FAMILY NOW?
HOW COULD YOU THINK I WOULD DO THAT?
YOU'LL GO WHEREVER YOU WENT TO SAY GOODBYE TO NICK.
AND YOU'LL GO BECAUSE IT'S AN ORDER.

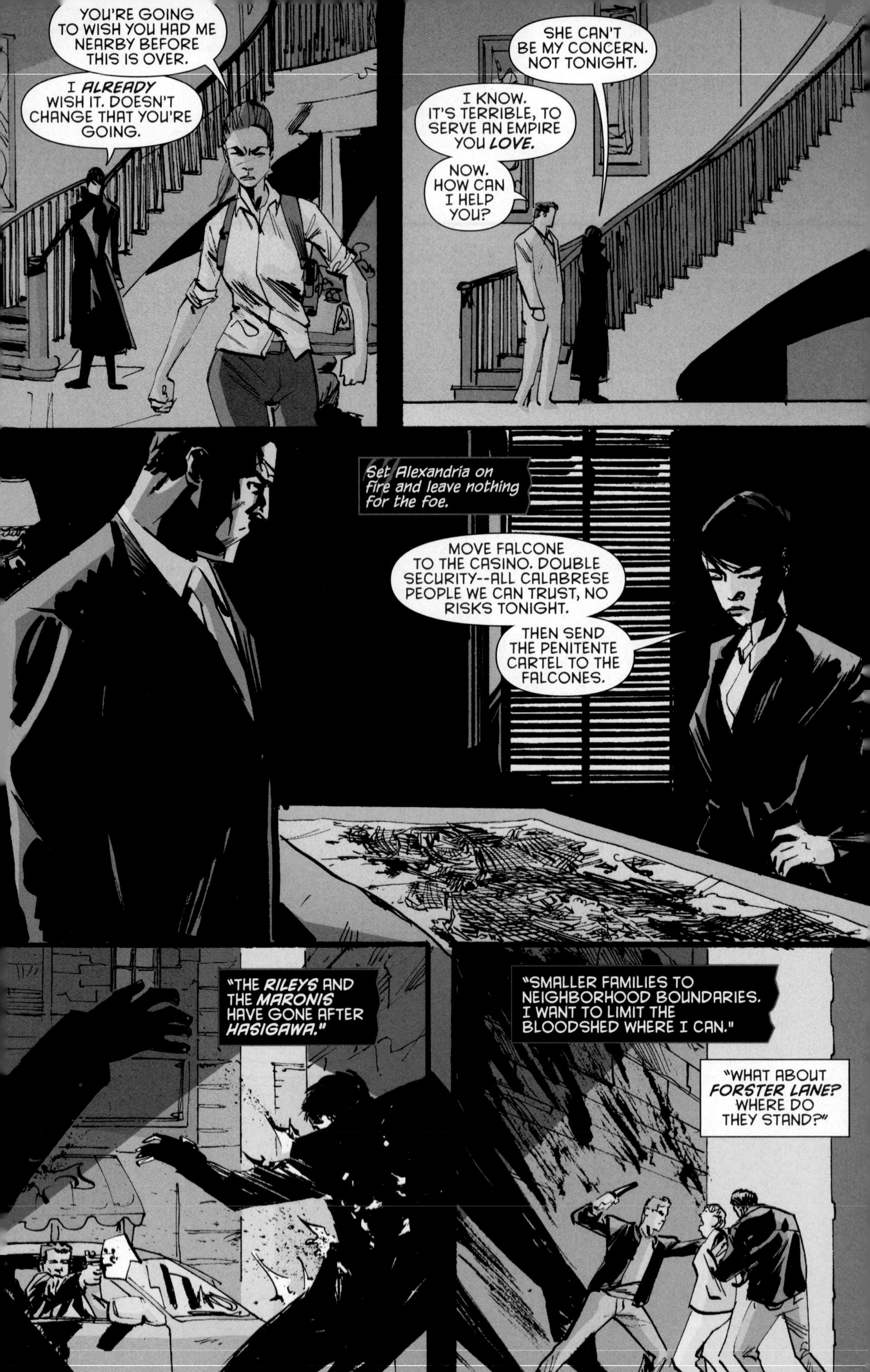

YOU'RE GOING TO WISH YOU HAD ME NEARBY BEFORE THIS IS OVER.
I *ALREADY* WISH IT. DOESN'T CHANGE THAT YOU'RE GOING.
SHE CAN'T BE MY CONCERN. NOT TONIGHT.
I KNOW. IT'S TERRIBLE, TO SERVE AN EMPIRE YOU *LOVE.*
NOW. HOW CAN I HELP YOU?
Set Alexandria on fire and leave nothing for the foe.
MOVE FALCONE TO THE CASINO. DOUBLE SECURITY--ALL CALABRESE PEOPLE WE CAN TRUST, NO RISKS TONIGHT.
THEN SEND THE PENITENTE CARTEL TO THE FALCONES.
"THE *RILEYS* AND THE *MARONIS* HAVE GONE AFTER *HASIGAWA.*"
"SMALLER FAMILIES TO NEIGHBORHOOD BOUNDARIES. I WANT TO LIMIT THE BLOODSHED WHERE I CAN."
"WHAT ABOUT *FORSTER LANE?* WHERE DO THEY STAND?"

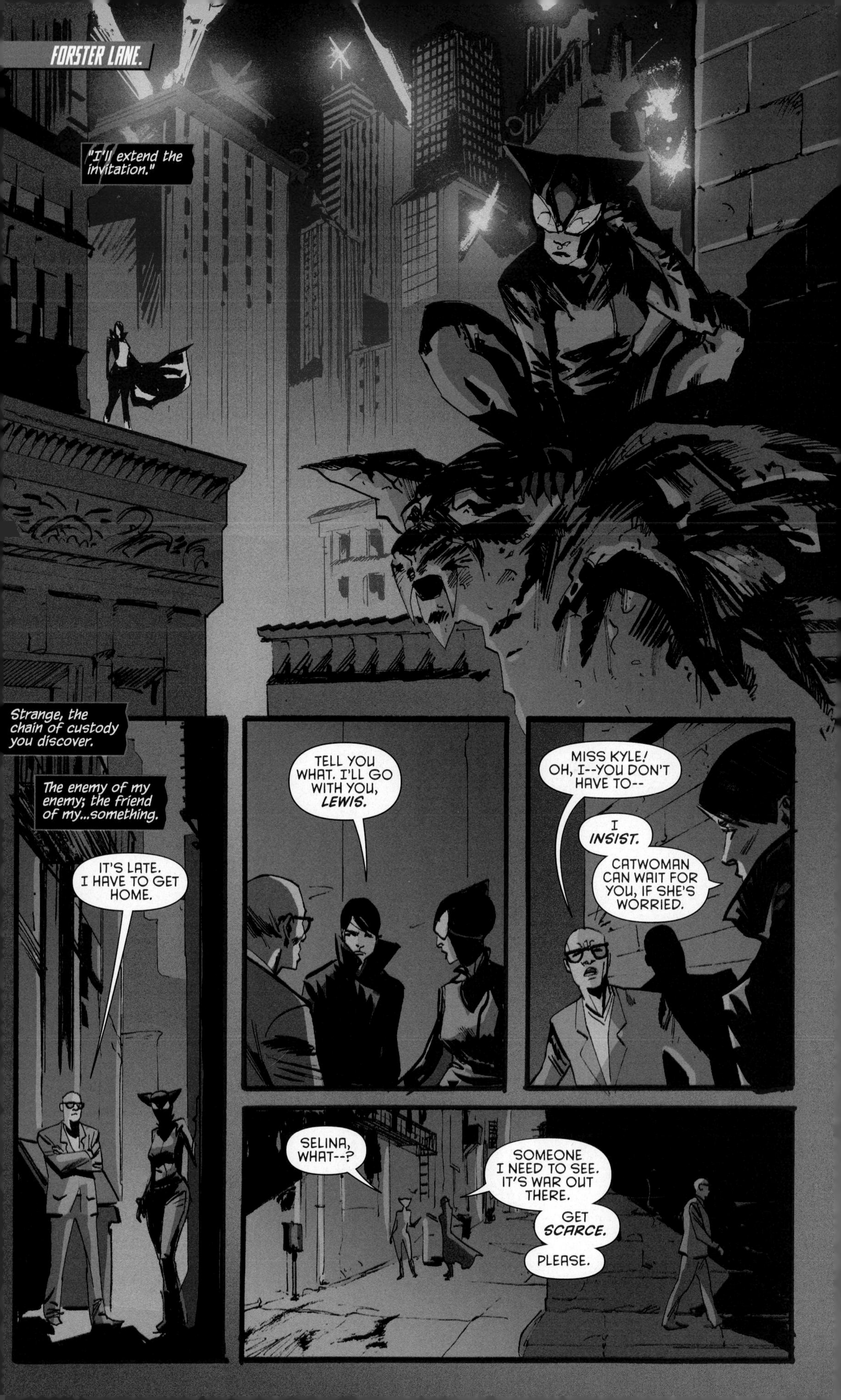
FORSTER LANE.
"I'll extend the invitation."
Strange, the chain of custody you discover.
The enemy of my enemy; the friend of my...something.
IT'S LATE. I HAVE TO GET HOME.
TELL YOU WHAT. I'LL GO WITH YOU, LEWIS.
MISS KYLE! OH, I--YOU DON'T HAVE TO--
I INSIST.
CATWOMAN CAN WAIT FOR YOU, IF SHE'S WORRIED.
SELINA, WHAT--?
SOMEONE I NEED TO SEE. IT'S WAR OUT THERE.
GET SCARCE.
PLEASE.

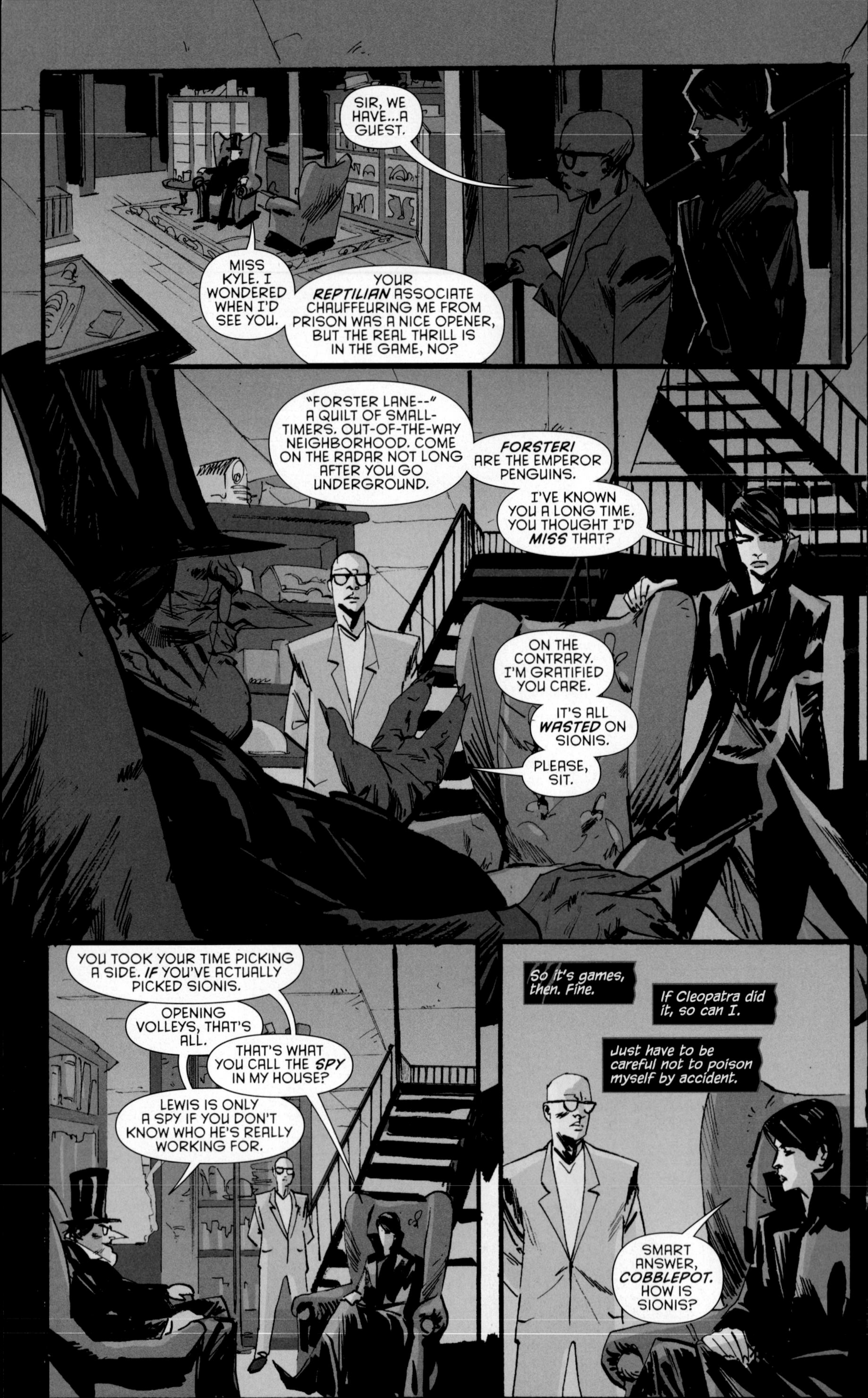
SIR, WE HAVE...A GUEST.
MISS KYLE. I WONDERED WHEN I'D SEE YOU.
YOUR REPTILIAN ASSOCIATE CHAUFFEURING ME FROM PRISON WAS A NICE OPENER, BUT THE REAL THRILL IS IN THE GAME, NO?
"FORSTER LANE--" A QUILT OF SMALL-TIMERS. OUT-OF-THE-WAY NEIGHBORHOOD. COME ON THE RADAR NOT LONG AFTER YOU GO UNDERGROUND.
FORSTERI ARE THE EMPEROR PENGUINS.
I'VE KNOWN YOU A LONG TIME. YOU THOUGHT I'D MISS THAT?
ON THE CONTRARY. I'M GRATIFIED YOU CARE.
IT'S ALL WASTED ON SIONIS.
PLEASE, SIT.
YOU TOOK YOUR TIME PICKING A SIDE. IF YOU'VE ACTUALLY PICKED SIONIS.
OPENING VOLLEYS, THAT'S ALL.
THAT'S WHAT YOU CALL THE SPY IN MY HOUSE?
LEWIS IS ONLY A SPY IF YOU DON'T KNOW WHO HE'S REALLY WORKING FOR.
So it's games, then. Fine.
If Cleopatra did it, so can I.
Just have to be careful not to poison myself by accident.
SMART ANSWER, COBBLEPOT. HOW IS SIONIS?

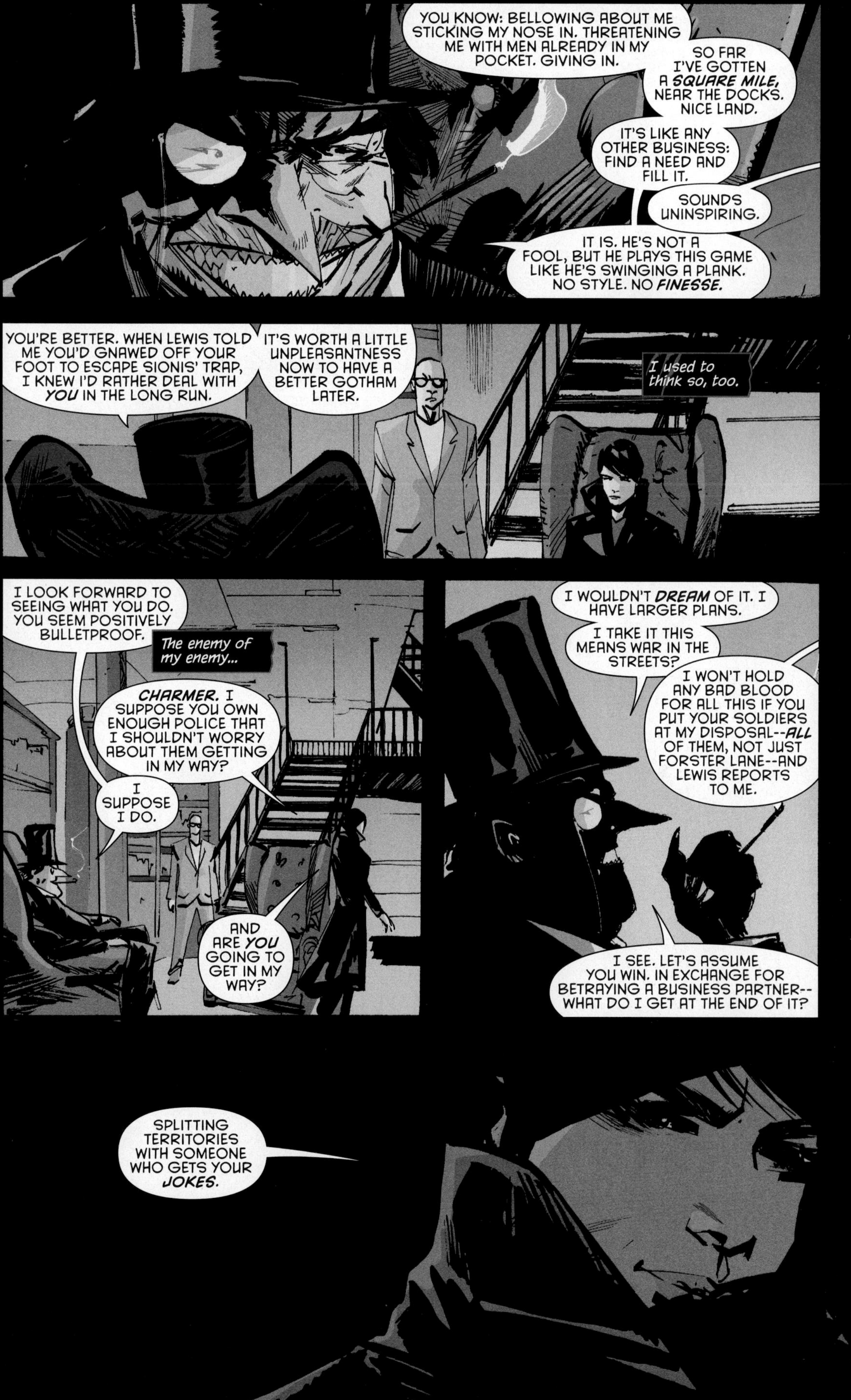
YOU KNOW: BELLOWING ABOUT ME STICKING MY NOSE IN. THREATENING ME WITH MEN ALREADY IN MY POCKET. GIVING IN.
SO FAR I'VE GOTTEN A *SQUARE MILE,* NEAR THE DOCKS. NICE LAND.
IT'S LIKE ANY OTHER BUSINESS: FIND A NEED AND FILL IT.
SOUNDS UNINSPIRING.
IT IS. HE'S NOT A FOOL, BUT HE PLAYS THIS GAME LIKE HE'S SWINGING A PLANK. NO STYLE. NO *FINESSE.*
YOU'RE BETTER. WHEN LEWIS TOLD ME YOU'D GNAWED OFF YOUR FOOT TO ESCAPE SIONIS' TRAP, I KNEW I'D RATHER DEAL WITH *YOU* IN THE LONG RUN.
IT'S WORTH A LITTLE UNPLEASANTNESS NOW TO HAVE A BETTER GOTHAM LATER.
I used to think so, too.
I LOOK FORWARD TO SEEING WHAT YOU DO. YOU SEEM POSITIVELY BULLETPROOF.
The enemy of my enemy...
CHARMER. I SUPPOSE YOU OWN ENOUGH POLICE THAT I SHOULDN'T WORRY ABOUT THEM GETTING IN MY WAY?
I SUPPOSE I DO.
AND ARE *YOU* GOING TO GET IN MY WAY?
I WOULDN'T *DREAM* OF IT. I HAVE LARGER PLANS.
I TAKE IT THIS MEANS WAR IN THE STREETS?
I WON'T HOLD ANY BAD BLOOD FOR ALL THIS IF YOU PUT YOUR SOLDIERS AT MY DISPOSAL--*ALL* OF THEM, NOT JUST FORSTER LANE--AND LEWIS REPORTS TO ME.
I SEE. LET'S ASSUME YOU WIN. IN EXCHANGE FOR BETRAYING A BUSINESS PARTNER-- WHAT DO I GET AT THE END OF IT?
SPLITTING TERRITORIES WITH SOMEONE WHO GETS YOUR *JOKES.*

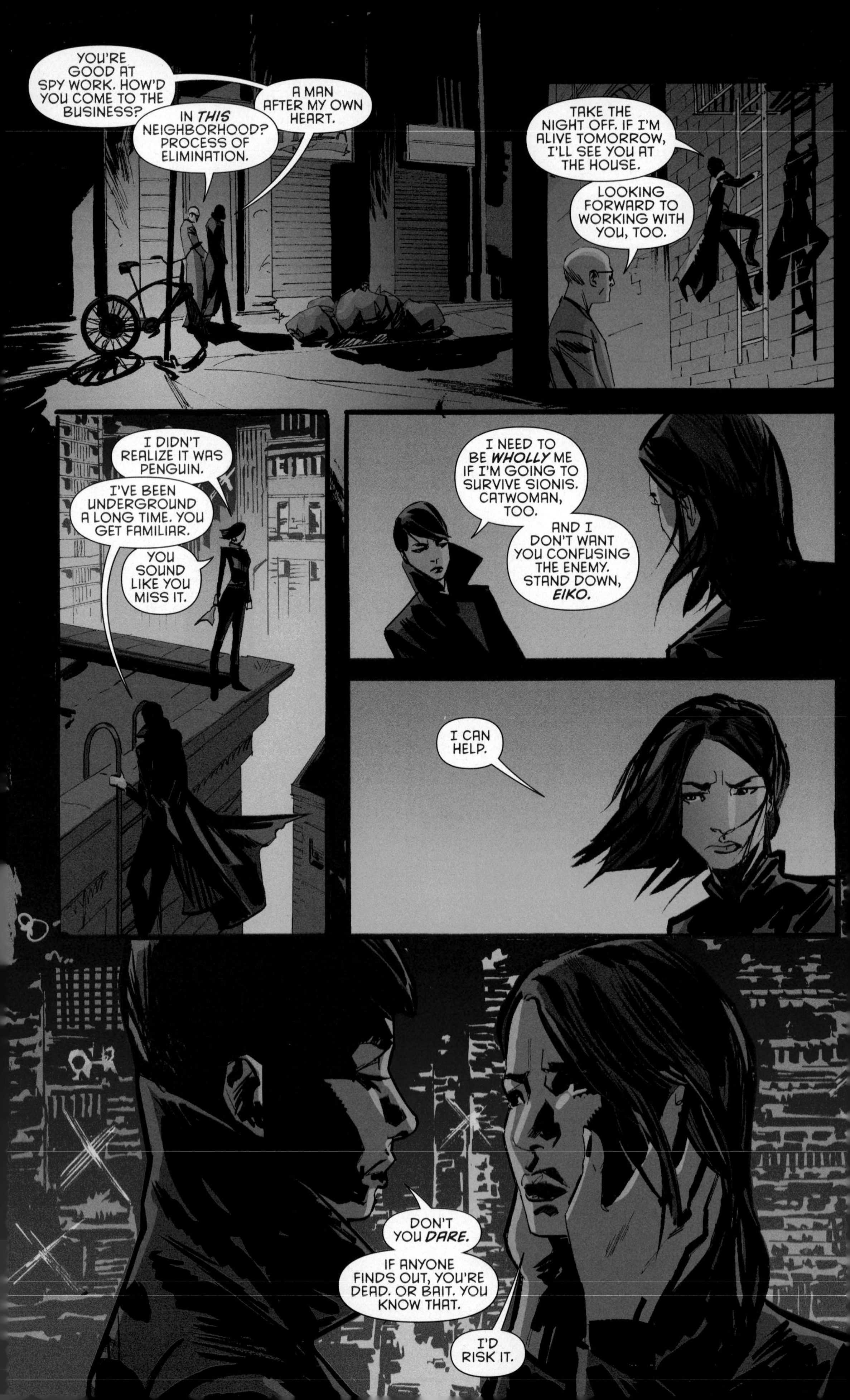

YOU'RE GOOD AT SPY WORK. HOW'D YOU COME TO THE BUSINESS?
IN *THIS* NEIGHBORHOOD? PROCESS OF ELIMINATION.
A MAN AFTER MY OWN HEART.
TAKE THE NIGHT OFF. IF I'M ALIVE TOMORROW, I'LL SEE YOU AT THE HOUSE.
LOOKING FORWARD TO WORKING WITH YOU, TOO.
I DIDN'T REALIZE IT WAS PENGUIN.
I'VE BEEN UNDERGROUND A LONG TIME. YOU GET FAMILIAR.
YOU SOUND LIKE YOU MISS IT.
I NEED TO BE *WHOLLY* ME IF I'M GOING TO SURVIVE SIONIS. CATWOMAN, TOO.
AND I DON'T WANT YOU CONFUSING THE ENEMY. STAND DOWN, *EIKO.*
I CAN HELP.
DON'T YOU *DARE.*
IF ANYONE FINDS OUT, YOU'RE DEAD. OR BAIT. YOU KNOW THAT.
I'D RISK IT.

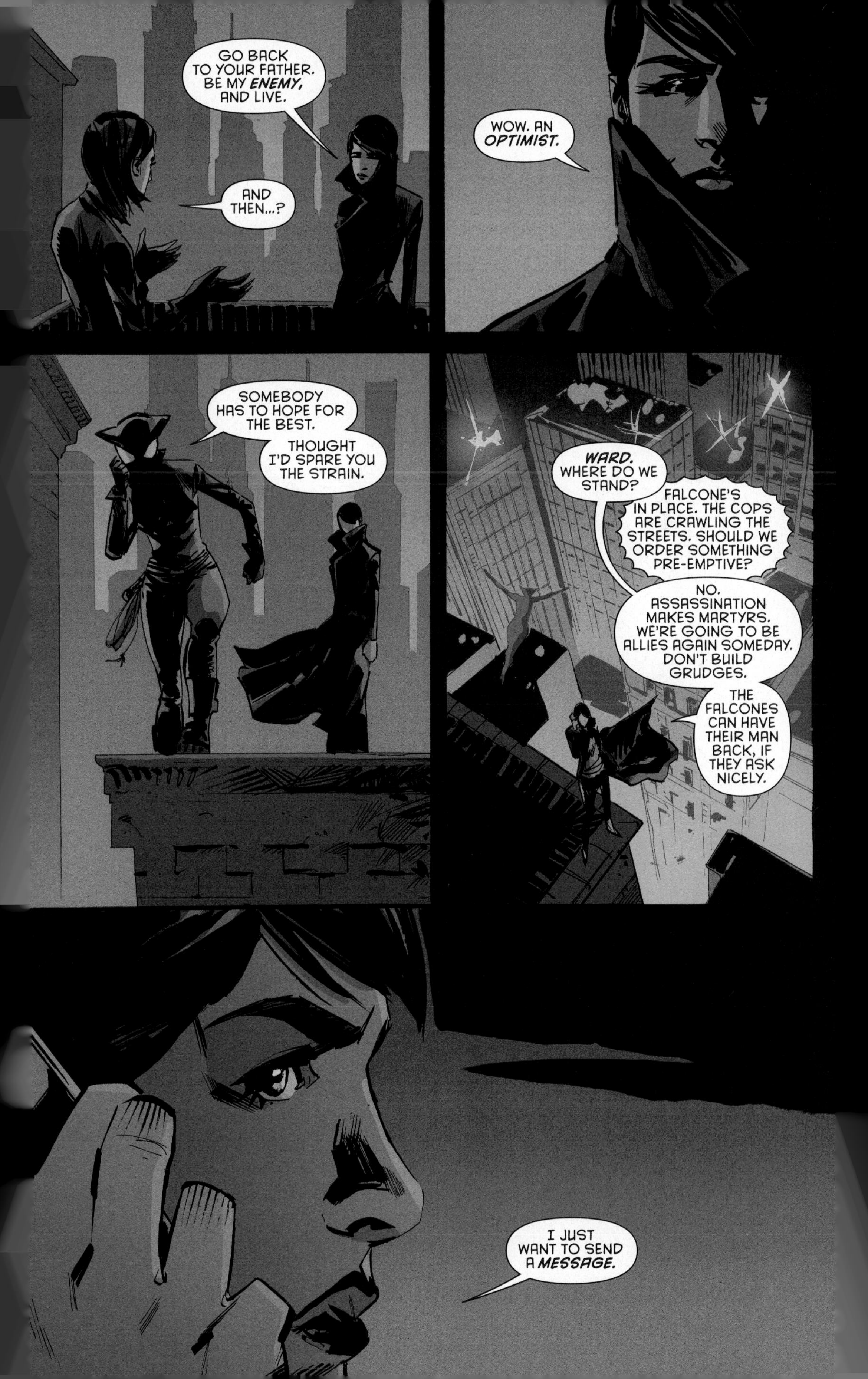
GO BACK TO YOUR FATHER. BE MY ENEMY, AND LIVE.
AND THEN...?
WOW. AN OPTIMIST.
SOMEBODY HAS TO HOPE FOR THE BEST.
THOUGHT I'D SPARE YOU THE STRAIN.
WARD. WHERE DO WE STAND?
FALCONE'S IN PLACE. THE COPS ARE CRAWLING THE STREETS. SHOULD WE ORDER SOMETHING PRE-EMPTIVE?
NO. ASSASSINATION MAKES MARTYRS. WE'RE GOING TO BE ALLIES AGAIN SOMEDAY. DON'T BUILD GRUDGES.
THE FALCONES CAN HAVE THEIR MAN BACK, IF THEY ASK NICELY.
I JUST WANT TO SEND A MESSAGE.

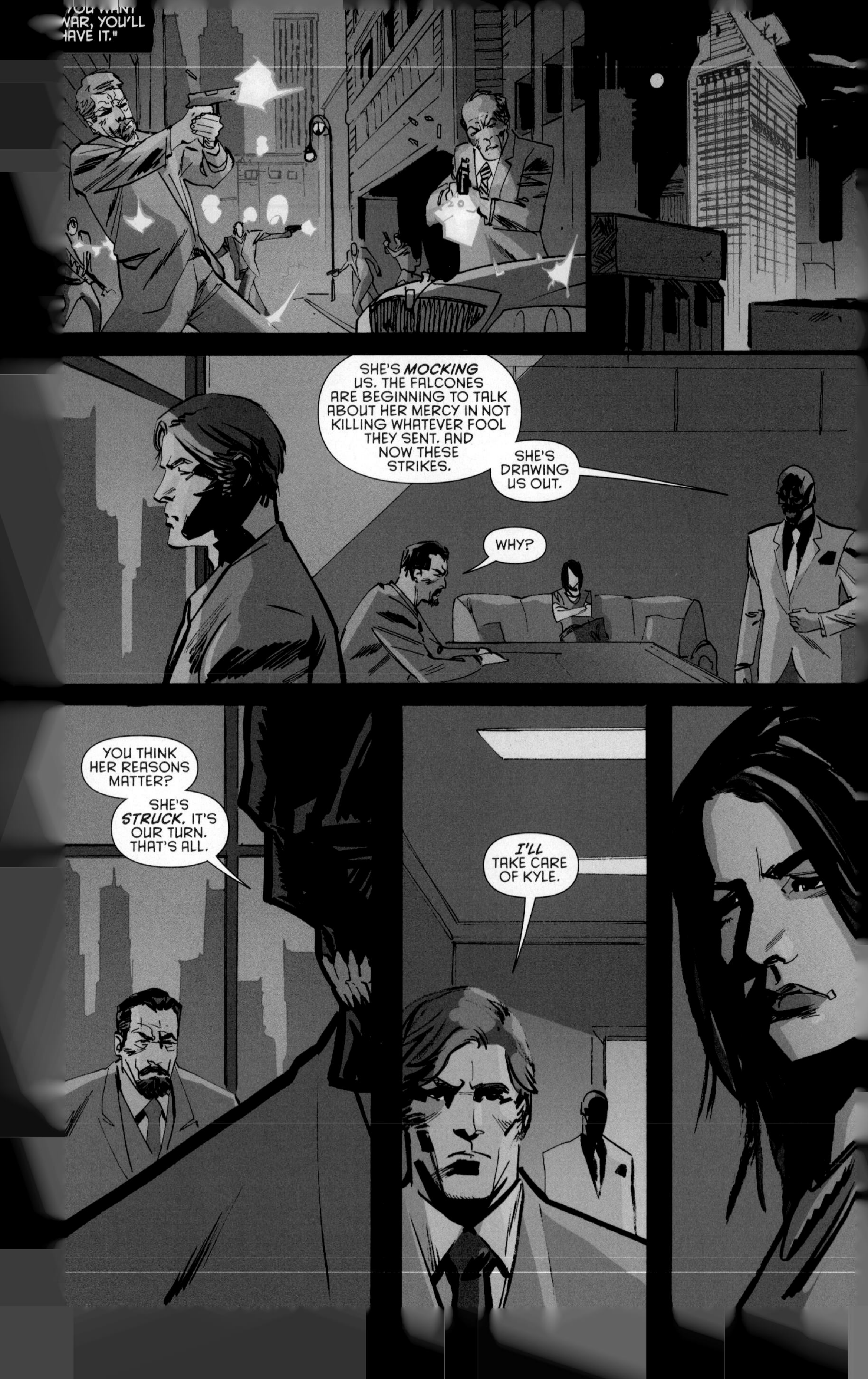
"YOU WANT WAR, YOU'LL HAVE IT."
SHE'S *MOCKING* US. THE FALCONES ARE BEGINNING TO TALK ABOUT HER MERCY IN NOT KILLING WHATEVER FOOL THEY SENT. AND NOW THESE STRIKES.
SHE'S DRAWING US OUT.
WHY?
YOU THINK HER REASONS MATTER?
SHE'S *STRUCK.* IT'S OUR TURN. THAT'S ALL.
I'LL TAKE CARE OF KYLE.

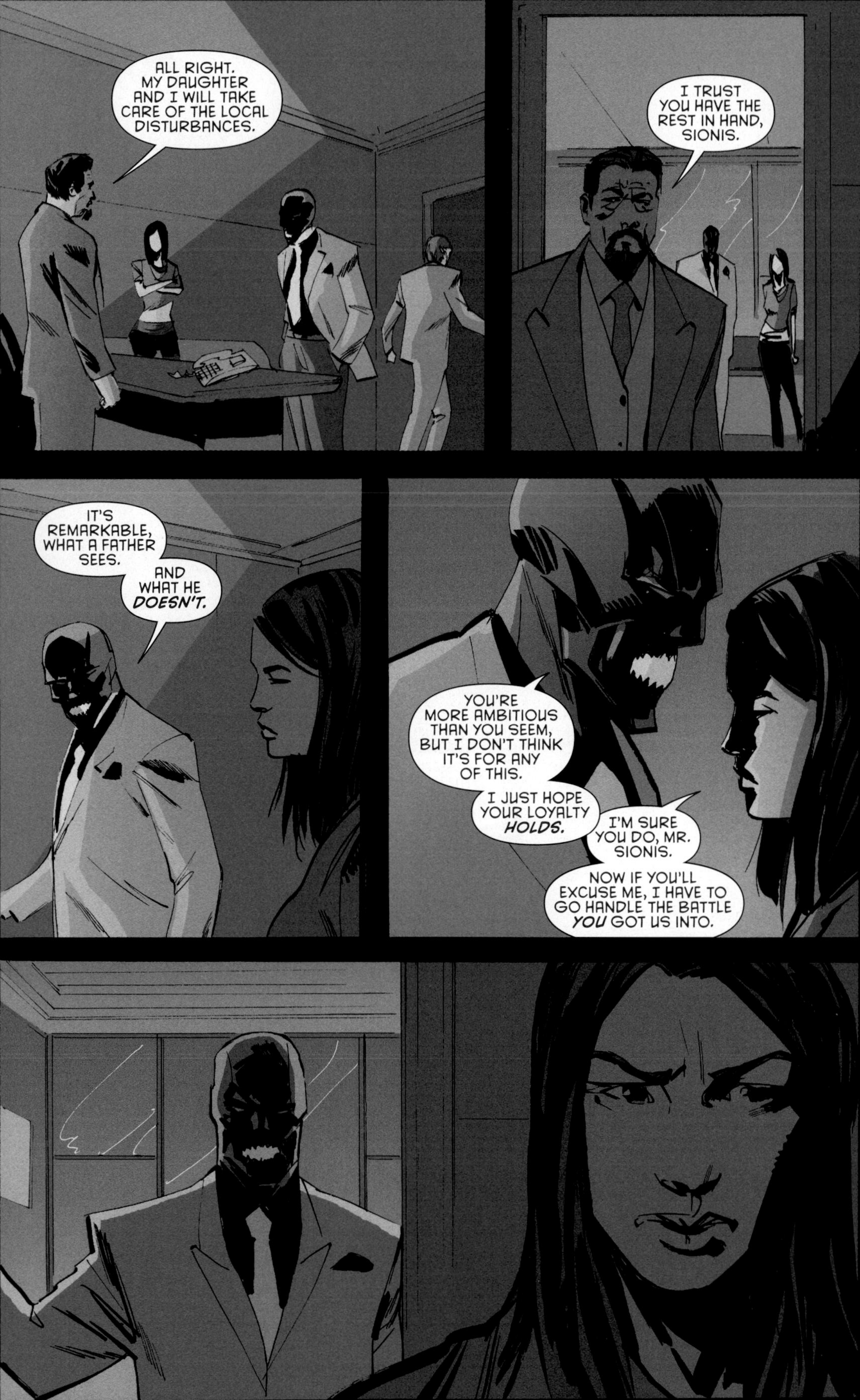
ALL RIGHT. MY DAUGHTER AND I WILL TAKE CARE OF THE LOCAL DISTURBANCES.
I TRUST YOU HAVE THE REST IN HAND, SIONIS.
IT'S REMARKABLE, WHAT A FATHER SEES.
AND WHAT HE *DOESN'T.*
YOU'RE MORE AMBITIOUS THAN YOU SEEM, BUT I DON'T THINK IT'S FOR ANY OF THIS.
I JUST HOPE YOUR LOYALTY *HOLDS.*
I'M SURE YOU DO, MR. SIONIS.
NOW IF YOU'LL EXCUSE ME, I HAVE TO GO HANDLE THE BATTLE *YOU* GOT US INTO.

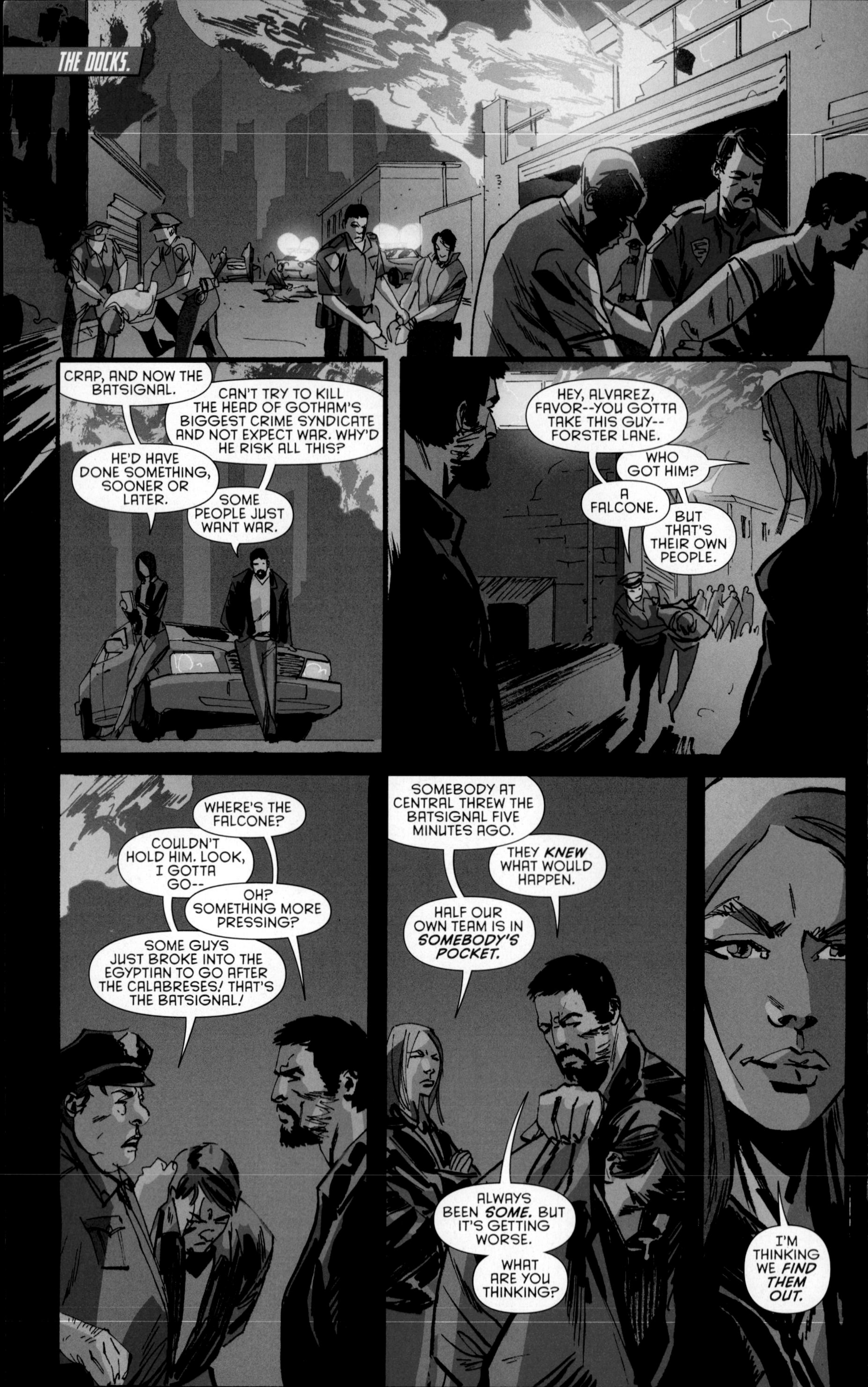
THE DOCKS.
CRAP, AND NOW THE BATSIGNAL.
CAN'T TRY TO KILL THE HEAD OF GOTHAM'S BIGGEST CRIME SYNDICATE AND NOT EXPECT WAR. WHY'D HE RISK ALL THIS?
HE'D HAVE DONE SOMETHING, SOONER OR LATER.
SOME PEOPLE JUST WANT WAR.
HEY, ALVAREZ, FAVOR--YOU GOTTA TAKE THIS GUY-- FORSTER LANE.
WHO GOT HIM?
A FALCONE.
BUT THAT'S THEIR OWN PEOPLE.
WHERE'S THE FALCONE?
COULDN'T HOLD HIM. LOOK, I GOTTA GO--
OH? SOMETHING MORE PRESSING?
SOME GUYS JUST BROKE INTO THE EGYPTIAN TO GO AFTER THE CALABRESES! THAT'S THE BATSIGNAL!
SOMEBODY AT CENTRAL THREW THE BATSIGNAL FIVE MINUTES AGO.
THEY KNEW WHAT WOULD HAPPEN.
HALF OUR OWN TEAM IS IN SOMEBODY'S POCKET.
ALWAYS BEEN SOME. BUT IT'S GETTING WORSE.
WHAT ARE YOU THINKING?
I'M THINKING WE FIND THEM OUT.

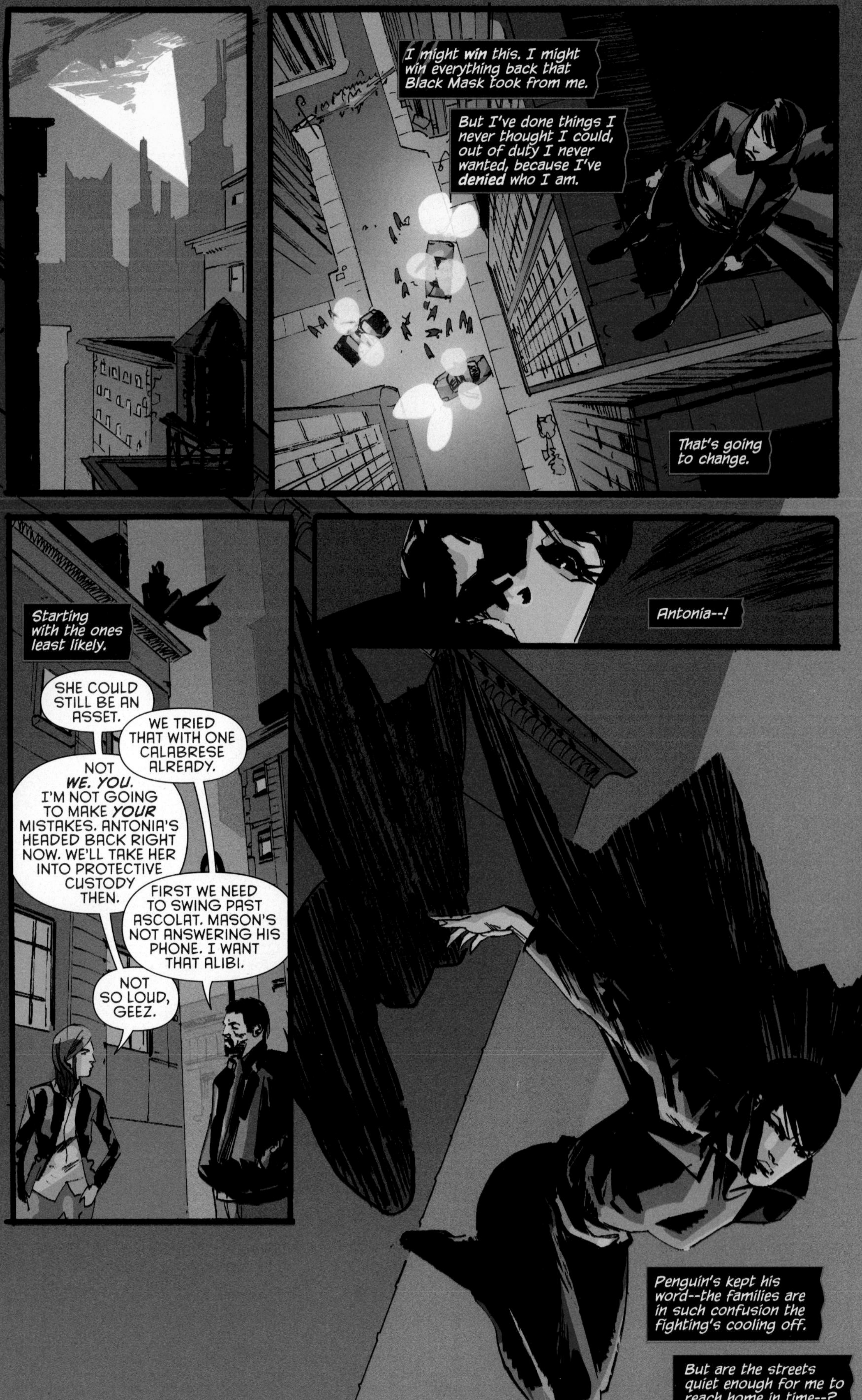

I might win this. I might win everything back that Black Mask took from me.
But I've done things I never thought I could, out of duty I never wanted, because I've denied who I am.
That's going to change.
Starting with the ones least likely.
SHE COULD STILL BE AN ASSET.
WE TRIED THAT WITH ONE CALABRESE ALREADY.
NOT WE. YOU. I'M NOT GOING TO MAKE YOUR MISTAKES. ANTONIA'S HEADED BACK RIGHT NOW. WE'LL TAKE HER INTO PROTECTIVE CUSTODY THEN.
FIRST WE NEED TO SWING PAST ASCOLAT. MASON'S NOT ANSWERING HIS PHONE. I WANT THAT ALIBI.
NOT SO LOUD, GEEZ.
Antonia--!
Penguin's kept his word--the families are in such confusion the fighting's cooling off.
But are the streets quiet enough for me to reach home in time--?

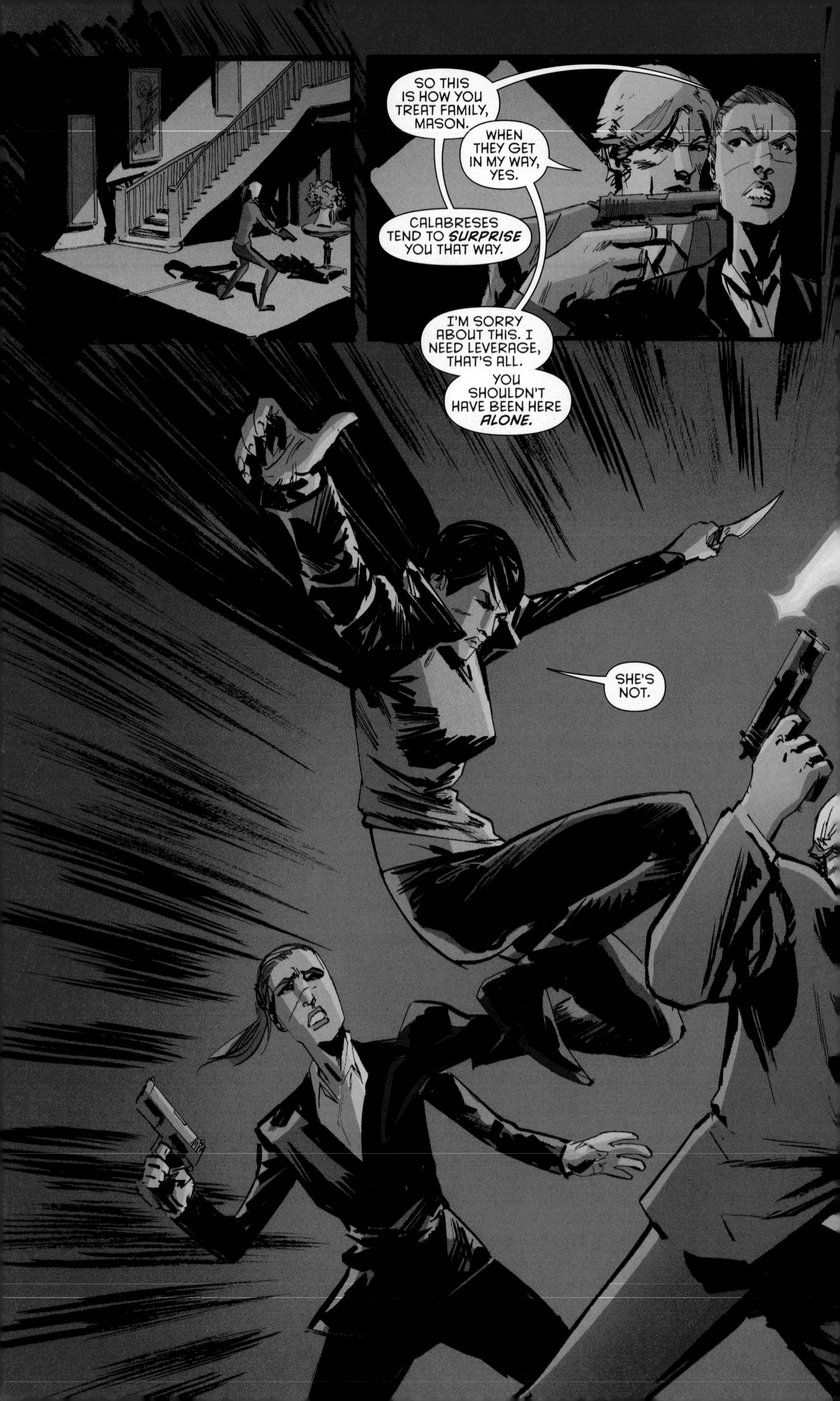

SO THIS IS HOW YOU TREAT FAMILY, MASON.
WHEN THEY GET IN MY WAY, YES.
CALABRESES TEND TO *SURPRISE* YOU THAT WAY.
I'M SORRY ABOUT THIS. I NEED LEVERAGE, THAT'S ALL.
YOU SHOULDN'T HAVE BEEN HERE *ALONE.*
SHE'S NOT.

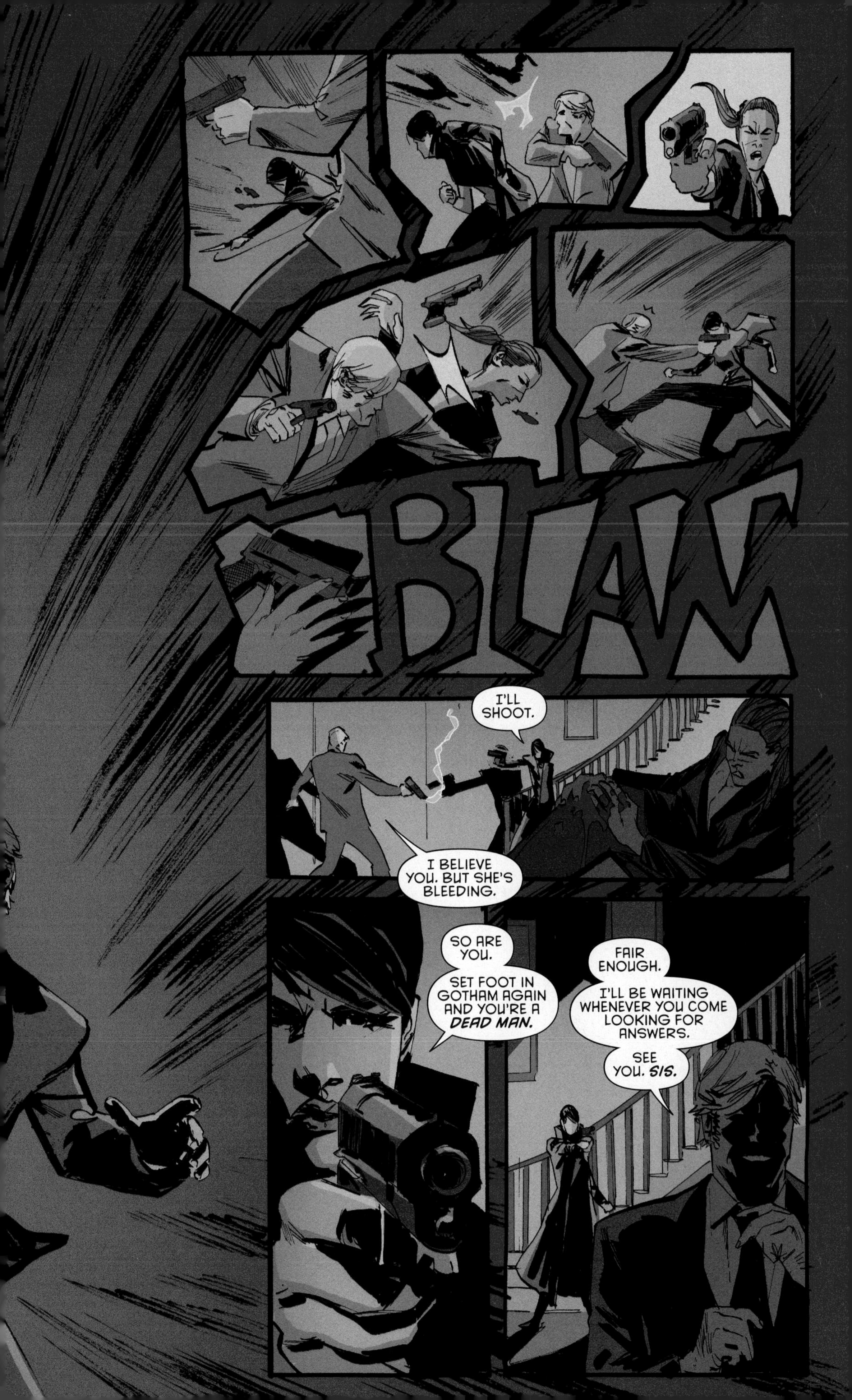
BLAM
I'LL SHOOT.
I BELIEVE YOU. BUT SHE'S BLEEDING.
SO ARE YOU.
SET FOOT IN GOTHAM AGAIN AND YOU'RE A DEAD MAN.
FAIR ENOUGH.
I'LL BE WAITING WHENEVER YOU COME LOOKING FOR ANSWERS.
SEE YOU. SIS.

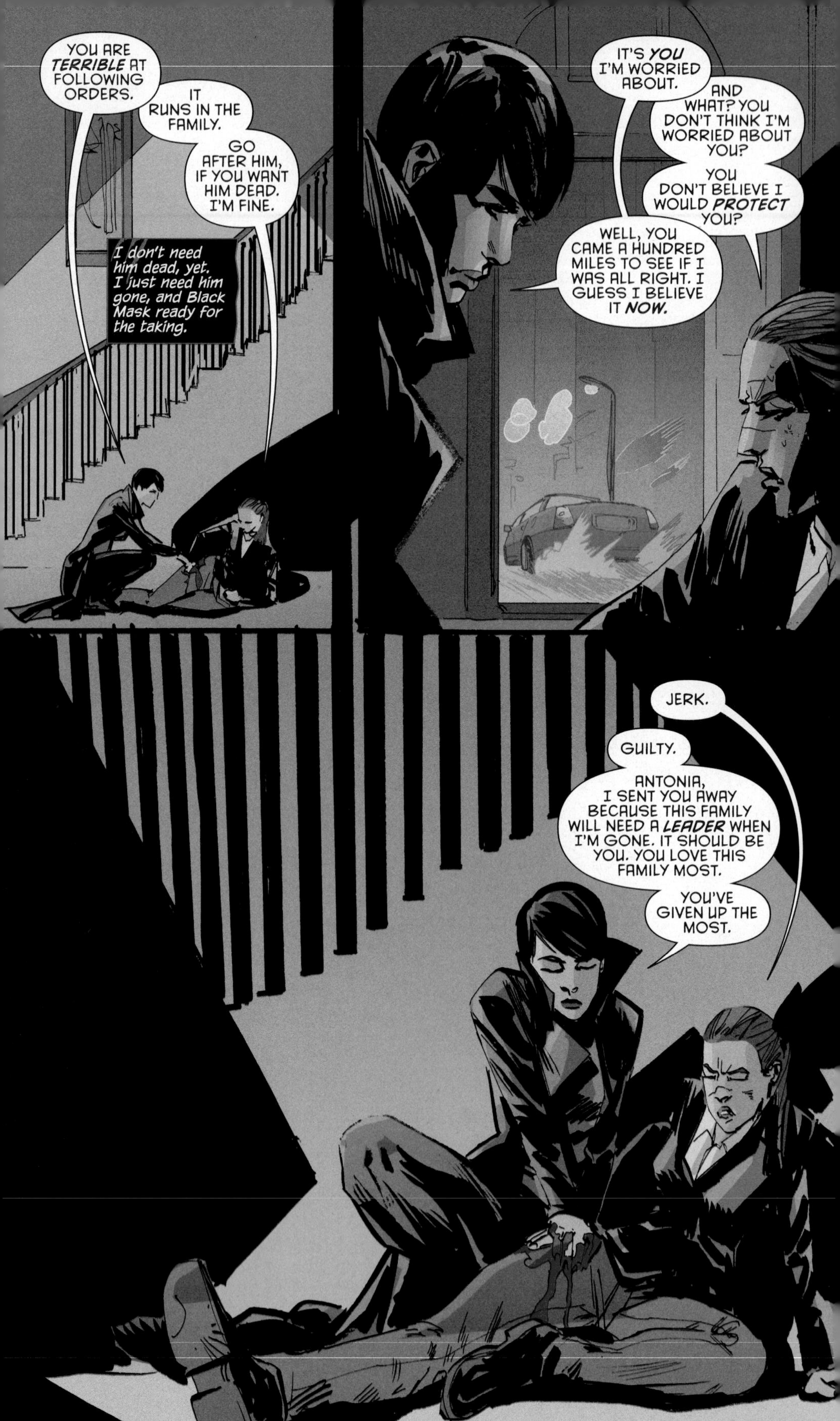
YOU ARE TERRIBLE AT FOLLOWING ORDERS.
IT RUNS IN THE FAMILY.
GO AFTER HIM, IF YOU WANT HIM DEAD. I'M FINE.
I don't need him dead, yet. I just need him gone, and Black Mask ready for the taking.
IT'S YOU I'M WORRIED ABOUT.
AND WHAT? YOU DON'T THINK I'M WORRIED ABOUT YOU?
YOU DON'T BELIEVE I WOULD PROTECT YOU?
WELL, YOU CAME A HUNDRED MILES TO SEE IF I WAS ALL RIGHT. I GUESS I BELIEVE IT NOW.
JERK.
GUILTY.
ANTONIA, I SENT YOU AWAY BECAUSE THIS FAMILY WILL NEED A LEADER WHEN I'M GONE. IT SHOULD BE YOU. YOU LOVE THIS FAMILY MOST.
YOU'VE GIVEN UP THE MOST.

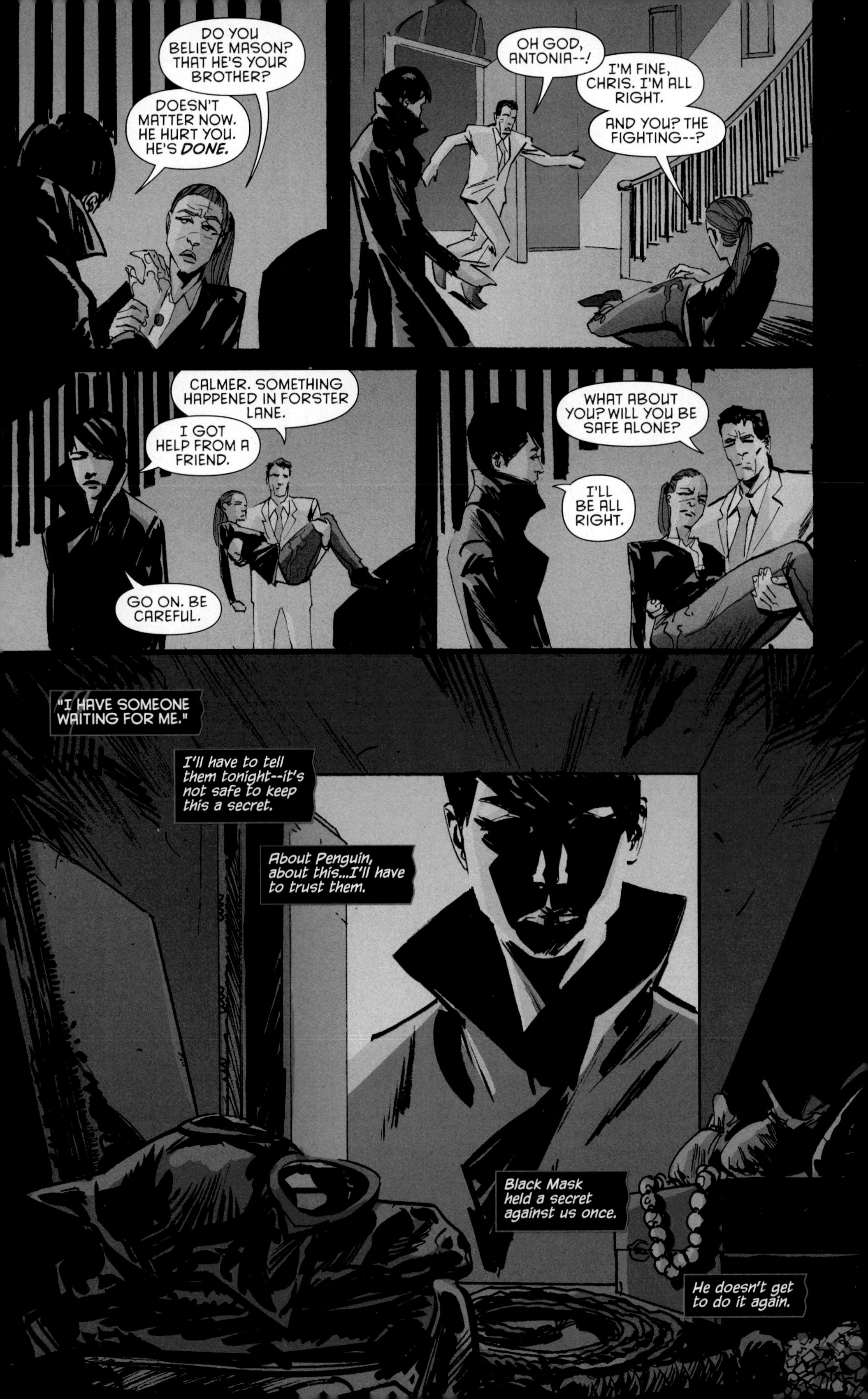
DO YOU BELIEVE MASON? THAT HE'S YOUR BROTHER?
DOESN'T MATTER NOW. HE HURT YOU. HE'S DONE.
OH GOD, ANTONIA--!
I'M FINE, CHRIS. I'M ALL RIGHT.
AND YOU? THE FIGHTING--?
CALMER. SOMETHING HAPPENED IN FORSTER LANE.
I GOT HELP FROM A FRIEND.
GO ON. BE CAREFUL.
WHAT ABOUT YOU? WILL YOU BE SAFE ALONE?
I'LL BE ALL RIGHT.
"I HAVE SOMEONE WAITING FOR ME."
I'll have to tell them tonight--it's not safe to keep this a secret.
About Penguin, about this...I'll have to trust them.
Black Mask held a secret against us once.
He doesn't get to do it again.

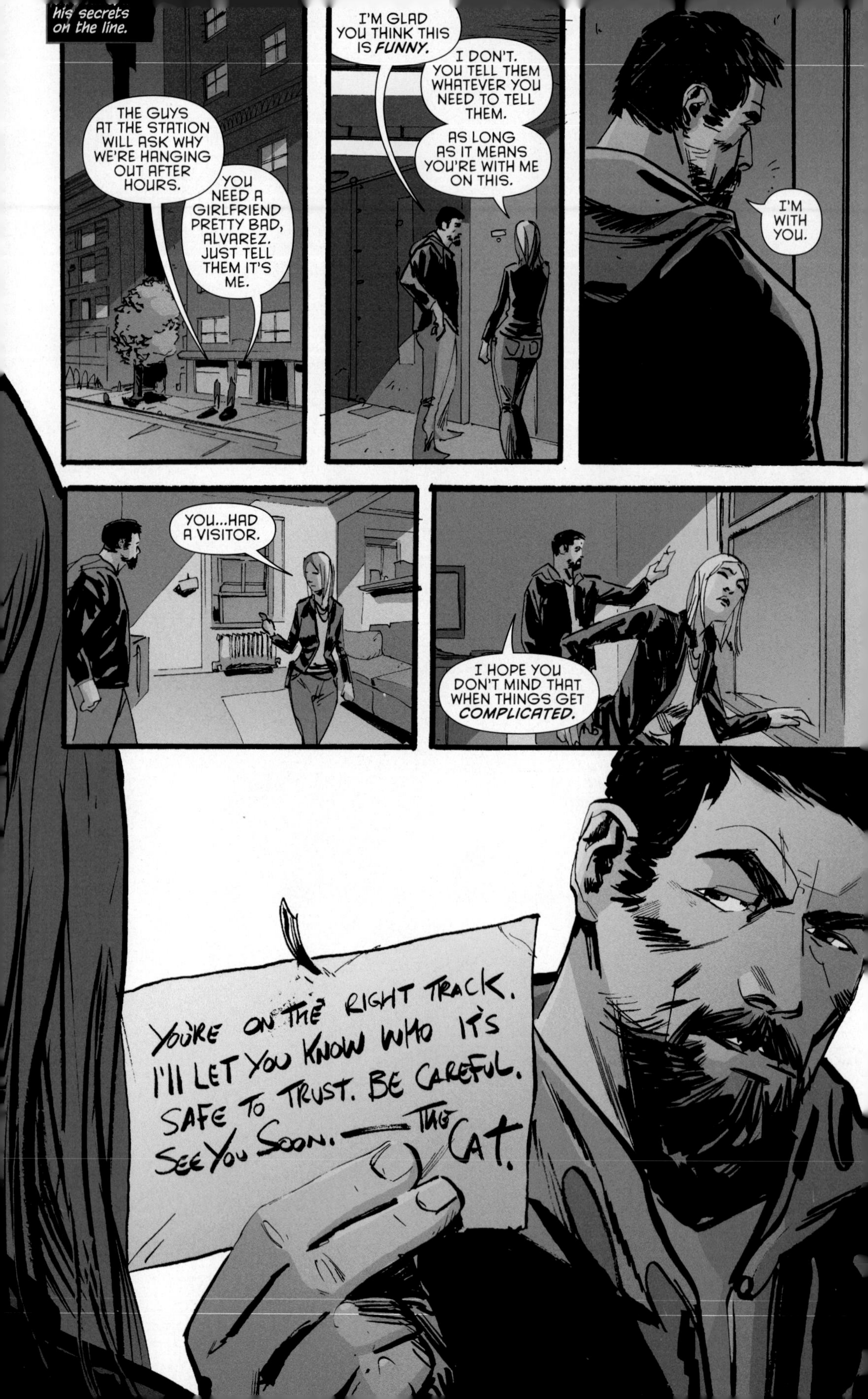
his secrets on the line.
THE GUYS AT THE STATION WILL ASK WHY WE'RE HANGING OUT AFTER HOURS.
YOU NEED A GIRLFRIEND PRETTY BAD, ALVAREZ. JUST TELL THEM IT'S ME.
I'M GLAD YOU THINK THIS IS *FUNNY.*
I DON'T. YOU TELL THEM WHATEVER YOU NEED TO TELL THEM.
AS LONG AS IT MEANS YOU'RE WITH ME ON THIS.
I'M WITH YOU.
YOU...HAD A VISITOR.
I HOPE YOU DON'T MIND THAT WHEN THINGS GET *COMPLICATED.*
YOU'RE ON THE RIGHT TRACK. I'LL LET YOU KNOW WHO IT'S SAFE TO TRUST. BE CAREFUL. SEE YOU SOON. —THE CAT.

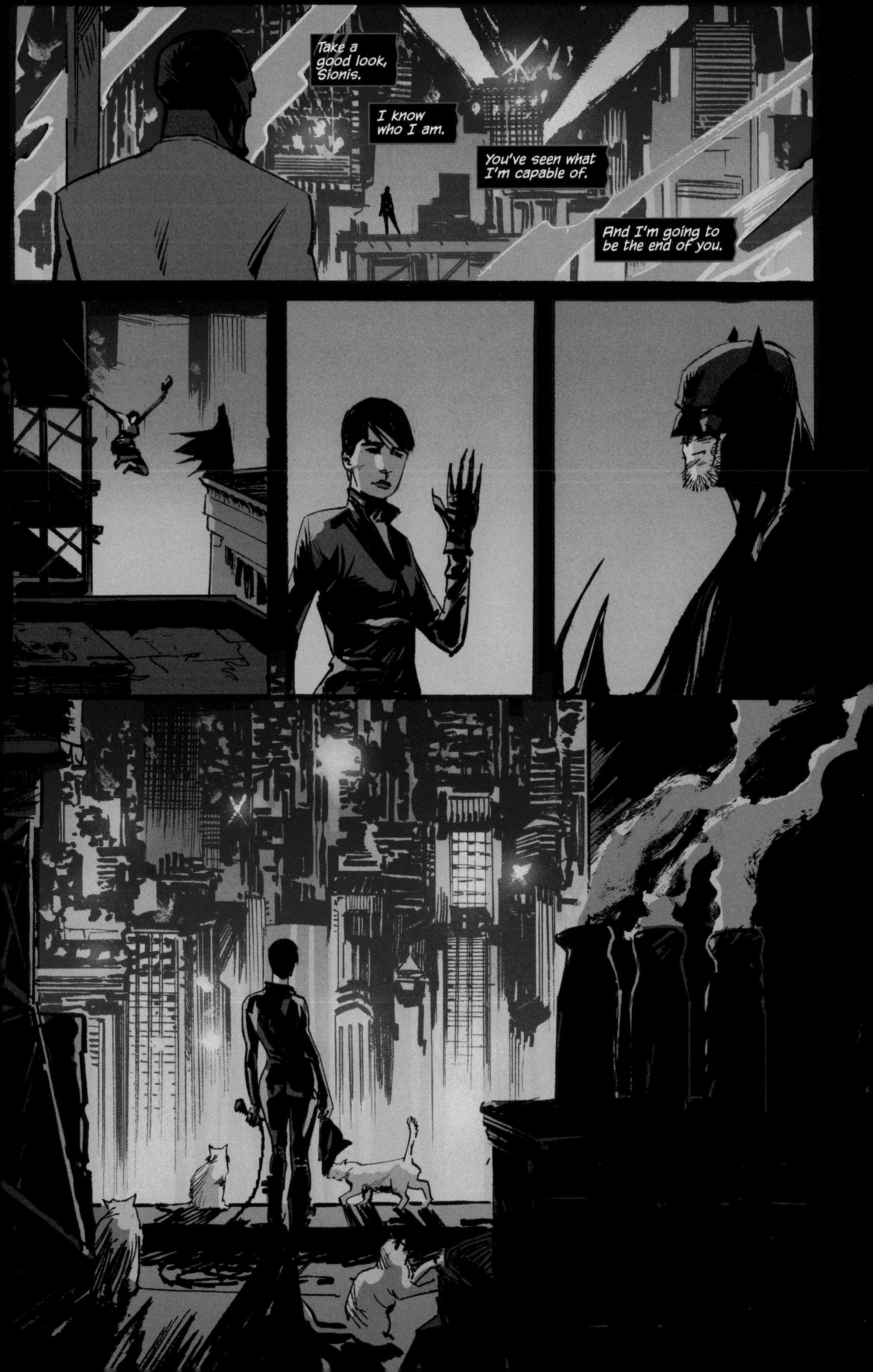
Take a good look, Sionis.
I know who I am.
You've seen what I'm capable of.
And I'm going to be the end of you.

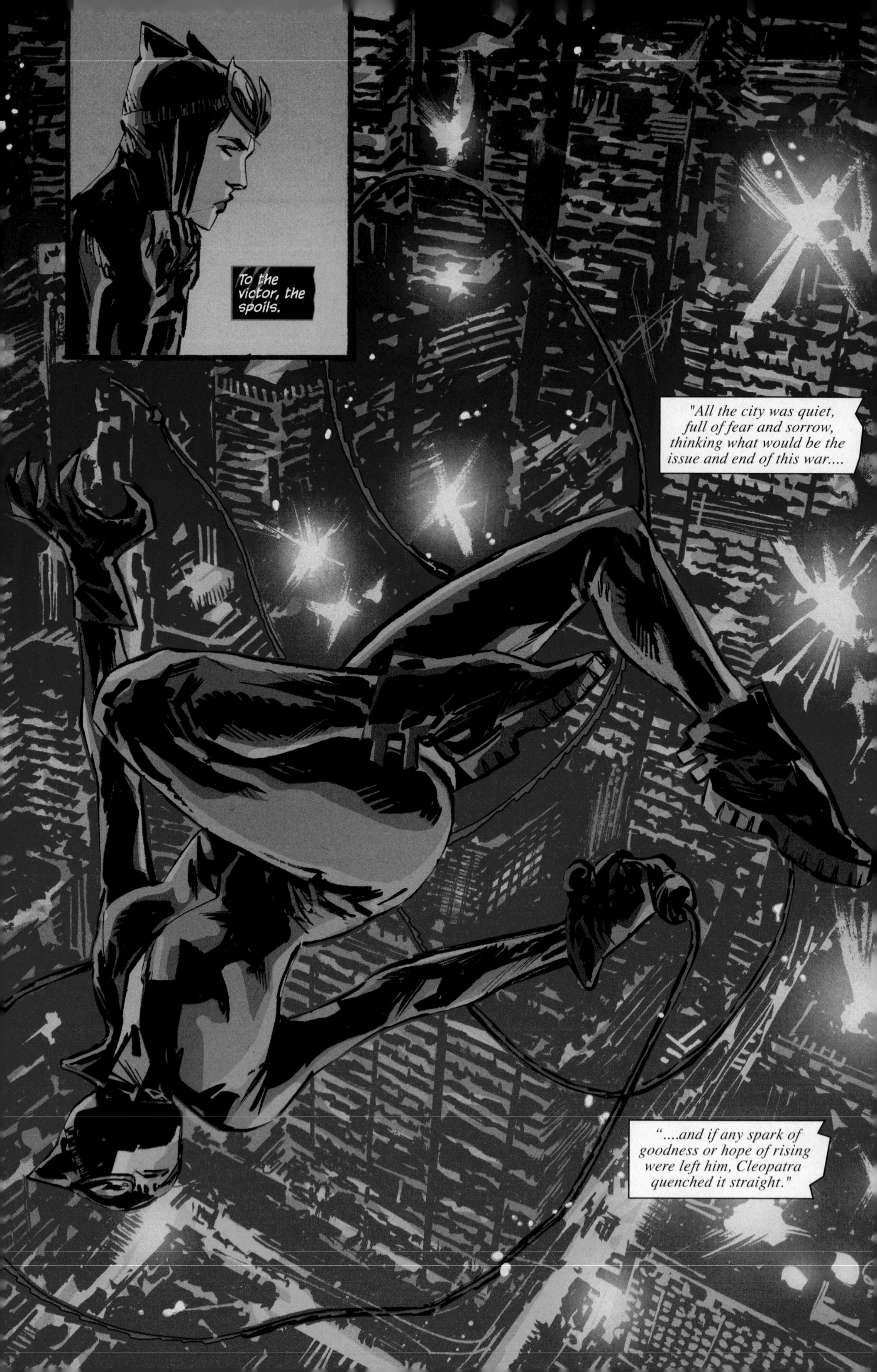
To the victor, the spoils.
"All the city was quiet, full of fear and sorrow, thinking what would be the issue and end of this war....
"....and if any spark of goodness or hope of rising were left him, Cleopatra quenched it straight."

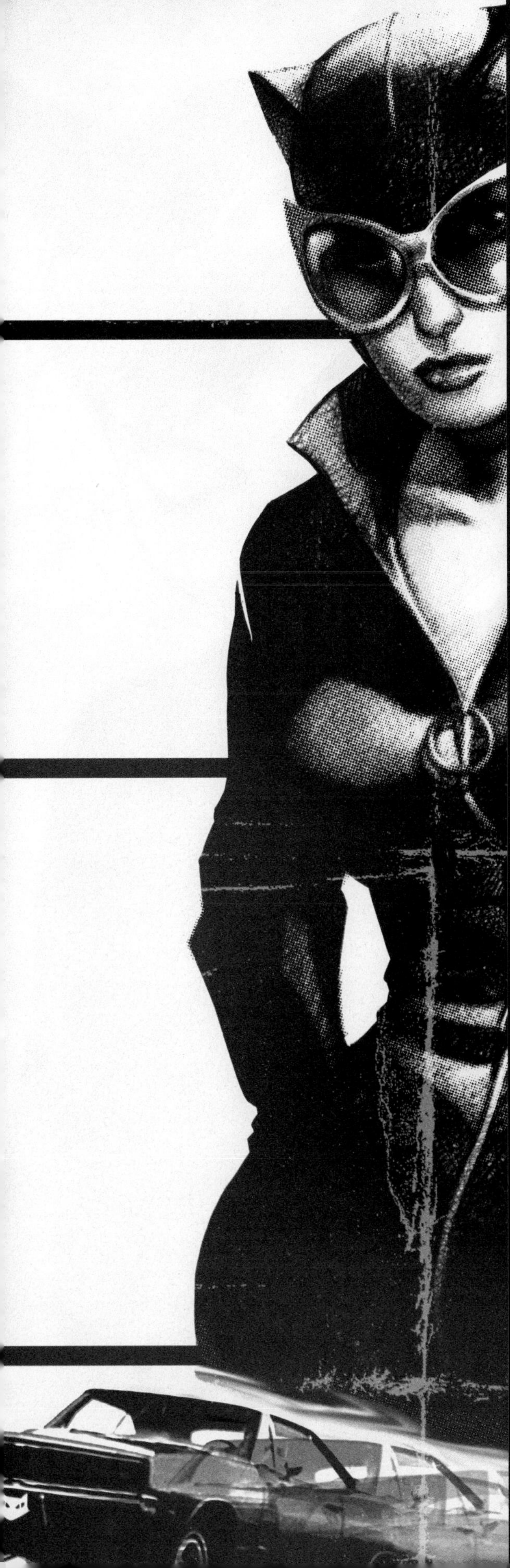

CATWOMAN COVER GALLERY

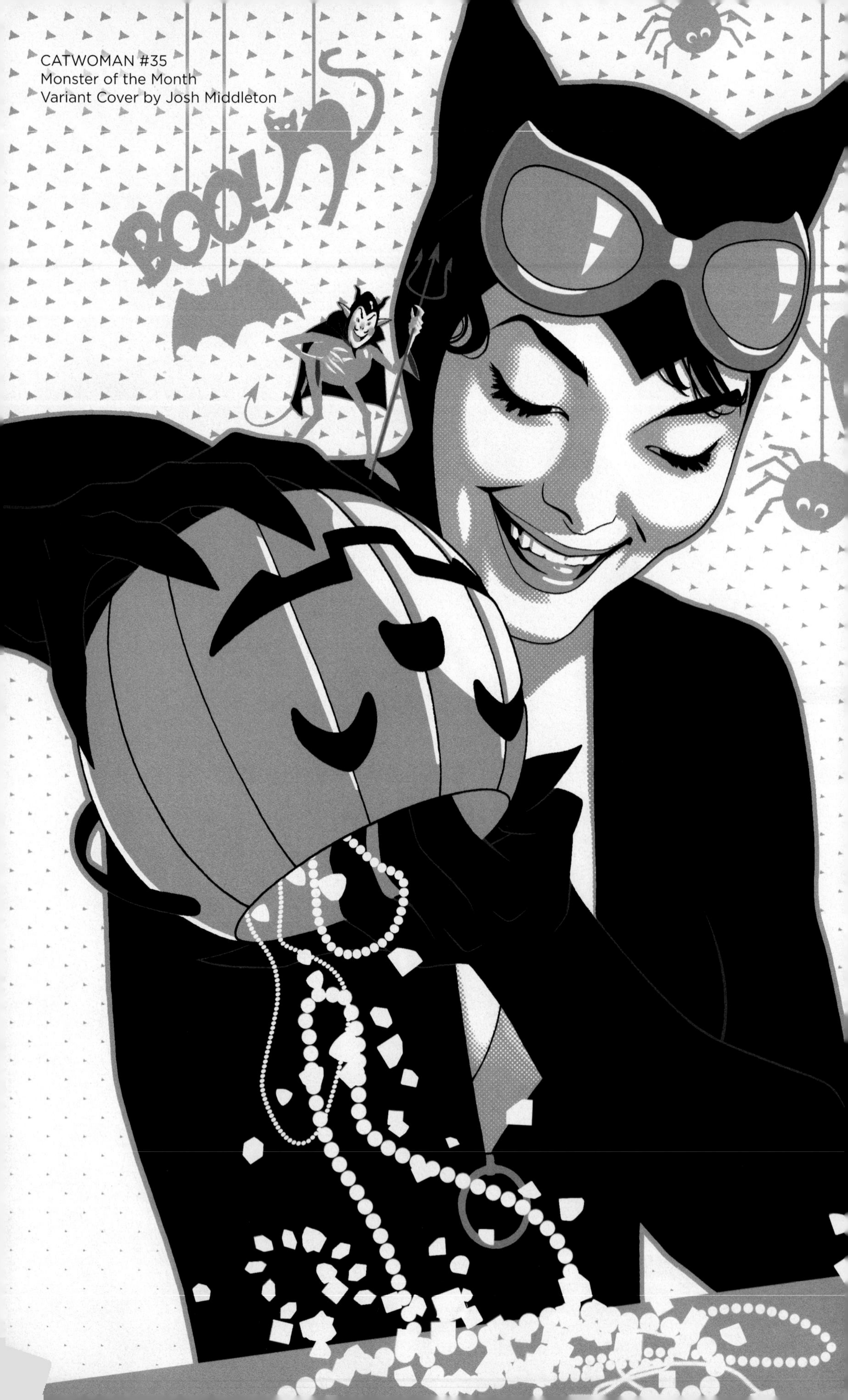
BOO!

CATWOMAN #35
Monster of the Month
Variant Cover by Josh Middleton

CATWOMAN #36
LEGO Variant Cover

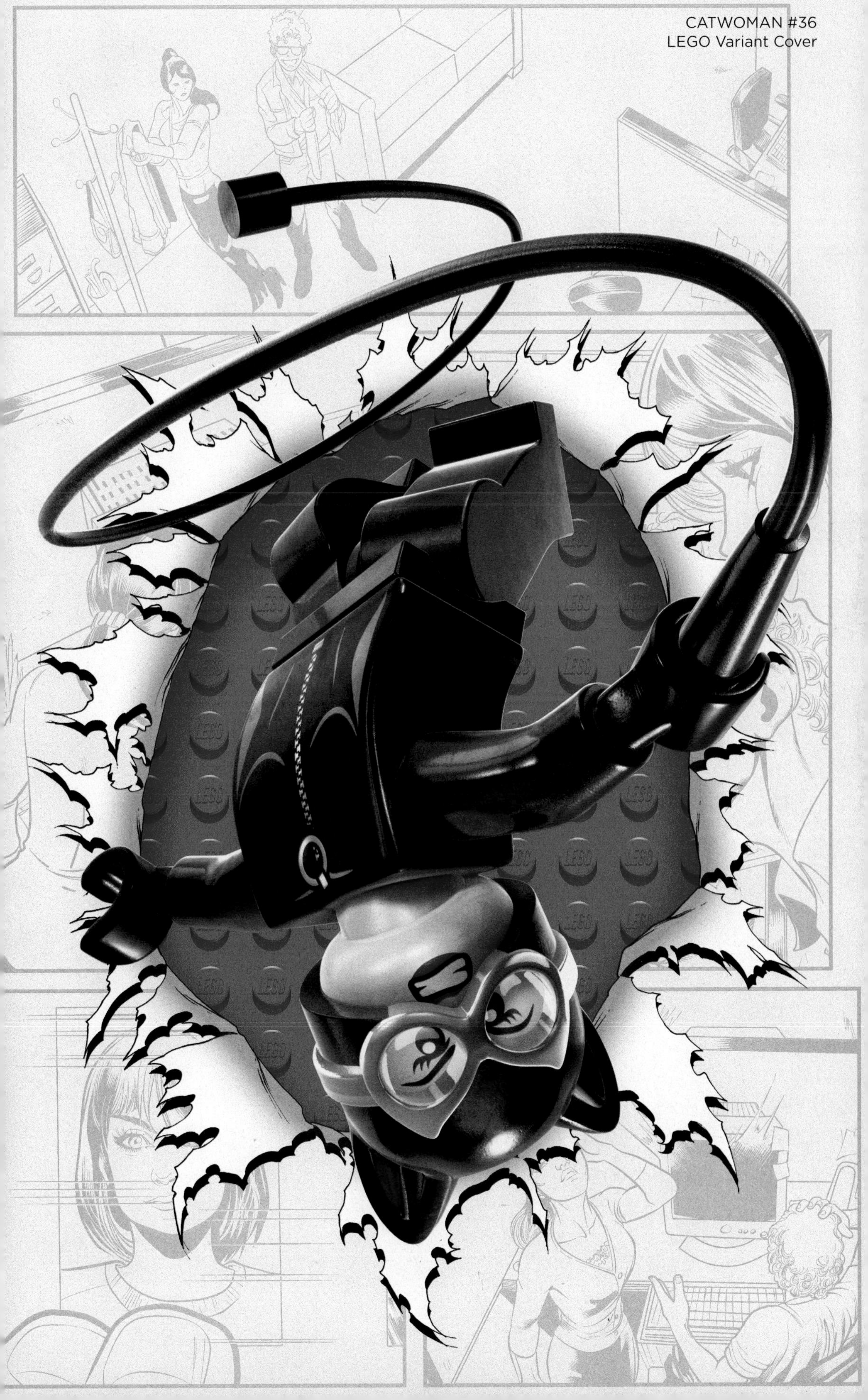

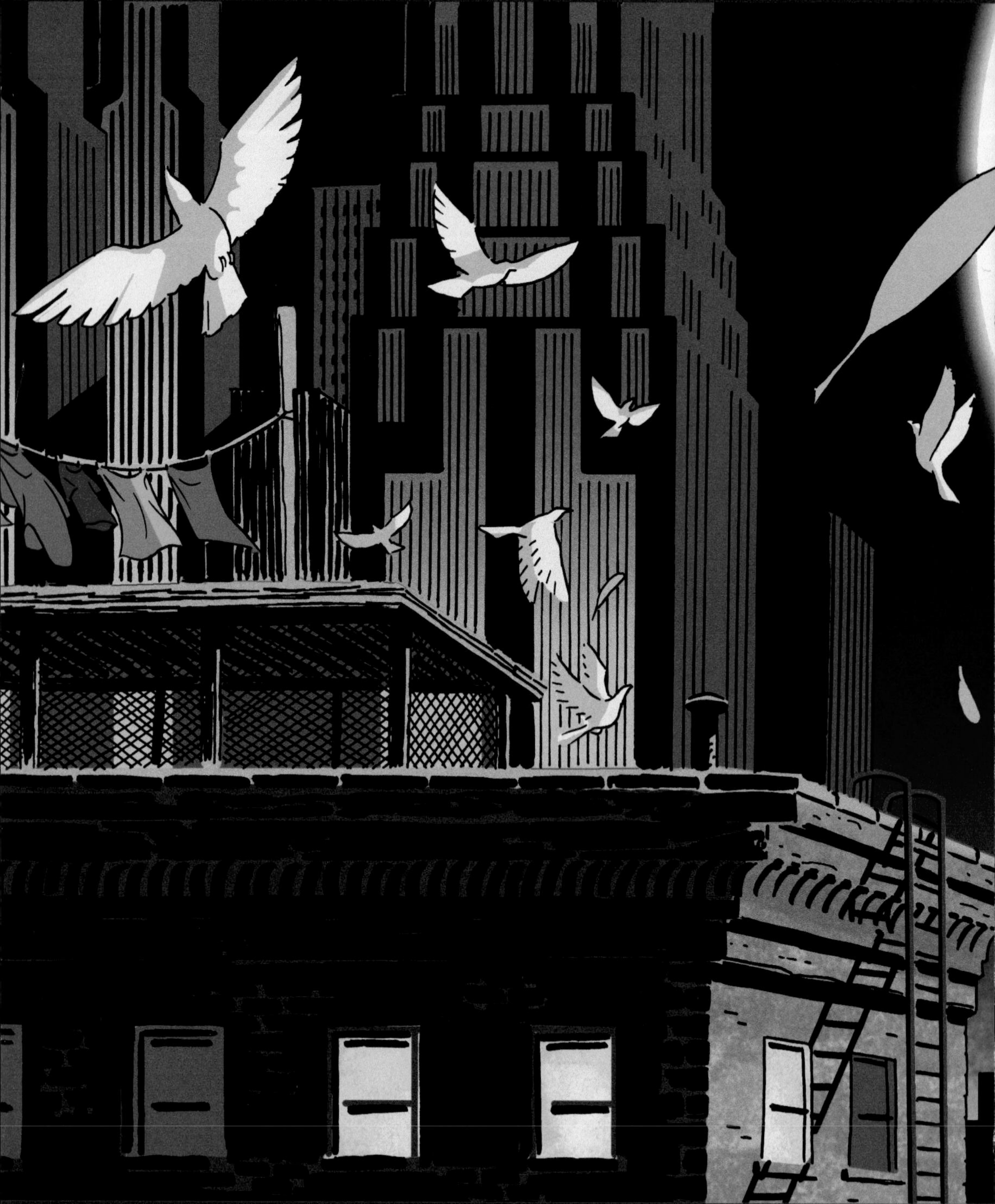

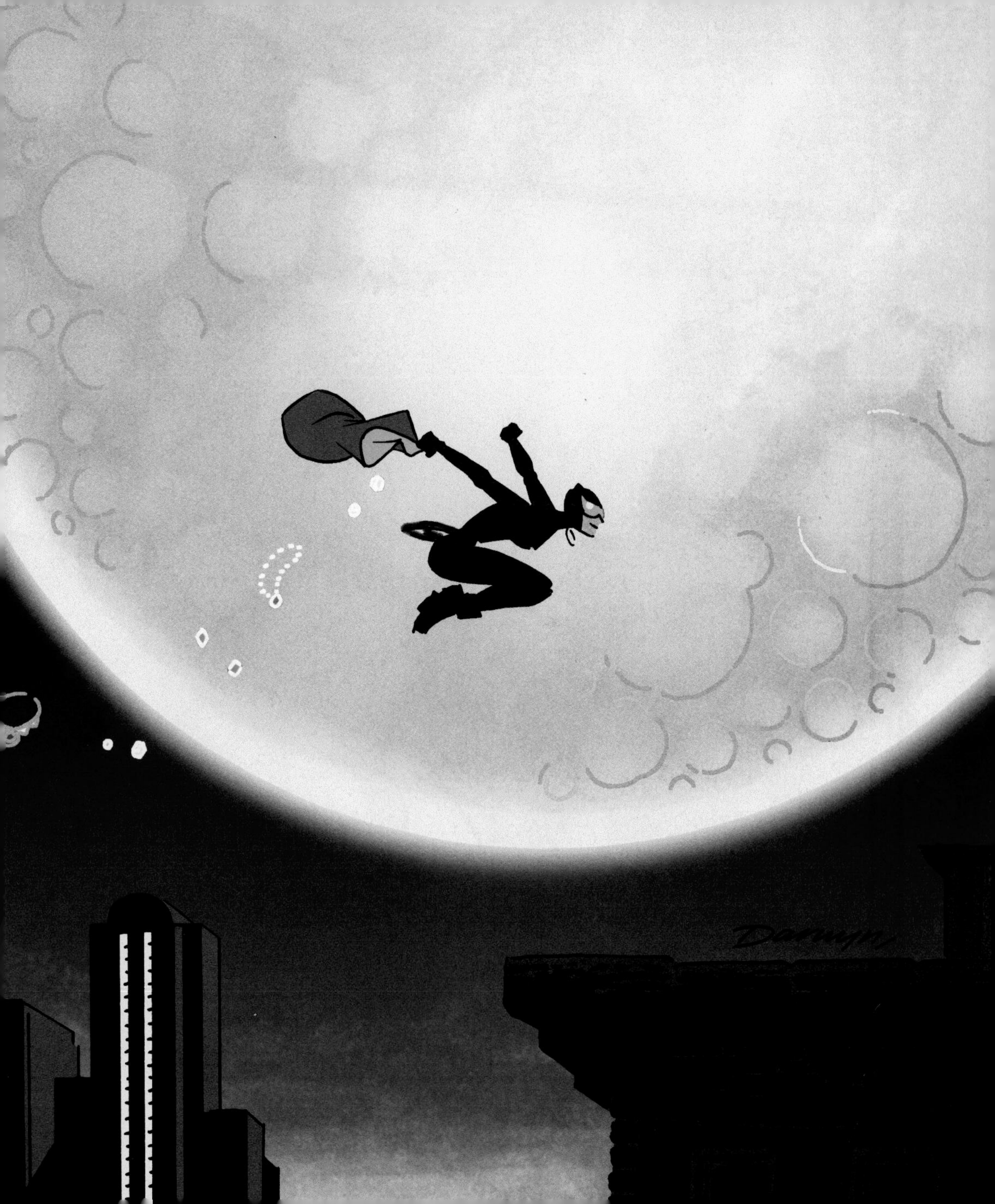
Darwyn

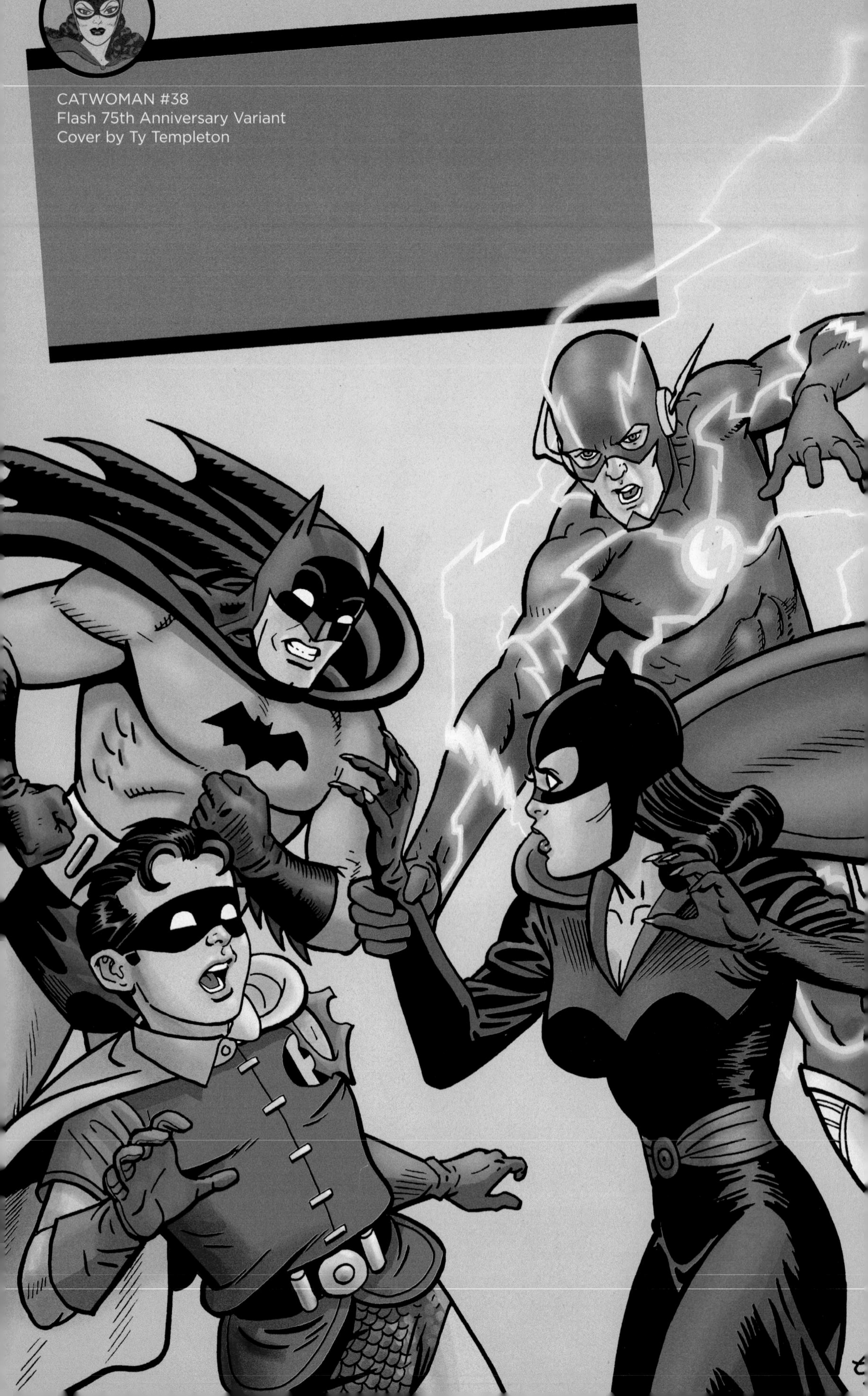

CATWOMAN #38
Flash 75th Anniversary Variant
Cover by Ty Templeton

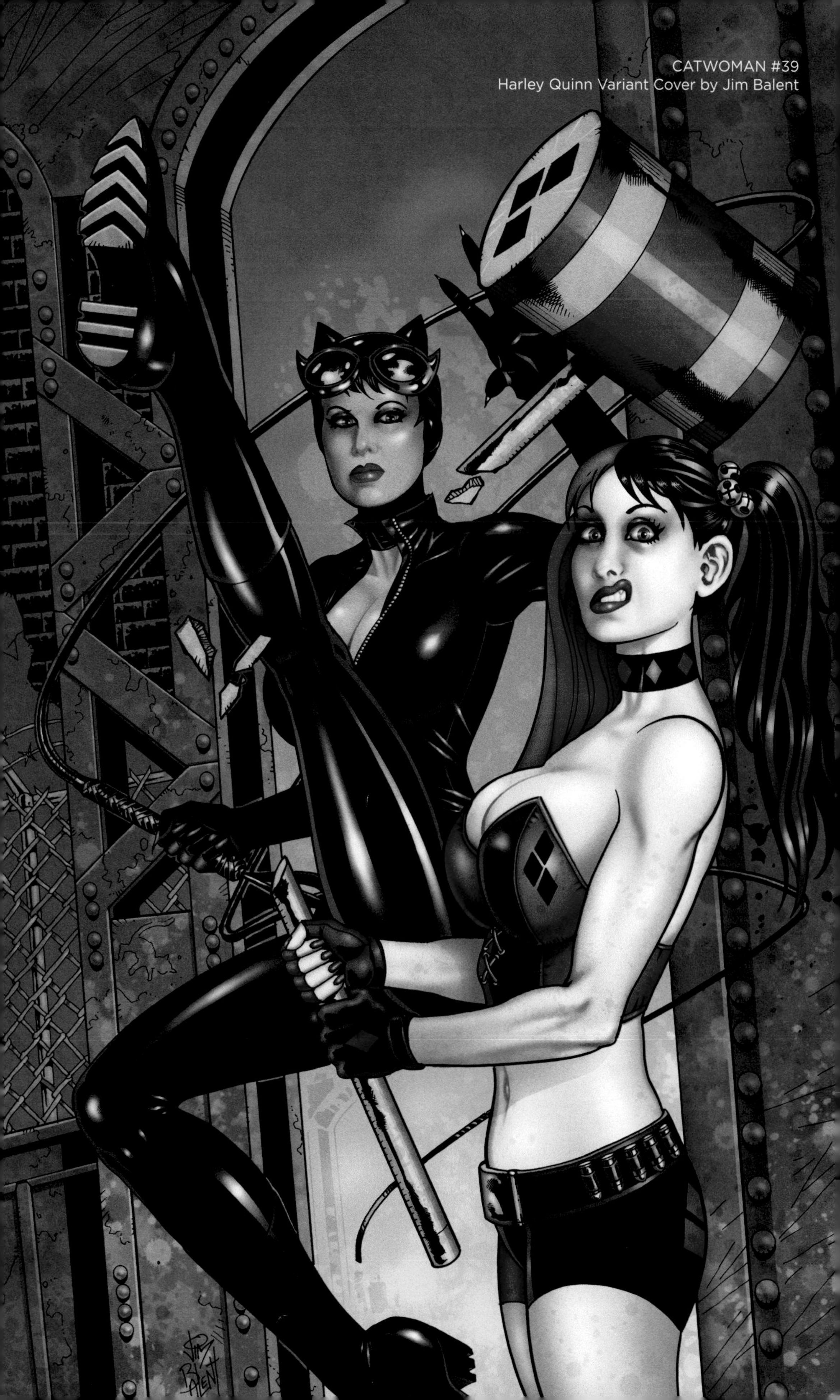

CATWOMAN #39
Harley Quinn Variant Cover by Jim Balent

CATWOMAN #40
Movie Poster Variant Cover by Dave Johnson

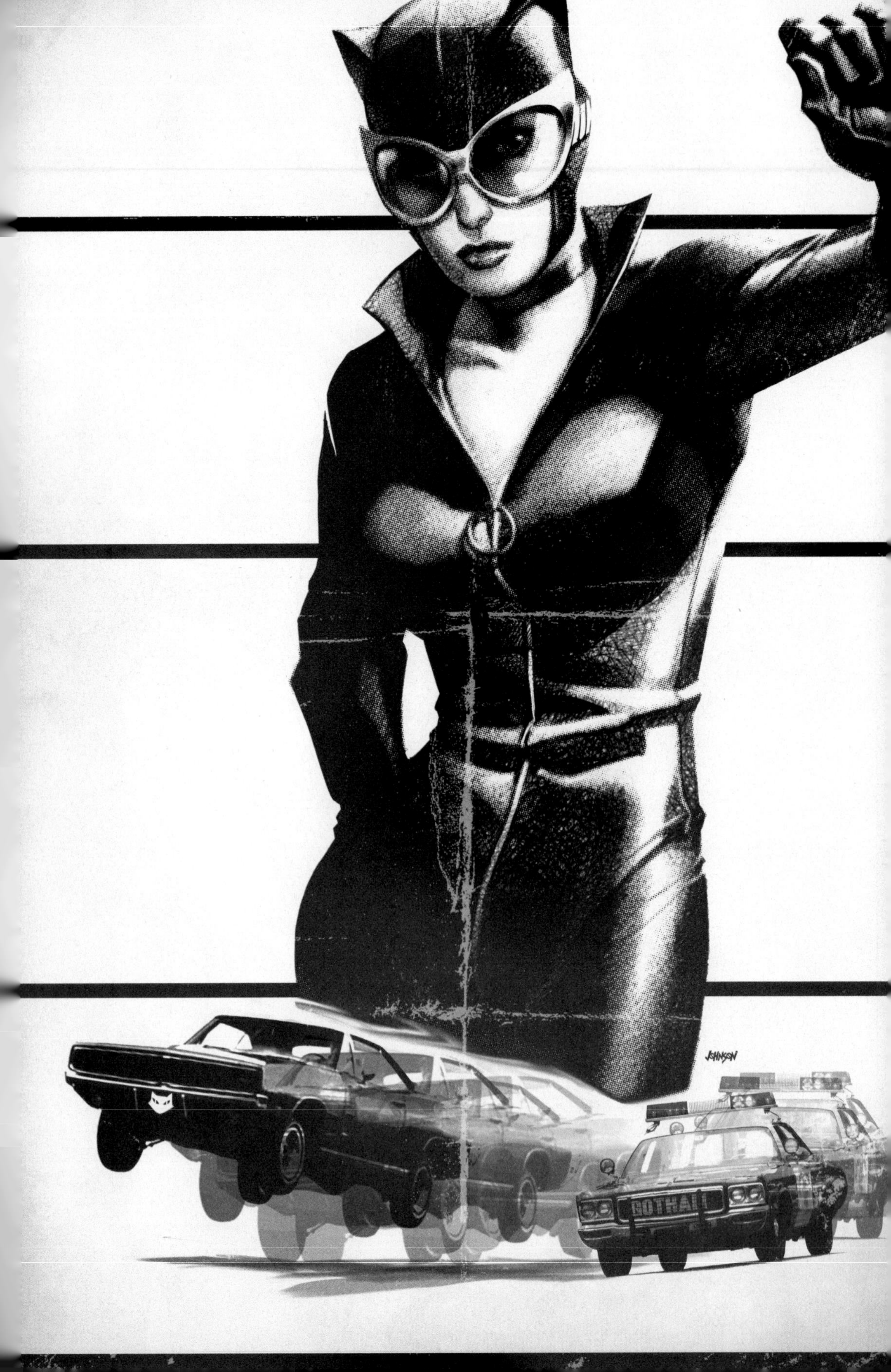
JOHNSON

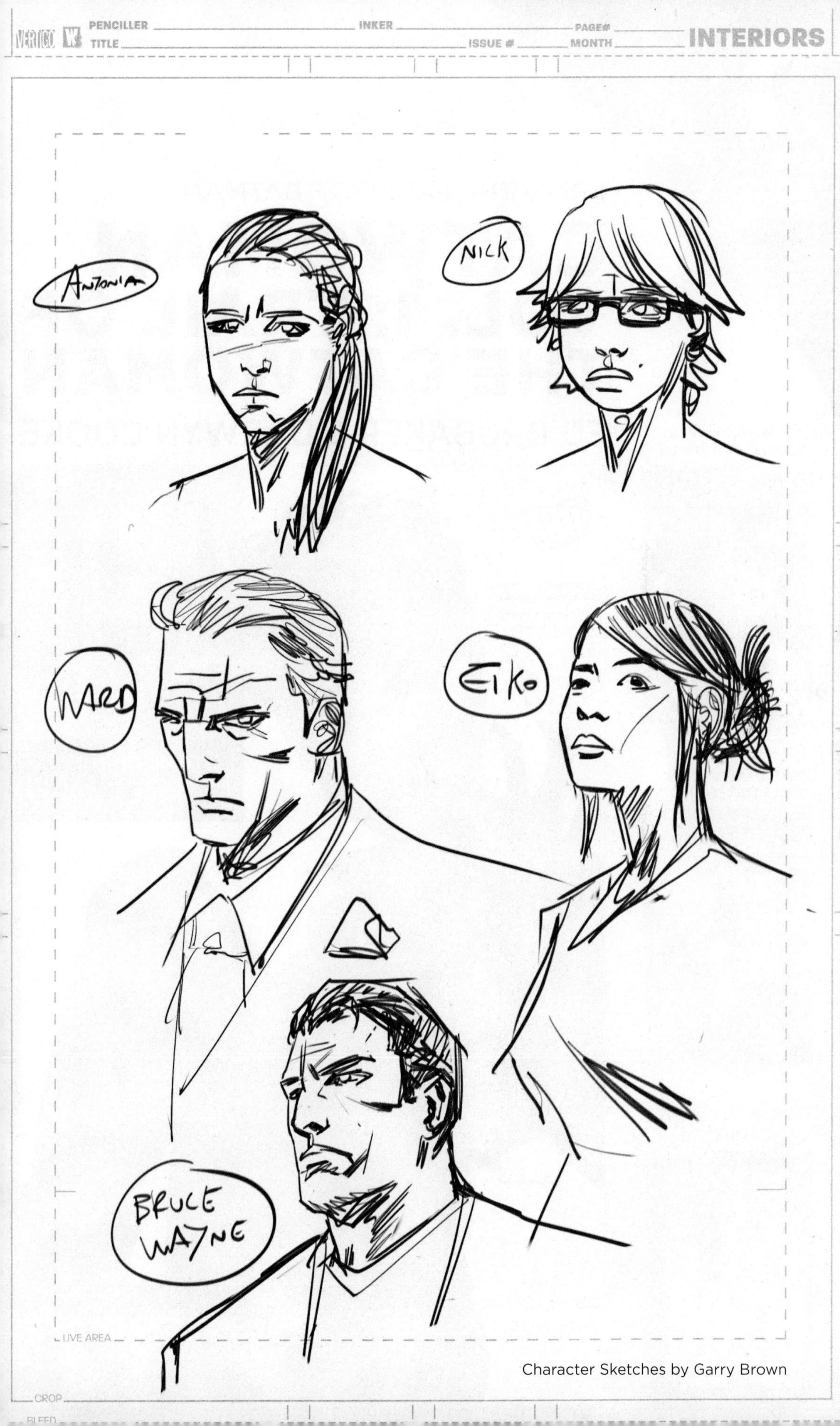
PENCILLER
INKER
PAGE#
TITLE
ISSUE #
MONTH
INTERIORS
ANTONIA
NICK
WARD
EIKO
BRUCE WAYNE
LIVE AREA
CROP
BLEED

Character Sketches by Garry Brown

DC COMICS™

FROM THE PAGES OF *BATMAN*

CATWOMAN VOL. 1: TRAIL OF THE CATWOMAN

ED BRUBAKER & DARWYN COOKE

CATWOMAN VOL. 2: NO EASY WAY DOWN

GOTHAM CITY SIRENS: STRANGE FRUIT

GOTHAM CITY SIRENS: UNION

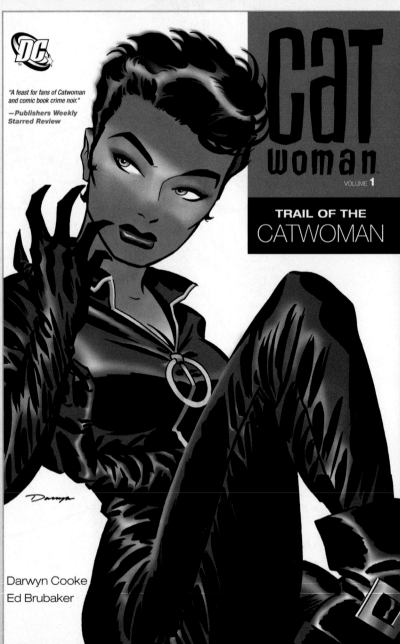

"A feast for fans of Catwoman and comic book crime noir."
—**Publishers Weekly Starred Review**

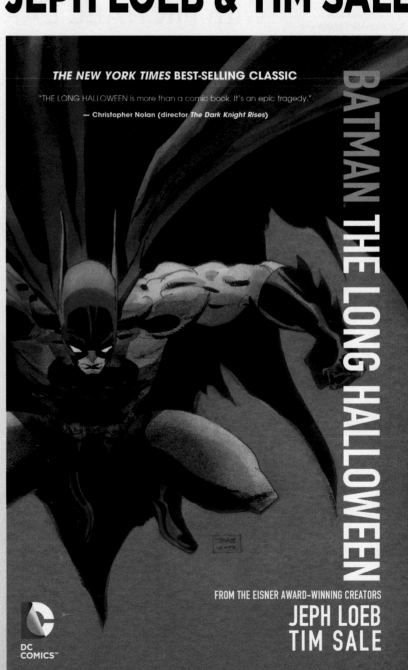

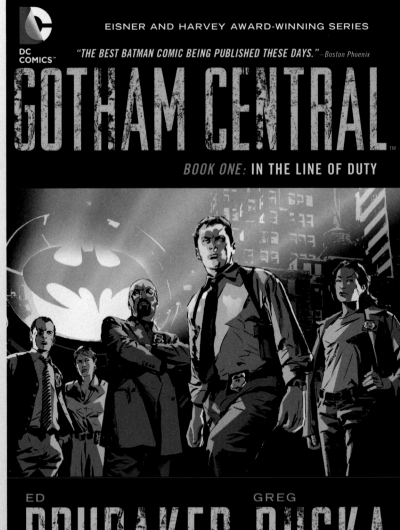

"Simone and artist Ardian Syaf not only do justice to Babs' legacy, but build in a new complexity that is the starting point for a future full of new storytelling possibilities. A hell of a ride."—IGN

START AT THE BEGINNING!

BATGIRL
VOLUME 1: THE DARKEST REFLECTION

BATGIRL VOL. 2: KNIGHTFALL DESCENDS

BATGIRL VOL. 3: DEATH OF THE FAMILY

BATWOMAN VOL. 1: HYDROLOGY

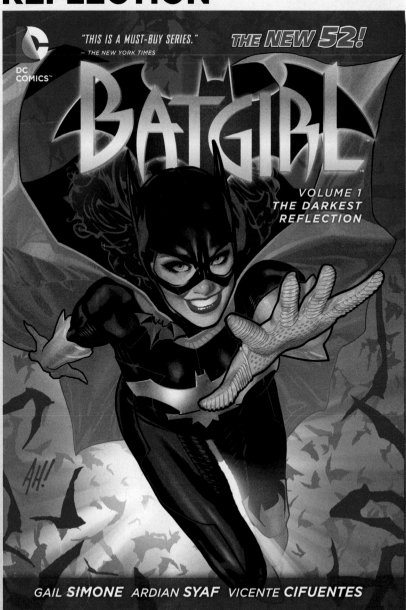

GAIL **SIMONE** ARDIAN **SYAF** VICENTE **CIFUENTES**

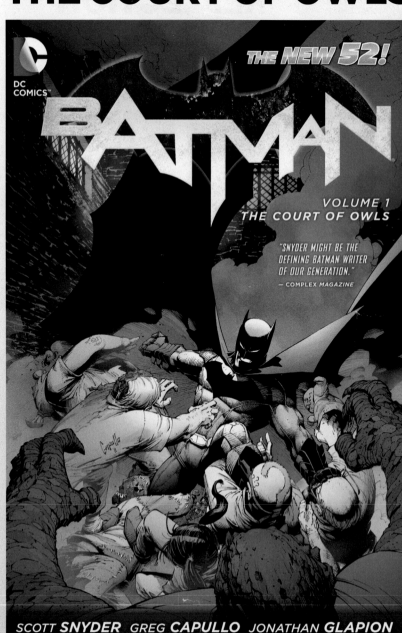